CIVIC H POLITICA REALITIES

26 in 26
Neighborhood Resource Centers
26 Neighborhood Strategies in a 26 month time fram
A Grant Funded by the LSTA
(Library Services & Technology Act)

CITY OF
RIVERSIDE

Riverside Public Library

CIVIC HOPES AND POLITICAL REALITIES

Immigrants, Community Organizations, and
Political Engagement

S. Karthick Ramakrishnan and Irene Bloemraad
Editors

Russell Sage Foundation • New York

The Russell Sage Foundation

The Russell Sage Foundation, one of the oldest of America's general purpose foundations, was established in 1907 by Mrs. Margaret Olivia Sage for "the improvement of social and living conditions in the United States." The Foundation seeks to fulfill this mandate by fostering the development and dissemination of knowledge about the country's political, social, and economic problems. While the Foundation endeavors to assure the accuracy and objectivity of each book it publishes, the conclusions and interpretations in Russell Sage Foundation publications are those of the authors and not of the Foundation, its Trustees, or its staff. Publication by Russell Sage, therefore, does not imply Foundation endorsement.

Library of Congress Cataloging-in-Publication Data
Civic hopes and political realities : immigrants, community organizations, and political engagement / edited by S. Karthick Ramakrishnan and Irene Bloemraad.
    p. cm.
  ISBN 978-0-87154-701-9
  1. Immigrants—United States—Political activity.   2. Immigrants—Social networks—United States.   3. Immigrants—Political activity.   4. Immigrants—Social networks.   I. Ramakrishnan, S. Karthick (Subramanian Karthick), 1975–   II. Bloemraad, Irene, 1972–
  JV6477.C6 2008
  324.086′9120973—dc22   2008002144

The paper used in this publication meets the minimum requirements of American National Standard for Information Sciences—Permanence of Paper for Printed Library Materials. ANSI Z39.48-1992.

Text design by Suzanne Nichols.

RUSSELL SAGE FOUNDATION
112 East 64th Street, New York, New York 10021
10 9 8 7 6 5 4 3 2 1

Contents

About the Authors

S. Karthick Ramakrishnan is associate professor of political science at the University of California, Riverside.

Irene Bloemraad is assistant professor of sociology at the University of California, Berkeley.

Kristi Andersen is Laura J. and L. Douglas Meredith Professor of Teaching Excellence in the Department of Political Science, Maxwell School of Citizenship and Public Affairs, Syracuse University.

Sofya Aptekar is a Ph.D. candidate in the Department of Sociology and Office of Population Research at Princeton University.

Maria Berger is a senior research advisor for the city of Delft.

Caroline B. Brettell is Dedman Family Distinguished Professor of Anthropology at Southern Methodist University and Dean ad Interim of Dedman College.

Els de Graauw is a post doctoral fellow at the Hauser Center for Nonprofit Organizations at Harvard University.

Shannon Gleeson is a Ph.D. candidate in the Graduate Group in Sociology and Demography at the University of California, Berkeley.

Rebecca Hamlin is a Ph.D. candidate in the Department of Political Science at the University of California, Berkeley.

Rahsaan Maxwell is a Transatlantic Postdoctoral Fellow with the German Marshall Fund for the 2008-2009 academic year.

Haven Perez is a Ph.D. candidate in the Department of American Studies and Ethnicity at the University of Southern California.

Deborah Reed-Danahay is professor of anthropology at SUNY Buffalo.

Kathy Rim is a Ph.D. candidate in the Department of Political Science at the University of California, Irvine.

LAURENCIO SANGUINO is a Ph.D. candidate in the Department of History at the University of Chicago.

FLORIS VERMEULEN is a researcher at the Institute for Migration and Ethnic Studies (IMES), Political Science Department, University of Amsterdam.

CELIA VIRAMONTES is an independent researcher and writer documenting the civic and political mobilization efforts of Mexican immigrant organizations in Southern California.

JANELLE WONG is associate professor of political science and American studies and ethnicity at the University of Southern California.

Acknowledgments

There is perhaps no greater time than the present to be examining the contours of immigrant civic participation. The chapters in this volume bring a variety of disciplinary perspectives to analyze the extent to which the civic hopes of community involvement lead to political benefits for immigrant groups and immigrant-serving organizations. The idea for this volume arose in the summer of 2005. We had both applied separately for grants from the Russell Sage Foundation on the topic of immigrant political incorporation, and thought that—given the emerging nature of this field of inquiry and our common interests—we could combine energies on an ambitious project together, and also draw in people working on similar projects elsewhere. After the first year of data collection for the Immigrant Civic Engagement Project, we broached the idea of an edited volume with colleagues in varied fields. Given the richness of our data collection efforts, we also wanted a volume that would plumb the intricacies of particular metropolitan areas and ethnic groups featured in the Immigrant Civic Engagement Project, which includes localities in the metropolitan areas of San Jose, Los Angeles, Orange County, Chicago, Central New Jersey, and Washington, D.C.

We put together a proposal, a draft introductory chapter, and gathered the enthusiastic involvement of scholars across the country. There was, however, one missing ingredient: we needed to get together to present working drafts and to make sure that the edited volume would hang well together. The Russell Sage Foundation provided that important link, as Karthick spent a semester on a visiting fellowship in the fall of 2006 and was granted a request to convene a working conference for contributors to the volume. We all spent two days together in New York in December, making presentations, commenting on each others' work, and soliciting the input from scholars at the foundation and in the region.

Thus, for several reasons, we are grateful first to the Russell Sage Foundation for supporting our research, as well as those of others studying immigrant political incorporation. Thanks especially to Aixa Cintrón-Vélez, Eric Wanner, and the board of the foundation for encouraging research in this area, and to the various reviewers of our project and the edited book. Thanks also to Suzanne Nichols for shepherding this book from its initial proposal to final publication.

At our working conference in New York, we benefited greatly from the involvement of Aixa Cintrón-Vélez, Orly Clergé, Héctor Cordero-Guzmán,

Katherine Ewing, Michael Fortner, Jane Junn, José Itzigsohn, Jitka Malečková, Pyong Gap Min, John Mollenkopf, and Dorian Warren. In developing our theoretical framework for this volume and the larger project, we also benefited from presentations at Syracuse University, the UCLA Migration Study Group, and at the annual meetings of the American Political Science Association and the American Sociological Association. Although we are surely forgetting the names of individuals who gave valuable feedback, we thank in particular Elizabeth Cohen, Adrian Favell, Rubén Hernández-León, Taeku Lee, Peggy Levitt, Melissa Michelson, Anthony Orum, Ricardo Ramirez, and Roger Waldinger.

We also acknowledge the support of our home institutions in valuing collaborative, interdisciplinary efforts such as this edited volume, and to entitites such as the Hellman Family Faculty Fund, The Institute for Governmental Studies, and the Institute for Research on Labor and Employment, all at UC Berkeley, and to the Public Policy Institute of California. The Immigrant Civic Engagement Project that inspired this volume would not have been successful without the assistance of truly exceptional research assistants. Some of these scholars have contributed their independent work in this volume, including Els de Graauw, Shannon Gleeson, and Rebecca Hamlin, while others such as Sofya Aptekar, Laurencio Sanguino, and Celia Viramontes have contributed chapters based on this larger data collection effort. In addition, we acknowledge the expert assistance of Kristel Acacio, Soo Jin Kim, Adam Orlovich, and Jennifer Paluch.

Finally, we thank our respective families for granting us the time to work on this volume and for continuing to provide encouragement and patience as we continue to work on publications from the Immigrant Civic Engagement Project. Our spouses (Brinda Sarathy and David St. Jean) have been particularly understanding in this regard, and for that we continue to be ever so grateful. We dedicate this volume to all of our families, of varying immigrant generations, and especially to children like Omji, Maxime, and Félix, who represent the future of political voice and civic engagement.

S. *Karthick Ramakrishnan and Irene Bloemraad*

Chapter 1

Introduction: Civic and Political Inequalities

In the spring of 2006, the United States experienced some of the largest, most widespread protest marches in its history, from massive demonstrations of a half million people or more in large cities such as Los Angeles, Chicago, and Dallas to unprecedented rallies in places like Schuyker, Nebraska, and towns across South Carolina. In total, several million demonstrators, with estimates ranging from 3.5 to 5 million, waved banners and walked in pro-immigration rallies from March 10 to May 1 (Bada, Fox, and Selee 2006; Wang and Winn 2006). The public, politicians, and even advocates for immigrant rights were taken unaware by the scale and breadth of these public protests. Yet, contrary to the depictions in many mainstream news outlets, the immigrant protests were not simply a spontaneous uprising against restrictive immigration legislation passed by the House of Representatives (ABC News 2006).[1] They arose instead from an existing scaffold of immigrant-serving organizations, the groundwork for such large-scale civic and political engagement already established by organizations ranging from immigrant advocacy groups and labor unions to religious institutions and transnational hometown associations (Wang and Winn 2006).[2] The protests of spring 2006 thus drew back the curtain on the rich and pervasive forms of community organization and mobilization operating within immigrant communities. They also showcased the political engagement of noncitizens who are, in large part, excluded from formal electoral politics.

The sudden visibility of immigrant community organizations and their ability to mobilize millions run counter to some recent studies of civic participation, which suggest that immigration is one of the primary reasons for declining civic engagement and the persistence of racial and ethnic gaps in participation (Gimpel 1999; Camarota 2001; Putnam 2007). Indeed, some of the steepest decreases in civic participation have coincided with the growing share of first- and second-generation immigrants in the United States, particularly those of Latin American and Asian origins. Other observers, less pessimistic, note that apparent group differences in participation may instead be the result of inaccurate measures of voluntarism that do not incorporate the different experiences of immigrants (Reynoso 2003; Vasquez 2003). These debates about the civic engagement of immigrants stand against a backdrop of scholarship suggesting that civic participation is declining for everyone: today's June Cleaver no longer helps out at the school bake sale and today's Ward Cleaver no longer belongs to his father's fraternal or local community organizations. These changes in civic participation are variously attributed to the societal transformations of postindustrial economies, the rise of private forms of entertainment, and the growth of expert-run member associations (Putnam 2000; Skocpol 2003).

Scholars and public officials alike worry about declines in civic engagement and social capital because of their troubling implications for democratic politics. Engagement with community organizations is often tied to political involvement and policy influence at all levels of government (Verba, Schlozman, and Brady 1995; Rosenstone and Hansen 1993). Thus declining levels of voluntarism may contribute to continuing declines in political interest and participation. Low levels of voluntarism may also adversely affect the provision of public goods in many communities, especially as cuts in government spending leave civic and voluntary organizations as major providers of social services. Implicit in these concerns is a strong belief that participation in the associational life of the United States is the underpinning of a robust democracy, a belief nurtured by a long historical narrative of America as a nation of joiners.

Taken together, these two strands of literature—on the causes of declining civic engagement and their consequences for democratic politics—warn that immigration and ethnic diversification are undermining the civic and political vitality of the United States and other liberal democracies (Putnam 2007). Before taking this large step, however, it is important to better account for the various forms of immigrant civic participation, especially with respect to immigrant- and ethnic-serving organizations. Studies suggesting that declines in civic participation may be related to immigration and ethnic diversification lack such a detailed understanding. As a consequence, several questions remain unanswered: To what extent are immigrants' community organizations, ranging from religious institutions to homeland associations and soccer leagues, transforming our taken-for-granted understandings of associational life? Will Sandeep Singh join—or be invited to join—the local Rotary Club? Will Mai Nguyen participate in the Chamber of Commerce, or will she feel unwelcome or unable to communicate effectively with other business owners? Will Rosa Hernandez have access to a Parent Teacher Association, ideally one that provides Spanish-language support? Will these immigrants join existing organizations, form their own groups, or will they lead private lives disconnected from collective, public-minded action? More generally, are stories of American civic (dis)engagement equally relevant to immigrants, or might immigrants revitalize community organizations?

This volume probes these questions of immigrant civic and political engagement, paying particular attention to community organizations and the processes linking them to political institutions (above) and to individual residents or constituents (below). We have organized the chapters to offer a better understanding of how immigrant civic engagement may vary across geographic contexts, national origins, and types of organization. Finally, we also draw attention to the political consequences of immigrant civic participation, especially as they relate to questions of inequality: To what degree do Americans open the doors of their clubs, associations and organizations to those not born in the United States? Will newer immigrant and ethnic organizations play the same role in local civic life and politics as suggested by older, pluralist narratives of American democracy, or do we find instead a stratified civic arena marked by group inequalities in political visibility and access to public officials?

This book thus asks whether the civic paths of immigrant participants lead to greater visibility and influence in politics, or whether such hopes dissipate in the face of political stratification. In particular, we focus on immigrant participation in formal and informal associations, and the interaction of immigrant-based organizations with mainstream political institutions as well as other collective groups in civic and political life. We strive to do this in a truly interdisciplinary manner, bringing together perspectives from political science, sociology, anthropology, ethnic studies, and history. With the study of contemporary immigrant community organizations still in its infancy, we need to think carefully about the factors that influence the growth and political relevance of such organizations, paying particular attention to the role of place, immigrant national origins, and organizational form. We also need to consider the interplay between community organizations and political institutions in other immigrant-receiving countries for the lessons they may provide for the United States. The result, we hope, is an innovative, thought-provoking account of immigrant organizing and the relationship between organizations and immigrants' civic and political engagement.

IMMIGRANT POLITICAL ENGAGEMENT: EXPANDING AND CHALLENGING WHAT WE KNOW

This volume is situated at the intersection of several research traditions in sociology and political science: literatures on immigrant adaptation, civic engagement, and minority political incorporation. As such, it seeks to address gaps in each tradition. The immigrant adaptation literature in sociology and related fields has focused primarily on economic, demographic, and other social outcomes, with much less attention to political and civic institutions and processes (see Alba and Nee 2003; Bean and Stevens 2003). The contemporary literature on civic participation and civic engagement, while rich in many ways, is largely silent on issues related to immigrant adaptation, focusing primarily on the native-born (Verba, Schlozman, and Brady 1995; Putnam 2000; Skocpol 2003). Finally, the literature on minority political incorporation in urban areas offers several potential insights to understand the incorporation of immigrants (Browning, Marshall, and Tabb 1984), though its focus on electoral mobilization may not be especially useful in explaining the political incorporation of immigrant residents, many of whom cannot vote (but see Jones-Correa 1998 and Wong 2006).

Indeed, several factors related to the immigrant experience may shape the extent to which residents form civic organizations and the extent to which such organizations are visible and influential in their local communities. Here we outline the reasons why it is important to draw particular attention to immigrants and the immigrant experience when considering civic and political engagement. We also provide a brief overview of the relevant literatures in sociology and political science on immigrant adaptation, civic engagement, and minority political incorporation.

Special Challenges—and Opportunities—of Immigration for Civic and Political Engagement

Our definition of *immigrant* rests on foreign birth and spans all legal statuses held by the foreign-born: naturalized citizen, legal permanent resident, legal temporary visitor (such as students or temporary workers, some of whom later become permanent residents), refugee or asylee, and undocumented or unauthorized resident.[3] As of 2006, more than 12.5 percent (37.5 million) of United States residents fit this definition of immigrant, more than the entire population of California and more than twice that of New England (U.S. Census Bureau 2006). We are also interested in the adult children of immigrants—often referred to as the immigrant second generation—because they can sustain, transform, or abandon the organizations of the first generation. Today, second-generation immigrants account for about 8 percent of the adult population in the United States and a slightly larger proportion of the adult citizen population.

The most obvious difference between the native-born and the foreign-born is the issue of legal status and access to formal membership through citizenship. Legal status critically informs the study of immigrant community organizations. The great majority of immigrants in the United States, about 65 percent, cannot vote because they have not applied for citizenship or are ineligible to do so.[4] Given this electoral exclusion and the generally lower propensity of naturalized citizens to vote, we may expect community organizations to play an even greater role in political representation for immigrants than for the native-born. At the same time, lack of citizenship or legal status may lessen the vitality and political influence of immigrant organizations, with noncitizens unable to provide voting blocs and with unauthorized immigrants reluctant to get involved in the public sphere. Differences in legal status may also affect whether immigrant joiners are more likely to participate in transnational associations targeted to the homeland or in organizations focused primarily on the host society.

We may also expect differences in civic and political engagement between refugees, who are eligible for government support and assistance from refugee settlement organizations, and economic or family migrants, who must largely rely on personal resources and the help of friends and family (Bloemraad 2006; Portes and Rumbaut 2006). About 7 percent, or 2.7 million, of the foreign-born are refugees or have previously held refugee status (Passel 2006). A related issue—important for any government-supported program directed to immigrant organizations—is the question of whether, and under what conditions, government assistance promotes the growth and sustenance of local organizations, or whether such support crowds out community-driven alternatives and undermines the autonomy of civic groups.

A third fundamental distinction between immigrants and native-born citizens lies in the cultural and linguistic distance that can separate the two groups. Although the fabric of American society is woven from diverse strands across regions and racial-ethnic groups, the linguistic and cultural gaps associated with foreign birth tend to be greater, especially among more recent arrivals to the United States (Hirschman, Kasinitz, and DeWind 1999).

One of the most important gaps is language. Despite fears in some corners that the United States is becoming a Spanish-speaking nation (Huntington 2004), English is without doubt the language of public and political discourse. Lack of English proficiency often emerges as a central barrier to immigrants' civic and political engagement within mainstream institutions (Ramakrishnan and Viramontes 2006). Language barriers also contribute to stratification between mainstream and ethnic organizations, because leaders in ethnic organizations often lack the linguistic skills to speak out in public hearings and apply for program grants or for nonprofit status (Ramakrishnan and Lewis 2005; Aptekar, chapter 8, this volume). Organizations in which immigrants can speak their native language consequently provide important spaces for newcomers to participate in the civic life of their adopted countries, and possibly in their home countries as well (chapter 13, this volume). To the extent that limited English skills might be characteristic of immigrants from a variety of class backgrounds, organizations that support such linguistic communities may provide a space for the kinds of cross-class alliances some see disappearing from mainstream America (Skocpol 1999).

Beyond language, immigrants may also face cultural gaps in understanding their new country's political institutions, its taken-for-granted norms about politics and civic activity, and the very ways that politics and civic engagement are understood and discussed. Immigrants must learn the ropes, so to speak, of their host country, and research indicates that those from authoritarian regimes are less prepared to participate in politics (Ramakrishnan 2005; Bilodeau 2005). On the other hand, immigrants from countries with stronger or more radical union traditions than in the United States may help reinvigorate the American union movement (La Luz and Finn 1998), and religious precepts from the homeland may give a distinctive spin on how immigrants get involved in community service (chapter 7, this volume). The immigrant experience can thus create obstacles to political and civic incorporation, but it can also rejuvenate or transform norms and practices in host societies.

Finally, immigrants may also get involved in transnational social fields where social, economic, and political activities collectively engage people in the homeland and the host country (Levitt and Glick Schiller 2004; Levitt 2001). An open question is whether transnational political and civic activities sap energies and resources that would otherwise involve immigrants in the adopted country, or whether the lessons learned and skills gained through transnational activities create a virtuous circle of civic and political engagement across borders (chapter 13, this volume).

In short, understanding immigrant civic and political engagement is important not only for the unique issues raised by immigration—from the importance of formal citizenship and legal status, to linguistic challenges and differences in culture—but also as a lens on general theories of civic and political engagement and as a hint of how organizational life may evolve in the decades to come.

The Immigrant Adaptation Literature: Its Relative Silence on Politics

Since the advent of the post-1965 wave of immigration, one of the most vigorous debates on immigrant adaptation has been over the continued relevance of immigrant assimilation and the utility of alternative frameworks such as reactive ethnicity or segmented assimilation. Classic models of immigrant assimilation in the United States viewed immigrant adaptation largely as a linear process. Scholars in this tradition disagreed over whether this process was marked by Anglo-conformity or the creation of a new melting-pot hybrid, and whether assimilation in some areas (such as acculturation to sociocultural practices) would inevitably lead to assimilation in others (Gordon 1964). However, they largely agreed that, with time and generational succession, immigrants would give up their distinctive languages, norms, identities, and practices, eventually becoming largely undifferentiated Americans (Park 1930; Warner and Srole 1945; Gordon 1964).

Scholars of the post-1965 wave of immigration to the United States are divided as to whether this older model applies to new immigrants. A number of scholars challenge the assertions of the classic assimilation model—of inevitable progression on matters such as cultural homogenization, intermarriage, occupational mobility, and the like—offering instead a model of segmented assimilation (Portes and Zhou 1993; Portes and Rumbaut 2006; Zhou 1999). These researchers note that integration experiences are heavily stratified by class and race: Depending on an immigrant group's class background, minority status, and their context of reception in the United States, they may follow a path of straight-line assimilation, assimilate downward into the American minority underclass, or advance socioeconomically while retaining their ethnic and cultural differences (Portes and Rumbaut 2006; Waters 1999; Zhou and Bankston 1998). In contrast, others favor a new assimilation model that forgoes the assumption of cultural homogenization and acknowledges the impact of multiculturalism in American life. These studies point to the continued relevance of certain critical aspects of the assimilation model—such as occupational mobility, intermarriage, English proficiency, and the pursuit of higher education—all of which are made possible by immigrants' desires for a better life and changes in social norms and legal frameworks that make discrimination less likely today than before (Alba and Nee 2003; Perlmann 2005).

This ongoing debate over immigrant adaptation has produced numerous empirical and theoretical studies, but neither the segmented assimilation nor the new assimilation frameworks have much to say about immigrant civic and political incorporation. For instance, Richard Alba and Victor Nee (2003) implicitly acknowledge the role of political institutions in shaping antidiscrimination laws, but they pay limited attention to the formation of civic organizations and groups' relative levels of politicization. The logic of the new assimilation approach nevertheless implies that immigrants and their children will increasingly choose to participate (and be welcomed to participate) in mainstream civic organizations and political activities. Similarly, the segmented assimilation model implies that class, legal status, and race will stratify entry and participation in political and civic affairs. However, as Portes and Rumbaut note, "the typology is largely based on the different *class* resources that immigrants bring with them, while . . . ethnicity regularly trumps class as a motive for collective mobilization" (2006, 182, emphasis in original). Nevertheless, a segmented assimilation approach to civic and political engagement would likely predict that nonwhite immigrants with socioeconomic resources will use ethnicity as an identity category and a source of organizational cohesion; minority immigrants of modest class backgrounds may join the (limited) organizations for poor minorities in the United States; and that white immigrants will blend over time into the American middle class mainstream.

Ultimately, however, these applications and approximations are unsatisfactory. Even though we can draw civic and political implications from the new assimilationist or the segmented assimilation frameworks, we lack detailed theoretical and empirical attention to civic organizations, political institutions, and processes of civic or political engagement. The present-day debate in the immigrant adaptation literature is largely silent on the role of civic and political participation or the formation of community organizations. We lack a clear understanding of the factors that catapult some organizations and groups to political prominence and leave others at the periphery of local influence, nor do we fully understand the role of state actors and mainstream social institutions in allocating and shaping power and access to political resources.

The Civic Participation Literature: Nascent Attention to Immigrants

A wealth of scholarship in political science shows that civic participation (also referred to as voluntarism or volunteerism) plays an important role in shaping political participation such as voting, writing letters to elected officials, and contributing money to politics. Even though the association of higher socioeconomic status with greater political participation is a widely applicable finding in the United States and other liberal democracies, more recent scholarship shows that such mechanisms often operate through prior forms of engagement, such as participation in religious institutions and other community organizations (Verba, Schlozman, and Brady 1995). Indeed, participation in civic activities can even help individuals overcome some of the disadvantages associated with lower socioeconomic status, providing residents with the civic skills and political information necessary to engage in politics (Verba, Schlozman, and Brady 1995; Lee 2002).

Scholarly attention to civic voluntarism received a considerable boost during the 1990s with Robert Putnam's work on associational life across Italy's various regions (1993) and in the United States (2000). One of Putnam's central claims regarding the United States is that civic voluntarism has declined over the past several decades, and that this has led to negative outcomes on matters ranging from interpersonal trust and confidence in government institutions to bureaucratic efficiency, economic development, and even public health outcomes. There have been several criticisms of Putnam's wide-ranging approach to civic voluntarism. Some involve disagreements over what has been responsible for the decline in voluntarism, with Theda Skocpol (2003) pointing to the rise of national, bureaucratic organizations disconnected from local concerns, and Jason Kaufman (2002) identifying competition from private insurance companies and changing norms regarding racial and gender exclusion.

Scholars have also called for a narrower and more detailed articulation of how civic voluntarism relates to political incorporation, particularly with respect to racial and ethnic minorities. For instance, Rodney Hero (2003) noted that Putnam's measures of social capital may predict improved outcomes for whites, but fail to do so—and, in some cases, even predict worse outcomes—for nonwhites. Kaufman offered a similar critique with respect to historical data on civic participation from the first half of the twentieth century, arguing that civic associations grew out of a process of competitive voluntarism, as new groups splintered along ethnic and religious lines and many native-born groups sought to maintain racial and gender exclusion. Thus, higher levels of voluntarism did not produce favorable outcomes for everyone in society, as members of excluded groups were worse off living in contexts of high voluntarism also characterized by strong biases in race, nativity, class, and gender.

Despite these vigorous debates about whether civic participation is declining, the causes for such declines, and the consequences for political participation, civic participation in contemporary immigrant communities has received much less attention. Part of this silence is due to the kinds of data currently available to scholars of civic and political engagement: surveys such as the 1990 Civic Participation Study (Verba, Schlozman, and Brady 1995) and the 2000 Social Capital Community Benchmark Survey (Putnam 2007) were not conducted in languages apart from English and Spanish, had relatively small sample sizes of Asian immigrant groups, and collected little information on respondents' national origins and immigration histories. Indeed, in the 2000 Social Capital Survey, there was no question regarding the nativity of survey respondents. Furthermore, even surveys such as the Current Population Survey, with detailed immigrant characteristics and large sample sizes (Ramakrishnan 2006), fail to include measures of voluntarism that adequately capture immigrant participation. For instance, measures that focus on involvement in neighborhood associations often ignore the role of hometown or home-region associations among Latino immigrants or the continuing connections between suburban immigrants and ethnic organizations in central cities (Jones-Correa 1998; Levitt 2001; Zhou 2001). In addition, it is unclear whether civic involvement in groups such as ethnic soccer leagues, storefront churches, and cultural associations has different implications for political participation than, say, involvement in mainstream churches, neighborhood associations, labor unions, and chambers of commerce.

Finally, the standard literature on civic participation gives relatively short shrift to organizations. Although organizations play a role in civic association models, such as that proposed by Sidney Verba, Kay Schlozman, and Henry Brady (1995), the focus is usually only on the extent to which organizations endow individuals with information, skills, and motivations to participate. Organizations are less likely to be the subject of independent study (but see Schlozman and Tierney 1986; Wong 2006; Strolovich 2007). Thus, scholars have paid less attention to the political stratification of organizations, in particular to inequalities over agenda setting and influence on politics and decision making at the local level. The limited focus on local stratification and influence is particularly problematic given that many community organizations operate at this level, rather than at the national level studied by scholars such as Skocpol (2003).

Scholars of immigrant politics have done a better job in examining community organizations and their role in shaping political power at the local level, but the findings from existing immigrant political incorporation studies have been limited to particular contexts and small-N comparisons (Jones-Correa 1998; Bloemraad 2006; García Bedolla 2005; Wong 2006). Although this volume is not a large-N study, we make explicit comparisons across contexts, groups, and organization types. A number of the chapters also come from the Immigrant Civic Engagement Project (chapters 2, 8, 9, and 13), and consequently share a methodology and are animated by a similar set of questions.[5]

The Literature on Minority Political Incorporation: A Need for New Models

Studies of community power, especially as they relate to ethnic and racial minority groups in the United States, offer a starting point in considering the interaction between community organizations and political institutions. A classic example of such an approach is Dahl's model of pluralist politics, developed from a case study of New Haven, Connecticut (1961). New Haven's population contained a significant proportion of European-origin immigrants and a small stratum of well-to-do Yankees. Dahl suggested that the nature of democratic politics in New Haven made decision making reliant on changing coalitions of actors, some of whom represented immigrant concerns. Significantly, Dahl argued that many immigrant issues stemmed largely from immigrants' working class background rather than their cultural or ethnic differences. He contended, as a result, that as immigrants and their descendants achieve upward mobility and social assimilation, ethnic groups pass through three stages of political assimilation, eventually becoming indistinguishable in their civic and political activities from others (1961, 32–36). This process, he posited, would also be furthered by the move of political administration toward greater bureaucratic and technical expertise. Dahl's characterization of ethnic politics as a temporary phenomenon was in line with the prevailing view of modernization theory during the 1960s.

In particular, modernization theory predicted that traditional views, institutions, and practices would get swept away and that more rational and economic interests would take hold.

However, dissenting voices in the political incorporation tradition argued that ethnic politics may be a more permanent part of political power and mobilization. Nathan Glazer and Daniel Patrick Moynihan (1963) raised this possibility in their examination of New York City with their observation that ethnic politics remain central to city politics. They argued that ethnicity remains a powerful force in political and civic life because it is emotionally salient to immigrants and their descendants, and because ethnic labels overlay socioeconomic distinctions, thereby providing relevant markers of political interests (Glazer and Moynihan 1975). The state can also encourage ethnic labels over class or other collective identifiers through its systems of categorization and the development of the welfare state. Michael Parenti (1967) developed similar arguments, but emphasized how socioeconomic advancement might reinforce the political salience of ethnicity: with more resources, immigrant groups and their children could better build civic organizations, may witness prejudice and discrimination more directly as they seek upward mobility, and may gain what he called the psychological strength to make political demands. According to these early alternative views, ethnic cohesion—reflected and reinforced in ethnically based civic organizations—facilitates political engagement and, by extension, immigrants' overall integration into American society.

Research on the political incorporation of American ethnic and racial groups further developed in the 1980s, with revisionist scholarship on urban political machines and more detailed attention to the empowerment of African Americans and Latinos. The revisionist scholarship accepted the premise that ethnicity was often a convenient way of packaging political coalitions, mobilizing voters, and providing benefits such as government jobs. However, these scholars challenged the notion that urban political machines arose because of immigration (Bridges 1984) or that such institutions were the natural friends of immigrant groups (Erie 1990; Gamm 1989). Instead, they argued, political parties mobilized immigrant groups selectively, including only those groups necessary to win office (the Irish, for instance) and ignoring the rest. These studies were useful in illustrating how immigrant and ethnic organizations were selectively incorporated into politics in the early 1900s, but were less so in explaining the incorporation of racial and ethnic minorities in the contemporary era, especially given the absence of strong local parties in the West, the decline of such institutions in the rest of the country, and the rise of African American protest power and electoral power in many urban areas.

The political consequences of African American protest activity were well documented by social movement scholars such as Douglas McAdam (1982) and Aldon Morris (1984), who showed that the civil rights movement was not simply an expression of disaffection among excluded groups but rather a multipronged strategy to advance group interests in the face of electoral exclusion and newly expanding opportunities for political change. The success of the movement also depended on a dense organizational infrastructure, including churches, teacher groups, and student groups, that mobilized participants and helped to shape public opinion on minority rights (McAdam 1982; Lee 2002). Yet despite the successes of the civil rights movement, scholars of minority politics in the mid-1980s began to question the relative value of protest strategies compared to electoral strategies in gaining influence, especially in local politics and policy. In their seminal work from 1984, *Protest Is Not Enough*, Rufus Browning, Dale Marshall, and David Tabb analyzed politics in the San Francisco Bay Area and found that protest politics were inadequate and electoral strategies more important for the political empowerment of African Americans and Latinos. These strategies included mobilizing group members, forming coalitions with other supportive groups, and getting racial and ethnic minorities elected to office. Thus, with the civil rights movement increasingly fading from view, electoral strategies became key to advancing the interests of racial minorities in the United States.

The framework of minority political incorporation by Browning, Marshall, and Tabb has proved influential to the study of Latino and African American empowerment (Hero 1992; Meier and Stewart 1991; Sonenshein 1997), but it faces several limitations when applied to immigrant populations. For one, electoral strategies are less applicable to immigrants in the United States than to the native-born populations who were part of most earlier studies of minority political incorporation. Naturalized citizens vote at lower rates than the native-born, two-thirds of immigrants do not have citizenship, and half of those without citizenship currently have no path to citizenship because they are undocumented. The limited utility of electoral mobilization is especially pronounced in new immigrant destinations, where a large proportion of the foreign-born population is recently arrived. However, the limits are also evident in more traditional destinations, where local governments sometimes respond to the needs of immigrant residents even without significant electoral pressures (Jones-Correa 2004; Lewis and Ramakrishnan 2004, 2007). Language barriers and fragmentation among community organizations and ethnic media are also more complex when considering Asian immigrants, given their greater levels of residential dispersion and linguistic and occupational diversity. Finally, with immigrants increasingly settling in suburban areas, the political opportunities, resources, and coalition partners available to immigrant groups are likely to be considerably different than those found in large, densely populated cities. Thus, even though the framework of minority political incorporation may continue to be relevant for long-term immigrant populations with high rates of citizenship, it needs to be expanded to include nonelectoral incorporation for those unable or unlikely to vote.

The upshot of all this is that existing integration models and political theories fit awkwardly with the contemporary immigrant experience. We need better conceptual and analytical tools with which to approach this field, and more detailed empirical information, especially with respect to community organizations and their relative involvement in political activities and policy issues.

In the remainder of this introduction, we lay out some of the concepts and tools we find helpful for understanding immigrant organizing and introduce the empirical studies showcased in the book.

CENTRAL THEMES AND COMPARISONS

The contributions to this volume all focus on organizations—whether founded and run by immigrants, or organizations that include substantial numbers of people with immigrant origins in their membership or clientele. By organizations, we mean more or less institutionalized collections of individuals that come together periodically for a common goal or activity. Organizations, and civic associations more generally, have always been considered central to American democracy. They take on added importance, however, when we consider the processes by which immigrants become part of American civic and political life. All newcomers, regardless of visa status, cannot immediately access American citizenship. Lack of citizenship shuts them out of the formal political system, such as voting and running for office, implying that immigrants' early civic and political socialization may occur first through local organizations, rather than through formal political groups such as parties. Even with citizenship, however, a growing body of research suggests that the workhorses of political integration of yesteryear, political parties, largely ignore or shut out new citizens or would-be citizens (Dahl 1961; Erie 1990; Jones-Correa 1998; Wong 2006). Finally, as figure 1.1 indicates, most immigrants today live outside the Northeast and the Midwest, regions most likely to have cities with partisan local elections and remnants of party machines. With no local partisan elections in the West and most areas of the South, local party organizations are largely irrelevant to the political mobilization of immigrants today (chapter 3, this volume). In these circumstances, we need to know whether other collective groups are stepping in to fill the breach, or whether our political life is becoming increasingly stratified not just by class, but also by immigrant origins and ethnicity.

This volume advances a framework for the study of immigrant organizing, offering a conceptual map for this type of research, profiling some of the most innovative scholarship in this area and setting an agenda for future research. The volume is motivated by three primary themes.

First, we want to understand the conditions under which organizations that speak for and bring together immigrants have visibility in their communities and have an impact on other civic and political actors. We thus develop the concepts of civic and political presence and weight to help researchers measure and evaluate organizational effects in the civic and political sphere. We also offer a wide-ranging list of factors that can help us understand these dynamics. These conceptual efforts are informed by frameworks around contexts of reception in North America (Portes and Rumbaut 1996; Reitz 1998; Bloemraad 2006) as well as the structuring influence of political institutions such as political parties, citizenship and voting rules, and government policies toward immigrants and refugees (Ireland 1994; Jones-Correa 1998; Koopmans et al. 2005; Wong 2006). In European studies of immigrant political incorporation, the concept of political opportunity structure (POS), taken from the social movements literature,

FIGURE 1.1   *Share of Foreign-Born Population By Region of Settlement in the United States*

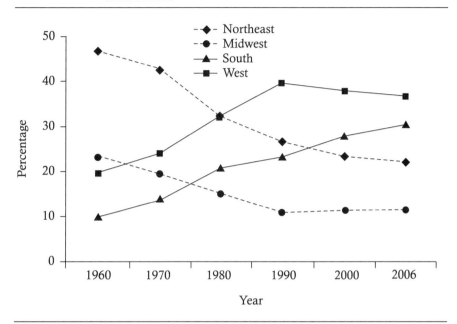

Source: Gibson and Lennon (1999); U.S. Census Bureau (2000, 2006).

captures the idea that institutional structures—and even discursive norms—channel civic and political engagement in distinct ways (for example, Koopmans et al. 2005; chapter 6, this volume). We cast a wide net in considering which factors may help us understand the nexus between immigrants, organizations, and the political system. As contemporary research in this area is still quite new, we want to reflect the range and breadth of questions that need to be explored.

Second, we introduce the idea of civic and political stratification, pointing out that all civic engagement and political organizing is not equal. Whereas many past studies of civic engagement and social capital take as their starting point the idea that participation is good in and of itself, we argue that studying immigrants' experiences highlights patterns of stratification in the degree to which immigrants are recognized in the civic sphere and are incorporated into community organizations (either through ethnic or mainstream organizations), and the extent to which local officials know of these organizations or acknowledge their importance. Although we are interested in how organizations affect individuals' attitudes, identities, and behavior—and a few of the contributions in this book discuss such dynamics explicitly—the volume's primary focus is on how organized collective actors affect or are affected by other organizations and institutions.

Third, we argue that comparative case studies are methodologically and conceptually invaluable for broadening our understanding of immigrant organizing and civic or political engagement. In particular, we highlight three types of comparison: the importance of the place in which immigrants organize (city versus suburb, regions within the United States. and variations across countries); the importance of the immigrant group that is organizing (national origin, religious background, group resources, and so on); and the importance of the type of organization that immigrants join (unions, churches, social services providers, hometown associations, and the like). To this end, the volume is divided into three sections—place, group, and organizational form—to help explain the political relevance of immigrant community organizations. Reading within and across these axes of comparison, we deepen our understanding of the political relevance of immigrant community organizations, in general, as well as the relative importance of place, group and type of organization in understanding similarities and differences in civic experiences and stratification.

Figure 1.2 brings various aspects of our theoretical framework together. The right side of the figure shows that civic stratification and political stratification are largely the result of processes and outcomes related to individual behavior and collective action. It is relatively straightforward to gauge level of civic and political stratification based on individual engagement: one obtains the rates of participation among various groups and compares their shares of the participating population to their shares of the overall population (DeSipio 1996; Ramakrishnan 2005). It is too simplistic, however, to rely exclusively on aggregations of individual behavior to gauge group inequalities on civic and political visibility, access, and influence. One must also take into account dynamics of collective action: the extent to which immigrants join existing organizations and create new ones, and the extent to which organizations are able to command political resources and take advantage of opportunities to gain visibility and influence in the policy process.

Collective dynamics involving community organizations and ethnic groups can be thought of as processes related to civic and political group-based *incorporation*, whereas dynamics involving individual participation and attitudes can be deemed relevant to questions of civic and political *assimilation*. Thus, in the language of contemporary assimilation, individual immigrants are assimilated when they have equal chances of being a member of a neighborhood association, Little League baseball club, or chamber of commerce, compared to native-born residents. The same would be true for political participation.

Thus, the contemporary scholarship on assimilation centers on questions of convergence in individual-level outcomes. In contrast, political incorporation suggests integration based on collective mobilization as a group of a particular background, ethnicity, culture, religion, or race. Such a pattern could suggest dynamics of segmented assimilation or processes of racialization hold sway. For

FIGURE 1.2   *Framework of Political and Civic Integration and Stratification*

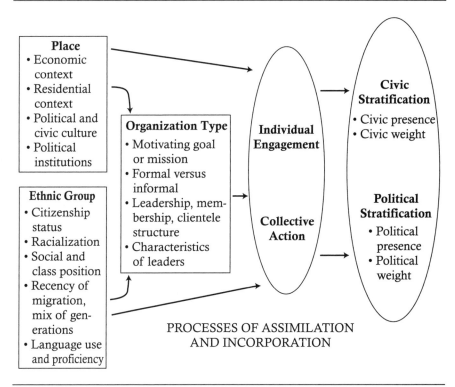

Place
• Economic context
• Residential context
• Political and civic culture
• Political institutions

Ethnic Group
• Citizenship status
• Racialization
• Social and class position
• Recency of migration, mix of generations
• Language use and proficiency

Organization Type
• Motivating goal or mission
• Formal versus informal
• Leadership, membership, clientele structure
• Characteristics of leaders

Individual Engagement

Collective Action

Civic Stratification
• Civic presence
• Civic weight

Political Stratification
• Political presence
• Political weight

PROCESSES OF ASSIMILATION AND INCORPORATION

Source: Authors' compilation.

example, we might say that Vietnamese Americans in Orange County, California, are politically incorporated because Vietnamese Americans play an important role in local, state, and congressional elections, because public officials see Vietnamese organizations as important players in local affairs, and because Vietnamese immigrants have regularly held protests against visits by cultural groups and government officials from Vietnam. It is possible that political incorporation at a group level may eventually lead to political assimilation at the individual level, though this empirical question can probably best be answered after multiple generations.

A third possibility is failed integration, in which immigrants do not become engaged in civic and political life, either as assimilated individuals or incorporated groups. Under this scenario, immigrants are either shut out or choose to remain outside civic and political spheres. In one way or another, all the chapters in this volume confront the question of whether and how immigrants get woven into the existing civic and political fabric of their new homes. By shining the spotlight on organizations, we place particular emphasis on group-based political incorporation.

ENGAGEMENT IN COMMUNITIES AND THE POLITY: DEFINITIONS

Because the study of civic and political engagement is rife with varying definitions and conceptualizations, we outline concepts used in this volume to facilitate greater transparency in comparisons. First, we suggest that participation in a community and in the polity can be conceptualized at three levels: the individual, the organizational, and the ethnic group. At each level, civic engagement refers to involvement in communal activities that have some purpose or benefit beyond a single individual or family's self-interest—either for a community organization, social group, or the general public. This could include volunteering for a local food bank, helping to organize the India Day Parade, or joining a cleanup day in a local park. Political engagement refers to involvement in activities related to the formal political system, often with the intention of influencing government policies and practices. Such involvement can be conventional (such as voting, running for office, or contacting officials) or unconventional (such as participating in protests and boycotts). We use the term *engagement* over *participation* to reflect aspects of involvement that go beyond the individual level, giving a more explicit role to government and organizational actors in producing engaged communities.

Although much current scholarship on civic engagement stems from an interest in how civic involvement spills over into the political sphere—an interest this volume shares—civic and political engagement should be conceptualized separately. The distinction is not merely academic: it is sharply felt by many immigrants. For instance, Kristi Andersen, in her chapter on parties and organizations in six U.S. cities, quotes a member of the Waco Hispanic Chamber of Commerce, who explained, "I didn't want to be in a political organization, I wanted to be in an organization that promoted business . . . and wanted to stay away from politics." Thus, immigrants may disavow interest in politics or perceive politics to be dirty and corrupt, but nonetheless be positively inclined toward civic endeavors and participate in community groups.

Yet self-defined nonpolitical activities can provide fertile grounds for later political engagement by making people more aware of current events, increasing participants' sense of personal and collective efficacy, teaching skills useful for politics and providing sites of mobilization around political or policy ends. For instance, participation in a chamber of commerce could well lead to direct or indirect political engagement when the chamber takes a position on local issues. Many Mexican hometown associations (HTAs) started as social and familial organizations, but some have recently become more involved in the politics of their home regions and places of settlement in the United States (chapter 13, this volume). Also, as Els de Graauw shows in her study of San Francisco (chapter 12, this volume), nonprofit social-service providers often get involved in a limited, yet important, form of political activity by serving as advocates and providing important information to government agencies. Indeed, as the chapters in this volume attest, outreach and mobilization by political actors can include not just political parties and candidates but also bureaucratic actors ranging from local government agencies to foreign embassies and consulates (see also Jones-Correa 2004; Ramakrishnan and Lewis 2005; chapter 4, this volume). An important goal of this volume is to compare the circumstances and conditions under which community organizations may be more or less likely to be drawn into the political process.

Civic and Political Engagement: The Individual Level

Although organizations and immigrant-origin groups are the primary focus of this volume, discussion of individual-level factors is inevitable. Table 1.1 summarizes some of the major individual-level indicators of civic and political engagement, distinguishing between people's behaviors and their attitudes or knowledge. We focus on adults rather than school-age children or adolescents, and our concern is largely with behavior rather than psychological orientations such as the development of civic norms, in-group trust or generalized trust. At a behavioral level, civic engagement can be measured as formal membership in a community organization, volunteering for a local group or initiative (that is, providing one's time and labor to a civic cause), donating money to a charitable cause, or taking a leadership role in an organization or initiative. Similarly, political engagement at the individual level can be measured by activities such as voting, supporting a political campaign, writing letters to elected officials, attending public forums, signing petitions, and participating in protests and rallies.

Civic and Political Engagement: The Organization Level

This volume focuses primarily on community organizations and their political relevance. Community organizations can range widely in their degree of formal organization (including incorporated or nonprofit status), leadership structure (ranging from flat to hierarchical), financial mechanisms (dues-paying, revenue-generating, grant-receiving, and so on), and territorial focus (cities or neighborhoods, domestic or transnational). We pay particular attention to organizational variation by activity type—such as transnational, arts and culture, social services, labor, advocacy, and religious- or faith-based—and we are sensitive to the potential for place-based variation in organizational coalitions and partnerships with government.

Within the immigration literature, organizations have taken a back seat to other collectives, notably the family and household unit, or the ethnic group. Immigrant households have received detailed attention as facilitators of migration

TABLE 1.1   *Measures of Civic and Political Engagement at the Individual Level*

	Civic Engagement	Political Engagement
Behavior	Being an associational member	Attending public forums
		Voting
	Contributing time and labor (volunteering)	Writing to elected officials
	Giving monetary contributions (donating)	Donating campaign money
	Assuming a leadership role	Doing campaign work
		Signing a petition
		Participating in protests, rallies, marches, or boycotts
Knowledge and attitudes	Information about civic opportunities	Political information
	Civic skills (enabling collective action)	Politically relevant skills
		Sense of political efficacy
		Trust in government
	Civic norms	Political interest
	Generalized trust in others	Party identification

Source: Authors' compilation.

and as sites of conflict and succor during integration (Kibria 1993; Pessar 1999). The ethnic or national origin group—often labeled as the ethnic or immigrant community—also receives attention as providing a potential economic enclave within which individuals can find work and entrepreneurs can set up businesses, or as a source of social networks and community norms that influences migration and incorporation (Portes and Bach 1985; Zhou and Bankston 1998; Menjívar 2000; Massey et al. 1998; Palloni et al. 2001).

Yet while studies of immigrant families and ethnic networks are invaluable for understanding migrants' experiences, the lack of attention to more formal organizations is problematic. From the perspective of political science, community organizations can be the building blocks of political engagement. They are attractive sites for politicians to mobilize would-be supporters, and they also provide individuals with skills, attitudes, and information relevant to political participation. The civic roots of political action have received considerable attention in political science during the last two decades (Verba, Schlozman, and Brady 1995; Rosenstone and Hansen 1993), but studies of immigrant civic participation are rare, and even rarer are those that tie together immigrant organizations to political institutions and processes.

From the perspective of sociology, the tradition of studying organizations dates back at least to Max Weber. Research in recent decades has considered the role of organizations in social movements, social capital formation, and in the development of a third sector between the market and the state (Salamon 1999; Van Til 2000; McAdam, Tarrow, and Tilly 2001). Yet most of these studies fail to consider whether immigrants engage in organizing to the same degree, in the same way, and with the same results as the native-born population. Much of this research has centered on organizational and nonprofit studies or contentious politics rather than on organizations' role in incorporating newcomers into mainstream political institutions, a key interest of this volume (but see Bloemraad 2005, 2006; Chung 2005; Marwell 2004).

Finally, social scientists studying urban environments have long noted the role of local civic organizations in influencing municipal politics and urban communities. Older work by these scholars included immigrants as an integral part of the urban story (Katznelson 1981; Glazer and Moynihan 1963). Today, however, immigrants live outside the traditional urban centers of yesteryear, having moved into metropolitan areas relatively new to immigration, suburban municipalities, and even rural areas. We do not yet know whether traditional accounts of urban politics and community engagement apply equally today, and to these new residential spaces (but see Oliver 2001; Jones-Correa 2004; Ramakrishnan and Lewis 2005).

Distinguishing Ethnic Groups from Political Communities

Finally, we need to define two other terms used in this volume: *groups*, denoted by ethnicity, and *communities*, denoted by geography and political jurisdiction. Individuals who share some attribute (or attributes) traditionally thought of as related to ethnicity—such as a common language, national origin, religion, racial classification, or cultural background—can form an ethnic group.[6] Ethnic groups can also include native-born citizens with similar origins, religious traditions, and so forth. We reserve the word *community* to talk about entities defined by a clear geographical jurisdiction. Because these geographical entities are legally defined—as towns, cities, counties, states, or even countries—they have some independent decision-making structures that control certain resources or rules in their jurisdiction. Although residents may not always feel unified in a sociological community, they form a necessary civic and political community because they must share public goods, compete over resources, and abide by similar policies. Communities are therefore made up of individuals, ethnic groups, and a variety of voluntary or nonprofit organizations.

CIVIC AND POLITICAL STRATIFICATION

Civic and political stratification can operate at any of the levels of analysis discussed so far: among individuals, organizations, ethnic groups, and political communities, though the primary focus here is on organizations and ethnic groups. In table 1.2, we offer a typology of civic and political stratification as they apply to organizations, although some of these measures can also be aggregated to the level of ethnic group and community. Because this is an emerging field of study, we want to set out a broad analytical framework from which subsequent chapters could draw.

One way to measure civic and political stratification is to compare the material resources of organizations, in terms of money, personnel, and physical space. How large is the group's budget? How large is the staff, or membership, or pool of volunteers? Does the organization have the exclusive use of a building or office space for meetings and activities, or must it constantly scramble to find space for events? For some organizations, such as unions or even 501(c)(3) nonprofits, resources can be specifically earmarked for political purposes (Berry 2003; chapter 12, this volume). For others, resources directed for general civic activities may be mobilized for political ends in rare instances, such as during the immigration protests and boycotts of spring 2006. One challenge researchers face is the lack of detailed and reliable information on organizations' material resources. This is especially true for detailed breakdowns of spending or overall budget information for informal associations and for small nonprofits not required to file 990 forms with the Internal Revenue Service.

One could argue that resources are at best an indirect measure of civic and political stratification, and that there are more direct ways to conceptualize the visibility and influence of community organizations as civic and political actors. In table 1.2, we advance a framework that distinguishes *presence*—visibility, legitimacy, and alliances—from *weight*—the extent to which organizations are taken seriously in policy decisions—with measures ranging from access to public officials to actual influence over the various stages of agenda setting, policy decision making, and policy implementation. Given the difficulties associated with establishing a particular group's influence in the policy process (which can be affected by multiple types of political opportunities, strategic decision making by many actors, and unintended consequences), we leave the definition of civic and political weight relatively open, capturing the extent to which organizations are able to have their interests represented at various stages of the policy-making process (Kingdon 1984; Hansen 1991).

More particularly, an organization's civic presence can be measured by its visibility among the general population and mainstream media: Do members of the community know about the organization? Do local journalists turn to the organization for stories or commentary on breaking news? Civic presence can also be measured by the degree to which organizations are isolated from, or connected to, other organizations when it comes to particular programs, events, and activities. Having allies, and the form that such alliances take, can act as a marker of prominence.[7] Finally, we can think about an organization's legitimacy, which can be based on whether it is formally recognized by the state through incorporation or nonprofit status, or the degree to which it is seen as a legitimate player by others in the civic sphere. These three facets of civic presence—visibility, alliances, and legitimacy—are analytically separate but may have important effects on each other.

TABLE 1.2   *Components of Civic and Political Stratification Among Organizations*

	Civic	Political
Resources	Budget Personnel (staff, volunteers, members, clients) Physical space, equipment	Expenditures, personnel, physical space, and equipment devoted to political activities
Presence	Visibility and recognition among general population, mainstream media Degree of isolation or connection to other organizations in civic activities Legitimacy—formal incorporation or state recognition Legitimacy—perceived as having a role in local governance	Visibility and recognition among government officials Organizational affiliations with elected and appointed officials Degree of isolation or connection to other organizations in political activities
Weight	Ability to advance interests in the civic realm Ability to influence allocations of resources to other organizations Ability to shape and influence civic projects involving multiple organizations	Ability to gain access to public officials Ability to have interests represented in agenda-setting policy decision-making and policy implementation Ability to influence allocations of power to other organizations

Source: Authors' compilation.

Analogous to civic presence is the notion of political presence, which is the extent to which organizations and ethnic groups are visible to government officials and other policy makers, and the extent to which they are seen as legitimate actors in the political community. Several chapters in this volume (2, 8, and 9) rely on such assessments by government officials of various community organizations across a range of activities. We can also measure political presence by examining the extent to which an organization has members who serve in local government, either as elected or appointed officials, or as high-placed civil servants within local bureaucracies (see chapters 3 and 6, this volume). Finally, we can consider organizational alliances that work toward explicit political ends, including links to groups such as political parties and lobbying organizations.

Civic and political presence are important measures of standing, showing the degree to which immigrants are recognized as full partners in their communities. Civic and political presence are also important precursors to influence in a community, what we term civic and political weight. The distinction hinges on the question of whether the state is significantly involved in the allocation of resources and power. Thus civic weight refers to the ability of an organization to advance its interests through actions that do not directly involve the state—for instance, a food service union urges consumers to boycott a major grocery store. Civic weight also refers to the ability of organizations to influence the allocation of resources to other organizations (for example, the United Way's distribution of funds to other organizations), as well as the ability of organizations to shape and influence projects that involve multiple organizations (for instance, if the local Lions Club spearheads a park clean-up day focused on certain local parks but not others).

By contrast, political weight refers to the ability of organizations to gain access to local government institutions and to influence the allocation of resources and power in ways that directly involve government. Thus, the ability of a neighborhood organization to get City Hall to block development of open space land would count as political weight, as would the ability of a PTA to get the school district to provide more language support to first-generation immigrant parents. As previous generations of social scientists have noted (Bachrach and Baratz 1970; Gaventa 1980), political influence can occur at the stage of actual policy making and implementation, but also during the agenda setting stage and in the actual formation of interests.[8] We can also differentiate weight depending on the types of outcomes that groups seek, such as policy changes, material benefits, electoral successes, or symbolic recognition. Thus, one organization may work to elect one of its members to office, another may try to change a local ordinance, and a third may seek to fly its national flag on a special day in front of City Hall. Finally, political weight can operate at various levels, from national politics to states, counties, school districts and local government. An organization may have political weight at one level of government and not others. For example, Caroline Brettell and Deborah Reed-Danahay profile an Indian organization that is active primarily on foreign policy issues but more silent on local affairs (chapter 7, this volume).[9]

INCORPORATION AND STRATIFICATION: CONTRIBUTING FACTORS

Explaining variations in civic and political engagement across immigrant and ethnic groups requires attention to a variety of potential influences. The chapters in this volume are organized to highlight the importance of three dynamics: the role of place, of national origins, and of organizational types. Table 1.3 attempts to summarize some of the main factors that relate to each dynamic. Our goal is to lay out a comprehensive analytical framework useful to many different situations; some chapters in this volume touch on certain aspects more than others.

TABLE 1.3   *Explaining Variation in Civic and Political Engagement*

	Component Factors
Place	City size
	Existence of ethnic enclaves; ethnic residential concentration
	Type of institutional arrangements or informal norms regulating interaction between government and private-non-profit sector
	Political-civic culture
	History of racial-ethnic relations and immigrant adaptation
	Traditions of volunteerism
	Definitions of legitimate public groups
	Preferences on taxation and government spending
	Political factors
	District versus at-large representation systems
	Partisan versus nonpartisan elections
	Political party competition
	Proportional versus plurality electoral systems
	Presidential versus parliamentary systems
	Federalism
Group	Socioeconomic status
	Legal status and citizenship status
	Recency of migration
	Mix of immigrant generations
	Language
	Fluency in English (or host country language)
	Existence and viability of language communities
	Status in host society
	Discrimination
	Model minority status
	Foreigner or guestworker status
Organization type	Motivating goal or mission (such as religious, social, advocacy, workplace issues)
	Formal versus informal
	Legal nonprofit status
	Resources
	Financial (including type of financing mechanisms such as fees, dues, fundraising, and so on)
	Personnel (volunteer, staff, and so on)
	Physical location
	Leadership and membership—clientele structure
	Characteristics of leaders (cultural competency, social capital)
	Connections to other groups, including national federations or international coalitions

Source: Authors' compilation.

The Importance of Place

We expect place to have important effects on immigrant civic and political engagement. Indeed, the chapters that follow repeatedly highlight how place affects immigrant organizing and its repercussions, both directly and by mediating the relative importance of group resources or organizational activities.

Many characteristics of place may affect immigrant organizing. For instance, ethnic organizations will probably be more numerous in ethnic enclaves than elsewhere because of greater numbers, visibility, ease of coordination, and support from ethnic businesses. However, the potential organizational penalty of residential dispersion is likely smaller for groups with more material resources—such as access to a car—and with more organizational skills, such as the ability to communicate by email and the Internet. In this way, dynamics of place intersect with other axes of difference, notably a group's resources.

More generally, the size of the city (which includes towns and other types of municipalities) likely matters, even after accounting for the proportion of immigrant or ethnic residents. Size matters because ethnic businesses and nonprofits can benefit from economies of scale with greater numbers of immigrant residents, and larger cities have greater capacity to provide translation services and community liaisons (Ramakrishnan and Lewis 2005). In this way, size might intersect with a third, analytically distinct, feature of communities: the types of formal institutional arrangements or informal norms communities use to manage interactions between government and civic groups. Larger cities generally have more resources, both financial and human, to set up regular channels of communication and interaction—such as formal boards, regular meetings, or a formal comment period for pending political decisions—but innovative smaller cities can also establish similar infrastructures. Finally, cities may do a better job of organizing sustained interaction between public officials and residents than larger jurisdictions such as states or national governments (chapter 4, this volume), reinforcing the notion that the local level is a particularly important arena for the study of immigrant civic and political engagement.

Cities, states and countries also differ, often substantially, on other factors, such as political and civic culture and the institutions structuring politics in a particular place. Measuring cultural influences is notoriously difficult, and it is usually even harder to show a cultural effect on civic and political outcomes. Nonetheless, it is clear that a community's cultural context (including its history of racial and ethnic relations, experiences with immigrant adaptation, traditions of volunteerism, definitions of legitimate public groups, and preferences on government spending and taxation) affects patterns of civic and political stratification, as well as individuals' abilities, interests and understandings of civic and political engagement (Bloemraad 2006; chapters 5 and 6, this volume).

Identifying relevant political institutional structures is easier than identifying cultural effects, and has a long tradition in political science. Thus, we know that systems of elections and representation (district versus at-large systems, partisan versus nonpartisan elections, proportional versus plurality electoral systems and presidential versus parliamentary systems) affect political participation and outcomes, as do the level of political party competition and the presence or absence of multiple political jurisdictions, such as under federalism. Intersections of institutions, ethnic residential patterns, and strategies of organization and mobilization together make attention to place critical in understanding the political and civic engagement of immigrants.

Group Resources and Immigrant Agency

Beyond place, we also expect variation in civic and political engagement across national origin groups because such groups often share common attributes, not only of language and culture, but also of socioeconomic and legal status, length of residence, and histories of discrimination. In general, we would expect community organizations to be stronger and more vibrant among immigrant groups of higher socioeconomic status and more stable legal status. We would also expect that the recency of immigration and the mix of immigrant generations within an ethnic group will influence the viability of ethnic organizations as well as the group's orientation toward domestic versus transnational issues and its visibility among those of the majority population.

Significantly, as some of the chapters in this volume highlight, the relationship between group resources and civic or political engagement, presence, and weight is not always straightforward. Particular organizational forms can mobilize resource-poor groups, and particularities of place can shut out even the most economically privileged immigrants. For instance, a group-resource perspective would accurately predict that Mexican immigrants—among the lowest-income immigrant groups in the country with the highest rates of unauthorized residents—tend to have fewer community organizations and less political presence among existing organizations. Notable exceptions occur, however, in large cities with strong social service infrastructures and long traditions of transnational activities (chapters 2, 9, and 13) and in cities where political machines are selectively incorporating Mexican immigrant groups into politics, such as in Chicago (chapter 9). On the other end of the socioeconomic spectrum, Indian groups with high average incomes and education levels have a relatively high incidence of community organizations, but their political presence and weight depend on the openness of political institutions. As Sofya Aptekar notes in chapter 8 of this volume, Indian organizations in Edison, New Jersey, find themselves shut out of local governance, and Laurencio Sanguino (chapter 9) finds that those in Chicago are relatively marginal players in local politics. Finally, Vietnamese organizations may be less prevalent and active in politics than Indian organizations in the Dallas/Fort Worth area (chapter 7), but in places where they are a large proportion of the adult citizen population, such as parts of Orange County in California, Vietnamese organizations are visible and influential in local affairs (chapter 2).

Beyond socioeconomic resources, the existence of relatively large language communities—as with the Spanish-speaking population, which draws from many countries of origins—facilitates organizations of cultural production and media. The religious makeup of a group can also be a resource, or a liability. If a group's primary religious identity overlaps with existing mainstream religious institutions, such commonalities could ease ethnic-mainstream bridges, as is the case for the largely Catholic Mexican-origin population in the United States. Other faith traditions might face greater obstacles, such as religious groups that are largely ethnically defined, such as Hindus and Sikhs; traditions that are not as easily organized in formal houses of worship, such as Buddhism; or religions that are stigmatized as problematic, such as Islam because of its perceived association with terrorism and fundamentalism.

Finally, religious bridges and gulfs raise the more general issue of how the reception and reactions of the larger host society bear on the nature, existence, and viability of immigrant community organizations. Religious discrimination may lead to a lower public profile among affected groups, though perhaps also to a high degree of within-group organizing. Similarly, the persistent image of a group as foreign may alter the visibility of domestically oriented ethnic organizations versus their transnational counterparts, and the image of an immigrant group as a model minority may lead to greater civic and political presence among organizations dedicated to business and education, but greater invisibility—by mainstream society and group elites worried about the group's image— for those organizations working on issues such as labor exploitation, mental health, and poverty. More generally, mainstream actors' racial categorization of immigrant groups, and their implicit or explicit racial hierarchies, will likely create opportunities for some groups and hardship for others.

What Sort of Organization?

The third central comparison in this volume contrasts types of organizations. In what ways does the type of organization in which immigrants and ethnic groups participate affect civic and political stratification? Getting some purchase on this question requires paying attention to the primary mission of the organization (for example, as religious, social, or political); the institutionalization of the organization (formal or informal, registered as a non-profit or not); and the organization's resources, as discussed earlier. Of particular interest is the extent to which organizations set up for one purpose, especially a nonpolitical purpose, might find themselves involved in local civic and political affairs (chapter 13, this volume), or whether a strong adherence to a particular purpose, say religious worship, keeps an organization and its members isolated from civic and political involvement at the local level (chapter 10, this volume). In a similar way, we can ask whether formalized 501(c)(3) status, the primary Internal Revenue Service registration for nonprofit organizations, helps immigrants' civic and political engagement by making it easier to receive funding from government or foundations, or whether it hurts local engagement because of legal restrictions on political activism (chapters 4 and 12, this volume). One notable finding reported in a couple of chapters is that organizations seen by some observers as apolitical or antithetical to engagement in domestic civic and political life, notably formal 501(c)(3) organizations and hometown associations, can indeed play an important role in the civic and political incorporation of immigrants.

Consideration of organizational type also requires attention to the internal dynamics of recruitment (recruitment to leadership and of members), decision making, and organizing, and to the external dynamics of cooperation and forming coalitions. Regarding the latter, we need to study the extent to which and ways in which local organizations ally with other organizations through informal coalitions, formally federated structures, local umbrella groups, or international networks of nongovernmental organizations. Here we must ask how well existing literatures on voluntary organizations, social movement organizations, and organizational behavior speak to the immigrant experience.

A TASTE OF WHAT'S TO COME

We end by briefly outlining the individual contributions to this volume, and the emergent themes that we observe across the various cases and different lenses used to understand immigrant organizing.

Part I of this volume explores place-based determinants of immigrant civic and political organizing, across localities in the United States and across different countries in Europe. In chapter 2, Karthick Ramakrishnan and Irene Bloemraad examine the incidence and political presence of community organizations across six cities in northern and southern California, paying attention to variations across national origin groups and between ethnic and mainstream organizations. Although differences across ethnic groups are significant, we also find variations across localities according to the size of a city, the city's ethnic makeup, and local government policies toward immigrants. We note that the presence of ethnic business districts can play an independent role in boosting the number of ethnic community organizations, though the lack of a corresponding electoral base limits the political presence and weight of such organizations.

Notably, party competition and party organizations are a relatively minor part of the story in these California cities, a finding echoed in Kristi Andersen's chapter on immigrant-serving organizations in six medium-sized cities throughout the United States. In chapter 3, Andersen examines the extent to which community organizations mobilize immigrants into politics in the absence of local party efforts, and finds that such mobilization is limited: community organizations serve as weak substitutes for the parties of yore. She notes that variations in the political relevance of immigrant community organizations depends on the city's geographic isolation from large metropolitan centers, its connection to refugee resettlement programs, and the presence of potential coalition partners such as unions and universities that can serve as allies to immigrant communities.

In chapter 4, the final U.S. place-based comparison, Shannon Gleeson shows the complexities of place within the federal American political system, where different levels of government and different administrative branches of the same government take distinctive tacks to immigrant labor issues. Comparing Houston, Texas, and San Jose, California, Gleeson argues that a more robust set of labor protections in California depresses organizing around Latinos' labor rights in San Jose relative to the more activist stance taken in Houston. A paradox thus emerges in Houston where a distant federal government combined with a weak state apparatus spurs local government to partner with a range of other groups, including community-based organizations, federal bureaucrats and even foreign consulates.

Place is important in explaining subnational variation in the United States, but there is good reason to expect even greater variation across national contexts (Koopmans 2004). Rahsaan Maxwell shows in chapter 5 how cross-national differences in political party outreach, perceptions of government neglect and the existence of robust race relations policies differentially channel the mobilization of Caribbean-origin communities in Great Britain and France. In the strongest example of party outreach in the volume, Maxwell finds that those of Caribbean origin are more integrated into British politics through the Labour Party than in France. He also details an interesting twist in the identity categories used by Caribbeans in the two countries: the French refusal to acknowledge ethnicity has ironically produced much greater ethnic mobilization in that country than in Great Britain, where Caribbeans organize instead around pan-ethnic affiliations.

Maxwell's attention to the context of reception, or political opportunity structure, is mirrored in chapter 6, which compares the number and networks of Turkish organizations in Amsterdam and Berlin. Floris Vermeulen and Maria Berger argue that the Dutch state's greater openness to ethnic organizing and its supportive policy of multiculturalism have lead to more Turkish organizations in Amsterdam and more of a civic community, as measured by horizontal ties between organizations. In Germany, where government and political actors distance themselves from migrant or ethnic organizing, Turks have fewer organizations, and those that do exist are ideologically polarized into largely separate networks. Interestingly, Vermeulen and Berger hint that some degree of civic or political incorporation at the group level produces uneven individual-level assimilation. More civic organizing in Amsterdam translates into greater political representation among local elected officials, but appears to lead to less individual-level participation. This is because Turkish organizations in Amsterdam have less reason to mobilize as compared to those living in Berlin.

Part II of the book holds place constant and focuses on diverse immigrant groups in a single city or metropolitan area. Distinctions between civic and political engagement are made more ambiguous in chapter 7, which looks at Indian and Vietnamese immigrants in the Dallas-Fort Worth area. Using ethnographic fieldwork and interviews, Caroline Brettell and Deborah Reed-Danahay argue that immigrant organizations, individually and as a constellation, need to be conceptualized as communities of practice where immigrants learn experientially about citizenship. Through organizational participation, those of Vietnamese and Indian origin not only learn civic and political skills, as other studies show, but they also create meanings of civic-mindedness and politics, a process of citizen-making. Their detailed descriptions of four immigrant organizations highlight the many and varied ways immigrants engage with each other and larger society.

In chapter 8, Sofya Aptekar examines Edison, New Jersey, a town that was long a suburb of working class and middle class white ethnics, but which recently has seen a demographic transformation in the rapid influx of highly skilled, professional Asian immigrants. Aptekar focuses on Indian and Chinese-origin residents in Edison, and shows that despite having substantial levels of human capital—traits that are usually linked to higher levels of political and civic engagement—immigrants in Edison are largely shut out of the political system by the entrenched Democratic machine. She also offers an intriguing glimpse into the various narratives of exclusion that public officials use, holding up Chinese immigrants as a model minority focused on education rather than politics, and treating Indians as potential trouble-makers.

Such intergroup differences show up even more starkly in chapter 9, which focuses on immigrant organizing in Chicago. Laurencio Sanguino shows, perhaps surprisingly, that Mexican immigrants enjoy a richer infrastructure of social service organizations and more political presence and weight among local officials than either Indian and Polish immigrants. As Sanguino suggests, the relative prominence of Mexican immigrant organizations is counterintuitive, given the comparatively lower levels of socioeconomic resources among Mexican immigrants and their higher likelihood of experiencing racial and ethnic discrimination. Sanguino also suggests that part of Mexican immigrants' organizational success lies in the long history of the group in Chicago, the relatively generous attitude of local officials and governments toward immigrants (including the undocumented), and the Mexican community's early institution-building around the nonprofit social service model.

Part III, which opens with chapter 10, concentrates on the consequences of organizational form: What is the effect of the type of organizations on immigrants' civic and political incorporation? Although this theme is touched on in other chapters, this section looks in-depth at a number of important organizational types: churches, unions, nonprofit service providers and immigrant hometown associations. Among these types of organizations, none are perhaps so central to the lives of many immigrants, and native-born Americans, as churches. Indeed, in chapter 10, Janelle Wong, Kathy Rim, and Haven Perez note that American residents of Latino and Asian origin make up increasingly large segments of the evangelical, Pentecostal, and charismatic Protestant traditions, either because of existing affiliations in their homeland or through conversion once in the United States. Given the regular, sustained interaction of congregants in these religious organizations, the importance of the church in members' lives, and the Christian Right's links to Republican Party, these churches could influence members' civic and political engagement in important ways. Assessing these possibilities, the authors conclude that pastors' mobilizing activities have been rather limited, congregants view political messages in church with a critical eye, and that any coalitions between native-born white Protestant churches and immigrant or minority churches contain fault lines as well as common ground.

Fault lines and common ground are also themes in chapter 11, in which Rebecca Hamlin focuses on unions' orientations to and organization of immigrants. She argues that in the face of declining union membership, many unions have become immigrant advocates as they try to organize a diverse, foreign-born workforce, including workers who do not have legal status in the United States. Given unions' historic reliance on voting numbers as one of many weapons in their political arsenal, incorporating immigrants into unions can be complicated, especially when dealing with a hierarchical, top-down organizational structure. Yet Hamlin documents the potential—and pitfalls—of unions in the political incorporation of immigrants, detailing the success of a bottom-up grassroots campaign to change the AFL-CIO's stance on undocumented workers.

Dealing with the needs of undocumented migrants and legal migrants without formal political voice in the electoral system is also a central theme in chapter 12, Els de Graauw's examination of immigrant social service providers in the city of San Francisco. De Graauw argues that though many observers assume that the legal status of 501(c)(3) organizations—a reference to the tax code governing these groups—prevents them from engaging in politics, immigrant social service providers play real and important roles in local and even state politics. She outlines the various ways such organizations advocate for clients and mobilize members, suggesting that they can be quite effective, especially around bureaucratic and regulatory politics. At the same time, she notes the limits of such organizations in promoting the wholesale incorporation of immigrants into the political system: social service advocacy is often limited to a relatively narrow set of issues, and mostly confined to particular local communities.

Finally, in chapter 13, Celia Viramontes grapples with the important question of whether groups formed out of nostalgia for the homeland and focused on community projects in immigrants' hometowns can facilitate civic and political engagement in the United States. Her chapter on Mexican hometown associations (HTAs) in Los Angeles speaks to a growing discussion over transnationalism and cross-national civic and political engagement.[10] She concludes that such hometown associations do indeed hold promise for bringing certain hard-to-reach groups into American civic and political life, especially the undocumented and recent migrants, since these are safe and comfortable spaces for immigrant participation. Fulfilling this promise, however, requires that hometown associations navigate a set of institutional and organizational stages, an evolution that she notes is far from inevitable.

ORGANIZATIONAL BAND-AIDS OR CIVIC BACKBONE?

Are immigrants' organizations and the mainstream organizations of which immigrants are a part the backbone for a new civic revival in the United States—as witnessed by the impressive show of strength during the spring 2006 rallies—or are such organizations merely band-aids, doing some good work with some people, but largely invisible and ineffectual in America's civic and political space? Do answers to this question differ in other countries, or even between cities and states in the United States?

Organizations Matter

This volume cannot provide definitive answers to these questions, but it does point out several promising paths. First, almost all of the chapters argue that immigrant organizations do important work, especially absent the traditional institutions of political incorporation. Many of the chapters find that political parties—especially in the United States, but also in Germany and France—have done relatively little to incorporate immigrants into the political system. In part, this might be because most immigrants do not have citizenship, because they lack the legal status to apply, they have not yet taken the steps to do so, or they are facing delays in naturalization due to processing backlogs. When noncitizens cannot directly access the political system through their votes, or face obstacles to electoral participation because of language barriers, they are more likely to need collective organizations to engage in representational politics.

But even when immigrants are citizens, it seems that many parties are not reaching out to newcomers. In U.S. regions such as the West and the Southwest, where more than 40 percent of the foreign-born live (U.S. Census Bureau 2006), party systems are weakened by nonpartisan local elections and other Progressive-era institutions such as the referendum and recall. In places such as New York and Chicago, parties remain important actors in local politics but are incorporating immigrant groups either piecemeal (Jones-Correa 1998; Wong 2006; chapter 9, this volume) or not at all (chapter 8, this volume). One exception to this story seems to be the United Kingdom, where the Labour Party has played an important role in minority political incorporation (chapter 5, this volume).

The decline or absence of political parties as vehicles of political incorporation might not matter, or not matter as much, if other organizations and institutions were taking their place. In examining the role of community organizations in fostering civic and political engagement, it is instructive to consider the putative role of parties in the political system. Political parties are important because they mobilize citizens to political ends, socialize political subjects by shaping political orientations or aggregating attitudes and opinions on policy, represent the interests of party members and voters, train individuals—elites as well as ordinary citizens—in political skills and provide resources to engage in the business of politics, simplify vote choices and help get candidates elected to political office, and help formulate, package, and pass public policy. Taken together, these functions represent the core of what may generally be termed political incorporation.

In the absence of party mobilization, do community organizations and civic associations act as parallel or alternative sites for political incorporation? The chapters in this volume suggest that community organizations can play a valuable role in political incorporation, although their roles are constrained in several ways.[11] As Kristi Andersen notes in chapter 3, community organizations are not federated in the same way as political parties, nor do they have the same enduring stakes and involvement in elections and everyday politics. Unlike political parties, community organizations are also more likely to focus on a smaller range of issues such as language access, worker protections, and U.S. foreign policy, making them more akin to interest groups than political parties (Schattschneider 1942). Also, as Celia Viramontes notes in chapter 13, many community organizations may only be informal associations, lacking the resources (such as paid staff, office space, and politically skilled leaders) to get involved in politics. Finally, immigrant-serving organizations also face some important internal constraints that may limit their political influence, including divisions over strategy and priorities (chapter 11, this volume), an estrangement from grass-roots membership with increased bureaucratization, and an over-reliance on charismatic authority that leads to difficulty in planning for leadership succession (Bloemraad 2002; Cordero-Guzmán 2005).

Even if community organizations are able to solve these internal constraints, they may still choose to eschew politics because they feel constrained by IRS rules governing political activities by nonprofits. As Jeffrey Berry and David Arons (2003) have noted, little-known IRS rules allow for nonprofit organizations to devote a percentage of their expenditures to political activities.[12] However, many nonprofits are reluctant to take on explicitly political roles for fear of running afoul of tax regulations (Chaves, Stephens, and Galaskiewicz 2004; Chung 2005). Yet, as Els de Graauw (chapter 12, this volume) and others (Bloemraad 2006; Wong 2006) show, even nonprofits that forswear political activity can play important roles in the political process, either through issue advocacy or by providing important policy information to elected officials and administrative agencies. Moving beyond nonprofits, chapters 4 and 11 show that unions can play an important role in issue advocacy and the formulation of public policy—although, as Gleeson notes, the involvement of local unions in the formulation of local policies depends on the state regulatory context. Even when unions are relatively strong and involved in politics, they may not take up issues dear to the day-to-day issues affecting immigrant workers at the local level. Dynamics of place—be they local, regional or national—clearly matter in explaining internal and external differences in the fate of immigrant organizing.

Organizational Inequalities

A second consistent theme across most chapters centers on civic inequality and political stratification. Our authors find organizational life in most immigrant communities, but it is unclear how much of this translates into real presence and influence among their fellow residents. Thus, even though immigrants clearly participate in a wide variety of organizations from hometown associations and unions to social service agencies and churches, many organizations with a substantial immigrant base have little visibility or weight in the political system.[13] Low levels of visibility and influence appear especially marked in suburbs and in newer-destination cities—places where the vast majority of immigrants now live (chapters 2, 3, and 8). Thus we can talk about civic and political stratification of organizations and groups in the United States, a stratification that also seems apparent, though perhaps along slightly different lines, in France, Germany, Great Britain, and the Netherlands.

What are the potential solutions to civic and political stratification? One possibility is proactive government policies directed toward immigrants, refugees, and ethnic groups. Supportive government policies can help level the playing field between ethnic and non-ethnic organizations by boosting the resources of organizations that serve marginalized communities (see chapters 2, 3, 9, and 6). Government assistance can also prove crucial in widening access to elected and non-elected officials among those organizations that receive funding (Jones-Correa 2001; Bloemraad 2006). By contrast, private sources of funding such as foundation grants, charitable giving, and support from ethnic businesses can help bridge resource gaps among community organizations and boost the civic presence of immigrant organizations. They are likely, however, to have a less direct impact on the access of such organizations to government officials. Finally, in addition to providing financial assistance, governments can also help mitigate levels of civic and political stratification by appointing immigrants to local boards and commissions and by creating special liaisons and commissions to foster communications with immigrant groups with limited English proficiency, low rates of citizenship, and little participation in local politics.

Other strategies for boosting the civic and political influence of immigrant organizations may include the creation of regional and national federations and collaborations or alliances with other organizations, whether mainstream, of the same ethnic group, of a different ethnic group, or transnational. One of the strengths of the party system in fostering political incorporation lies in its hierarchical structure and symmetry with U.S. federalism. As Theda Skocpol (2003) argued about fraternal groups and other historic civic associations, federated structures are more likely to bring ordinary people into politics. Of the organizations highlighted in this volume, few follow such a traditional federated structure. One exception is unions, and as chapter 11 makes clear, there are opportunities for individuals to affect important change by working within a federated organization structure. At the same time, organizational leaders will have a harder time maintaining institutional cohesion as various affiliated locals have their own interests and agendas. In the case of unions, the inability to resolve such differences contributed to the breakup of the AFL-CIO, and arguably further weakened organized labor's ability to speak with a strong, unified political voice. Because relatively few Americans are represented by unions, and even a smaller proportion of immigrants are union members, unions cannot be a panacea for immigrants' political incorporation.

Beyond unions, almost all of the other organizations showcased in this volume either are stand-alone organizations or form shifting horizontal coalitions with local groups, often on a temporary basis. The nonprofit social service providers discussed in chapter 12 engage in important advocacy work within the city of San Francisco, but their ability to affect national policy—including immigration policy—is limited by their lack of permanent relationships to actors in other places and in Washington, D.C. Similarly, Andersen notes in chapter 3 that across her six-city comparison, immigrant organizations in those cities with more developed coalitional structures are more likely to enjoy a greater presence in local decision-making bodies. Wong, Rim, and Perez show in chapter 10 how issues related to immigration and civil rights have the potential to unravel political coalitions among Evangelical groups, and in chapter 6 Vermeulen and Berger provide more general lessons of how the form and shape of coalition structures can have important consequences for political participation. In chapter 2, Ramakrishnan and Bloemraad show that mainstream organizations and ethnic organizations are largely disconnected from each other in terms of day-to-day participation in the civic and political lives of their communities. Future research needs to look more carefully at the dynamics of coalition formation: how it is done in the civic arena (and not just around particular electoral contests); the forms it takes; and the relationship between coalition form and political or civic outcomes.

Coalitions can also form across international borders, bringing in issues of transnational political and civic involvement. A central question is whether transnational engagement by immigrants in the United States hurts or helps incorporation into the American civic and political landscape. On the one hand, transnationalism can hurt incorporation into the receiving country if money sent home for community development projects decreases the resources immigrants can put into building civic organizations in the host country. On the other hand, the desire to send money home for community projects may encourage organizing that would have been absent without the transnational interest in homeland development.

Some have wondered whether transnational activism saps civic and political energies away from U.S.-based concerns by promoting an exclusive (and implicitly parochial) interest in the homeland. The research reported in this volume suggests the opposite: concern about homeland issues helps push immigrants to engage in the American system. This can happen through transnationalism from above, as with Mexican consular activities around hometown associations or labor violations, or from below, as immigrants translate homeland concerns into domestic U.S. politics (Smith and Guarnizo 1998). For example, Brettell and Reed-Danahay document in chapter 7 how Indian immigrants in the Dallas-Fort Worth area have learned about the workings of American politics by trying to influence U.S. foreign policy toward India. Future research might consider whether such transnationalism from below happens more readily when the immigrant group is relatively well-educated and well-off, as in the case of Indians in Texas and Cubans in Miami (Torres 2001). Where communities have relatively fewer resources, such as Mexican immigrants in most regions in the United States, perhaps some support from above facilitates both the building of transnational organizations and their (re-)orientation to U.S. politics.

Finally, potential solutions to civic and political stratification may lie well beyond the control of local governments and community organizations, and depend instead on sudden changes in political opportunities and more systematic changes in the nature of political contestation. For instance, immigrant-serving organizations have been relatively marginal to politics in most regions of the United States, but for a few months in early 2006, they were at the epicenter of some of the largest political debates over federal and local immigration policies. The challenge of using external threats and other political shocks for mobilization lies in maintaining the momentum from such events into lasting civic and political engagement. This is where the role of organizations becomes critical.

In the case of the immigrant protests, after the explosion of activity in spring of 2006, it became evident by the fall that movement leaders were unable to bring more than a few thousand protesters to the streets. Once Congress had reached a stalemate on immigration legislation, it was difficult for leaders to forge a more proactive and pro-immigrant agenda.[14] It is quite possible, then, that more sustainable solutions to mitigating civic and political stratification between immigrant and nonimmigrant organizations require systematic changes to the political system. These may include government support for organizations, such as for immigrants in the Netherlands or for refugees in the United States, the creation of district, proportional- and cumulative-voting systems of representation (Lublin 1997; Brockington et al. 1998), the extension of noncitizen voting rights at local and perhaps higher-level offices (Hayduk 2006), or measures intended to increase party competition such as open primaries and balanced electoral districts.

The upshot from the contributions here is that immigrant civic organizations have the potential to be vehicles of political engagement, but that much of that power depends on their ability to build wide-ranging coalitions with mainstream and ethnic organizations, to draw on assistance from government and private sources, to create federated structures, to harness the positive returns to homeland participation, and to take advantage of political events that facilitate organizing. One of the major challenges is to maintain gains made as a result of such developments and to prevent backsliding in political presence and weight when external funding dries up and political opportunities close.

Despite heated debates around border control and national immigration policy in the United States and other industrialized democracies, the issue of immigrant integration and the local challenges accompanying large-scale migration also remain important. It is clear that in many American cities, immigrants have transformed workplaces, schools, and neighborhoods. They are also establishing civic groups, although such organizations remain invisible to government officials in many places across the United States. Similar patterns of activism and stratification can be found in other countries around the world. We hope this book will help spark further intellectual debate and scholarly attention to whether immigrants' participation and organizing will (re)invigorate the civic ideals of Western democracies, or whether inequalities in resources, outreach, and recognition will continue to sow the seeds of civic and political stratification for the foreseeable future.

NOTES

1. Peter Prengaman, "Immigration March Draws 500,000 in LA," Associated Press, March 25, 2006.
2. Randal Archibold, "Immigrants Take to U.S. Streets in Show of Strength," *New York Times*, May 2, 2006, 1.
3. Those who are foreign-born to American citizen parents—and who are thus themselves American citizens at birth—would generally not be included in the category of immigrant.
4. According to demographer Jeffrey Passel (2006), in 2005, only 35 percent of the foreign-born were naturalized citizens, 32 percent were noncitizen legal permanent residents, 30 percent were unauthorized migrants without legal status, and three percent were temporary legal migrants such as students and temporary workers.

5. We outline the common methodology of the Immigrant Civic Engagement Project, of which we are principal investigators, in chapter 2. The common set of questions that animate this project is laid out later in this chapter.

6. In this formulation, an ethnic group is a descriptive classification: individuals with some common trait can be grouped together to compare the group to other individuals with different backgrounds. We do not assume that sharing a language, origin, religion, or racial classification necessarily or naturally makes people come together in a sociological community. Indeed, a central question for the study of immigrants' political and civic engagement is to ask when certain characteristics become salient for group identity and political mobilization, and how the make-up and salience of ethnic identity or common ethnicity might vary across time and places. We thus concur with the predominant view of ethnicity as a social construction; to help us get at the dynamics of these constructions, we use the concept of ethnic group to make comparisons between immigrants.

7. On the importance of alliances and the form they take, see the network analysis by Dirk Jacobs and Jean Tillie (2004) and Floris Vermeulen and Maria Berger, chapter 6 in this volume.

8. There are various ways in which social scientists have measured political influence—some have relied on reputational measures of influence among the general population (Hunter 1953), while others have measured influence based on particular decisions (Dahl 1961), and others still argue for more in-depth case study work on a particular issue, from identity formation and issue gestation through the agenda setting, policy-making, and policy implementation processes (Gaventa 1980).

9. Although civic and political presence and weight are loosely operationalized across this volume, we can establish the kinds of evidence that scholars would need to better specify these measures. Thus, for instance, robust measures of civic presence would require content analysis of mainstream news sources, network analysis of organizational activists, and surveys that measure the visibility of organizations among the general population and various ethnic populations. Similarly, robust measures of civic weight would need to rely on information about transfer of resources across organizations, and other evidence from in-depth interviews, news reports, and archival records that indicate the extent to which some organizations have a greater hand in shaping projects involving multiple organizations. Finally, measures of political presence would require in-depth interviews with elected officials regarding the visibility of organizations (mainstream, ethnic, and panethnic) across various issues while measures of political weight could rely on interviews with elected officials and organization leaders, as well as content analysis of news coverage and public records such as city council agendas and minutes.

10. Indeed, some imply that in addition to an individual-level political assimilation or group-based political incorporation account of immigrants' civic and political integration, we can speak about a third, transnational model (Portes and Rumbaut 2006). Such a model recognizes that immigrants' political attention is not necessarily or uniquely focused on their country of residence, but also on their countries of origin. The expansion and lowered cost of international communication and transportation clearly broadens the scope of possible participation. It is unclear, however, whether enlarging our view of civic and political engagement across international borders necessarily changes the models by which we understand incorporation into the new system. As others have pointed out, transnationalism remains a strongly nation-bounded model; immigrants have a foot in multiple countries, but the fact that

these are countries—with their particular histories, institutions, and discursive structures—remains highly salient (Smith and Guarnizo 1998; Waldinger and Fitzgerald 2004).

11. A well-developed body of research argues that participation in civic groups, even ones with no political interests, plays an important role in teaching individuals the skills and aptitudes needed for political engagement, outside formal parties (compare Verba, Schlozman, and Brady 1995; Putnam 2000). These arguments operate at the meso-micro level, suggesting that organizational settings help with individual skill building. The focus in this volume is more squarely centered on meso-macro dynamics: to what extent do organizations represent the interests of members or of immigrant groups in the political arena, and do they successfully mobilize immigrants into the political system in such a way as to provide immigrants with visibility and weight in political discussions, decision making, and policy implementation.

12. The H election that 501(c)(3) organizations may take has a sliding scale—where those with budgets under $500,000 can devote up to 20 percent of expenditures on direct lobbying, and those with larger budgets have a lower percentage, but potentially larger absolute amount, they can give to lobbying (Berry and Arons 2003, 55).

13. These findings are in line with other studies that report low visibility and influence for immigrant organizations in local politics. For instance, Michael Jones-Correa (1998) found that one-party dominance in New York diminished the political influence of Latino immigrants and immigrant organizations, and Ramakrishnan and Lewis (2005) found in a 300-city study of California that city council members rank labor unions and immigrant advocates among the lowest in influence over matters that come before city hall, and rank developers, neighborhood associations, and mainstream business associations the highest.

14. Rachel Swarns and Randal Archibold, "Immigration Movement Struggles to Regain Momentum Built in Spring Marches," *New York Times,* September 11, 2006, 11.

REFERENCES

ABC News. 2006. "Country Braces for Immigrant Protests." *Good Morning America,* May 1, 2006.

Alba, Richard, and Victor Nee. 2003. *Remaking the American Mainstream: Assimilation and Contemporary Immigration.* Cambridge, Mass.: Harvard University Press.

Bachrach, Peter, and Morton Baratz. 1970. *Power and Poverty.* New York: Oxford University Press.

Bada, Xóchitl, Jonathan Fox, and Andrew Selee, editors. 2006. *Invisible No More: Mexican Migrant Civic Participation in the United States.* Washington: Woodrow Wilson International Center for Scholars.

Bean, Frank D., and Gillian Stevens. 2003. *America's Newcomers and the Dynamics of Diversity.* New York: Russell Sage Foundation.

Berry, Jeffrey M., and David F. Arons. 2003. *A Voice for Nonprofits.* Washington: Brookings Institution Press.

Bilodeau, Antoine. 2005. "Political Socialization and Democratic Commitment among Immigrants from Authoritarian Regimes in Australia and Canada." Paper presented at the annual meeting of the American Political Science Association, Marriott Wardman Park, Omni Shoreham, Washington Hilton, Washington, D.C., September 1, 2005.

Bloemraad, Irene. 2002. "The North American Naturalization Gap: An Institutional Approach to Citizenship Acquisition in the United States and Canada." *International Migration Review* 36(1): 193–228.

————. 2005. "The Limits of Tocqueville: How Government Facilitates Organizational Capacity in Newcomer Communities." *Journal of Ethnic and Migration Studies* 31(5): 865–87.

————. 2006. *Becoming a Citizen: Incorporating Immigrants and Refugees in the United States and Canada*. Berkeley, Calif.: University of California Press.

Bridges, Amy. 1984. *A City in the Republic : Antebellum New York and the Origins of Machine Politics*. Cambridge and New York: Cambridge University Press.

Brockington, David, Todd Donovan, Shaun Bowler, and Robert Brischetto. 1998. "Minority Representation under Cumulative and Limited Voting." *The Journal of Politics* 60(4): 1108–25.

Browning, Rufus P., Dale Rogers Marshall, and David H. Tabb. 1984. *Protest Is Not Enough: The Struggle of Blacks and Hispanics for Equality in Urban Politics*. Berkeley, Calif.: University of California Press.

Camarota, Steven. 2001. *The Slowing Progress of Immigrants: An Examination of Income, Home Ownership, and Citizenship, 1970–2000*. Washington: Center for Immigration Studies.

Chaves, Mark, Laura Stephens, and Joseph Galaskiewicz. 2004. "Does Goverment Funding Suppress Nonprofits' Political Activity?" *American Sociological Review* 69(2): 292–316.

Chung, Angie Y. 2005. ""Politics Without the Politics:" The Evolving Political Cultures of Ethnic Non-Profits in Koreatown, Los Angeles." *Journal of Ethnic and Migration Studies* 31(5): 911–29.

Cordero-Guzmán, Héctor. 2005. "Community Based Organizations and Migration in New York City." *Journal of Ethnic and Migration Studies* 31(5): 899–909.

Dahl, Ronald A. 1961. *Who Governs? Democracy and Power in an American City*. New Haven, Conn.: Yale University Press.

DeSipio, Louis. 1996. *Counting on the Latino Vote: Latinos as a New Electorate*. Charlottesville, Va.: University of Virginia Press.

Erie, Steven P. 1990. *Rainbow's End: Irish–Americans and the Dilemmas of Urban Machine Politics, 1840–1985*. Berkeley, Calif.: University of California Press.

Gamm, Gerald H. 1989. *The Making of New Deal Democrats : Voting Behavior and Realignment in Boston, 1920-1940*. Chicago, Ill.: University of Chicago Press.

García Bedolla, Lisa. 2005. *Fluid Borders: Latino Power, Identity, and Politics in Los Angeles*. Berkeley: University of California Press.

Gaventa, John. 1980. *Power and Powerlessness: Quiescence and Rebellion in an Appalachian Valley*. Urbana-Champaign, Ill.: University of Illinois Press.

Gibson, Campbell, and Emily Lennon. 1999. *Historical Census Statistics on the Foreign-Born Population of the United States: 1850-1990*. U.S. Census Bureau Working Paper (29). Washington: U.S. Government Printing Office.

Gimpel, James. 1999. *Migration, Immigration and the Politics of Places*. Washington: Center for Immigration Studies.

Glazer, Nathan, and Daniel Patrick Moynihan. 1963. *Beyond the Melting Pot*. Cambridge, Mass.: MIT Press.

————. 1975. "Introduction." In *Ethnicity: Theory and Experience*, edited by Nathan Glazer and Daniel P. Moynihan. Cambridge, Mass.: Harvard University Press.

Gordon, Milton M. 1964. *Assimilation in American Life: The Role of Race, Religion and National Origins*. New York: Oxford University Press.

Hansen, John Mark. 1991. *Gaining Access: Congress and the Farm Lobby, 1919–1981*. Chicago, Ill.: University of Chicago Press.

Hayduk, Ronald. 2006. *Democracy for All : Restoring Immigrant Voting Rights in the United States*. New York: Routledge.

Hero, Rodney. 1992. *Latinos and The U.S. Political System: Two-Tiered Pluralism*. Philadelphia, Pa.: Temple University Press.

———. 2003. "Social Capital and Racial Inequality in America." *Perspectives on Politics* 1(1): 113–22.

Hirschman, Charles, Philip Kasinitz, and Josh DeWind. 1999. *The Handbook of International Migration: The American Experience*. New York: Russell Sage Foundation.

Hunter, Floyd. 1953. *Community Power Structure: A Study of Decision Makers*. Chapel Hill, N.C.: University of North Carolina Press.

Huntington, Samuel P. 2004. *Who Are We? The Challenges to America's National Identity*. New York: Simon & Schuster.

Ireland, Patrick R. 1994. *The Policy Challenge of Ethnic Diversity: Immigrant Politics in France and Switzerland*. Cambridge, Mass.: Harvard University Press.

Jacobs, Dirk, and Jean Tillie. 2004. "Introduction: Social Capital and Political Integration of Migrants." *Journal of Ethnic and Migration Studies* 30(3): 419–27.

Jones-Correa, Michael. 1998. *Between Two Nations: The Political Predicament of Latinos in New York City*. Ithaca, N.Y.: Cornell University Press.

———. 2001. "Institutional and Contextual Factors in Immigrant Naturalization and Voting." *Citizenship Studies* 5(1): 41-56.

———. 2004. "Racial and Ethnic Diversity and the Politics of Education in Suburbia." Paper presented at annual meeting of the American Political Science Association, Chicago, Ill., September 2, 2004.

Katznelson, Ira. 1981. *City Trenches: Urban Politics and the Patterning of Class in the United States*. Chicago, Ill.: University of Chicago Press.

Kaufman, Jason. 2002. *For the Common Good? American Civic Life and the Golden Age of Fraternity*. New York: Oxford University Press.

Kibria, Nazli. 1993. *Family Tightrope: The Changing Lives of Vietnamese Americans*. Princeton, N.J.: Princeton University Press.

Kingdon, John W. 1984. *Agendas, Alternatives, and Public Policies*. Boston, Mass.: Little, Brown.

Koopmans, Ruud. 2004. "Migrant Mobilisation and Political Opportunities: Variation Among German Cities and a Comparison with the United Kingdom and the Netherlands." *Journal of Ethnic and Migration Studies* 30(3): 449–70.

Koopmans, Ruud, Paul Statham, Marco Giugni, and Florence Passy. 2005. *Contested Citizenship: Immigration and Cultural Diversity in Europe*. Minneapolis, Minn.: University of Minnesota Press.

La Luz, Jose, and Paula Finn. 1998. "Getting Serious about Inclusion." In *A New Labor Movement for the Century*, edited by Gregory Mantsios. Boston, Mass.: Allyn and Bacon.

Lee, Taeku. 2002. *Mobilizing Public Opinion: Black Insurgency and Racial Attitudes in the Civil Rights Era*. Chicago, Ill.: The University of Chicago Press.

Levitt, Peggy, 2001. *The Transnational Villagers*. Berkeley, Calif.: University of California Press.

Levitt, Peggy and Nina Glick Schiller. 2004. "Conceptualizing Simultaneity: A Transnational Social Field Perspective on Society." *International Migration Review* 38(3): 1002–39.

Lewis, Paul, and S. Karthick Ramakrishnan. 2004. "Open Arms? The Receptivity of Cities and Local Officials to Immigrants and Their Concerns." Paper presented at annual meeting of the American Political Science Association, Chicago, Ill. September 3, 2004.

———. 2007. "Police Practices in Immigrant–Destination Cities: Political Control or Bureaucratic Professionalism?" *Urban Affairs Review* 42(6): 874–900.

Lublin, David. 1997. *The Paradox of Representation: Racial Gerrymandering and Minority Interests in Congress.* Princeton, N.J.: Princeton University Press.

Marwell, Nicole P. 2004. "Privatizing the Welfare State: Nonprofit Community Organizations." *American Sociological Journal* 69(2): 265–91.

Massey, Douglas S., Joaquin Arango, Graeme Hugo, Ali Kouaouci, Adela Pellegrino, and J. Edward Taylor. 1998. *World's in Motion: Understanding International Migration at the End of the Millennium.* New York: Oxford University Press.

McAdam, Douglas. 1982. *Political Process and the Development of Black Insurgency, 1930–1970.* Chicago, Ill.: University of Chicago Press.

McAdam, Doug, Sidney Tarrow, and Charles Tilly. 2001. *Dynamics of Contention.* New York: Cambridge University Press.

Meier, Kenneth J., and Joseph Stewart, Jr. 1991. *The Politics of Hispanic Education: Un Paso Pa'lante Y Dos Pa'tras.* Albany, N.Y.: State University of New York Press.

Menjívar, Cecilia. 2000. *Fragmented Ties: Salvadoran Immigrant Networks in America.* Berkeley, Calif.: University of California Press.

Morris, Aldon. 1984. *The Origins of the Civil Rights Movement: Black Communities Organizing for Change.* New York: Free Press.

Oliver, J. Eric. 2001. *Democracy in Suburbia.* Princeton, N.J.: Princeton University Press.

Palloni, Alberto, Douglas S. Massey, Miguel Ceballos, Kristin Espinosa, and Michael Spittel. 2001. "Social Capital and International Migration: A Test Using Information on Family Networks." *American Journal of Sociology* 106(5): 1262–98.

Parenti, Michael. 1967. "Ethnic Politics and the Persistence of Ethnic Identification." *American Political Science Review* 61(3): 717–26.

Park, Robert E. 1930. "Assimilation, Social." In *Encyclopedia of the Social Sciences,* edited by E.R.A. Seligman and A. Johnson. New York: Macmillan.

Passel, Jeffrey S. 2006. *The Size and Characteristics of the Unauthorized Migrant Population in the US: Estimates Based on the March 2005 Current Population Survey.* Washington: Pew Hispanic Center. Accessed at http://pewhispanic.org/files/reports/61.pdf.

Perlmann, Joel. 2005. *Italians Then, Mexicans Now: Immigrant Origins and Second-Generation Progress, 1890 to 2000.* New York: Russell Sage Foundation.

Pessar, Patricia R. 1999. "The Role of Gender, Households, and Social Networks in the Migration Process: A Review and Appraisal." In *The Handbook of International Migration: The American Experience,* edited by Charles Hirschman, Phillip Kasinitz, and Joshua DeWind. New York: Russell Sage.

Portes, Alejandro, and Robert L. Bach. 1985. *Latin Journey: Cuban and Mexican Immigrants in the United States.* Berkeley, Calif.: University of California Press.

Portes, Alejandro, and Rubén G. Rumbaut. 1996. *Immigrant America: A Portrait,* 2nd ed. Berkeley, Calif.: University of California Press.

———. 2006. *Immigrant America: A Portrait,* 3rd ed. Berkeley, Calif.: University of California Press.

Portes, Alejandro, and Min Zhou. 1993. "The New Second Generation: Segmented Assimilation and Its Variants." *Annals of the American Academy of Political and Social Science* 530: 74–96.

Putnam, Robert D. *Making Democracy Work: Civic Traditions in Modern Italy.* Princeton, N.J.: Princeton University Press.

———. 2000. *Bowling Alone: The Collapse and Revival of American Community.* New York: Simon & Schuster.

———. 2007. "*E Pluribus Unum*: Diversity and Community in the Twenty-first Century." *Scandinavian Political Studies* 30 (2): 137–74.

Ramakrishnan, S. Karthick. 2005. *Democracy in Immigrant America: Changing Demographics and Political Participation.* Stanford, Calif.: Stanford University Press.

———. 2006. "But Do They Bowl? Race, Immigrant Incorporation, and Civic Voluntarism in the United States." In *Transforming Politics, Transforming America: The Political and Civic Incorporation of Immigrants in the United States,* edited by Taeku Lee, Karthick Ramakrishnan, and Ricardo Ramirez. Charlottesville, Va.: University of Virginia Press.

Ramakrishnan, S. Karthick, and Paul Lewis. 2005. *Immigrants and Local Governance: The View from City Hall.* San Francisco, Calif.: Public Policy Institute of California.

Ramakrishnan, S. Karthick, and Celia Viramontes. 2006. *Civic Inequalities: Immigrant Volunteerism and Community Organizations in California.* San Francisco, Calif.: Public Policy Institute of California.

Reitz, Jeffrey G. 1998. *Warmth of the Welcome: The Social Causes of Economic Success for Immigrants in Different Nations and Cities.* Boulder, Colo.: Westview Press.

Reynoso, Julissa. 2003. "Dominican Immigrants and Social Capital in New York City: A Case Study." *Latino Perspectives* 1(1): 57–78.

Rosenstone, Steven J., and John Mark Hansen. 1993. *Mobilization, Participation, and Democracy in America.* New York: Macmillan.

Salamon, Lester M. 1999. *America's Nonprofit Sector: A Primer,* 2nd ed. New York: Foundation Center.

Schattschneider, E. E. 1942. *Party Government.* New York: Holt, Rinehart and Winston.

Schlozman, Kay Lehman, and John Tierney. 1986. *Organized Interests and American Democracy.* New York: HarperCollins.

Skocpol, Theda. 1999. "Advocates Without Members: The Recent Transformation of American Civic Life." In *Civic Engagement in American Democracy,* edited by Theda Skocpol and Morris P. Fiorina. Washington: Brookings Institution Press.

———. 2003. *Diminished Democracy: From Membership to Management in American Civic Life.* Norman, Okla.: University of Oklahoma Press.

Smith, Michael P., and Luis Guarnizo. 1998. *Transnationalism from Below.* New Brunswick, N.J.: Transaction Publishers.

Sonenshein, Raphael J. 1997. "Post Incorporation Politics in Los Angeles." In *Racial Politics in American Cities,* 2nd edition, edited by Rufus Browning, Dale Rogers Marshall, and David Tabb. New York: Longman Press.

Strolovich, Dara. 2007. *Affirmative Advocacy: Race, Class, and Gender in Interest Group Politics.* Chicago, Ill.: University of Chicago Press.

Torres, Maria de los Angeles. 2001. *In the Land of Mirrors: Cuban Exile Politics in the United States.* Ann Arbor, Mich.: University of Michigan Press.

U.S. Census Bureau. 2000. Census 2000 SF3 data. Accessed at http://factfinder .census.gov/.

———. 2006. American Community Survey. Accessed at http://factfinder.census.gov/.

Van Til, Jon. 2000. *Growing Civil Society: From Nonprofit Sector to Third Space.* Bloomington, Ind.: Indiana University Press.

Vasquez, Manuel. 2003. "Latino Immigrants in Southern Florida: Some Theoretical Reflections." Paper prepared for presentation at the Annual Meeting of the Latin American Studies Association, Dallas, Tx., March 27–29, 2003.

Verba, Sidney, Kay Lehman Schlozman, and Henry E. Brady. 1995. *Voice and Equality: Civic Voluntarism in American Politics.* Cambridge, Mass.: Harvard University Press.

Waldinger, Roger, and David Fitzgerald. 2004 "Transnationalism in Question." *American Journal of Sociology* 109(5): 1177–95.

Wang, Ted, and Robert C. Winn. 2006. *Groundswell Meets Groundwork: Recommendations for Building on Immigrant Mobilizations.* A Special Report from the Four Freedoms Fund and Grantmakers Concerned with Immigrants and Refugees. New York.

Warner, Warner Lloyd, and Leo Srole. 1945. *The Social Systems of American Ethnic Groups.* New Haven, Conn.: Yale University Press.

Waters, Mary C. 1999. *Black Identities : West Indian Immigrant Dreams and American Realities.* New York: Russell Sage Foundation.

Wong, Janelle. 2006. *Democracy's Promise: Immigrants and American Civic Institutions.* Ann Arbor, Mich.: University of Michigan Press.

Zhou, Min. 1999. "Segmented Assimilation: Issues, Controversies, and Recent Research on the New Second Generation." In *The Handbook of International Migration: The American Experience,* edited by Charles Hirschman, Phillip Kasinitz and Joshua DeWind. New York: Russell Sage.

———. 2001. "Immigrant Neighborhoods in Los Angeles: Structural Constraints, Ethnic Resources, and Varied Contexts for the Adaptation of Immigrant Children." Paper presented at the Weiner Inequality and Social Policy Seminar. John F. Kennedy School of Government, Harvard University.

Zhou, Min, and Carl L. Bankston III. 1998. *Growing Up American: How Vietnamese Children Adapt to Life in the United States.* New York: Russell Sage Foundation.

Part I

The Importance of Place

S. Karthick Ramakrishnan and Irene Bloemraad

Chapter 2

Making Organizations Count: Immigrant
Engagement in California Cities

The past decade has seen a spate of studies on civic volunteerism and its relationship to political participation (Verba, Schlozman, and Brady 1995; Putnam 2000;
Skocpol 2003). At the same time, the number of immigrants living in the United
States has grown dramatically, from an estimated 24 million in 1995 to 37 million a decade later (U.S. Census Bureau 2000; Passel 2006). Despite increasing
numbers, studies of civic participation among immigrant residents are rare, and
rarer still are studies of immigrant community organizations and their relationship to politics (Wong 2006). As we argued in the introduction, questions of civic
and political inequality necessitate a focus on community organizations and,
where possible, comparisons between ethnic organizations and what are typically thought of as nonethnic or mainstream organizations.

This chapter focuses on the political presence of ethnic and nonethnic organizations across cities in California. Perhaps nowhere in the country are issues of
civic inequalities across immigrant and racial groups more important than in
California, where no racial group can claim majority status and where first-generation immigrants account for more than one in four state residents. We know
that immigrant numbers do not easily translate to civic and political participation at the individual level (DeSipio 1996; Ramakrishnan 2005). Less understood is what happens at the organizational level with respect to civic and political inequality.

Political presence refers to the extent to which organizations and ethnic
groups are recognized by government officials and other local policymakers. Differences in the relative prominence of local organizations in the eyes of government officials can be considered a measure of civic and political stratification. In
this chapter, we show that immigrant associations garner much less attention—
indeed, are poorly known—by those involved in political decision making. In
many cases, elected officials remain largely ignorant of the activities and characteristics of ethnic organizations in their cities, despite substantial immigrant and
ethnic minority populations. The result is a double stratification of American
civic and political life for foreign-born residents: first, immigrants face a relative
paucity of civic voluntary organizations open to them, and second, the organiza-

tions in which they do participate engage in more marginal interactions with American political institutions.

Perceptions of immigrants' minimal political presence are not necessarily objective assessments of immigrants' disinterest in political and civic affairs. Rather, organizational disparities in numbers and resources, the limited efforts of mainstream organizations to increase their ranks with immigrant or ethnic members, and the perceptions of public officials act in some ways as self-fulfilling prophecies. To the extent that immigrant or ethnic organizations remain off the radar screens of decision makers, these organizations suffer from having less funding, restricted access to corridors of power, less knowledge of the political system, and less recognition as legitimate voices of residents. Political presence—or invisibility—can create virtuous or vicious circles, reinforcing the prominence of some local organizations to the detriment of others.

We find that the incidence and political presence of immigrants and ethnic organizations are not merely a function of the resources and strategies of minority populations. They also vary in important ways by locality: place matters. Certain cities seem more favorable sites for immigrant organizing and their political recognition than other cities. In particular, we highlight the importance of three sets of factors: those related to demographic characteristics, such as the size of a city and its ethnic groups; an ethnic group's economic resources as manifest through the creation of ethnic business districts; and those related to political institutions and opportunity structures, including government financial assistance, party competition, and the election of ethnics to elected office. We find that demographic characteristics and place-based economic resources play powerful roles in explaining the growth of ethnic organizations. However, factors related to political institutions and opportunities are important in shaping whether such organizations are politically prominent or remain on the margins of politics.

EVALUATING POLITICAL PRESENCE: RESEARCH DESIGN AND METHODS

This chapter reports on the findings of the Immigrant Civic Engagement Project[1] in California. We chose three counties as the basis for subsequent sampling and analysis: Santa Clara (San Jose area), Los Angeles, and Orange. In each county, we conducted case studies of two cities of varying size, analyzing their community organizations, immigrant populations, political institutions, and elected officials. The cities were chosen with an eye towards variation in city size, socioeconomic status, and immigrant national origins (table 2.1). Given the existing scholarship on immigrant community organizations and political engagement in large cities such as Los Angeles and New York (Jones-Correa 1998; Rogers 2006; Wong 2006), we chose municipalities ranging in size from about 100,000 to nearly 1 million. We chose cities where we would get some variation in national origins but have a few instances of overlap (Vietnamese and Mexicans in Orange

TABLE 2.1   *Select Characteristics of Case Study Cities*

	Population (2005)	Foreign-Born (Percent)	Median Income (Dollars)	Top Two National-Origin Groups
Anaheim (Orange County)	329,000	38	52,000	Mexico, Vietnam
Garden Grove (Orange County)	192,000	45	52,000	Vietnam, Mexico
Glendale (Los Angeles County)	195,000	54	50,000	Iran, Armenia
San Jose (Santa Clara County)	887,000	38	71,000	Mexico, Vietnam
Sunnyvale (Santa Clara County)	133,000	44	74,000	India, China
West Covina (Los Angeles County)	116,000	32	53,000	Mexico, Philippines

Source: U.S. Census Bureau (2005).
Note: Income and population rounded to nearest 1,000.

County and in the San Jose metropolitan area), to better examine the relative importance of group characteristics and local contexts.

In each city, we conducted two rounds of interviews. The first involved elected officials and staff in local agencies and departments such as school districts, arts commissions, and parks-recreation. The second round of interviews involved leaders and staff of mainstream and ethnic community organizations, based on samples that were stratified by activity type and ethnic group, including nonethnic or mainstream organizations. In each city, we conducted twenty to twenty-five interviews with government officials and organization leaders, for a total of about 130 interviews.

All interviews were structured and standardized across the Immigrant Civic Engagement Project cities (see also chapters 8, 9, and 13, this volume). To reduce any bias due to social desirability, respondents were told that the study focuses on civic participation in general and questions related to immigration, race, and ethnicity were placed toward the end of the interview. The elected officials were selected at random after an initial stratification based on race-ethnicity, and agency staff were selected based on their relevance to civic participation or social service provision.

Government officials were asked to name prominent local organizations in various activity categories. They were then asked about organizations catering to particular ethnic groups, and asked to comment on the civic participation of immigrants and the nature of racial and ethnic relations in the city. We thus measure political presence by gauging the visibility and perceived influence of community organizations among elected officials, such as mayors and city council members, and among local bureaucrats who are in a position to know about community organizations, such as parks and recreation officials and arts and culture commission members. The interviews with elected officials and nonelected policy makers help establish the political presence of local groups in the eyes of public officials. Here, we operationalize political presence based on the average number of ethnic organizations mentioned by officials in any given city, as well as more qualitative assessments about the visibility of ethnic organizations versus mainstream ones.[2]

The second round of interviews involved the leaders and staff of organizations operating in these cities. In each city, we built an organizational database based on information from GuideStar, Melissa DATA, and local ethnic directories (see appendix). We sought to enumerate all civic organizations in each city of interest, though our sources admittedly best cover formal nonprofit organizations. We supplemented this list with organizations and informal associations mentioned by our first round of interviewees. The database was then classified according to the organization's primary mission in a manner consistent with national surveys of voluntarism (for example, children's education, adult education, sports, arts and culture, multiservice, and religious). These categories were further subdivided into ethnic versus nonethnic-specific organizations. These subdivided categories served as stratified samples from which we selected organizations at random.[3] In the interviews, we asked organization leaders a series of questions regarding the organization's history, funding sources, and the characteristics of staff, volunteers, members, and clients. We also asked about any challenges the organization faced and the involvement of members and staff in various political activities.

Identifying Ethnic and Mainstream Organizations

One of the central comparisons motivating this chapter is the distinction between ethnic or immigrant organizations, on the one hand, and mainstream organizations on the other. Ethnic organizations have missions (either through formal statement or communicated through interviews) that clearly direct their activities to a particular ethnic or immigrant group, or which have a substantial proportion of their clientele, members, or leadership drawn from a particular national-origin group or a coalition of immigrant and ethnic populations. In contrast, organizations labeled as mainstream primarily cater to a nonimmigrant population and are usually made up of U.S.-born whites, though they may have some diversity in membership or clientele. As we show in this chapter, using a label such as mainstream is an implicit recognition of systems of inequality that prompt officials to sort organizations between those they classify as ethnic and others. For example, an organization may be composed entirely of native-born whites, but will not be referred to as a white organization. Thus, by making the analytic distinction between ethnic and mainstream organizations—a distinction readily made by our interview respondents—we are able to give an accurate account of political stratification, especially around immigrants' political incorporation.[4]

It was often easy to distinguish between ethnic and mainstream community organizations, based on whether they make reference to national origin groups or racial-ethnic categories in the organization's title and mission. For instance, it is relatively obvious that groups such as Korean Community Services (Garden Grove) and Grupo de Autismo (Anaheim) are ethnic organizations. Others, such as Friends of Anaheim Public Library, can be labeled as mainstream. In some instances, however, there are groups with mainstream-sounding names that are primarily ethnic. To take one example, We Give Thanks, a philanthropic organization that runs a Thanksgiving dinner and toy-giving program in Anaheim, is managed by a local Mexican restaurant and composed primarily of Latino volunteers. Similarly, ACCESS California (Anaheim) is an Arab American organization that works on issues of health access, immigration services, and women's empowerment. For these groups, information on ethnic composition is not apparent from the organization name but can be obtained from mission statements and interviews with organization leaders and staff.[5] Finally, even though African American organizations are not a focus of the qualitative fieldwork in our study, they do appear in our analysis of nonprofit organizations. Given the way we define mainstream and ethnic organizations and their respective places in systems of civic and political stratification, we find it more justified to group African American organizations with nonwhite ethnic organizations than with mainstream organizations that have no ethnic designation.

City Comparisons: Background and Context

Finally, before moving on to our findings, it is worth elaborating the historical, demographic, and social contexts of our case study cities (see table 2.1 and figure 2.1).

Anaheim   Located thirty-five miles southeast of downtown Los Angeles, Anaheim is one of the most ethnically diverse cities in Orange County. Like other areas east of Los Angeles, the city was known for its citrus groves until the 1950s, when the growth of defense industries, the development of freeways, and the opening of the Disneyland theme park led to rapid population growth. Although tourism accounts for a significant portion of employment among the city's residents (10 percent), it still lags behind manufacturing (20 percent), education, health, and social services (14 percent), and retail trade (12 percent).[6] In the last two decades, the city has gone from being a majority-white city to a majority-Latino city, the city's Hispanic population more than doubling from about 83,000 in 1990 to 175,000 in 2005. Today, about 91 percent of Latinos in Anaheim are of Mexican origin, and the remainder are primarily from Central America. Those of Vietnamese origin account for about 28 percent of the city's 41,000 Asian residents, and Filipinos for 18 percent.

   Residential segregation in the city is fairly high for Latinos, who had an isolation index of .67 in the 2000 census, but is considerably lower for Asian–Pacific Islanders, for whom it was .30.[7] Latinos are heavily concentrated in central Anaheim, and western Anaheim has significant populations of whites, Latinos, and

FIGURE 2.1   *Map of Case Study Cities in California*

Source: U.S. Geological Survey (2008).

Asians (particularly Vietnamese). This western area has also seen a growing Arab American community with local businesses concentrated along Euclid Avenue. Finally, eastern Anaheim, also known as Anaheim Hills, is predominantly white and Republican, but has also seen a growing Filipino population in the last decade. The city has dealt with different kinds of racial and ethnic tensions in recent years, including concerns over the police department's cooperation with immigration authorities, violence against Arab immigrants after September 11,

2001, and disputes between Latinos and Vietnamese over the building of a Catholic parish named after a patron saint of Vietnam in the nearby city of Santa Ana (Associated Press 2003).

Garden Grove   Garden Grove was filled with orange groves until the 1950s, when the postwar population boom led to the city's incorporation in 1956. A decade after its founding, Garden Grove had a large residential population but no major industries. In the 1970s, the city launched major redevelopment efforts with a new civic center and other projects in the downtown area.[8] During this time, the collapse of the Republic of Vietnam and the subsequent "boat people" crisis led to an influx of refugees into Garden Grove and neighboring Westminster. Korean-owned businesses also began to spring up along Garden Grove Boulevard.[9] Today, Asians and Pacific Islanders (API) account for 34 percent of the city's population, and the Latino population for about 40 percent. As in Anaheim, an overwhelming proportion of Latinos in Garden Grove are of Mexican ancestry (90 percent). Among the API population, Vietnamese vastly outnumber Koreans, accounting for 73 percent and 9 percent, respectively, of the Asian resident population.

Residential segregation among Latinos is lower in Garden Grove than in Anaheim (.58) but is higher for Asians (.59). We also found several instances of racial and ethnic tensions between the various ethnic groups in the past few years. For instance, the *Orange County Weekly* has reported heightened level of ethnic conflict between Vietnamese and Latino youth in schools, prompting the Orange County Human Relations Commission to sponsor in-school workshops between the two groups. A spokesman for the Garden Grove Police Department's Vietnamese Outreach program also reported efforts by the police and the Orange County Human Relations Commission to sponsor what are called living room chats between the Latino and Vietnamese community members.[10] Finally, both Korean and Latino community leaders have expressed frustrations with their political marginalization, especially in relation to the Vietnamese who have enjoyed a significant measure of electoral success and influence in city hall.[11]

Glendale   A city of about 200,000 immediately north of Los Angeles, Glendale is the third largest city in Los Angeles County, behind Los Angeles and Long Beach. It is also the third largest financial center in California, with retail and service industries dominating the local economy and accounting for 83 percent of occupational employment among the city's residents (City of Glendale 2008). The city experienced considerable population growth after its incorporation in 1906 through World War II, but has since slowed down because of the lack of available land for new housing. The notable exception was during the construction boom of the 1980s, when single-family homes were converted into multi-family dwellings in the southern and central portions of the city. In 2005, the city was still majority non-Hispanic white (63 percent), 19 percent Latino, and 15 percent Asian American. However, those of Armenian ancestry are the largest ethnic group (28 percent) and, in the 2000 census, enough of them checked off the Other racial category to reduce the proportion of non-Hispanic white-only residents to 54 percent. In most of our interviews with government officials and organization leaders, respondents saw Armenians as distinct from the white, Protestant population in the city. Indeed, the distinctiveness of the group is evident to even the casual observer, with not only Armenian restaurants, but also schools, international relief organizations, and scores of ethnic businesses with Armenian language signs.

Residential segregation in Glendale is fairly low when compared to other cities in our analysis, with an isolation index of 0.27 for Asians and 0.36 for Latinos. However, racial and ethnic diversification in the city has brought some notable tensions. For instance, Armenians bristled at the city's decision to maintain a ban on outdoor commercial grilling, calling it an insult to Armenian culture, while many native-born white residents resent the increasing political clout of the Armenian population.[12] There is also a history of violence between Armenian and Latino students in one of the high schools, although some community activists have created an organization to promote intercultural understanding.

San Jose The tenth largest city in the United States, San Jose spans almost 175 square miles and was home to 887,000 residents in 2005. San Jose became the first incorporated city in California in 1850, and today is the county seat of Santa Clara County. A major farming community until the 1960s, San Jose began a phase of industrialization in the postwar period. Today, San Jose is considered the heart of Silicon Valley and is home to major corporations such as Cisco Systems, IBM, Adobe Systems, and Hewlett-Packard. It is also one of the cultural centers of the South Bay. The city's population in 2005 was divided about evenly between whites (32 percent), Latinos (31 percent), and Asians (30 percent). Blacks accounted for only 3 percent of the total population. In terms of national origin groups, those of Mexican ancestry are by far the largest (28 percent), followed by Vietnamese (10 percent).

Residential segregation in San Jose is fairly high, with an isolation index of 0.65 for Latinos and 0.60 for Asians and Pacific Islanders. Indeed, the city ranks as the fifth highest in the country for residential segregation among Asians and Pacific Islanders (U.S. Census Bureau 2005). The Mexican Heritage Plaza, located in the largely immigrant east side, is a venue for major theater companies such as Teatro Visión and musical groups such as the thirty-year-old mariachi group, Los Lupeños. The Mexican Heritage Plaza, despite its name, hosts many other ethnic arts and cultural groups as well. Many Vietnamese businesses and residents cluster in the Tully-Senter area, though there is no designated business district for Vietnamese in San Jose, and attempts to designate such a district have foundered on controversies over proposed names (Corcoran 2005; Joshua Molina, "San Jose Council Again Shoots Down 'Little Saigon' Name," *San Jose Mercury News*, March 5, 2008, accessed at http://www.mercurynews.com/ci_8459305).

Because housing prices in the city continue to be among the highest in the nation, affordable housing remains a contentious debate in the city. In 1995, for example, the City of San Jose faced outcries from the homeless community for deciding to turn an abandoned hotel into retail shops rather than low-income housing. Labor is another contentious issue. Of late, many groups have rallied against many large high-tech corporations to demand better working conditions for janitors, and an aggressive unionization effort has ensued. Social relations between racial and ethnic groups are seen as relatively harmonious, however, although the area saw a spike in hate crimes toward Arabs, Sikhs, and Muslims in the months following September 11, 2001. The county government's establishment of a hate crime hotline, and outreach efforts by groups such as the South Bay Islamic Association, have helped to reduce such incidents over the past few years.

Sunnyvale   Sunnyvale is a city of about 130,000 residents some ten miles north of San Jose in the heart of Silicon Valley. The area was known primarily for its fruit orchards until World War II, and agriculture brought immigrants from China, Italy, Japan, and Portugal to the area. High-tech industry and employment has been an important part of the city since 1956, when Lockheed Martin established its headquarters there. Today, the city is home to many high-tech corporations such as Advanced Micro and Yahoo! Inc. Sunnyvale is one of an increasing numbers of cities in the United States that is majority minority, with non-Hispanic whites (39 percent) and Asians (38 percent) accounting for nearly equal shares of the population in 2005, and Latinos accounting for 17 percent. Asian Indians account for 13 percent of the total population, while Chinese- and Mexican-origin residents account for 11 percent each.

Residential segregation is slightly higher for Asians in Sunnyvale than for Latinos (isolation index of 0.46 vs. 0.35, respectively), though the overall levels of segregation are lower than in other cities in our study. There are clear differences between north and south Sunnyvale: the north is home to mobile parks and other low-income housing developments, and the south to high-skilled workers and the more affluent. Our interviews and news analysis indicate that racial and ethnic tensions in the city were generally low, with no major conflicts in the past five years.

West Covina   West Covina is a city of about 116,000 residents in the eastern end of Los Angeles County. At the time of its incorporation in 1923, it had a population of only 535, but residents chose to incorporate to prevent the construction of a sewage treatment facility serving neighboring Covina. Population growth was slow in the early years, but began to grow with the construction of the Los Angeles freeway system in the postwar period. Today, the city has a majority Latino population of 54 percent, an Asian American population of 21 percent, and a white population of 16 percent. Manufacturing, education and social services, and retail account for about 57 percent of employment among city residents, professionals for another 11 percent, and the service-sector for another 19 percent.

Residential segregation in West Covina is high when compared to other cities in our analysis, with an isolation index of 0.58 for Asians and 0.68 for Hispanics. According to the 2000 census, the difference in household income between Latinos ($52,000) and whites ($51,600) is not significant, but Asian households earned an average of $58,000. Political and civic institutions remain largely undiversified, evident in that only one of the city's five council members is nonwhite, and that most organizations that are active or involved in politics have predominantly white memberships. Interviews with government officials in West Covina do not show much ethnic tensions, but the visibility of nonwhite groups is generally low.

FINDINGS: CONDITIONS OF CIVIC AND POLITICAL STRATIFICATION

We first compare the share of ethnic and mainstream organizations in the cities we studied and provide a more detailed examination of the organizational share of particular national origin groups. Next, we examine the political presence of mainstream and ethnic organizations, paying particular attention to those activities that bear a significant relationship to political engagement. Finally, we consider the importance of various place-based factors in accounting for the incidence and political presence of ethnic organizations across our various cases.

Organizational Incidence and Shares

When analyzing our databases of nonprofit organizations, we find significant disparity in the relative number of mainstream and ethnic organizations. In the six cities we studied, ethnic organizations account for 1,058 civic organizations, or about 13 percent of the total number of organizations (see table 2.2).[13] Remarkably, this proportion is similar across almost all the cities studied, ranging from 11 percent in Sunnyvale to about 13 percent in Glendale. In comparison, the overall proportion of the foreign-born population in these cities stands between 32 percent in West Covina to 54 percent in Glendale, or if we use the minority population as a reference point, from 37 percent in Glendale to 77 percent in West Covina. Clearly organizational incidence does not appear to reflect population demographics.

The only exception to this trend is Garden Grove, where the ethnic share of community organizations is 28 percent, more than double the others. As we shall see, the high numbers of Korean and Vietnamese organizations in the city may be related to the presence of business enclaves (Korean immigrants) and ethnic electoral power (Vietnamese). However, it is significant that even in a city such as Garden Grove, the proportion of ethnic organizations is substantially lower than the proportion of foreign-born residents.

The difference between ethnic and mainstream organizations is apparent not only in their sheer numbers but also in the types of activities in which they engage. Table 2.3 presents the spread of ethnic and mainstream organizations across various types of activities. The first set of figures shows the distribution of organizations across all the cities considered while the second set of figures excludes San Jose.[14] Regardless of the figures used, some clear patterns emerge. Mainstream organizations are more likely than ethnic organizations to be concentrated among civic groups and those focused on education, sports, and health. Ethnic organizations are more likely to be concentrated in religious activities and the provision of social services. Also, perhaps not surprisingly, ethnic organizations are also more concentrated in transnational activities and those re-

TABLE 2.2   *Select Organization and Population Characteristics in Six California Cities*

	Ethnic Organizations	Mainstream Organizations	Total Organizations	Proportion Foreign-Born, 2006	Proportion Nonwhite, 2006
Anaheim	12%	89%	1,193	38%	64%
Garden Grove	28	77	533	45	67
Glendale	13	88	1,388	54	37
San Jose	11	89	4,183	38	64
Sunnyvale	11	90	689	44	54
West Covina	12	89	397	32	77

Source: U.S. Census Bureau (2005).
Note: The proportion of nonwhites equals 100 percent minus the proportion of non-Hispanic whites.

TABLE 2.3   *Distribution of Activities by Ethnic and Mainstream Organizations*

	With San Jose				Without San Jose			
	Ethnic		Mainstream		Ethnic		Mainstream	
Advocacy	44	*4%*	92	*1%*	26	*5%*	43	*1%*
Agricultural	1	*<1*	16	*<1*	0	*0*	5	*<1*
Animal care	0	*0*	40	*1*	0	*0*	25	*1*
Arts-music	161	*16*	374	*6*	64	*11*	173	*6*
Business-professional	86	*8*	777	*12*	32	*6*	298	*10*
Citizenship-government	6	*1*	14	*<1*	5	*1-*	10	*<1*
Civic	73	*7*	663	*10*	18	*3*	359	*12*
Disabled	6	*1*	84	*1*	5	*1*	38	*1*
Education	44	*4*	658	*10*	24	*4*	404	*13*
Environmental	1	*<1*	53	*1*	1	*<1*	21	*1*
Health	30	*3*	418	*7*	14	*2*	197	*6*
Homelessness	0	*0*	8	*<1*	0	*0*	6	*<1*
Housing	2	*<1*	140	*2*	1	*<1*	81	*3*
Labor union	0	*0*	121	*2*	0	*0*	51	*2*
Multiservice	123	*12*	518	*8*	64	*11*	172	*6*
Poverty	8	*1*	58	*1*	6	*1*	27	*1*
Public safety-emergency	2	*0*	50	*1*	0	*0*	32	*1*
Recreation	24	*2*	479	*8*	18	*3*	252	*8*
Religious	307	*30*	1338	*21*	219	*39*	709	*23*
Sexual orientation	1	*<1*	7	*<1*	0	*0*	2	*<1*
Shelter	3	*<1*	33	*1*	3	*1*	14	*0*
Sports	7	*1*	296	*5*	5	*1*	144	*5*
Transnational	77	*8*	37	*1*	56	*10*	26	*1*
Veterans	8	*1*	68	*1*	3	*1*	32	*1*
Total		*100*		*100*		*100*		*100*

Source: Authors' compilation.
Note: Column percentages in italics.

lated to advocacy and arts, music, and culture. Nonetheless, due to the considerably larger overall number of mainstream associations in each city, mainstream organizations still outnumber their ethnic counterparts in each activity category, with the notable exception of transnational activities.

So far, we have examined differences in the relative proportion of ethnic and mainstream groups as a share of all community nonprofit organizations, grouping all racial and ethnic organizations together. However, there are significant national origin differences among the immigrant and ethnic populations of the cities in this study. Our exploration of organizational shares would be incomplete without taking into account the particular national origin groups within each city. Table 2.4 consequently presents the number of community nonprofit organizations for the top two national origin groups in each city, with the exception of Garden Grove, where Koreans are included as a third group because of the unusually high number of community organizations. Organizational share is compared to the group's relative proportion in the general population. Column B presents the group's relative percentage of the total city population, column C indicates the total number of organizations per ethnic group, column D calculates the percentage of a group's organizations as a share of all organizations in the city, and column E provides a ratio of each group's organizational share compared to its share of the resident population.

The greatest absolute proportions of immigrant and ethnic organizations are among Koreans and Vietnamese in Garden Grove and among Armenians in Glendale (column D). Relative to their numbers in the total population, Koreans in Garden Grove, Vietnamese in Garden Grove and Anaheim, and Filipinos in West Covina show the greatest organizational incidence (column E). Indeed, Koreans in Garden Grove are the only group with an organizational share larger than their population share. This is notable because their share of the total population is only 3 percent, far behind Mexicans and Vietnamese, who together account for more than 60 percent of the city's population. Although the presence of Korean community organizations in Garden Grove does not reflect the resident population in the city, it finds a parallel in the large number of Korean-owned businesses in the malls dotting Garden Grove Boulevard. Ethnic business districts may foster the growth of ethnic organizations, as we discuss momentarily.

It is also worth noting that those cases with the lowest ratio of ethnic organizations per population are Mexican groups in Anaheim, Garden Grove, San Jose, and West Covina. Given relatively lower levels of education and income for this group, and higher incidences of noncitizenship, including undocumented status, such findings are perhaps not surprising. However, given the sheer numbers of Mexican-origin residents in California, the low incidence of formal organizations speaks directly to the issue of civic and political stratification, especially for this population.[15]

Political Presence

We have seen that the number of mainstream organizations far outstrips the number of immigrant or ethnic organizations in a city and that this pattern holds true across most types of civic activities. The share of ethnic organizations is con-

TABLE 2.4   *Distribution of Organizations for Select National-Origin Groups*

		A	B	C	D	E
		Proportion of Population	Number of Organizations	As Proportion of all Organizations	Ratio (D/B)	Political Presence
Anaheim	Mexican	48%	26	2%	0.03	medium
	Vietnamese	4	11	1	0.23	low
Garden Grove	Vietnamese	25	36	7	0.23	high
	Korean	3	61	11	2.25	low
	Mexican	36	18	3	0.09	low
Glendale	Armenian	28	76	5	0.17	high
	Mexican	12	20	2	0.13	low
San Jose	Mexican	28	41	2	0.03	high
	Vietnamese	10	71	2	0.12	medium
Sunnyvale	Indian	13	14	2	0.12	low
	Chinese	11	12	2	0.15	low-medium
West Covina	Mexican	47	10	2	0.05	low
	Filipino	9	7	2	0.20	low-medium

Source: Authors' compilation.
Note: Population proportions were derived from the 2000 census, using the ethnic question for Latinos (Hispanic or Latino, of any race), the race question for Asian groups, and ancestry for Armenians.

sistently lower than the share of immigrants or nonwhites in the resident population. There is good reason to think that such disparities may be meaningful for political presence, but we cannot make claims of civic inequality based on these statistics alone. For instance, there may be only one Vietnamese advocacy group in a city, but it may hold hig-hly visible rallies and protests relating to transnational matters or local affairs. Put another way, political presence may be related to the number of groups in a city, as a sheer organizational count implies, but it might also relate to specific organizational strategies and activities. A more direct measure of political presence relies on reports from local officials best positioned to assess the visibility and influence of civic organizations in local affairs.

In our interviews with local informants, local elected officials, and the staff of various city and county bureaucracies, we asked what organizations they considered to be prominent on a range of activities and issues (including arts, music and culture, education, the environment, health, poverty, labor, and advocacy). As indicated earlier, we operationalize political presence based on the average number of ethnic organizations mentioned by officials in any given city, as well as more qualitative assessments about the visibility of ethnic versus mainstream organizations. Thus, for instance, public officials in a city might note the existence of many Latino cultural organizations but also mention that they have never interacted with anyone from those organizations. By contrast, officials in the same city may note that Vietnamese organizations organize prominent cultural events and fundraisers, and are very active in public hearings and local elections. Thus, we would rank Latino organizations in the city as having low political presence, and Vietnamese organizations as having high political presence. A summary of our political presence measures is given in the last column of table 2.4. To provide context to these summary measures, we offer narrative examples focusing on three types of activity groups—arts and culture, advocacy groups, and civic associations. We chose these groups because of the high prevalence of the first in immigrant and ethnic groups, and the more obvious connections of the second and third to civic and political engagement.

Although a disproportionate number of ethnic organizations focus on issues of arts, music, and culture, public officials mostly mentioned mainstream groups as being the most prominent, including city symphonies, playhouses and historic theaters, and mainstream dance and music groups. In Sunnyvale, for instance, a spokesperson for the arts commission noted that most of the cultural groups applying for co-sponsorship and use of city facilities are mainstream organizations such as theater groups, the Sunnyvale Art Club, and the Sunnyvale Photo Club. Although a few ethnic groups had reserved rooms in the past, the spokesperson could not recall any group in particular that would be considered prominent.[16] In larger cities such as San Jose and Garden Grove, informants were able to name a few ethnic organizations, such as the Mexican American Community Services Agency (MACSA) in San Jose and the India Community Center in Sunnyvale. In many instances, however, these were multiservice agencies or community centers, and not specific arts and culture groups.

When we asked about the prominent advocacy groups in their city, many informants mentioned neighborhood associations and business groups. Indeed, in West Covina, one elected official noted that the chamber of commerce was the only significant advocacy group around:

> Well, you've got the chamber of commerce—that is a business advocacy group. . . . We really don't have a lot of other organized advocacy groups in West Covina. The people who come to the city council meetings are either regular attendees—I call them gadflies—who are oftentimes fielding questions not centered around any particular issue. . . . Sometimes neighborhoods will get stirred up over issues. But not a lot of other organized groups, other than the chamber of commerce, who is there to represent and promote business.

Similarly, in Glendale, Latino advocacy organizations were rarely mentioned, even though Hispanics account for one in every five residents. Instead, the chamber of commerce and the downtown business association were both seen as prominent advocacy groups, and homeowners associations were named as strong and active. It was clear that Latinos were not an important part of these associations.

In the larger cities we studied, informants had no problem coming up with names of ethnic advocacy organizations, such as Hermandad Mexicana and Los Amigos in Anaheim, and MACSA and SIREN (Services, Immigrant Rights, and

Education Network) in San Jose. In smaller cities and suburbs, officials often had trouble naming ethnic organizations. In Glendale and West Covina, for instance, informants either did not know of any organizations providing advocacy or services to Latino immigrants, or they presumed that immigrant residents were accessing services in larger cities such as nearby Los Angeles or Pasadena. In Glendale, the only ethnic organizations mentioned as having vocal advocacy presence were Armenian, though the city's Latino population is nearly as numerous as its Armenian population. According to one official,

> there is the Armenian National Committee, western regional office, and they often advocate for additional governmental assistance to Armenian youth programs and they advocate on behalf of Armenians groups that feel they've been discriminated against. . . . There are other groups but they're not quite so active. There's a Hispanic Business Professionals Organization, and there's also a Filipino Professional Association as well, but I don't really see them advocating all that much.

Finally, when we asked local officials about prominent civic associations, they tended to mention established mainstream groups such as the Rotary Club, local chambers of commerce and homeowners associations. Informants also identified strong neighborhood associations in cities with formal relationships between city government and neighborhood associations, such as San Jose, Sunnyvale, and Anaheim. Although no particular ethnic organizations were mentioned, informants in cities such as San Jose and Anaheim did note that immigrants have a say in local affairs in neighborhoods with large numbers of Latino residents, but the same does not appear to be the case in areas with Vietnamese populations. One informant in San Jose noted that, under the Strong Neighborhood Initiative, the city was able to provide bilingual support in Spanish for association meetings, which in turn encouraged participation by immigrant residents with limited English proficiency:

> They are very active in particular neighborhoods. In District 5 [Strong Neighborhood Initiative] programs are held bilingually—where a large number of SNI constituents are monolingual or bilingual Spanish. The advisory committee [for the district] meets bilingually, and so there is great turnout.

Informants also cited particular neighborhood associations in cities, such as Glendale, where residents are concerned about limiting commercial development. There was no indication, however, that immigrants were involved in these antigrowth associations and movements.

Thus, even though immigrants constitute a sizable share of the resident population in many of our case study cities, their community organizations have only a limited political presence when compared to mainstream organizations. Not only do groups such as the chamber of commerce and neighborhood associations have more visibility and influence in city hall than advocates for immigrants (Ramakrishnan and Lewis 2005), mainstream organizations also have greater political presence in seemingly nonpolitical activities such as performing arts and civic concerns.

Given these findings, we need to ask whether the mainstream organizations are offsetting these disparities by incorporating immigrants into their fold. Our evidence from the various case study cities in California indicate that, for the most part, mainstream organizations conduct only limited outreach to Latino and Asian immigrant residents. When we asked the leaders of mainstream organizations about the extent of immigrant involvement within their organizations, most responded that, in general, immigrants are not likely to participate in civic organizations beyond those with which they most closely identify. For instance, the president of one civic club noted that "many of them [immigrants] prefer, at least until they get comfortable with the community and language, to stay close to their church or ethnic group, rather than getting out and mixing. That's a challenge we're facing that's affected membership."[17] In terms of specific outreach efforts to incorporate immigrants, the president of a chamber of commerce cited such activities as mixers and interaction with businesses, clients, and vendors. These arenas, however, are traditional sites of social networking for the mainstream community and may be less effective in recruiting from ethnic or immigrant communities.

There is some evidence that mainstream organizations have a greater degree of success in incorporating second- and third-generation immigrants. This is especially true among multiservice organizations and PTAs. For instance, PTA groups in most of our cities reported that first-generation immigrant participation is minimal, but that second- and third-generation Latino and Asian immigrant participation is growing. Similarly, an officer in the Garden Grove Boys and Girls Club noted the growing number of young Latino, Asian, and Filipino staff members within the organization who had previously been club members or had grown up in the neighborhood. This trend suggests that early exposure to, and experiences with, organizations and groups can play a decisive role in promoting participation by successive generations. However, membership and staff involvement within these organizations have not yet translated into greater leadership roles for immigrants.

EXPLAINING HOW PLACE MATTERS

From this analysis, it appears that Vietnamese and Armenian immigrants generally have a greater number of organizations relative to their individual numbers, and a higher level of political presence than other national origin groups, most notably Mexican immigrants. These differences can be attributed to factors such as human capital, economic resources, the context of reception greeting migrants to the United States (that is, unauthorized versus recognized refugees) and contexts of civic and political socialization in the homeland and adopted country. However, even after taking into account sources of group variation, we still find differences in the organizational share and political presence of groups

TABLE 2.5   *Political Presence and its Relationship to Other Place-Based Factors*

		Political Presence	Co-Ethnics on City Council in 2006 (Total in Parentheses)	Party Competition (100 = Democrat-GOP split)[a]	Democrat Share of Electorate
Anaheim	Mexican	medium	2 (5)	91	37
	Vietnamese	low	0 (5)	91	37
Garden Grove	Vietnamese	high	1 (5)	96	39
	Korean	low	0 (5)	96	39
	Mexican	low	0 (5)	96	39
Glendale	Armenian	high	3 (5)	96	39
	Mexican	low	1 (5)	96	39
San Jose	Mexican	high	3 (11)	82	49
	Vietnamese	medium	1 (11)	82	49
Sunnyvale	Indian	low	0 (7)	87	46
	Chinese	low-medium	2 (7)	87	46
West Covina	Mexican	low	1 (5)	84	49
	Filipino	low-medium	0 (5)	84	49

Source: Authors' compilation.
[a] Excludes independents.

across our cities. For instance, Mexicans and Vietnamese in Anaheim, Garden Grove ,and San Jose have similar group characteristics, but their organizational density and political presence vary, as we have seen in table 2.4 and further elaborated in table 2.5). Here, we pay detailed attention to place and associated factors such as city size, group size, the presence of ethnic business districts and the role of political access and outreach.

City Size and Group Size

One of the ways in which place can affect the number and political presence of ethnic organizations is through the total population of the city and of particular ethnic groups. There are good reasons to believe that larger cities and cities with larger numbers of a particular group should have more ethnic organizations. In larger cities, governments are more likely to have the bureaucratic capacity to develop and implement policies to support or engage with local immigrant populations (Ramakrishnan and Lewis 2005). Such support or engagement may encourage the establishment of organizations. It may also facilitate organizations' political contact with city government, boosting political presence. Bigger local governments usually mean more access points for city residents, including newcomer populations. A small town may have only a handful of local officials with whom residents can interact. This situation can facilitate access for those in-the-know and with the right networks, but become an obstacle for immigrants who face language barriers and have only more recently settled in a community.

Size might also matter in that a critical mass of immigrants may be necessary to establish and maintain immigrant-serving organizations, and this is less likely in smaller cities or in larger cities with small immigrant populations. The number of ethnic group members may translate into the number of organizations in a city, and organizational numbers may in turn feed into immigrant political presence: with more ethnic organizations, there is a greater chance that at least one of them will be visible to local decision makers. The *share* of an ethnic population in a particular city, rather than absolute numbers, may also matter for political presence, especially when this translates into a significant share of the local electorate. On the other hand, if other factors—such as the socioeconomic characteristics of ethnic groups or the absence or presence of local party competition—play a more important role in political presence, then the sheer number of organizations or people may drive the number of organizations but have little impact on political presence.

Considering first the incidence of ethnic organizations, the available evidence, as reported in table 2.5, suggests a positive association between the number of such organizations and the size of the city (correlation of 0.5), one that still holds when San Jose is excluded from the analysis (correlation of 0.3). There is also a positive correlation (0.3) between the number of organizations for an ethnic group and that group's total population in the city. These relationships hold when we control for ethnic composition and other place-based factors such as the degree of party competition in the city. This suggests that immigrant groups do need a critical mass of both their own members and of the city around them to establish multiple organizations. However, the factors that encourage organizational founding in large cities also affect other residents, potentially reducing immigrants' overall share of city organizations, while still increasing their numbers compared to other, smaller cities.

Turning next to differences in political presence across groups and locales, we find positive relationships with city size (0.44) and ethnic group size (0.58) that hold up in both the bivariate and multivariate contexts. However, when we dig deeper into comparisons across locales for particular ethnic groups, we find mixed evidence regarding group size and political presence. For example, the Vietnamese share of the total population is a better predictor of organizational visibility among elected officials than their absolute numbers. Thus, Vietnamese organizations in Garden Grove have greater political presence than those in San Jose, though the Vietnamese-origin population in San Jose is nearly twice as large, but constitutes a much smaller overall percentage of the city's residents. On the other hand, absolute numbers seem to matter more for Mexican immigrants: elected officials in San Jose are more likely to name Latino and Mexican organizations than those in Anaheim and West Covina, even though the proportion of Mexican-origin residents is smaller in San Jose (28 percent) than in Anaheim (48 percent) and is the same in West Covina (27 percent). As we shall soon see, these seemingly disparate findings for the political presence of Vietnamese and Mexican immigrants may be explained not by group size per se, but rather by the interaction of group size with other factors related to the political opportunity structures in these cities.

Our data also suggest two other important dynamics regarding city size. First, there is a disadvantage in political presence for immigrant organizations in cities that are neighbors to others with much larger immigrant populations. Thus, for instance, many officials in Glendale and West Covina knew little about organizations serving Latino immigrants and thought that most were accessing services in nearby Los Angeles and Pasadena. This is seemingly contrary to the findings in chapter 3 of this volume, where long distances to large cities hampered the growth of immigrant community organizations. However, both dynamics may indeed be true. Shorter distances may be a barrier in suburban contexts, where officials assume that immigrant residents are only interested in activities elsewhere, and larger distances may be a barrier in rural areas, where long distances to large ethnic population centers mean that local immigrant groups feel isolated and unable to form effective coalitions with urban organizations. Finally, population size does not always translate into political presence, because low rates of citizenship can dampen the visibility of immigrant organizations among local government officials, which is evident in the lack of attention accorded to Mexican immigrants in Glendale when compared to the local Armenian population. So, even though city size and group size generally predict the incidence of ethnic organizations, the relationships get more complicated when we examine political presence.

Ethnic Business Districts

The size of a city, the size of an immigrant group, and the relative price of commercial rents may also lead to the formation of an ethnic business district. Once established, ethnic business districts may encourage the creation and survival of ethnic community organizations. First, such districts provide locational advantages to organizations serving immigrant residents—not only can they draw volunteers, clientele and money from the owners and patrons in such districts (Zhou 2001), they may also help build community leadership among business owners (Min 1996). The existence of ethnic business districts may also help increase the political presence of community organizations, as individual business owners and business associations interact with local government agencies and elected institutions—either to pass favorable policies, such as the creation of ethnic heritage districts, or to minimize the costs associated with other policies, such as noise ordinances and parking regulations (Corcoran 2005). Finally, ethnic businesses may also increase the viability of ethnic media and language communities (Bonacich and Modell 1980; Zhou and Cai 2002) that could help organization-building, though it is unclear whether such language communities would increase or decrease a group's visibility and influence among elected officials.

The existence of an ethnic business enclave is one of the most likely explanations for the high proportion of Korean community organizations in Garden Grove. Based on the resident population alone, we would not expect many Korean organizations in Garden Grove, given that Koreans make up only 3 percent of the overall resident population and are much less numerous than Latinos or Vietnamese. However, there is a thriving Koreatown in Garden Grove, with businesses that serve residents in nearby cities such as Fullerton, Buena Park, and Anaheim. Our interviews with Korean community organization leaders indicate that the existence of a business district was an important consideration in where to locate their organization, and that the district made their organizations more viable: in addition to shopping, people could go to church, and drive their children or the elderly to various clubs or activities. For Korean organizations in Garden Grove, the presence of an ethnic business district has a positive, causal relationship to the number of Korean community organizations.

In other instances, however, it is difficult to distinguish the positive effects associated with ethnic business districts from those associated with large ethnic populations. It may be tempting to associate the number of Vietnamese organizations in Garden Grove with the existence of a Little Saigon business district, but one cannot rule out the possibility that the large Vietnamese resident population in the city drives both outcomes. Similarly, though there are many Armenian businesses and Armenian community organizations in Glendale, it is difficult to assert any causal relationship because both likely stem from Glendale's large and prosperous Armenian population.

Finally, moving from organization numbers to political presence, we find a limited relationship between political presence and the existence of an ethnic business district. In Garden Grove, the ethnic business district has certainly made the Korean community more visible to local elected officials, but we find little evidence that Korean organizations—other than the business association—are visible to public officials. Even Korean business leaders feel politically marginalized in city hall, especially in relation to the Vietnamese population. For instance, the president of a Korean umbrella organization noted that one key issue facing the community is the lack of a community center. Despite attending city council meetings and public hearings pertaining to future developments, and attempting to get the nod from the city to develop such a proposal, the city offered a project to another developer.[18] Another organization leader noted that Vietnamese in Garden Grove were politically ascendant in local school boards and the city council, but that Koreans had seen a taste of political influence only briefly in the late 1990s, with the election of a Korean immigrant to city council, and were unlikely to be influential in local politics again. Thus, although ethnic business districts may help the growth of community organizations in cities without large ethnic populations, they have only a limited independent effect on the political visibility and influence of such organizations because there is no electoral base to bolster their political demands such organizations may have.

Government Policies and Programs

As we argue, a key factor affecting organization-building and political presence is the degree of access to local government and the degree to which city governments and political actors reach out to immigrant communities. Of course, this contention risks building a circular argument: local government may reach out to those groups perceived as most politically present, which in turn spurs further organizing, and reinforces the group's relative advantage in the eyes of public officials. Indeed, we believe that such virtuous circles—or their opposite—regularly occur in local politics. At the same time, we can identify numerous cases where an idea for an organization or the need for a particular service existed for a long time, but transformed into an established organization only after outreach or connections to people in government. This suggests that, even though independent grassroots organizing can clearly lead to organizational flourishing and political presence, access and outreach can also have independent effects.

One example of outreach lies in government policies and programs directed to refugees, ethnic groups or racial minorities. Government aid and assistance can foster communication between decision-makers and those targeted by the programs, they can open access points to elected and nonelected officials, and they can provide direct resources to organizations, helping them remain viable and even expanding their activities (Bloemraad 2006). Even beyond financial assistance, local government policies on matters such as neighborhood empowerment and law enforcement can have a significant influence on the political presence of immigrant and ethnic community organizations.

Government policies are relevant to notions of place because they often vary across local jurisdictions. Policies that promote the political presence of immigrant organizations can originate from the federal, state, county, or local level. Often higher levels of government will provide funds, such as federal refugee resettlement monies or federal community block grants, to city or county governments. These in turn use this money, sometimes in conjunction with their own resources, to run programs or provide grants to local community organizations. The politics of who receives these funds can influence civic and political stratification between groups. For instance, the federal Office for Refugee Resettlement (ORR), housed in the Department of Health and Human Services, funds employment preparation and job placement services, skills training, English-language instruction, programs of social adjustment for the victims of torture, as well as direct cash assistance and medical assistance to individual refugees, but nonrefugees are generally barred from such programs and funding.[19]

The existence of immigrant assistance programs, especially language training and employment placement, can foster political participation by lowering language barriers or providing more resources with which to engage in politics. More important for the focus here, these programs and services usually are offered by local community organizations through grant and contract systems, providing financial resources to keep these organizations alive and even expand their activities, often beyond the initial populations identified by grantmakers (Bloemraad 2006; chapter 3, this volume).[20] For instance, the largest and most prominent immigrant-serving organization in Garden Grove is the Orange County Asian and Pacific Islander Community Agency (OCAPICA). The organization started in 1997 with funding from the county government to provide for the public health needs of Asian and Pacific Islander (API) populations in Garden Grove and nearby cities. Today, the organization has nine paid staff and scores of volunteers, and has expanded its focus to after-school activities, assistance with citizenship applications, and advocacy on civil rights issues. The organization has also hosted policy mixers in which elected officials interact with community members and leaders of other API organizations in the area. OCAPICA has been able to sustain this expansion by relying on support from private foundations and charitable organizations. However, without the initial (and continuing) support from county government, it would be a considerably smaller organization with little political presence in the area. Beyond the case of OCAPICA, other organizations such as MACSA and SIREN in San Jose are further examples of how government financial support raises the political presence of social service providers above that of many other immigrant and ethnic organizations (see also chapters 9 and 12, this volume).

Local government policies can also affect the organizational vitality and political presence of immigrant-serving community organizations by establishing formal mediating or consultative bodies and programs. For instance, Santa Clara County has a commission designed to address the needs of immigrant residents. In Santa Clara County, the Immigrant Relations and Integration Services (IRIS) office collaborates with community partners to provide direct services such as assistance with citizenship applications, immigrant leadership classes, and immigrant community education. Our interviews indicate that collaborations tend to increase the visibility of immigrant-serving organizations in the minds of local elected officials.

At the same time, there is the risk that the direct government provision of social services will hinder the growth of community organizations by crowding out grassroots organizing (but see Bloemraad 2005, 2006; Chaves, Stephens, and Galaskiewicz 2004). It is also possible that direct service provision dampens the establishment of multiple organizations, but that subcontracting social services to one or two key organizations raises the prominence of those organizations in the minds of policy makers. This is arguably the case for organizations, such as SIREN, that work with agencies in Santa Clara County. Here immigrants may face a trade-off between enjoying political presence through one or two organizations, but not having the full diversity of their group represented to local officials. The tendency of government sponsorship to simultaneously raise the prominence of particular organizations while dampening the growth of new ones merits further exploration, with attention to differences in factors such as whether government services are provided directly or indirectly through organizations, and whether local governments have discretion in social service spending or whether the disbursement of funds are determined by national formulas and guidelines.

Finally, it is important to note that local governments may also enact unsupportive (or restrictive) policies toward immigrant residents. In the previous year, many local governments have considered or passed ordinances that forbid renting apartments to illegal immigrants or that mandate the deportation of unauthorized immigrants in local police custody. It is still too early to assess the effects of such policies on immigrant-serving organizations. On the one hand, we would expect such ordinances to have a dampening effect on civic participation among immigrants. Indeed, our interviews with Latino organization leaders in Anaheim indicated that a rash of highly publicized ICE raids in the previous few years made many Latino immigrants reluctant to participate in community organizations.[21] However, immigrant-serving organizations may also receive more political visibility as a result of such controversies, though presumably their political influence may be limited in areas with strong restrictionist movements. An initial examination of the relationship between organizing or political presence, on the one hand, and city and police cooperation with federal immigration authorities or language ordinances, on the other, found no clear correlation in our six-city study. It is very likely the effect of restrictionist policies takes a while to work out—by hurting current or future organizations, or by spurring reactive organizing—and such effects are probably sensitive to the duration of restrictions. Further longitudinal research is needed on this topic.

Party Competition and Ethnic Elected Officials

Political context may influence the growth and political presence of ethnic organizations in other ways. The political science literature on minority political incorporation (Browning, Marshall, and Tabb 1984; Bobo and Gilliam 1990; Barreto, Segura, and Woods 2004) suggests that descriptive representation (that this, the election of coethnics to political office) increases the political influence of racial and ethnic minorities. Some may consider the election of ethnic officials to itself be a measure of political presence of an ethnic group. However, our examination of political presence focuses on the attributes of organizations, not resident populations. We would thus expect the election of ethnics to local office in our cities to increase the political presence of ethnic organizations among other council members. Indeed, the election of coethnics may increase the viability and incidence of ethnic organizations through the allocation of funds and the appointment of ethnic organization leaders to boards and commissions (Ramakrishnan and Lewis 2005).

In our case study cities, we do find a positive association between the presence of ethnics on city council and the political presence of organizations in the city (table 2.5). However, it is difficult to assign causal weight to this relationship because it may be the size of the ethnic population that is driving both outcomes. Thus, for instance, Vietnamese organizations in Garden Grove may be visible to elected officials in the city because they represent a significant and growing voting bloc, a factor that also explains why there is a Vietnamese American on the city council.[22] At the same time, ethnic group size is not an adequate argument because the substantial Mexican-origin populations in many of our cities generally have low incidences of ethnic organizations and limited political presence. To evaluate the hypothesis regarding the importance of elected officials, it will be important to do follow-up work to determine whether the election of Mexican-origin politicians in Anaheim and San Jose results in more civic organizations in the future.

It is also important to note that the presence of ethnic elected officials does not guarantee a group's overall political presence. This may especially be true in instances where common racial identities belie important national origin differences—see, for example, the sentiment among Korean leaders in Garden Grove that their interests are not represented by Vietnamese elected officials in city hall. Even with members of the same nationality, divisions in party loyalties or the absence of a sense of linked fate may limit the political visibility of ethnic organizations. For example, in Glendale, one local government official noted that, even with Latinos in city hall, Latino organizations remained largely invisible to government officials:

> The thing is, what's really frustrating to me, my understanding is Latinos make up also a third of the population here also and it's very difficult to get anybody from the Latino community to show up or be a representative. . . . I find them very uninvolved and very invisible in Glendale and then we also have two council people that are Latino and they're not too much of a help. . . . Dario Fromer is our assemblyman and he's Latino. . . . I have just not figured out how to get to the Latino community here.

The presence of ethnic elected officials is one of several possible factors related to the political opportunity structure in these localities that may help explain the political presence of ethnic organizations. Other factors that may be relevant include party competition, the dominance of liberals and Democrats in the electorate, and the existence of district versus at-large electoral systems. If, as other studies suggest, greater party competition will lead to greater mobilization among immigrant communities (Jones-Correa 1998; Wong 2006), we should also expect a corresponding increase in the political presence of ethnic organizations. However, we do not find any clear relationship between the level of party competition in a city and the political presence enjoyed by ethnic organizations (see table 2.5). Not only do cities with strong party competition have significant variations in the political presence of groups within the city, we also find instances, such as in San Jose, where Mexican organizations have a fairly high degree of political presence despite low levels of party competition.

Even if party competition is not significant in these cities, the dominance of liberals and Democrats in the electorate may still make a difference for political presence because of the election of officials sympathetic to minority interests (Browning, Marshall, and Tabb 1984). Our results, however, indicate otherwise: we find a very weak relationship between the dominance of Democrats in the electorate and the political presence of ethnic organizations (see table 2.5). It is quite possible that the lack of significance of these party competition and party control variables stems from limited variation on these measures in California and the lack of local partisan elections in the state. However, evidence suggests that, even with varying rules on local partisan elections and more significant variation in party competition, such factors still do little to explain the political presence of ethnic organizations (see chapter 3, this volume).

Finally, the presence of district versus at-large electoral systems may also make a difference with respect to the political presence of ethnic organizations. Indeed, the political reformers of the Progressive era who led the change away from district to at-large elections were often motivated by a desire to restrain the political power of minorities and immigrants and shift power away from neighborhoods (Bridges 1997; Judd and Swanstrom 1994). Studying the contemporary period, scholars have found that district elections are indeed better than at-large systems in promoting the election of minorities to elected office and giving greater attention to neighborhood interests and constituency service (Welch and Bledsoe 1988). Given that San Jose is the only city with district elections in our sample, we cannot easily distinguish the effects of city size and district elections on the political presence of ethnic organizations. Still, it is instructive to examine differences among Mexican and Vietnamese organizations in San Jose with those in other cities such as Glendale and Garden Grove. Mexican organizations seem to benefit from being in a district-system city such as San Jose because Latinos constitute a majority of residents in three of ten council districts (City of San Jose 2006), even though the proportion of Mexican-origin residents is smaller in San Jose (28 percent) than in Anaheim (48 percent) and is similar to West Covina (27 percent). Given the comparatively low rates of American citizenship among Mexican immigrants, the district system not only ensures that more Latinos get elected to City Hall, but also seems to increase the visibility of Latino organizations in these ethnic majority districts. In contrast, given the comparatively high rates of American citizenship among Vietnamese immigrants, being in an at-large system is not as much of a disadvantage. Indeed, Vietnamese residents (and, by extension, Vietnamese organizations) seem to benefit more from the at-large system in Garden Grove, where they form an important voting bloc for all council seats, than from the district system in San Jose, where they sway the outcome in only one district.

CONCLUSIONS

This study has shown that civic participation is often characterized by group inequalities, with mainstream organizations having considerably higher levels of political presence than ethnic organizations. Measures of civic participation that treat all civic participation the same—whether it be the chamber of commerce, the rotary club, or the Korean American Federation—ignore crucial components of group inequalities that include financial resources, access to future resources, and various aspects of social and cultural capital that relate to an organization's relative political prominence and influence in local affairs. Not only do mainstream groups have more political presence, they also do little to recruit immigrants and nonwhites into their ranks of members and leaders. This, in turn, lays the groundwork for persistent gaps in immigrant political incorporation at the local level.

When seeking to explain variation in organizational incidence and political presence across our cases, we find that city size and group size generally predict the number of ethnic organizations, but such relationships are more complicated when looking at political presence. We also find that ethnic organizations are more numerous in places with ethnic business districts, even if such places do not have many ethnic residents. However, the lack of an electoral base in such places limits the political presence of organizations founded due to the locational advantages associated with ethnic business districts.

In considering factors such as city size, group size, and ethnic business districts, it is also important to note the potentially exceptional case of cities that are nationally prominent for particular immigrant and ethnic communities. For instance, Glendale has the highest numbers of Armenians in the United States, accounting for about one in five residents of Armenian heritage in the country. As a consequence, it is one of the major centers for Armenian American organizing at a national scale, with two national Armenian newspapers and several national organizations headquartered in Glendale (though Watertown, Massachusetts, and the Boston metropolitan area are also important in this regard). Similarly, the northern parts of Orange County are considered the geographic home of much Vietnamese American advocacy and activism, with the epicenter of political strength in Westminster but also drawing on populations in nearby Garden Grove, Santa Ana, and Anaheim. This has been the case ever since the original resettlement of Vietnamese refugees in 1975 and 1976 established Orange County as of the four main resettlement camps in the area. The most prominent Vietnamese news organizations and political groups in the country are in Orange County, but the San Jose area is now slowly growing in prominence. The role of these nationally prominent cities thus cannot simply be reduced to factors such as city size, ethnic group size, and ethnic business districts—though all three are clearly present on a large scale for Armenians in Glendale and Vietnamese in Orange County. Histories of early settlement and subsequent resettlement, and the importance of these areas to their respective ethnic populations at the national level, also play important roles in shaping the prominence of these ethnic organizations in local politics. The cases of Vietnamese in Orange County and Armenians in Glendale also point to the possibility of length of residence as a potential explanatory factor in accounting for differences in political presence across groups. However, this explanation would not account for the relatively low political presence of other long-standing immigrant groups in our study including Mexican immigrant organizations in many cities and Korean organizations in Garden Grove.

Finally, we find that government assistance to immigrants helps boost the viability of a few ethnic organizations, but that the direct provision of services may dampen the growth of new ethnic community organizations. We found modest relationships for other aspects of local political opportunity structures such as district versus at-large elections and local party competition, findings echoed in chapter 3 of this volume, which focuses on medium-sized cities across the United States. At the same time, the interrelationships between ethnic organizations and local parties may be quite different in our cities than in strong-party cities such as Chicago (chapter 9) and Edison, New Jersey (chapter 8), with intraparty divisions being more important than interparty rivalry. We also expect that political contexts take on more weight when the comparison is made across different national contexts (chapters 5 and 6, this volume).

It is difficult, based on a snapshot view of civic and political engagement among immigrant communities in the United States today, to predict whether ethnic organizations will surmount the problems they currently face in terms of diminished resources and lower political presence compared to mainstream community organizations. In our cities, many local officials attributed the political marginality of such groups to their insular orientations, focusing exclusively on ethnic residents instead of the larger population in the city. In some cases, insularity does not seem to harm the visibility and influence of politically ascendant immigrant groups, such as the Armenians in Glendale and the Vietnamese in Garden Grove. For these groups, high rates of citizenship and large shares of the voting-eligible population render moot the liability of insularity, whether perceived or real. Even in the same cities, however, other groups, such as Mexicans and Koreans, remain on the margins of civic life—the former due to their low rates of citizenship and low socioeconomic status, and the latter because the prevalence of ethnic businesses and community organizations is not bolstered by a large voting population.

It is quite possible that with higher rates of citizenship and economic advancement among Latino immigrants in the next decade or two, their ethnic organizations will gain more political visibility and influence in these medium-sized cities. Our findings can only be suggestive in this regard because our data is not based on longitudinal data, and is instead a cross-sectional comparison across cities and major immigrant-origin groups. Our findings suggest that it is not simply the passage of time that makes a difference with respect to the political presence of immigrant-origin groups. Thus, for instance, many Korean organizations in Garden Grove remain marginal in the eyes of public officials, even though many may have been created before counterpart mainstream organizations and Vietnamese organizations with relatively high levels of political presence. With growing populations, higher rates of citizenship acquisition, and increased political participation, immigrant groups can hope to overcome the marginality that currently befalls many ethnic organizations. Absent such empowerment, however, we may continue to see stratification in civic and political life in many immigrant-destination cities, both between mainstream and ethnic organizations, and across various national-origin groups.

APPENDIX

Organizational Directories

We derived our list of organizations for sampling and interviewing from several sources.

1. Melissa DATA and GuideStar

Melissa DATA is a for-profit corporation specializing in bulk mailings. It sells a database of 1.3 million nonprofit organizations, with contact name, mailing address, type of organization (based on the Internal Revenue Service (IRS) Code of 1986, which defines the category under which an organization may be exempt), tax I.D. number, and assets and income information when available. GuideStar is a nonprofit, registered 501(c)(3) established to provide readily accessible nonprofit data, mainly to the nonprofit sector. (It also tailors its data for business, grantmakers, government, donors, media, researchers, and other entities.) A central goal is transparency, so that donors can make informed decisions before committing funds. GuideStar provides information on 1.5 million nonprofit organizations, which it claims are all the tax-exempt nonprofits registered with the IRS. GuideStar data come from IRS 990 forms and the IRS Business Master File. Nonprofits included in the database can voluntarily add their annual reports, audited financial statements, letters of determination, and other documents. Both databases are limited in that they include only those groups that have officially filed for tax-exempt status with the IRS. Consequently, they offer good coverage of large, established groups, but their coverage of small groups is more spotty.

2. Local, publicly available directories

To generate a more exhaustive list of ethnic organizations, we used ethnic telephone directories wherever possible—we could use only those directories printed in English or Spanish, given the language skills of the researchers involved in this project.

3. Snowball samples

In addition to these publicly available data, we included those organizations that were mentioned in our informant interviews of government officials as well as in our organizational interviews.

This project has benefited from the institutional support of the Russell Sage Foundation and the Public Policy Institute of California, and the valuable research assistance of Kristel Acacio, Sofya Aptekar, Shannon Gleeson, Els de Graauw, Rebecca Hamlin, Soo Jin Kim, Jennifer Paluch, Laurencio Sanguino, Crissa Stephens, and Celia Viramontes. The authors bear sole responsibilities for any errors.

NOTES

1. The Immigrant Civic Engagement Project (ICEP) examines the political consequences of immigrant civic participation in cities from the Chicago, Central New Jersey, Washington D.C., San Jose, Los Angeles, and Orange County metropolitan areas. This research was funded largely by the Russell Sage Foundation and the Public Policy Institute of California. Other chapters in this volume derived from ICEP include those by Aptekar, Sanguino, and Viramontes.
2. Early debates over community power between elitist and pluralist scholars centered around whether assessments of influence should be based on general reputations (elitists) or on influence over particular issues and decisions (pluralists). Our method stakes a middle ground by relying on reputational assessments from those in political power, while also probing for which organizations are most prominent on particular topics. Many elitist scholars relied instead on more general assessments of influence.
3. In each case, we made several attempts to contact an organization staff member or group leader. In the event of lack of contact or response, we selected at random from the remaining organizations within the stratum.

4. We use the label mainstream because it accurately describes the dominant civic and political institutions in the United States today, most of which are composed of native-born whites. Some scholars may dispute this distinction, either from a normative standpoint (ethnic organizations should be considered as part of mainstream American life) or a descriptive one (ethnic associations are redefining what is considered mainstream in American society and politics). We leave aside the normative argument. There is certainly some merit to the descriptive claim with, for instance, the adoption of official holidays honoring ethnic heroes or incorporating ethnic elements or themes in city festivals. However, because this study is primarily concerned with how immigrant civic participation matters for influence and participation in politics, we base our distinction on the views of local officials and organizational elites, most of whom make ready differentiations between ethnic and mainstream organizations.

5. Admittedly, our method of refining the ethnic versus mainstream measure is subject to measurement error because we do not have access to information about mission statements and memberships for all organizations. Thus, we may indeed have more ethnic organizations than we show in this analysis. However, given the small proportion of mainstream organizations that were reclassified using more intensive searches and interview methods, our findings regarding gaps between the share of the resident population and the share of the organizational universe still holds. Also, we have no reason to believe that this measurement error varies across the case study cities, making such error less relevant for this chapter's focus on comparisons across groups and cities.

6. U.S. Census Bureau (2000).

7. "The isolation index measures 'the extent to which minority members are exposed only to one another,' (Massey and Denton [1998], p. 288) and is computed as the minority-weighted average of the minority proportion in each area" (U.S. Census Bureau 2000).

8. Jim Tortolano, "The Boom of WWII and Modern Day Garden Grove," *Garden Grove Journal*, accessed at http://ggjournal.com/history2.html.

9. The Vietnamese community and business sector has flourished along Brookhurst Street, turning it into an extension of Little Saigon (Westminster). This represents one of the major ethnic enclaves in Garden Grove. The other is represented by Koreatown, which stretches over a half mile along Garden Grove Boulevard.

10. Gustavo Arellano, "When Immigrants Attack," *Orange County Weekly*, July 18, 2004, 15.

11. Based on interviews with city officials and staff of community-based organizations.

12. As the *Los Angeles Times* noted in 2006, "Mayor Dave Weaver, who opposes lifting the ban, believes that the debate has gotten too bitter and denounced his Armenian American colleagues on the council for 'using the race card'" (David Pierson, "Passions Flame Over Kebabs," November 4, 2006, accessed at http://www.burning issues.org/forum/phpBB2/viewtopic.php?t=56&sid=26550ae3da635378bd605718 bc4e52c6).

13. These figures do not include the informal associations mentioned by local informants but not listed in any of the directories we used. They are not included because there is no predetermined universe of all such organizations to which our snowball samples can be compared.

14. It is important to present both figures because San Jose is a large city, a regional capital of sorts, where certain types of community organizations may be more likely than others.

15. The lower incidence of Mexican (or Latino) organizations might also stem from the more informal nature of some of these associations. As outlined in the methods section of this chapter and the appendix, we relied heavily on organizational sources drawing from registered nonprofit organizations. For those who are undocumented or believe they might return home—as is regularly the case among Mexican immigrants—many ethnic organizations remain informal and hard to capture through standard organizational directories. See, for example, Viramontes in this volume.

16. Interviews with arts commission members in other cities and counties revealed a growing interest in conducting community outreach, because of the relative invisibility of immigrant and ethnic organizations relative to mainstream ones. In many cases, however, lack of organizational capacity among ethnic arts and culture groups remains a barrier.

17. Organizational interview, April 1, 2005.

18. Organizational interview, August 2, 2004.

19. In the 2004 fiscal year, the total appropriations for the various domestic refugee resettlement programs were almost $450 million. The state of California received $17.7 million in cash and medical assistance, funds that generally go directly to refugees, as well as $9.4 million for social services and $5.3 million in targeted assistance, funds which go to state and county governments, as well as nonprofit service providers, to run programs for refugees. All three of the counties we consider received funds under the Targeted Assistance program directed to areas with high refugee populations or refugee concentrations. Los Angeles County received $1.9 million in FY 2004, Orange County received $420,000 and Santa Clara received $570,000. Unfortunately, ORR's public reports do not break these figures down by city; the 2004 report to Congress can be found at http://www.acf.hhs.gov/pro grams/orr/data/arc.htm (accessed March 6, 2008).

20. Beyond the pure financial transfers, which largely increase individuals' and organizations' ability to be political active and present, the very existence of these programs creates bridges between minority populations and local decision-makers. For county governments to justify the continued flow of fund to their area, they must coordinate with local organizations on the county's needs, the services offered and the resources expended. Such reporting activities necessarily build personal relationship and knowledge of ethnic organizations. The existence of such programs also opens access points to elected office-holders and nonelected officials.

21. Organizational interview, May 5, 2005; government official interview, July 6, 2004.

22. There is also the possibility of endogeneity, with the presence of ethnic organizations making the election of ethnics possible, and not the other way around. As we have seen with Korean organizations in Garden Grove, however, it is difficult to translate organizational numbers to electoral strength when there is no electoral base that underpins such organizations.

REFERENCES

Associated Press. 2003. "Orange County Priest Seeks Cultural Understanding in New Parish." *The Association Press State and Local Wire*, June 8, 2003.

Barreto, Matt, Gary Segura, and Nathan Woods. 2004. "The Effects of Overlapping Majority-Minority Districts on Latino Turnout." *American Political Science Review* 98(1): 65–75.

Bloemraad, Irene. 2005. "The Limits of Tocqueville: How Government Facilitates Organisational Capacity in Newcomer Communities." *Journal of Ethnic and Migration Studies* 31(5): 865–87.

————. 2006. *Becoming a Citizen: Incorporating Immigrants and Refugees in the United States and Canada.* Berkeley, Calif.: University of California Press.

Bobo, Lawrence, and Franklin D. Gilliam. 1990. "Race, Sociopolitical Participation, and Black Empowerment." *American Political Science Review* 84(2): 377–93

Bonacich, Edna, and John Modell. 1980. *The Economic Basis of Ethnic Solidarity: Small Business in the Japanese American Community.* Berkeley, Calif.: University of California Press.

Bridges, Amy. 1997. *Morning Glories: Municipal Reform in the Southwest.* Princeton, N.J.: Princeton University Press.

Browning, Rufus P., Dale Rogers Marshall, and David H. Tabb. 1984. *Protest Is Not Enough: The Struggle of Blacks and Hispanics for Equality in Urban Politics.* Berkeley, Calif.: University of California Press.

Chaves, Mark, Laura Stephens, and Joseph Galaskiewicz. 2004. "Does Government Funding Suppress Nonprofits' Political Activity?" *American Sociological Review* 69(2): 292–316.

City of Glendale. 2008. *Come Home to Glendale.* Accessed March 17, 2008, at http://www.ci.glendale.ca.us/cdh/chg_links.asp.

City of San Jose. 2006. "Demographic Trends Census Brief," City of San Jose Planning Division. Accessed at http://www.sanjoseca.gov/planning/Census/briefs/race_ethni city.asp.

Corcoran, Katherine. 2005. "San Jose Neglects Ethnic Tourism." *San Jose Mercury News,* October 10, 2005.

DeSipio, Louis. 1996. *Counting on the Latino Vote: Latinos as a New Electorate.* Charlottesville, Va.: University Press of Virginia.

Jones-Correa, Michael. 1998. *Between Two Nations: The Political Predicament of Latinos in New York City.* Ithaca, N.Y.: Cornell University Press.

Judd, Dennis R., and Todd Swanstrom. 1994. *City Politics: Private Power and Public Policy.* New York: HarperCollins College Publishers.

Min, Pyong Gap. 1996. *Caught in the Middle: Korean Merchants in America's Multiethnic Cities.* Berkeley, Calif.: University of California Press.

Passel, Jeffrey S. 2006. *Size and Characteristics of the Unauthorized Migrant Population in the U.S.: Estimates Based on the March 2005 Current Population Survey.* Washington: Pew Hispanic Center.

Putnam, Robert. 2000. *Bowling Alone: The Collapse and Revival of American Community.* New York: Simon & Schuster.

Ramakrishnan, S. Karthick. 2005. *Democracy in Immigrant America: Changing Demographics and Political Participation.* Palo Alto, Calif.: Stanford University Press.

Ramakrishnan, S. Karthick, and Paul Lewis. 2005. *Immigrants and Local Governance: The View From City Hall.* San Francisco: Public Policy Institute of California.

Rogers, Reuel. 2006. *Afro-Caribbean Immigrants and the Politics of Incorporation: Ethnicity, Exception, or Exit.* New York: Cambridge University Press.

Skocpol, Theda. 2003. *Diminished Democracy: From Membership to Management in American Civic Life.* Norman: University of Oklahoma Press.

U.S. Census Bureau. 2000. Census 2000 SF3 data. Accessed at http://factfinder .census.gov/.

————. 2005. American Community Survey. Accessed at http://factfinder.census.gov/

U.S. Geological Survey. 2008. "California County Map with Selected Cities and Towns." Accessed at http://nationalatlas.gov/printable/reference.html#California.

Vasquez, Manuel. 2003. "Latino Immigrants in Southern Florida: Some Theoretical Reflections." Paper prepared for presentation at the Annual Meeting of the Latin American Studies Association. Dallas, Tex., March 27–29, 2003.

Verba, Sidney, Kay Lehman Schlozman, and Henry E. Brady. 1995. *Voice and Equality: Civic Voluntarism in American Politics.* Cambridge, Mass.: Harvard University Press.

Welch, Susan, and Timothy Bledsoe. 1988. *Survey of City Council Members in Large American Cities, 1982.* Ann Arbor, Mich.: Institute for Social Research University of Michigan.

Wong, Janelle. 2006. *Democracy's Promise: Immigrants and American Civic Institutions.* Ann Arbor, Mich.: University of Michigan Press.

Zhou, Min. 2001. "Immigrant Neighborhoods in Los Angeles: Structural Constraints, Ethnic Resources, and Varied Contexts for the Adaptation of Immigrant Children." Paper presented at the Wiener Inequality and Social Policy Seminar, John F. Kennedy School of Government, Harvard University. Boston, Mass., October 29., 2001.

Zhou, Min, and Chen Cai. 2002. "The Chinese Language Media in the United States: Immigration and Assimilation in American Life." *Qualitative Sociology* 25(3): 419–40.

Kristi Andersen

Chapter 3

Parties, Organizations, and Political Incorporation: Immigrants in Six U.S. Cities

New arrivals to the United States settle in places with varied political and social characteristics. This paper is concerned with how immigrants move toward a situation where they have a place at the table in local politics: where their organizations and their leaders are consulted, where their members are seen as valuable constituents, where their interests are seen as part of the political calculus.

The U.S. Census Bureau estimates that the United States is currently home to about 31 million foreign-born adults over eighteen (2004). Approximately 59 percent of those are noncitizens, none of whom can vote except in local elections in few places[1] and many of whom are reluctant to participate in almost any sort of political activity for fear of drawing the attention of federal agencies, a particular danger in the post-9/11 world. Imagine placing these foreign-born denizens on a continuum from, at one extreme, undocumented, short-term or circular immigrants to, at the other, long-naturalized citizens. Reasonable people might disagree about where to draw the line, but most Americans would agree that our political system is benefited if the people toward the latter end of this continuum are full participants in American political and civic life. Conversely, the political system's stability and democratic values are threatened if high rates of immigration produce large numbers of nonparticipating, unrepresented, disengaged residents.[2]

This research examines six medium-sized American cities in 2004 and asks first whether political incorporation of immigrants appears to be taking place at a similar pace and in a similar manner in these places. I then investigate the role of parties in working to naturalize, register, and mobilize immigrant groups in these cities—and ask if, as suggested by the research, parties are basically absent, in what ways are other organizations stepping up to connect members of immigrant groups to local (and state and national) political machinery? What can comparisons among these cities suggest about the conditions under which the local organizational context works or doesn't work to incorporate immigrants? Some of the aspects of place that may differentially shape immigrant incorporation include the political and geographical isolation of the city; the historical existence of a significant refugee stream among the city's immigrants; and the types and strengths of the connections between immigrant-related organizations and between these organizations and other civic and political organizations in the community. I suggest that the fundamental step of naturalization is facilitated by community organizational capacity which is sometimes based partially on organizational spillover from refugee programs. The next step of group representation in decision making seems to be related to the strength of connections between immigrant groups and the larger community—in the form of political allies and supportive organizations.

THE SIX-CITY STUDY

This exploratory research examines midsized cities—Chico, California; Fort Collins, Colorado; Lansing, Michigan; Spokane, Washington; Syracuse, New York; and Waco, Texas. Traditionally, immigrants to the United States have concentrated in a relatively small number of gateway cities, and much of the research on political incorporation of immigrants, historically and contemporary, has focused on these cities. Though the traditional gateway cities are still popular destinations, newcomers are also settling in states and cities that have previously experienced little immigration, so that a focus on nongateway cities is increasingly important (for a good data-based overview of the different categories of gateway metropolitan areas: former, continuous, post-World War II, emerging, re-emerging, and pre-emerging, see Singer 2004). And though immigrants to gateway cities typically join established communities or have easily available models of other established immigrant communities, immigrants in these smaller cities are more isolated. How does such establishment and incorporation happen in these situations?

The cities studied were comparable on four dimensions: the size of the metropolitan area (100,000 to 500,000 MSA population); the size of the immigrant population (4 to 10 percent of the total population); the proportion of temporary or transient residents (such as college students) in the metropolitan area (cities chosen were close to the national average on this dimension); and the timing of the city's immigrant population's arrival in the United States (again, close to the national average in terms of percentage of foreign-born arriving between 1990 and 2000). The cities varied in terms of the diversity of their immigration streams (the two cities with homogeneous migrants, Fort Collins and Waco, have primarily Mexican immigrants), the bases of their economies, and their relative affluence. Table 3.1 provides basic demographic and economic information about the six cities (census data is for SMSAs).

In each city a research assistant conducted fifteen to twenty unstructured interviews (averaging about an hour each) with elected officials (or people who managed their campaigns); political party leaders; and heads or staff members of organizations that provided services to immigrant groups, advocated for immigrant rights, or were otherwise relevant to understanding the position of immigrant groups in that city. These interviews took place in the spring and summer of 2004, with the exception of Syracuse.[3] We also scrutinized the cities' and

TABLE 3.1 Economic, Political, and Demographic Characteristics of Six Cities

	SMSA Population	Percentage Foreign-Born	Immigrant Diversity	Party Control[a]	Economy	Wealth
Chico-Paradise, CA	203,171	7.7	heterogeneous	Republican	service	poor
Ft. Collins-Loveland, CO	251,494	4.3	homogeneous	Republican	mixed	rich
Lansing-E. Lansing, MI	447,728	4.6	heterogeneous	Democratic	mixed	rich
Spokane, WA	417,939	4.5	heterogeneous	Republican	service	average
Syracuse, NY	732,117	4.3	heterogeneous	Democratic	mixed	average
Waco, TX	213,517	6.1	homogeneous	Republican	mixed	poor

Source: U.S. Census Bureau (2003a), tables P1, P23, PCT19, P49, P53, and P52.
[a] Party control: based on average presidential vote 1996, 2000, and 2004, and control of city government in 2004.

counties' websites and examined media coverage of issues related to immigration, immigrant groups, and minority politics in each city, and made use of appropriate census and voting data as well.

ASSESSING IMMIGRANT POLITICAL INCORPORATION

There are a number of ways of conceptualizing and measuring immigrant incorporation. Fundamentally, incorporation is the process of becoming a part of a community's political practices and decision making. Becoming a naturalized citizen is perhaps the most basic step and one which has been used to make historical comparisons among groups and over time (compare Gavit 1922; Valelly 2005; Bloemraad 2006a, 2006b).[4] Naturalization is required in order to vote (in the vast majority of elections in the United States), run for office or (sometimes) serve on local boards or commissions; in the present post-9/11 context, even an immigrant with a green card or legal visa may think twice about participating in demonstrations or signing petitions, though they would have every right to do so.

Voting is the most commonly used indicator of political participation, but in situations where survey data is not available, it is challenging to estimate voting rates for particular groups by using aggregate analysis. Later I look at naturalization rates, at representation of immigrant groups in governmental institutions, and at local government responsiveness to immigrants.[5]

The density and concentration of communities, the existence of organizational networks, the existence of political entrepreneurs in the new communities, the incentives to create cross-group coalitions, and the receptiveness of local political parties—among other contextual factors—will shape the ways that immigrants are involved in politics. For example, Waldinger (1996) argued that the institutional structures of Los Angeles and New York (the party systems, at-large versus district level representation, the traditions of ethnically balanced slate-making, etcetera) have meant that New York immigrants are more easily incorporated than those in Los Angeles. States vary quite a bit in the extent to which immigrants have naturalized, and this is true even among states with similar patterns of immigration (see Andersen 2006).

Naturalization Rates

Most research aimed at explaining variations in naturalization rates, as suggested above, has focused on group characteristics (there are consistent variations in naturalization by sending country) and on individual attributes. There has been some attention paid to the impact on naturalization rates of California's Proposition 187 as well as the similar mid-1990s federal legislation, all of which changed the incentive structure for naturalization. But in general there has been little focus on politico-geographical variation in naturalization (or in other measures of incorporation). Much as Bloemraad (2006b, 12) argued that U.S.-Canada differences can be illuminated through an institutional approach, it

FIGURE 3.1 *Naturalization Rate for Six Cities and Their States, 2000*

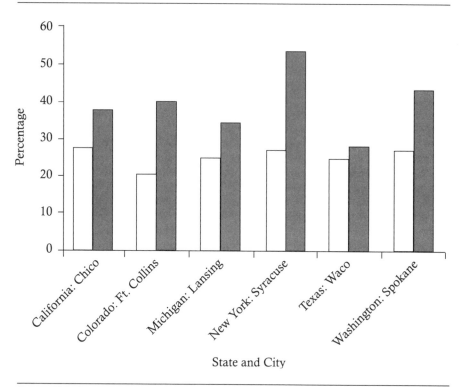

State and City

Source: U.S. Census Bureau (2003a, table P23).

seems reasonable to suggest that cross-state or cross-city variations within the United States are worth studying. Figure 3.1 shows the overall naturalization rate in 2000 for the six cities and for the states in which they are located.

It is worth noting that all of the cities have higher naturalization rates than their states as a whole, and that the rank ordering of states according to extent to which their foreign-born residents have naturalized is not consistent with the rank ordering of the cities. The variation between states is narrow (about three percentage points), while the variation among the cities is quite broad: from Waco's 28 percent to Syracuse's 53 percent. Some portion of this variation might be due to variations in the timing of immigration to each of the six cities, but the six cities are relatively similar in this regard: on average a bit fewer than half of their immigrants entered the United States before 1980, about a third since 1990, and the remainder between 1980 and 1990.[6]

Because these cities vary in the makeup of their immigrant populations, it makes sense to examine naturalization rates among more or less comparable groups. Table 3.2 compares naturalization rates for those who arrived between

TABLE 3.2   *Naturalization Rates by City and Origin, 2000*

	Chico	Ft. Collins	Lansing	Spokane	Syracuse	Waco
Pre-1980						
Mexican	37.4%	63.2%	54.1%			43.2%
European			77.8	81.3%	82.9%	
Asian	73.4		74.4	82.9	76.8	
1980 to 1990						
Mexican	41.8	32.4	29.9			24.8
European			58.5	41.9	44.8	
Asian	66.6		62.4	66.6	56.2	

Source: U.S. Census Bureau (2003b, table PCT48).

1980 and 1990 and those who arrived before 1980, by city and (where there are more than 1,000 members of the group in the city) by country or region of origin.

There are a number of interesting comparisons here. First, as previous research has found, likelihood of naturalization increases with length of time in the United States. The average levels of naturalization among these groups and cities are 71 percent for immigrants arriving before 1980 and 53 percent for those arriving between 1980 and 1990. There is one exception to this pattern: a somewhat higher rate of naturalization among the 1980 to 1990 arrivals in Chico, for which the contentious immigration politics of California during the 1990s may be responsible. Second, as we have come to expect, differences among groups are unmistakable: specifically, Mexicans are less likely to naturalize than other immigrants. Third, and most relevant to this research, differences among the six cities are also pronounced. The patterns are not clear or consistent, however. City differences for European immigrants are quite a bit larger among more recent arrivals. The opposite is true for Mexicans: there are greater city-to-city differences in naturalization rates for the pre-1980 immigrants. Group comparisons must be made at a very general level: Asians include various nationality groups, and even Mexican immigrants may vary from city to city in their class or occupational backgrounds. Nonetheless, some of the differences are striking. For example, almost two-thirds of long-established Mexican immigrants in Fort Collins are citizens, but only a little more than one-third of the comparable group in Chico has naturalized. Lansing and Spokane show quite different naturalization rates for newer European immigrants. Although explaining these differences is not my goal here, the existence of such variability is consistent with situations in which local parties are not widely organizing and facilitating naturalization, but rather where group-specific organizations vary in their capacity for incorporation (and their focus on naturalization).

Levels of Political Representation

If we define immigrant political incorporation as a situation in which new groups have a place at the table politically, then it is also important to assess the extent to which members of immigrant groups have been appointed or elected to public office in the six cities. In terms of the concepts used in the present volume, political representation may be seen as an indicator of political presence. Have members of immigrant groups begun to run for office? Many scholars have argued that a key ingredient to improving political participation is to ensure that elected officials share similar backgrounds and experiences as the constituencies they represent. Such representation ensures that minority concerns make it onto the public agenda, reduces political alienation among minorities and increases their trust in democratic processes, thereby improving democratic institutions' legitimacy (Mansbridge 1999). "By appearance alone, statements, or symbolic gestures" descriptive representatives "send cues to their co-ethnic constituents that they will be more responsive to their needs" (Pantoja and Segura 2003, 443–44). Pantoja and Segura found that among Latino voters in Texas and California, descriptive representation increased their sense of political efficacy, voter turnout, and trust in government.

I examined the websites of city and county offices and agencies to identify members of immigrant groups who had been elected or appointed to office.[7] It should be noted that the structures of city and county governments vary dramatically. In some places, city clerks are elected; in others, they are appointed. Some cities have few elected officials and many appointed officials. Some rely more heavily than others on volunteer commissions and boards. Whether local legislators are elected on a district or at-large basis might be expected to have an impact on representation, but all these cities except Chico have some form of district elections on the local level.[8] Lansing's system is mixed (four at large, four district) and the other four cities have district-based elections.[9] In any case, the representation column in table 3.3 provides the percentage of immigrant group members (as far as could be determined from names) in city and county elected and top appointed positions, and the following paragraphs supply some narrative background for the numbers.[10]

Chico had a Vietnamese city council member and several Hispanics in appointed positions (planning commission board, assistant director of public works, assistant school superintendent), but in general very few Hispanic or Asians occupied positions on commissions and committees (some elected, some appointed). There were substantial numbers of Latinos serving in the state senate and the state assembly.

The Fort Collins mayor at the time of our study was Mexican American. There were a number of Hispanic members of volunteer boards and commissions (Affordable Housing Board, Citizen Review Board, Human Relations Commission, Landmark Preservation Commission, and so on). Two Larimer County magistrates were Hispanic, but no one on the city council (seven members) or the school board (ten members) or in any of the county offices other than the magistrates.

Lansing's mayor, Tony Benavides, was Latino and was elected in part based on a coalition of Latino and black voters. There were no Hispanics or other immigrant group members on the city council. Of the nine members of the board of education, one was Hispanic. Two members of the Ingham County Board of Commissioners were Hispanic, as was a circuit court family division judge. Appointed members of advisory boards include people with varied ethnic backgrounds: Japanese, Mexican, Syrian, Afghan, and Vietnamese.

In Spokane, no elected officials were from immigrant groups. There were a fairly large number of appointees, however, including Hispanics and people from the Vietnamese, Chinese, Russian, Hmong, and Native American communities. For example, the Policy Advisory Committee had members representing the Hispanic Business Professionals' Association, the Native American Community, the Russian American Communication Agency, the Vietnamese Community, and the Spokane Hmong Association. Others served on the Aging and Long-Term Care Board, the Human Services Advisory Board, the Youth Commission, the Human Rights Commission, the Regional Transportation Council, and the City/County Historic Landmark Committee.

In Syracuse, the most visible minority official was the Puerto Rican president of the Common Council, a strong advocate for the Hispanic and minority communities. The commissioner of community development was Hispanic, as was one school board member The city-county Human Rights Commission included a Chinese-American member, an African American, a Native American, and a Latina, but I found no elected or appointed members of the Vietnamese, Bosnian, or other immigrant or refugee communities.

In Waco, of the six members of city council, one was Latino. The seven-member school board had one Latino member. Other Latinos included a justice of the peace, the chief of police, and the assistant city manager. At the state level, about a fifth of the state assembly was Hispanic. The McLennan County office-holders, including auditor, clerk, tax assessor, treasurer, and sheriff, were all white.

Interest Representation

To what extent are the needs and preferences of immigrant groups represented in local government decisions and policies? As discussed in the introductory chapter, political influence can occur at many stages in the policy process, and groups and organizations may have varied political goals. Local governments vary greatly in their willingness and ability to reach out to new groups; news accounts over the past year describe cities designating themselves safe zones for immigrants, and others that have tried to make it illegal to fly non-American flags.

As Michael Jones-Correa (2005) found in the Washington suburbs, school officials in these six cities were often receptive to the needs of immigrants. For example, we were told by people in Lansing and Spokane about the favorable orientation of school districts. Lansing public schools have been very receptive to suggestions about Muslim cultural practices and preferences, and Spokane's city school district was described as being helpful, establishing an equity office to provide more resources to local immigrant and refugee families with children in public schools.[11]

In Fort Collins, whose mayor in 2004 was a conservative Hispanic Republican, the city library has a bilingual section, bus routes are published in Spanish, and city council meetings provide translation.[12] The Waco-McClennan County

TABLE 3.3   *Summary of Political Incorporation Measures*

	Naturalization Rate	Naturalization Rate, 1980 to 1990 Arrivals	Immigrant Representation in Local Government	Government Responsiveness
Chico	37.8%	38.9%	4.4%	medium
Fort Collins	39.5	50.9	10.9	low
Lansing	34.6	55.1	17.8	high
Spokane	43.0	53.8	12.3	low
Syracuse	53.0	58.4	5.4	medium
Waco	28.2	35.4	11.9	medium

Source: Author's compilation.

Public Health District partners with the Community Race Relations Coalition to educate people about health disparities, although at the same time there has been resistance to distributing materials (from the city government and the schools) in Spanish as well as English.

The government responsiveness column in table 3.3 presents a considerable simplification of this aspect of political weight. This measure was derived primarily from data available on the websites of local governments. In particular we focused on the web pages of each city's mayor or city council, policy department, social services department, city school district, board of elections, and personnel department. Each was coded as to whether they had pages in languages of the city's immigrant groups, mentioned immigration or immigrants positively, mentioned ethnic-racial diversity positively, identified office or staff member to deal with immigrant-related issues, offered staff diversity training, contained links to immigrant or refugee groups, or evidenced special programs to recruit immigrant employees. The ordinal rankings in the last column of table 3.3 follow the results of this procedure, with two exceptions, which were supported by information from official sources, media accounts, and informants as to the difficulty faced by immigrant groups when they deal with local government officials and agencies.[13]

This summary presents a complicated picture, suggesting that incorporation is multidimensional and context-dependent. Syracuse, for example, has the highest overall naturalization rates, and Lansing and Spokane (as well as Syracuse) have relatively high rates for 1980 to 1990 arrivals (all of whom should presumably have had enough time to naturalize). However, Syracuse lags in representation and (to a lesser extent) responsiveness, whereas Lansing is high on both those measures. The responsiveness measure here, it is important to note, looks at local—that is, county, city, and school district—government. In some cases—Spokane, for example—the state-level responsiveness is relatively higher. At the other end of the spectrum, Chico's immigrants have been slow to naturalize and are not significantly represented in local government, but the city government (with at least some progressive elected officials) reflects greater openness to immigrant concerns than one might expect. Waco's naturalization rates are similarly low, but this city has somewhat higher representation and government attention to immigrant concerns.

PARTIES AND INCORPORATION

Historically, political parties played a key role in this process (see, for example, Erie 1988; Sterne 2001; Valelly 2005), routinely easing the naturalization process for many immigrants.[14] Before the 1870s, the major source of immigration was northwestern Europe, and once arrived in the United States, many of these people dispersed to rural areas and small communities across the country. Rules governing naturalization and voting were lax; local parties frequently helped immigrants to naturalize, as well as providing them with material assistance and facilitating employment. In more than twenty states before 1910, primarily the South and Midwest, aliens were permitted to vote if they merely declared their intention to become citizens. Partly in reaction to the new streams of immigrants from Southern and Eastern Europe beginning roughly in the 1880s, and partly as a function of the general Progressive desire toward rationalization, laws and practices were tightened. For example, in all but two of the states mentioned above, aliens' voting privileges were revoked by constitutional amendment (for the impact of increasingly nationalized rules on state variation in naturalization rates, see Bloemraad 2006a).

Parties' success during the late nineteenth century (a period of high turnout, at least in the North) depended on mobilizing voters, so logically they had an interest in new potential voters, where they settled, and whether they were allowed to vote. Political parties "subsidized the naturalization/voting sequence—through providing advice, personal assistance, and material incentives for naturalization and participation to foreign-born residents" (Valelly 2005, 7). In addition, many civic groups, often directly or indirectly related to parties, emerged to provide naturalization assistance to immigrants. Some of these were nationality based clubs and groups, as Roy Peel meticulously described for New York City in his 1935 *Political Clubs of New York City*. At the same time, the political parties created "committees and bureaus to assist the alien in getting naturalization" (Gavit, 1922, 32). Michael Jones-Correa, in *Between Two Nations,* provided a good discussion of the traditional views of the parties as mobilizers of immigrants as well as the more recent revisionist views, but concludes overall that the political parties of the late nineteenth and early twentieth century did provide channels for the incorporation of immigrants (1998, chapter 4).

In the early twentieth century, local Democratic and Republican party organizations continued to prosper in situations where dependent populations could be motivated by means of service provision and jobs to supply votes and political manpower. During the 1920s and 1930s, those dynamics were especially beneficial to the national Democratic Party, whose constituency was significantly reshaped with the incorporation of first- and second-generation immigrants. From that point until the late 1960s, immigration declined dramatically and the political incorporation of immigrants faded from national consciousness.

Parties have undergone dramatic changes over the past hundred years or so, and these changes have implications for the relationship between parties, on the one hand, and immigrants and immigration policy, on the other. Although there is a great deal of scholarly debate about the extent to which parties have declined on various dimensions, there is consensus that the level of individual identification with the parties has decreased. Election campaigns and voter decision making are more candidate-centered than in the past, and parties' power increasingly derives from their important roles as providers of services and funds to candidates rather than from their grassroots organizational vigor. American political parties are no longer mass parties. Steven Rosenstone and John Hansen (1993), among others, made it clear that parties increasingly act strategically to target those whose behavior is predictable, and thus who are already participants in the political system. The new technologies and the data sources available to parties' and candidates' organizations make it possible for them to succeed in a low-turnout era, by fine-tuning appeals, targeting supporters and ignoring large blocs of nonregistered, nonvoting, or unpredictable voters.

Thus parties no longer serve the important role that they once did either in naturalizing immigrants or including new citizens in political activities. Michael Jones-Correa's study of South American immigrants in Queens gives evidence of this shift. His research indicates that "rather than lowering the costs for marginal political players, the Queens Democratic party . . . raises them." Jones-Correa explained: "If actors are at the margins of electoral politics, as immigrants are, then they are ignored; if political players rise to the challenge of the machine, they are thwarted. Only if the new political actors succeed in mobilizing themselves on their own does the party organization attempt to bring them into its cycle" (1998, 70). In comparative work on community organizations in New York City and Los Angeles, Janelle Wong found that "political machines and party organizations today are no longer the driving force behind minority immigrant political mobilization" (2006, 52).

Naturalization and Registration

Similar claims can be made about parties in these six cities. In general, political parties—by which I mean both local party organizations and candidate organizations—simply do not see encouraging naturalization as part of their responsibility, nor (apparently) as providing a potential electoral advantage. In interviews with party leaders and elected officials (and their staffers) at the city, state, and congressional levels, there was little evidence that local parties facilitated naturalization in the ways that were common a hundred years ago.

Party and candidate organizations are barely more involved in registration drives. The response to questions about voter registration was, essentially, that "somebody else does it." A Texas Congressman's campaign staffer was vague on registration or get-out-the-vote (GOTV) activities: "In the past we worked with the Democratic Party and other organizations to do a comprehensive get out and vote effort." What organizations? "Well, there are a few loosely affiliated local groups that just kind of flow together to do a get out and vote effort."[15] Party officials sometimes implied that candidate organizations were more likely to conduct voter registration drives. But for these organizations, strapped for time and resources, encouraging nonvoters (including immigrants) to register was low on their list of priorities. A Colorado state senator said she had had a bilingual volunteer go door to door on Election Day to get out the vote, but that her campaign did not have the capability to mount voter registration drives.[16] Candidates or elected officials would sometimes mention that the party did that sort of thing. The leader of the Onondaga County (Syracuse) Republican Party was not atypical. Although he had raised the party's level of activity in terms of fund-raising and recruiting candidates, when asked about voter registration efforts, he admitted, "we haven't done as good as we should. . . . We have some plans to do it this year. I have a couple people who, once the weather clears, are going to be prepared to start going out and start running some booths and tables."[17]

Outreach

It is clear that in most of these places, officials have been elected pretty much on their own (sometimes in nonpartisan elections) or with very little organizational support by their parties. Thus reaching out for them may mean some attempts to speak to or visit immigrant communities at election time; but their responses to this question more generally had to do with reaching out through the bureaucracy—making sure that there were Spanish-language books in the libraries, publishing informational pamphlets in appropriate language, or perhaps supporting the institution of a Human Rights Commission. It also meant maintaining some contact with group leaders in immigrant communities. But this is often fairly minimal. The director of the Americanization League of Syracuse, which provides various services to immigrants, was mostly positive about his relationship with offices of congressmen, senators, and other officials, but perceived that they were not paying much attention to new groups as constituents. "The elected officials around this community are very good. I'd like to see some of them once in a while show up and say something at the Naturalization Board. I mean, a new citizen is potentially a new voter."[18]

Explaining Parties' Inertia

Politicians' and parties' lack of interest in mobilizing new populations is consistent with the research of Jones-Correa, Wong, and others. Clearly, the lack of resources (and, possibly, the perceived need to use resources for advertising) may discourage party organizations from undertaking intensive voter registration drives. It is also the case that mounting outreach efforts introduces uncertainty to situations where local parties may have a very accurate knowledge of the demographic and geographic parameters of their support base. The fact that in these smaller cities the immigrant groups are absolutely and relatively small means that the payoff for introducing such uncertainty may not be sufficient to outweigh the costs.

Interviews with elected officials and their staffers illustrate this reasoning. A staff member for a Michigan state senator said that elected officials do have databases of potential voters in the area, with name, address, socioeconomic data, and ethnicity, if known. They try to determine who is likely to vote and who they might vote for, and make their decisions based on that. With scarce resources, he said, it doesn't make sense to go out and try to mobilize everyone.[19]

Especially in situations where seats were safe, elected officials and their staff members were quick to say that immigrant groups were "just like any other group." A California staffer said, for example, that he tries to view Hispanic and Hmong groups similarly to how he views growers or right-to-lifers—as groups that have specific interests and perspectives, entitled to the same services as other constituents. He attends their events, meets with their leaders, learns about their issues, and lets them know that he cares about their concerns. But, he emphasized, "we don't solicit their involvement. If they come to us, we're happy to help out, but we don't see it as our job to go out and offer them services."[20] He then pointed out that his boss occupied a pretty safe seat.

Although politicians frequently used the sleeping giant metaphor to talk about the Hispanic electorate in general and in their districts, they also frequently pointed out that Hispanics' numbers were small, their voting turnout was low, and they weren't organized as a community. Repeatedly, politicians termed immigrant groups not visible. This was particularly true when immigrants were dispersed through the metropolitan area, rather than in identifiable ethnic neighborhoods (for the impact of residential concentration or dispersion, see Leighley 2001).[21]

There was also the occasional protestation that it was the individual's responsibility to register and vote, not the party's responsibility to motivate them. A city council member in Chico, asked if he encouraged naturalization, voter registration (in general and among immigrant groups in particular), said he didn't. Parties may do some of it, he explained, but "if you're a resident of a particular community [you have a] responsibility to be active in the community, to vote, but if you choose not to be active. . . ."[22]

Finally, even though it may be fair to claim that political parties, in general, do not make it a high priority to attract new supporters from these immigrant communities, the existence of connections to the parties can serve to educate group leaders and members about the advantages of getting involved in elections and presenting themselves as a significant constituency. In Waco, for example, an organization now called the Latino Women's Coalition was formerly Latino Democratic Women. They have conducted voter registration drives in local high schools and in the Hispanic churches, St. Frances and Sacred Heart, and have also done some door-to-door voter registration. In fact, Waco is probably the city with the closest connections between immigrant communities and the parties—the Latino Women's Coalition, office-holders, and Hispanic branch of the Republican Party, a chapter of the Republican National Hispanic Assembly.[23] In this context, it is worth noting that though Waco has a low naturalization rate and a relatively weak network of immigrant-related organizations, Hispanics are reasonably well represented in local government and the state legislature, and the analysis of the city and county websites, as well as information about the city-sponsored neighborhood programs, suggest that in Waco, immigrants have been able to work through both political parties to help them move toward political incorporation.

The six states under consideration are all above the national mean in terms of conventionally measured party competition—the Ranney index (see Gray, Hanson, and Jacob 1999). In the 2004 presidential election, Lansing was Democratic by a comfortable margin; Syracuse was more precariously Democratic. All other cities voted for Bush, led by Waco, where the Republican plurality made up a huge 32 percent of the total vote. The remaining cities—Spokane, Chico, and Fort Collins—voted Republican but with much smaller pluralities (5 to 12 percent). Overall, the parties in these states and cities are fairly representative of the broad majority of state and local parties. Both major parties have a presence, but, as we have seen, this presence is mostly evident during election campaigns; these are not well-institutionalized organizations engaging in recruitment and mobilization. Where the parties are, arguably, a bit stronger—in Waco and Lansing—this may have resulted in somewhat greater representation of immigrant groups in local offices. Where parties are weak, self-recruitment is the norm, and representation is lower.

LOCAL ORGANIZATIONS AND INCORPORATION

Because political parties no longer invest time and energy to link new groups to elected and appointed officials and because most local and state governments in the United States do not have explicit policies fostering political incorporation, the voluntary sector becomes critical, a site where individuals and families are able to acquire the knowledge and skills to navigate and interact with the larger society and particularly with the political and governmental systems. Sidney Verba, Henry Brady, and Kay Schlozman's research (1995) has demonstrated at the individual level how civic associations build these skills and resources. Here I am concerned with the capacity of the relevant organizations and their ability to move collective activity in an explicitly political direction. I describe and categorize the immigrant-related organizations in the six cities, paying particular attention to the extent to which they take on incorporative functions, either deliberately or as a consequence of other activities. Table 3.4 contains an overview of the range of organizations in each city.

Only a few organizations reported initiating or participating in active efforts to naturalize immigrants or register voters. These were usually connected with national or state-wide organizational efforts, for example, on the part of the Southwest Voter Registration Education Project (SVREP). Of the seventy-eight organizations on which we have at least some information, fewer than ten ap-

TABLE 3.4   *Functional Categorizations of Organizations Studied in Six Cities*

	Chico	Fort Collins	Lansing	Spokane	Syracuse	Waco	Number in Category
Legal rights and services	2	1	1	2	0	0	6
Advocacy	4	2	2	1	1	2	12
Capacity building	4	3	2	6	6	3	24
Human services	4	5	5	8	4	4	30
Business	1	0	0	3	1	1	6
Total in city	15	11	10	20	12	10	78

Source: Author's compilation.

Note: Legal services: visas, civil and criminal law, pro bono counsel; advocacy: lobbying, protest, partisan politics; capacity building: organizing, leadership training, social capital development; human services: charities, social welfare, public health, recreation; business: chamber of commerce, professionals' association.

pear to include voter registration, voting, or other forms of participation as even a secondary part of their mission. Many did report that they "encouraged" naturalization or registration, or (even more weakly) "had forms available" for voter registration.

A good example of this is Syracuse, which is a bit unusual in having a nonprofit organization which provides services to both refugees and immigrants. The Americanization League, founded in 1916 as a resettlement agency, currently has three staff members and is funded by the Onondaga County Legislature and given space by the Syracuse City School District. The organization is specifically focused on assisting immigrants with the process of obtaining permanent residency, with the naturalization process, and in dealing with the former Immigration and Naturalization Service. As for voter registration, they do have the forms to fill out "if someone asks for it."[24]

When particular issues arise, local organizations do act to mobilize their constituents. In early 2004, anticipating the 2004 election and Muslims' perceptions of discrimination, the American Muslim Center in Lansing set up voter registration tables at the mosque after services and made efforts to publicize this within the community. A staff member of California Rural Legal Assistance (CLRA) mentioned that they planned to encourage members of the Latino and Hmong communities to attend an upcoming meeting soliciting public comment on county housing policies.[25] In Syracuse, organizations reported having engaged in lobbying efforts around issues having to do with immigration policy— for example, protesting the post-9/11 reduction in quotas—and involving members of the immigrant communities with activities such as letter-writing.[26]

An interesting example of immigrants wanting more political involvement in the context of an agency not seeing its role as facilitating political action comes from Lansing. Every year, Lutheran Refugee Services arranges a summer retreat in Maryland for the Sudanese boys resettled in Lansing. At one such retreat, several of the boys were disappointed that despite being so close to Washington, the retreat organizers had not set up any meetings with elected officials. The boys had wanted to meet with their representatives personally to push for greater American involvement in resettling Sudanese people living in refugee camps. Instead, they decided to skip the retreat's official functions and to write a collective letter to their representatives to publicize recent attacks on the refugee camps.[27]

In summary, of the organizations that provide services to or organize immigrants in these cities, many encourage naturalization. A number of the social service organizations, for example, make the relevant application forms available, and some offer ESL classes. The six legal rights organizations and a few of the advocacy organizations go a step further by offering advice and help with the process. But only eight of the organizations on which we have some information appeared to take an active role in pushing voter registration or engaging in get-out-the-vote drives. On the other hand, these organizations do help immigrants develop knowledge and skills critical to civic and political participation. They offer forums where officials can speak to the public and provide opportunities for people to work together, organize events, and gain information about the community.

PLACE AND POLITICAL INCORPORATION

Three aspects of place, I argue, help to shape opportunities for political incorporation of immigrants. These are the geographical location of a city, specifically its relative isolation vis-à-vis other population centers; whether it has been a refugee resettlement center; and its larger political context, especially the existence of liberal allies and links between immigrant groups and other organizations.

Isolation

A hundred years ago, many immigrants settled in inner cities, eventually moving also to suburbs surrounding those cities. These settlement patterns facilitated coalitional behavior among immigrant groups and connections between immigrant organizations and other kinds of organizations, such as parties, unions, civic associations, and business groups. The current dispersion of immigrants to new areas[28] mean that immigrant families have little access to social and political capital—in the terms used here, immigrant groups may have little political presence and virtually no political weight. Geographical isolation exacerbates this situation.

Groups that have the provision of social services as their primary mission may encourage voter registration but do not typically focus on political organization. Organizations that can be characterized as capacity-building—for example, Chico's Hispanic Resource Council; Lansing's Refugee Development Center; Syracuse's Southeast Asia Center; El Centro at Colorado State University in Fort Collins—are often concerned with organizing the community and building leadership, but less often with specific political skill-building. California organizations such as the Central Valley Partnership for Citizenship have general commitments to encourage naturalization and to "assist migrants, immigrants, and refugees organizing to claim their rightful place in the civic, cultural, and economic life of the Valley."[29] Others, like California Rural Legal Assistance, are more concerned with protecting the rights of immigrants and poor people. A CRLA staff member based in a town near Chico discussed the recent recognition by CRLA that attention should be paid to developing the political skills and strengths of immigrants rather than just dealing with their legal issues. "We ought to think about how we can encourage our clients to develop their own political power. They need to know that whether or not they are citizens they have a right to communicate with government officials."[30] At the time of the interview, however, this idea was merely at the talking phase.

The push to engage in more explicitly political activities often comes from statewide or regional organizations which have the resources (for example, legal staff, money to hire student interns) to work on registration drives, grassroots lobbying, or other political activities. In 2004 the Fort Collins area was among the targets for voter registration on the part of the Center for Peace, Justice, Environment (CJPE), which worked with the Colorado Progressive Coalition (CPC) to register voters. CJPE found that there were more than 6,000 people in the Fort Collins area who were eligible to vote but not registered, of whom 1,600 were Latino. They planned to set up tables, engage in door-to-door education, and distribute mailings to voters to educate them about the issues, including issues related to immigration. In fact, the CPC-CJPE efforts were lauded during the 2004 campaign by Truemajority.org as particularly effective.[31]

Thus the political activity levels of local organizations often depend on the choices made by state-level organizations as to where to organize, and the leaders of the statewide groups may not feel that small or isolated cities are worth the effort. For example, the major organizations that focus on Latino communities are completely absent in the area north of Sacramento where Chico is: there are no local chapters of MALDEF, La Raza, UFW, or ACLU. These organizations cannot afford the field staff to cover such a large, sparsely populated area, and the fact that the area is so overwhelmingly white and conservative may help shape their decisions about where to focus their efforts.[32] When this research was being conducted, Columbia Legal Services (CLS) was in the process of closing its Spokane office. With a heavy reliance on state funding, a statewide budget crisis had forced CLS to close several of its local offices. In this context, people in Spokane talked about the fact that "everything was in Seattle" and those in Fort Collins complained about the distance to Denver, where many advocacy organizations had their headquarters.

The disadvantages of geographical isolation were felt mostly in the western cities: Chico, Spokane, and Fort Collins. Syracuse and Lansing are located in much more densely populated areas; both are accessible to the state capital and other population centers. Though driving distances in Texas are long, Waco is less than 100 miles from Fort Worth, Dallas, and Austin.

The staff member at California Rural Legal Assistance in Chico who was quoted regarding a focus on citizenship observed that the organization had a sister organization in Sacramento, the California Rural Legal Systems Foundation, and pointed out that citizenship and immigration is one of their areas of focus. "We work with, we collaborate with them and, so when we do get issues involving immigration or citizenship we, I say we refer, but it sounds pretty distant, and sometimes it is. Sometimes it's you know, here's a phone number, go call these people."[33] Similarly, in Fort Collins, the Catholic Charities office does not have staff or resources specifically devoted to immigration or refugee issues, but if someone comes to them with an immigration question, they usually refer them to the Immigration Office at Catholic Charities' Denver headquarters. Still, Denver is at least an hour away, so these services are a little more difficult for Fort Collins residents to access. "People from the Denver office sometimes come up to Fort Collins to give workshops, but it doesn't happen very often."[34] More recently, the establishment of the small advocacy group Fuerza Latina has been a help to those trying to provide services to immigrants.[35]

Although problems associated with geographical isolation were mentioned much less frequently in Waco, Lansing, and Syracuse, they surfaced sometimes even in these cities. One Michigan State faculty member in Lansing said that even though the city is only an hour west of Detroit, the distance can undermine a sense of continuity or common interest that might exist between immigrants dispersed among the two cities.[36]

In Syracuse, the founder and former director of the Refugee Resettlement Program pointed to the related issue of the size of the immigrant population. Where there are more refugees (for example, in Minnesota), Hmong and Laos are involved in "much more political activity; they recognize that they have power." But the relatively small population in Syracuse means that "politicians are not going to bother."[37]

In addition to illustrating the challenges to mobilization thrown up by geography, this discussion is consistent with Theda Skocpol's argument in *Diminished Democracy* that "democratic leverage" to confront a variety of political problems "can only be addressed with concerted national commitment." Building better local organizations and organizational capacity is not enough (Skocpol 2003, 258).

Refugee Resettlement

Whether or not a city has had significant streams of refugees may be important because refugees are entitled to government-funded assistance, delivered through nonprofit organizations such as World Relief and Catholic Charities, from their moment of arrival until they achieve some self-sufficiency. U.S. State Department goals say that should happen within 135 days of their arrival. These organizations provide resettlement and housing assistance, social services (Medicare, Medicaid, TANF, SSI), help with status adjustment, and job placement assistance. They also offer classes in English, American history, and civics in preparation for the citizenship exam. The existence of these institutions, and their usually strong connections with state and local social welfare and educational bureaucracies, may spill over and benefit economic immigrants in addition to refugees. Irene Bloemraad's recent research comparing Portuguese and Vietnamese immigrants in the United States and Canada, made the case that "government support, including funding, technical assistance and normative encouragement, plays an important role in building immigrant communities' organizational capacity" (2006b, 2).

This spillover effect is both material and symbolic. Organizations involved in refugee resettlement may broaden their mission to serve nonrefugee immigrants, and people who work with refugees may develop organizational skills, legal knowledge, and political connections which can be useful to other immigrant groups. In addition, I believe that the positive media treatment given to refugees may have the effect of adding legitimacy not only to the particular refugees (such as those in Syracuse, where numerous stories were published about the Sudanese "Lost Boys" resettled locally) but to other refugee groups and to immigrants more generally.

Both effects can be seen in Lansing, which has a very diverse array of immigrants, including those from Cuba, Bosnia, Sudan, Sierra Leone, Vietnam, and Afghanistan. The Refugee Development Center (RDC) of Lansing, associated with a Lutheran church, offers programs in American Lifeskills (including driving) and sees its mission as educating the larger community about the refugees' experiences and talents. The staff of the RDC has been entrepreneurial in fundraising and has explicitly tried to provide refugees with "an opportunity to begin to create social capital in a very safe environment for them."[38] Lansing refugees (and other immigrants, to a lesser extent) are also served by Catholic Charities. A number of these organizations combined forces in 2003 to produce a cookbook called *A Taste of Freedom: A Culinary Journey with American's Refugees*. This was sold locally and regionally and its proceeds were donated to refugee services. The personal accounts accompanying the recipes present the struggles of refugees in narratives that are very similar to the "immigrants reaching for the American dream" stories traditionally used to construct Americans' understanding of the melting pot.

Spokane also had inflows of refugees, including Vietnamese and Hmong, as well as a number of Russian and East European evangelical Protestants. As the numbers have ebbed, at least one of the refugee resettlement agencies (Catholic Charities), shifted its mission to serve farm worker communities, helping these as well as refugees navigate the social welfare bureaucracy, adjust their immigration status, and naturalize; their biggest clientele is no longer Russian but Hispanic. One of the most frequent services they provide is to help immigrant women leave abusive white husbands without losing their permanent resident status.[39]

Syracuse's refugees include significant numbers from Eastern Europe (particularly Bosnia and Herzegovina) and more than 1,000 Vietnamese, now joined by growing numbers of Hmong and Burmese. Syracuse is also home to several groups of African refugees, including Sudanese and Somalis. The people and organizations who work with refugees and immigrants in Syracuse form a dense organizational network. Business interests, organized through the Metropolitan Development Association, work closely with the service-providing groups to identify, train, and support potential new employees. Businesses were also drawn into the letter-writing and lobbying campaign initiated by the refugee resettlement agencies—two dozen agreed to write letters or make calls to Washington objecting to the post-9/11 restrictions on refugees.[40]

Neither Waco nor Fort Collins, among our six cities, has significant numbers of refugees, and thus lack some of the organizational resources (human and material) which have been useful in developing immigrant communities in the other three cities. Chico is home to a number of Hmong refugees, including secondary migrants, but they are served primarily by voluntary agencies in Sacramento. Interestingly, in Waco the local congressman's office seems to provide many of the services that, in Spokane, Lansing, or Syracuse, are provided by the refugee organizations (and spill over to nonrefugee immigrants). The office had a staff person with some training in immigration law, who speaks at local community centers and deals with visas, status adjustment, and citizenship problems.[41]

Thus I would suggest that a city's history as a substantial refugee resettlement area not only increases the likelihood that immigrants and refugees will have their material needs met, but also creates an organizational legacy that may be used, depending on the goals and skills of the groups involved, to encourage and empower immigrant groups. Additionally, though this claim would be difficult to support empirically, the existence of substantial numbers of refugees may increase public sympathy for nonrefugee immigrants.

Political Connections

Finally, the organizational capacity within immigrant communities can be boosted when institutions and groups construct helpful links with larger umbrella groups and with well-positioned individuals and organizations. The immigrant groups in these cities are not large enough to be automatically politically relevant and are for the most part residentially dispersed. A plurality of the immigrant-related organizations are service providers and others are primarily cultural or economic (see table 4.2), and thus community leaders may not see political mobilization—naturalization, registration, and voting—as a major goal. Even if immigrant groups have come together in an organization, have elected officers, planned and executed projects, raised funds, perhaps rented a space, they may not see any connection between their organizational goals and the political system. For example, in Chico neither the Hispanic Chamber of Commerce nor the Hispanic Resource Council have been involved organizationally in politics or had much connection with elected officials. An explicit statement about the disconnect between business organizations and politics came from a Waco member of the board of the Hispanic Chamber of Commerce "I got involved when a friend of mine brought me into the Chamber a few years ago . . . I didn't want to be in a political organization, I wanted to be in a business organization that promoted businesses . . . and wanted to stay away from politics."[42]

When organizations do want to advocate for immigrants' rights, mobilize members to act politically, or change policy, they benefit from being formally or informally linked to other organizations. If these organizations operate at the state level, the linkage also has the consequence of allowing the local groups to work on state-level policies and campaigns. One small success story in this regard involves a fairly new Fort Collins organization, Fuerza Latina (FL), "an organization of immigrants for immigrants." The winner of Fort Collins' 2004 Human Relations Award, FL sponsored workshops on employment rights and visits from the Mexican consulate and worked in support of a controversial ordinance to bar city employees from asking an individual's immigration status without just cause. But it had only a couple dozen active members, and though they received at least one grant and a fair amount of media attention, they operated on a shoestring. FL benefits from its position within the umbrella organization the Center for Peace, Justice, and Environment (CJPE). This organization administered FL's grant, and provided resources to fund leadership trainings and an activist conference. Moreover, through CJPE, FL is connected with a network of organizations operating at the statewide level, such as the Rocky Mountain Immigration Advocacy Network, the Colorado Immigrant Rights Coalition, and the Colorado Progressive Coalition.

In Washington as well, immigrant groups are sometimes able to seek and receive more assistance at the state level than at the local level. The Washington State Hispanic Affairs Commission is an advisory group established by the governor's office to provide the state's Hispanic residents with input into the governor's decisions. It also sets the governor's legislative agenda for Hispanic issues. The commissioner from Spokane, who is also involved in the Hispanic Business and Professional Association, makes efforts to channel information and resources from the state level down to local groups.[43] Statewide organizations advocate for immigrants' rights and provide pro bono legal services for immigrants in both Washington (Columbia Legal Services) and California (California Rural Legal Assistance), and staffers of these organizations are often a resource for smaller, local organizations.

Lansing and Syracuse are the only cities among the group with much of a union presence. In Syracuse, union members are predominantly public service employees, and most immigrant and refugee employment is in nonunionized manufacturing and service sectors. In Lansing, on the other hand, it is fairly clear that the immigrant communities benefit from the union presence. Unions are important, several of our informants said, especially the United Auto Workers, because General Motors employs many immigrants in the Lansing area, and membership happens along ethnic-kinship channels. The Service Employees International Union, which has organized state employees and many local government employees in Michigan, is also strong. Union membership among immigrant groups provides organizational skills and facilitates cooperation among different Latino groups, such as Mexicans and Cubans.[44] As well, Democratic Party connections with the unions means that immigrants in Lansing have a higher likelihood than immigrants in the other cities of forging links to political parties.[45]

In several of the cities we studied, local colleges and universities were significant providers of liberal sympathizers, funding, or programmatic resources for immigrant groups. This was least true of Waco (Baylor is viewed as quite conservative and did not seem to be perceived as particularly relevant) and Spokane.

California State University at Chico, Colorado State University (CSU) in Fort Collins, Syracuse University, and Michigan State University in Lansing, however, are important sources of allies. At Chico, student volunteers set up an ESL tutoring program for immigrant and migrant parents, held while their children were attending catechism classes (the church provided space and publicity). They added a citizenship emphasis when they found that people wanted English skills to pass the citizenship test. Colorado State hosts the National Hispanic Institute–Collegiate Leadership Network—at CSU, El Centro student service—to serve and support Chicano and Latino students.

It is difficult to sustain organizational momentum, of course, when it is based on student volunteers, but student organizations (including MECHA, or Movimiento Estudiantil Chicano de Aztlan, which exists at both Chico and Colorado State) and other organizations have helped with voter registration and GOTV drives. Universities can also bring together leaders of community groups and other practitioners with researchers and teachers, encouraging connections and new thinking about immigrant-related issues. For example, Cal State Chico sponsored an all-day conference "about and for members of the Hmong community" on campus in March 2003. The conference was addressed by the highest elected Hmong official nationwide, Mee Moua, a state senator from Minnesota, and by the first Hmong attorney in California. The University's Center for Economic Development, in conjunction with the local Hispanic Chamber of Commerce, sponsored a Hispanic Marketing Conference later the same year. [46]

Michigan State University has a number of programs focusing on migrant workers and researchers have also received recent funding to support projects in the Muslim Community. The College Assistance Migrant Program (CAMP) holds intensive twelve-week courses to help local farm workers—Chicanos, Mexicans, Cubans, Haitians—obtain their GEDs so that they can find better jobs in other sectors of the economy. MSU has received grants from the federal Department of Education to develop programs "to assist migrant youth and adults with completion of their high school degree and enhance their educational and career opportunities." The MSU FACT program—Families and Communities Together, a partnership among MSU faculty, MSU extension, and community groups to help solve pressing social needs—has funded the project Muslim Immigrants: Social, Cultural and Religious Issues of Youth, Families and Schools in the Greater Lansing Area.[47]

These accounts suggest that the existence of institutions such as universities and organizations that are prepared to provide both symbolic and material support can help to build organizational capacity. Because government support is relevant only for refugee-related organizations and only for relatively circumscribed purposes, and because groups are small, the existence of allies is critical.

A final story illustrates the role of allies, as well as the important of organizational entrepreneurialism, political experiences, and a commitment to coalition-building. A business association in Spokane, AHANA (African American, Hispanic, Asian, Native American) has made explicit attempts to influence the local political process through the parties. This organization's director (of Filipino origin) is a Vietnam veteran who returned to the University of Washington after his military service, where he began his extensive experience as an advocate and union organizer. In his view, politicians in Spokane make almost no mention of immigrant communities and tend to gloss over their concerns by saying that they are trying to deal with the entire Spokane community's interests, not just those of a few small groups. Even though AHANA does receive some funding for operating costs from the city and county, the day we interviewed its director, the mayor's office had held a conference on economic development but failed to invite anyone from the minority community until the last minute. To improve this situation, AHANA has tried to consolidate minority groups' power and to develop closer relations with local politicians. This is complicated by the fact that many members of the minority communities don't vote because they don't think that politicians care about them or that politics is relevant to their lives. AHANA has put together a candidate forum to advance the minority community's concerns to local candidates.[48] In July 2005, AHANA approached local Democratic leaders, asking for more support. Their argument stressed the commonality of values between AHANA and the Democrats, and contained an implied political threat as well, saying that local Republican candidates had actually been "more aggressive than Democrats" in seeking support from AHANA."[49]

CONCLUSIONS

Though each of these cities has its own immigration story, rooted in its history, geography, and economy, I believe there are some patterns here worth following up in future research.

The data in table 3.5 suggest that high naturalization rates are assisted by either a more diverse and numerous set of organizations dealing with immigrants or the existence of a refugee stream with attendant organizational spillover. These two variables overlap. Additionally, high naturalization rates in turn help groups become visible and significant to political decision makers. Levels of representation, on the other hand, are heightened in situations where immigrant groups have strong allies in unions and other progressive organizations or in the relatively rare cases where local organizations are part of federated structures.

In examining these six cities, each with relatively small immigrant populations, I found that the many and varied organizations that serve, advocate for, and sometimes mobilize immigrants and refugees were frequently poor in resources, isolated, and overwhelmed by demands and tasks. Their primary goals were not explicitly political, though they certainly tried to influence local decisions and local institutions. Yet these are the institutions that are often immigrants' and refugees' first connections with American civic life, and may be the

TABLE 3.5   *Factors Facilitating Political Incorporation*

	Dependent Variables		Independent Variables		
	Naturalization	Representation	Organizational Capacity[a]	Refugees?	Allies
Chico	low	low	medium	no[b]	weak
Fort Collins	medium	medium	medium	no	medium
Lansing	medium	high	medium	yes	strong
Spokane	medium	medium	high	yes	medium
Syracuse	high	low	low	yes	weak
Waco	low	medium	low	no	weak

Source: Author's compilation.
[a] Number of organizations, diversity of organization functions.
[b] Chico has refugees, but refugee programs are administered from Sacramento.

organizations that help them learn English, connect them with employers, advise them on their immigration status, provide venues for them to meet local officials, and connect them with nonimmigrant neighbors to work on community issues.

It is oversimplifying things to make a black-white distinction between the immigrant experiences in 1906 and 2006 with regard to the means by which the individual is linked to political and civic life. Certainly mutual benefit associations, homeland cultural and sports groups, charities, settlement houses, and other kinds of organizations were important in 1906. Nonetheless, it is a significant difference that well-organized, competitive political parties existed in almost all locales and in many of those places parties saw the mobilization of immigrants as an important organizational goal.

Two implications of this shift are illustrated by the six-city study described here. One is that groups and organizations that contribute to the political incorporation of immigrants in these cities intersect with governments and the policy arena in more diffuse ways than parties did in 1906. Parties and their local leaders focused on strategies to win elections and control governments, which in turn created incentives for them to encourage and facilitate naturalization, registration, and voting. Present-day organizations have multiple sorts of connections with governments: they may receive local, state, and federal grants; they may have government contracts to help settle refugees; they may be advocating single policy issues or promoting the interests of particular immigrant or ethnic groups; they may be mostly focused on helping clients navigate government bureaucracies. The point is that for the most part their environment does not provide strong incentives to mobilize immigrants electorally. They may advise naturalization for a host of reasons, and help with the process, but if more of their clients naturalize it doesn't benefit the organization in the same way that high levels of naturalization benefited Tammany Hall. One could argue that this changed situation has advantages: it may help individuals acquire a variety of political skills (organizing protests, writing letters, dealing with bureaucrats) which are important in today's politics, rather than merely the capacity to participate in electoral politics. But to the extent that voting, and understanding the power of the vote, is the basic building block of our democratic system, I think that the present system is less supportive of participatory democracy.

The second implication has to do with the nature of these organizations. They are, in general, free-standing local organizations, not parts of larger organizations or federations. The exceptions here are League of United Latin American Citizens (LULAC), MALDEF, and SVREP, which are national or regional (in the case of SVREP) organizations with local branches. But, as we have seen, many smaller cities, such as the ones in this study, have not been organized or targeted by these organizations. Theda Skocpol's historical research on American associational life argues that the federated, trans-local character of nineteenth- and early twentieth-century associations contributed significantly to their efficacy and to the civic skills of their members. "Federations were especially vital in building an American democracy in which ordinary people could participate, gain skills, and forge recurrent ties to one another—not just locally but also across communities, states, and regions" (2003, 124). Though Skocpol does not discuss political parties, a similar argument applies to party organizations during the same period: they provided channels of upward mobility, allowed local organizations to share resources, and exposed local Democrats and Republicans to broader constituencies and issues at the state, regional, and national level.

It follows that the success in the task of political incorporation, especially in places like the cities in my study, hinges on connections. Immigrant communities in these smaller cities need to be able to make connections—with other immigrant and nonimmigrant groups, with liberal allies, and with the political system. Being in a city that has served as a refugee resettlement point seems to add to this bridging capacity, as does the existence of large research universities and statewide organizations that may have the resources to encourage and fund political action. These allies can also help when localities are characterized by anti-immigrant sentiment or organizations. Parties can provide similar resources, but we didn't find that this happened anywhere but (possibly) in Waco and (to some extent) in Lansing. Finally, individuals who have had experience as student activists, organizing labor, or working in electoral campaigns may help provide the capacity for groups to make explicitly political linkages. Thus the ability to build coalitions and forge connections, both within the community and with groups outside the community, is critical.

Similar conclusions were reached by the authors of *Building the New American Community* (2004), sponsored by the Office of Refugee Resettlement and the Migration Policy Institute. This project also focused on smaller cities (Lowell, Massachusetts, Nashville, Tennessee, and Portland, Oregon) and one of the main findings was that coalitions were "vectors for integration." "Relative to large gateway cities," these small cities, the report finds, "tend to have less fully developed institutional relationships and networks that facilitate integration." Building coalitions by "engaging the resources of several levels of government and their agencies, businesses, private organizations and a broad spectrum of community-based partners" characterizes the difficult road to the political incorporation of immigrant groups (Ray 2004, v).

An earlier version of this paper was presented at the annual meetings of the American Political Science Association, 2005, Washington, D.C. I am grateful to Linda Fowler and John Berg for comments on that version of the paper. For research assistance I am happy to thank Brett Heindl, Gae Hee Song, Camilla Olson, and John Mero. The research was supported by the Carnegie Corporation of New York and by the Daniel Patrick Moynihan Institute of Global Affairs of the Maxwell School, Syracuse University.

NOTES

1. In parts of Maryland, including Takoma Park, noncitizen residents can vote in local elections. Legislatures in San Francisco and Washington, D.C., are considering similar measures. In New York City, parents with children in the public schools were able to vote in school board elections before 2004. Good information about the immigrant voting rights movement is available at the Migration Information Source, www.migrationinformation.org/USfocus/display.cfm?id=265 (for a comprehensive discussion of immigrant voting rights, see Hayduk 2006).

2. David Brooks put it even more strongly in a *New York Times* op-ed piece on August 4, 2005 ("Trading Cricket for Jihad"), though he was talking primarily about social roots rather than explicitly political connections: "Countries that do not encourage assimilation are not only causing themselves trouble, but endangering others around the world as well." (Accessed at http://www.nytimes.com/2005/08/04/opinion/04brooks.html?_r=1&incamp=article_popular&oref=slogin.)

3. The Syracuse study was conducted as a pilot study in the winter of 2002 and 2003 (see Andersen and Wintringham 2003). As is clear in table 3.1, the Syracuse SMSA is somewhat larger than the others. In addition, some of the information collected differs a bit from our later protocols.

4. The importance of naturalization has increased since mid-1990s legislation moved toward limiting access to public benefits and rights to those who are citizens. "Even so," Michael Fix and his colleagues noted, "few public policies promote naturalization. No notice is sent to refugees and immigrants when they become eligible to naturalize. Comparatively little public funding underwrite language and civics classes to help legal immigrants pass the citizenship exam" (Fix, Passel and Sucher 2003, 1).

5. There is a good deal of research which contributes to explaining variations in the voting rates of immigrant groups. Some studies focus on individual-level variables (see Junn 1999; Bass and Kasper 2001; Cho 1999; Minnite and Mollenkopf 2001, for the impact of contextual variables, see Jones-Correa 1998; DeSipio 2001; Pantoja, Ramirez, and Segura 2001; Ramakrishnan and Espenshade 2001; and Ramakrishnan 2005).

6. The variation among the cities in terms of timing is fairly small. Syracuse has a somewhat larger proportion of recent immigration; Waco has a larger proportion of the 1980 to 1990 immigrants. Thus, without Syracuse, the proportions of immigrants arriving since 1990 have only a ten percentage-point range.

7. There are many limitations to this approach. Names (particularly but not only women's names) are not always reliable indicators of people's ethnicity. It is impossible to determine on the basis of this kind of research whether, say, someone named Rodriguez is a first- or second-generation immigrant or a member of a family that has lived in the United States for generations. On the other hand, these errors are probably randomly distributed across the six cities.
8. Chico has another barrier to the representation of minority groups: many live in an unincorporated area adjacent to the city, which has neither city services nor council representation, and many Hmong live in a small rural town outside the city.
9. A number of people we spoke with in Waco described how changing from at-large to district elections in the 1980s (as a result of a lawsuit) almost immediately increased the number of black and Latino city council members (and, possibly as a result, of other black and Latino elected officials).
10. The number of positions surveyed ranged from forty-two (Waco) to 155 (Spokane).
11. Interview with Michigan State University researcher who has studied Muslims in public school system; interview with Spokane-based member of state Hispanic Affairs Commission, February 27, 2004. A recent controversy in a small town near Spokane demonstrates that the "bureaucratic incorporation" described by Jones-Correa, and which I believe characterizes these six cities also, does not exist everywhere. In late 2003 in Brewster, Hispanic students were warned by the principal that "their future would likely be that of their parents, working in the orchards." The principal, frustrated by fights in the school, called twenty-seven of them to a meeting and "told [them] that their Washington Assessment of Student Learning scores were lower than those of Anglo students, they showed less respect for one another than Anglo students, and they were bringing one another down." They were not allowed to leave the meeting room without signing a behavior contract agreeing to various disciplinary actions, including expulsion, if further violations of rules. Parents were not informed; a letter had been drafted but not sent "because of difficulty getting it translated into Spanish" (*Spokesman-Review*, February 1, 2004).
12. Interview with Fort Collins mayor, May 25, 2004.
13. The exceptions: Syracuse would have ranked low according to the website measure, and was moved to medium. Fort Collins would have ranked medium and was moved to low.
14. In this discussion I focus on the role of local parties (for an interesting discussion of the ways national parties have dealt with immigration policy and immigrant incorporation, see Valelly 2005; see also historical examples cited in Ueda 2001, 298).
15. Interview with staffer for Texas congressman, March 30, 2004.
16. Interview with Colorado state senator, May 12, 2004.
17. Interview with chair of Onondaga County Republican Party, February 23, 2003.
18. Interview with Americanization League director, February 23, 2003.
19. Interview with staff member for Michigan state senator, January 23, 2004.
20. Interview with representative of California politician's district office, April 29, 2004.
21. However, residential concentration doesn't appear to be sufficient to create group visibility. Syracuse had many more census tracts with over 10 percent foreign-born than the other five cities, but politicians there did not exhibit a particularly higher level of consciousness about the immigrant groups in these areas.
22. Interview with Chico City Council member, April 27, 2004.
23. Interview with Republican Party official, March 26, 2004.
24. Interview with director of Americanization League, February 23, 2003.
25. Interview with CLRA staffer, April 27, 2004.

26. Interview with Catholic Charities staff member, November 24, 2002; also mentioned in Refugee Assistance Program interview.
27. Interview with LRS director, February 3, 2004.
28. For example, a recent study of immigrants in Nebraska, which had the largest percentage increase in immigrants of any Midwestern state between 1990 and 2000, found substantial groups of Latino immigrants in very small cities and towns (Gouveia and Powell 2007).
29. CVP website, http://www.citizenship.net/index.shtml, accessed on August 12, 2005.
30. Interview with CLRA staffer, April 27, 2004.
31. Interview with director of Center for Peace, Justice, Environment, May 25, 2004. By late September of 2004, the CPC website (http://www,progressivecoalition.org/) cited 550 new registrants in Fort Collins.
32. Two of our cities—Spokane and Waco—have chapters of LULAC, Latin American Citizens United. Waco's has existed for some time; Spokane's was formed in 2004, apparently in response to perceptions of discrimination against Hispanics in a school district near Spokane.
33. Interview with CLRA staff member, April 27, 2004.
34. Similar distance issues were voiced with regard to RMIAN, the Rocky Mountain Immigrant Advocacy Network, with forty to fifty attorneys who are mostly in the Denver area.
35. Interview with Catholic Charities staff member, May 27, 2004. Fuerza Latina, which was specifically set up to organize and advocate for immigrants, was established in 2003 and has received some small grants to do community outreach and leadership development.
36. Interview with MSU sociologist, December 3, 2003.
37. Interview with former director of Refugee Resettlement Program, Syracuse, January 13, 2003.
38. Interview with director of Refugee Development Center, January 30, 2004.
39. Interview with director of Refugee and Immigrant Services, Catholic Charities, February 23, 2004.
40. Interview with Catholic Charities staff member, November 4, 2002.
41. Interview with staff member in local congressional office, March 25, 2004.
42. Interview with member of the board, Waco Hispanic Chamber of Commerce, March 25, 2005.
43. Interview with member of Hispanic Affairs Commission, February 27, 2004.
44. Interview with faculty member in Latino/Chicano Studies program, MSU, January 19, 2004.
45. Interviews with staffers for assembly member and state senator, January 23, 28, 2004.
46. *Chico Enterprise-Record*, March 16 and August 8, 2003.
47. Michigan State University website, accessed at http://www.fact.msu.edu/proj ects/2001/muslim_immigrants.html.
48. Interview with AHANA director, February 20, 2004.
49. Spokane Democrats website, accessed at http://www.spokanedemocrats.org/index.cfm?page=ahana.cfm.

REFERENCES

Andersen, Kristi. 2006. "In Whose Interest? Political Parties, Context, and the Political Incorporation of Immigrants" In *New Race Politics in America: Understanding Minority and Immigrant Voting,* edited by Jane Junn and Kerry Haynie. Cambridge: Cambridge University Press.

Andersen, Kristi, and Jessica Wintringham. 2003. "Political Parties, NGOs, and Immigrant Incorporation: A Case Study." Paper presented at the Midwest Political Science Association meetings. Chicago, Ill., April 3–6, 2003.

Bass, Loretta E., and Lynne M. Kasper. 2001. "Impacting the Political Landscape: Who Registers and Votes among Naturalized Citizens?" *Political Behavior* 23(1): 101–30.

Bloemraad, Irene. 2006a. "Citizenship Lessons from the Past: The Contours of Immigrant Naturalization in the Early Twentieth Century." *Social Science Quarterly* 87(5): 927–53.

———. 2006b. *Becoming a Citizen: Incorporating Immigrants and Refugees in the United States and Canada.* Berkeley, Calif.: University of California Press.

Cho, Wendy K. Tam. 1999. "Naturalization, Socialization, Participation: Immigrants and (Non-) Voting." *Journal of Politics* 61(4): 1140–55.

DeSipio, Louis. 2001. "Building America, One Person at a Time: Naturalization and Political Behavior of the Naturalized in Contemporary American Politics." In *E Pluribus Unum? Contemporary and Historical Perspectives on Immigrant Political Incorporation,* edited by Gary Gerstle and John Mollenkopf. New York: Russell Sage Foundation.

Erie, Steven. 1988. *Rainbow's End: Irish Americans and the Dilemma of Urban Machine Politics, 1840–1985.* Berkeley, Calif.: University of California Press.

Fix, Michael E., Jeffrey S. Passel, and Kenneth Sucher. 2003. "Trends in Naturalization." Brief No. 3 in *Immigrant Families and Workers: Facts and Perspectives.* Washington: Urban Institute Press.

Gavit, John P. 1922. *Americans by Choice.* New York: Harper and Brothers.

Gouveia, Lourdes, and Mary Ann Powell. 2007. "Second-Generation Immigrants in Nebraska: A First Look." *Migration Information Source.* Washington: Migration Policy Institute. Accessed at http://www.migrationinformation.org/Feature/display.cfm?id=569.

Gray, Virginia, Russell Hanson, and Herbert Jacob. 1999. *Politics in the American States: A Comparative Analysis,* 7th ed. Washington: CQ Press.

Hayduk, Ronald. 2006. *Democracy for All: Restoring Immigrant Voting Rights in the United States.* New York: Routledge.

Jones-Correa, Michael. 1998. *Between Two Nations: The Political Predicament of Latinos in New York City.* Ithaca, N.Y.: Cornell University Press.

———. 2005. "The Bureaucratic Incorporation of Immigrants in Suburbia." Paper presented at Russell Sage Foundation conference Immigration to the U.S.: New Sources and Destinations. New York, February 3–4, 2005.

Junn, Jane. 1999. "Participation in Liberal Democracy: the Political Assimilation of Immigrants and Ethnic Minorities in the United States." *American Behavioral Scientist* 42(9): 1417–38.

Leighley, Jan. 2001. *Strength in Numbers? The Political Mobilization of Racial and Ethnic Minorities.* Princeton, N.J.: Princeton University Press.

Mansbridge, Jane. 1999. "Should Blacks Represent Blacks and Women Represent Women? A Contingent 'Yes'." *Journal of Politics,* 61(3): 628–57.

Minnite, Lorraine C., and John H. Mollenkopf. 2001. "Between White and Black: Asian and Latino Political Participation in the 2000 Presidential Election in New York City." Paper presented at meetings of the American Political Science Association. San Francisco, Calif., August 30–September 2, 2001.

Pantoja, Adrian D., and Gary M. Segura. 2003. "Does Ethnicity Matter? Descriptive Representation in Legislatures and Political Alienation Among Latinos." *Social Science Quarterly* 84(2): 441–60.

Pantoja, Adrian D., Ricardo Ramirez, and Gary M. Segura. 2001. "Citizens by Choice,

Voters by Necessity: Patterns in Political Mobilization by Naturalized Latinos." *Political Research Quarterly* 54(4): 729–50.

Peel, Roy V. 1935. *The Political Clubs of New York City.* New York: G. P. Putnam Sons.

Ramakrishnan, S. Karthick. 2005. *Democracy in Immigrant America: Changing Demographics and Political Participation.* Stanford, Calif.: Stanford University Press.

Ramakrishnan, S. Karthick, and Thomas J. Espenshade. 2001. "Immigrant Incorporation and Political Participation in the United States." *International Migration Review* 35(3): 870–907.

Ray, Brian K. 2004. *Building the New American Community: Newcomer Integration and Inclusion Experiences in Nontraditional Gateway Cities.* Washington: Migration Policy Institute.

Rosenstone, Steven J., and John Mark Hansen. 1993. *Mobilization, Participation, and Democracy in America.* New York: Macmillan.

Singer, Audrey. 2004. "The Rise of New Immigrant Gateways." Living Cities Census Series. Washington: Brookings Institution.

Skocpol, Theda. 2003. *Diminished Democracy from Membership to Management in American Civic Life.* Norman, Okla.: University of Oklahoma Press.

Sterne, Evelyn Savidge. 2001. "Beyond the Boss: Immigration and American Political Culture from 1880 to 1940." In *E Pluribus Unum? Contemporary and Historical Perspectives on Immigrant Political Incorporation,* edited by Gary Gerstle and John Mollenkopf. New York: Russell Sage Foundation.

Ueda, Reed. 2001. "Historical Patterns of Immigrant Status and Incorporation in the United States." In *E Pluribus Unum? Contemporary and Historical Perspectives on Immigrant Political Incorporation,* edited by Gary Gerstle and John Mollenkopf. New York: Russell Sage Foundation.

U.S. Census Bureau. 2003a. *United States Census* 2000. Summary File 3. Accessed at http://www.census.gov/Press-Release/www/2002/sumfile3.html.

———. 2003b. *United States Census* 2000. Summary File 4. Accessed at http://fact finder.census.gov/servlet/DatasetMainPageServlet?_ds_name=DEC_2000_SF4_U &_program=DEC&_lang=en.

———. 2004. Current Population Survey. Foreign-Born Population of the United States, Detailed Tables (PPL-176). Washington: Government Printing Office (March).

Valelly, Richard M. 2005. "Why Then But Not Now? Immigrant Incorporation in Historical Perspective." Paper presented to weekly workshop, of the Center for the Study of Democratic Politics, Princeton University, April 14, 2005.

Verba, Sidney, Henry Brady, and Kay Lehman Schlozman. 1995. *Voice and Equality: Civic Voluntarism in American Society.* Cambridge, Mass.: Harvard University Press.

Waldinger, Roger. 1996. "From LAX to Ellis Island: Immigrant Prospects in the American City." *International Migration Review* 30(4): 1078–87.

Wong, Janelle. 2006. *Democracy's Promise: Immigrants and American Civic Institutions.* Ann Arbor, Mich.: University of Michigan Press.

Shannon Gleeson

Chapter 4

Organizing for Immigrant Labor Rights: Latino Immigrants in San Jose and Houston

Federal labor standards, ranging from wage and overtime guarantees to workplace safety, generally are meant to protect all workers in the United States, regardless of immigrant status. States can enact statutes that improve upon these standards, but must at least enforce these basic protections. Such provisions take on an added importance in the context of declining unionization rates. Foreign-born workers are less likely than native-born to be represented by a union, and, overall, Latinos have the lowest levels of unionization.[1] Given increasing levels of Latino migration, how do low-wage Latino workers, especially those who are undocumented immigrants, ensure and advocate for their labor rights both individually and collectively? When do local governments get involved in advocating for migrant rights, and what forms do these coalitions take?

In this chapter, I explore the impact that differing state labor policy contexts have on strategies for protecting the rights of low-wage workers, particularly Latino immigrants. I focus on two cities with distinct state labor policies: Houston, Texas, and San Jose, California. Texas labor policy generally only replicates federal minimum standards, it is a Right to Work state with one of the lowest rates of union representation, and it is the only state in the nation that does not require employers to provide workers' compensation insurance. By contrast, California has a strong history with robust labor standards.

I draw on interviews conducted in San Jose and Houston with key immigrant labor unions, community organizations, and labor standards enforcement agencies. Interviews with Latino immigrant workers in each city also inform the analysis. I find that the policy context in each state, and local institutions in each city, shape the opportunities local governments and civil society organizations have to intervene on behalf of workers, in surprising ways. Despite the more favorable state opportunity structures in California, organization around basic Latino immigrant labor rights is greater in Houston. Here I explore the dynamics of this paradox, and the process by which community coalition members have garnered political presence and political weight in each city.

LABOR RIGHTS ORGANIZING

Labor rights are a common site for civic action and collective mobilization. A good deal of research has highlighted the progress that labor unions have made in organizing immigrants. Some of the most prominent union victories include the Service Employees International Union "Justice for Janitors" campaign, which for two decades rallied for the rights of immigrant workers. Immigrants, who used to be thought of as not organizable have in fact become the focus of the labor movement. This is especially the case since the AFL-CIO passed a resolution to "stand in solidarity with immigrant workers," and even went on record to call for amnesty for all undocumented workers and their families (AFL-CIO 2007; Bacon 2000). The national Change to Win coalition, which split from the AFL-CIO with a mission to increase union organizing efforts, also represents a large sector of the immigrant low-wage workforce.

Inspirations such as the Justice for Janitors campaign suggest that organizing immigrant workers may indeed be the key to revitalizing American unionism, but it is not at all clear that unions' efforts will be sufficient to address the needs and concerns of low-wage immigrant workers. In fact, the continued saliency for basic labor standards is strongest in nonunionized work settings, which is where the vast majority of Americans, and especially immigrants, work. However, though traditional labor unions are the quintessential organization for addressing worker rights, they are not the only form of collective mobilization (Fine 2006; Jayaraman and Ness 2005). Given the low levels of unionization, particularly for Latino immigrants, it is important to understand the circumstances under which these workers are able to make claims on their labor rights, particularly outside of the union context.

One might expect that in places where policies more vigorously protect individual labor rights, this would also create an opening for civic engagement on the issue, beyond simply union activity. In the case of gay and lesbian rights, Ellen Andersen (2005) develops the concept of a "legal opportunity structure," which she argues differs from political opportunity structures because they are based on the available legal stock, which in turn shapes the types and strength of potential social movements. Similarly, I argue that in the case of advocating for immigrant labor rights, a legal-administrative opportunity structure also exists that determines to what extent workers (especially those in a nonunionized context) are encouraged to make claims on their rights either individually, or at a more collective level. As I explain, local governments can be key catalysts for this civic engagement.

METHODOLOGY

This research employs a comparative case study method. I examine two cities with very different legal-administrative structures for addressing labor rights: Houston is characterized by a weak state structure and active local government-community coalition, whereas San Jose relies primarily on a strong state legal apparatus and an evolved labor union history. The significance of the comparison between this thick versus thin policy context is that it determines not only the range of accepted labor conditions and the importance attached to worker rights, but also the strategies that workers and their advocates use to address these concerns.

Table 4.1 details state variation in major labor and employment policy context. Whereas Texas wage and hour standards generally replicate federal minimums, California standards are much stronger.[2] Texas is a Right to Work state where labor union membership is just one-third of that in California (5.3 percent versus 16.5 percent). California also provides more strenuous discrimination protections than do federal anti-discrimination statutes, which are enforced by the Equal Employment Opportunity Commission.[3] Worker health and safety standards in California are governed by a state agency, the California Occupational Safety and Health Administration, whereas Texas relies on the federal agency. Furthermore, Texas is the only state in the nation where employers are not required to carry workers' compensation insurance.[4]

In addition to differing standards, California and Texas also vary substantially in terms of claims filed on these protections. In 2005, California and Texas had, respectively, 16,118,662 and 10,255,292 employed individuals. The same year, 9,402 and 10,192 total charges were filed with the Equal Employment Opportunity Commission or partner Fair Employment Practices Agency (FEPA), respectively for each state.[5] The U.S. Department of Labor processed violation claims for 14,249 and 17,541 employees, respectively for each state, that year.[6,7] This data suggests that levels of both discrimination and wage and hour claims are higher in Texas, even adjusting for the size of the employed population.[8]

Comparative Case Study Approach: Why San Jose and Houston?

Despite overarching federal policies and distinct state policy contexts, I find that local innovation and institutions also matter. Several excellent studies have chronicled the shift within the labor movement toward being more inclusive of immigrants. For example, one of the high-profile success stories has been Los Angeles (for example, Milkman 2000, 2006). Through her review of four sectors in Los Angeles (janitorial, residential construction, truck transportation and apparel), Milkman argued that, in fact, "immigrant workers may be easier to organize than their native counterparts" (2006, 133). However, Milkman explained, Los Angeles is also a demographically and historically exceptional story of working class immigrant organizing, "Nowhere in the United States is there more palpable evidence of the potential for today's working class immigrants to reenact the drama of union upsurge that brought earlier generations of newcomers to the United States into the economic mainstream of the 1930s and 1940s" (2006, 187).

TABLE 4.1 *State Variation in Labor Policy (2005)*

State	State OSHA Plan?	Minimum Wage	Right to Work State?	Union Representation	State	State OSHA Plan?	Minimum Wage	Right to Work State?	Union Representation
Alabama	N	5.15	Y	11.7	Montana	N	5.15	N	12.2
Alaska	Y	7.15	N	24.1	North Carolina	Y	5.15	Y	3.9
Arizona	Y	5.15	Y	7.7	North Dakota	N	5.15	Y	9.2
Arkansas	N	5.15	Y	6.0	Nebraska	N	5.15	Y	9.5
California	Y	6.75	N	17.8	Nevada	Y	5.15	Y	15.1
Colorado	N	5.15	N	9.4	New Hampshire	N	5.15	N	11.5
Connecticut	~	7.10	N	17.0	New Jersey	~	5.15	N	21.7
Delaware	N	6.15	N	12.9	New Mexico	Y	5.15	N	10.7
Florida	N	5.15	Y	7.2	New York	~	6.00	N	27.5
Georgia	N	5.15	Y	6.0	Ohio	N	5.15	N	17.2
Hawaii	Y	6.25	N	26.7	Oklahoma	N	5.15	Y	6.4
Idaho	N	5.15	Y	6.3	Oregon	Y	7.25	N	15.7
Illinois	N	6.50	N	17.6	Pennsylvania	N	5.15	N	15.0
Indiana	Y	5.15	N	13.2	Rhode Island	N	6.75	N	16.8
Iowa	Y	5.15	Y	13.5	South Carolina	Y	5.15	N	3.3
Kansas	N	5.15	Y	9.5	South Dakota	N	5.15	Y	8.2

State				
Kentucky	Y	5.15	N	10.8
Louisiana	N	5.15	Y	7.4
Maine	N	6.35	N	13.6
Maryland	Y	5.15	N	15.0
Massachusetts	N	6.75	N	14.9
Michigan	Y	5.15	N	21.4
Minnesota	Y	5.15	N	16.4
Mississippi	N	5.15	Y	9.7
Missouri	N	5.15	N	12.6
Tennessee	Y	5.15	Y	6.6
Texas	N	5.15	Y	6.2
Utah	Y	5.15	Y	6.1
Vermont	Y	7.00	N	13.0
Virginia	Y	5.15	Y	6.2
Washington	Y	7.35	N	20.4
Washington, D.C.	N	6.60	N	12.8
Wisconsin	N	5.15	N	17.2
West Virginia	N	5.15	N	15.5
Wyoming	Y	5.15	Y	9.5

Source: Author's compilation.

Note: The federal Occupational Safety and Health Administration (OSHA) sets standards for working conditions. These include things like shade and water availability for farm workers, appropriate scaffolding or trench construction, or limits on exposure to toxic chemicals. Some states have created their own state OSHA programs, which receive 50 percent of their enforcement funds, and 90 percent of their funds for consultation services, from the federal government. States are encouraged to form their own state programs, though less than half have not. State OSHA standards must be "at least as effective as" federal standards, but can include additional regulations as well. California OSHA standards contain many additional provisions above the federal baseline. (Connecticut, New Jersey, and New York plans cover public sector employees only.)

Employees in Right to Work states do not have to formally join (pay dues to) a union even after it is recognized by the company through an election or other negotiations. That worker however still remains protected if a union is elected to represent workers. This difference changes the dynamics of union organizing in that it makes recognition potentially more difficult, in addition to reducing the resources a union has through membership.

Consequently, this chapter focuses on cities that are emblematic of the regulatory dynamics in each state, but not radically divergent in terms of local innovations and resources. I thus excluded the capital cities in each state (that is, Sacramento and Austin), global cities such as Los Angeles and New York, and also border cities such as El Paso and San Diego, which have a distinctive demographic character. I selected Houston and San Jose due to their similar demographic and economic profile (see table 4.2). Houston is the fourth largest city in the United States (the largest in Texas), and San Jose is the tenth largest city in the country (the third largest in California next to Los Angeles and San Diego).

Houston and San Jose also have distinct economic and labor histories. According to one historian, Houston was a town built on speculative growth and the spirit of unfettered capitalism (Feagin 1988). Houston's economic growth was originally fueled by cotton, timber, and the railroads, though it quickly became captivated by the booming oil industry. The oil industry is still dominant, but Houston is also a major port of entry, known for its biomedical research, aeronautics (with NASA located nearby), and financial services. Houston's sprawling housing and economic development has spurned considerable demand for construction and service workers (for example, hotels, restaurants, janitorial services), all of which rely heavily on immigrant labor.

The labor movement in Houston centers around the Harris County AFL-CIO (HC AFL-CIO), which has recently spearheaded many immigrant rights initiatives, but not without heated debate. In the midst of huge demographic shifts that have pushed the Latino population over the former white majority, the established white union leadership (characterized by several key building trades unions) has contested many of the efforts to bring immigrant rights into the forefront of the HC AFL-CIO's work. The HC AFL-CIO has also worked closely with local coalitions such as the Justice and Equality in the Workplace Project, which rests largely on the political support of Mayor Bill White (in his second term in 2006) and the mayor's Office of Immigrant and Refugee Affairs. The Houston city council is comprised of fourteen members (five at-large). Though elections are technically nonpartisan, conservative sentiments run strong on the council,[9] reflecting the large Republican electorate in the area.[10]

San Jose was known until the 1960s as the Valley of Heart's Delight, though is now considered the capital of Silicon Valley. Today, companies such as Cisco Systems, Adobe, eBay, HP, Apple, IBM, and countless other start-ups, dot the landscape. Unlike Houston, San Jose has had a historically small African American population; however, more than a third of the San Jose population is foreign-born. Before the 2000 tech bust, San Jose and surrounding cities were also home to a dense concentration of electronic manufacturing plants, which employed mostly immigrants. Since the recession that followed, many of these immigrants and other low-skilled workers have moved into the service sector.

The now well-known Justice for Janitors campaign garnered one of its first victories in San Jose more than a decade ago, and one of its more recent in late 2006 in Houston. Whereas organizations such as the Silicon Valley

TABLE 4.2 *Profile of Case Studies: San Jose and Houston (2005)*

	San Jose, California	Houston, Texas
Total population	916,220	2,074,828
One race (percent)		
White	47.0	52.3
Black or African American	2.9	24.7
Asian	30.5	5.0
Hispanic-Latino of any race (percent)	32.2	41.9
Foreign-born (percent)	38.6	27.8
Europe	5.4	3.8
Asia	57.8	15.7
Africa	1.5	3.8
Oceania	0.3	0.1
Latin America	34.0	75.8
Northern America	1.1	.8
Industry (percent)		
Agricultural, forestry, fishing and hunting, mining	0.2	2.1
Construction	7.6	12.0
Mining	20.8	8.6
Wholesale trade	3.0	4.1
Retail trade	10.1	9.9
Transportation, warehousing, utilities	3.2	5.6
Information	3.4	1.5
Finance, insurance, real estate, rental and leasing	5.8	6.8
Professional, scientific, management, administrative, waste management services	15.1	13.9
Educational services, health care, social assistance	15.9	17.9
Arts, entertainment, recreation, accommodations, food services	8.2	9.2
Other services, except public administration	4.3	6.1
Public administration	2.4	2.3
Median household income	$73,804	$39,682
Families living in poverty (percent)	7.7	17.0

Source: Author's calculations from American Community Survey 2006, accessed at http://factfinder.census.gov/home/saff/main.html?_lang-en.

Leadership Group (formerly the Silicon Valley Manufacturing Group) and Joint Venture Silicon Valley have worked on issues relevant largely to the working elite and business owners, the South Bay Labor Council (SBLC) has positioned itself squarely against the political agenda of such groups and the local Chamber of Commerce. The SBLC created Working Partnerships USA in 1995 as its research and advocacy arm, to work with community organizations on issues such as child care, affordable housing, and union neutrality. The SBLC is also intimately involved in local politics. The former SBLC political director and vice mayor in 2005, Cindy Chavez, lost a bid for the mayor's seat in a heated race in 2006. The San Jose city council is comprised of ten members. Although San Jose is known as a Democratic city, long-embedded business interests present challenges to labor organizing. The newly elected mayor, Chuck Reed, received significant support from the business community, and the largely conservative and demographically significant Vietnamese community.

Interview Sampling Strategy

This analysis relies on sixty interviews with key governmental and organizational informants in San Jose and Houston.[11] I focus on those agencies and groups with direct jurisdiction over, or otherwise involved with, protecting labor rights. My goal was to interview all relevant government and community actors who are involved in shaping the focus and direction of labor standards enforcement in each city. The first group of interview informants included federal, state, and local labor standards enforcement agencies with the job of enforcing state and local statutes and processing claims. I interviewed a representative of all the agencies, with one exception, as outlined in table 4.3.

Because government actors are by no means the only relevant influence on shaping the creation and implementation of policy, I also interviewed all relevant nongovernment organizational actors. To identify this group of organizations, I relied on directories of nonprofit organizations[12] in each city as well as on resources and referrals provided by government agencies.[13] I interviewed low-income legal service providers, unions, and community and advocacy groups that focused on labor or employment issues. I targeted agency leaders, such as directors, lead counsel, and union business agents. Table 4.4 details the type of organizations interviewed in each city.[14]

I aimed to interview the sister organization in each place, wherever relevant. However, as I discuss, because the state apparatus and union strength in San Jose was so dominant, very few community advocacy organizations saw labor and employment as one of their major concerns. Conversely, in Houston, where unions were weak and the state apparatus was very weak and the local government played a larger role in conjunction with community actors, more community organizations saw labor and employment as a central part of their organizing mission. Yet, in Houston, unlike in San Jose, no viable nonprofit legal resources were available for low-wage aggrieved workers.

TABLE 4.3 *Overview of Interviews with Labor Standards Enforcement Agencies*

Labor Issue	Houston, Texas	San Jose, California
Union organizing	National Labor Relations Board, Region 16	National Labor Relations Board, Region 20
Wage and hour	Department of Labor-Wage and Hour Division, Houston Office, Houston Office Texas Workforce Commission, Labor Law Section, Austin Office	Department of Labor, Wage and Hour Division, San Jose Office Department of Industrial Relations, Labor Standards Enforcement, San Jose Office
Health and safety	Occupational Safety and Health Administration (OSHA), Houston South Area Office	Department of Industrial Relations Cal/OSHA, Oakland Office
Discrimination	Equal Employment Opportunity Commission, Houston Office Texas Workforce Commission, Civil Rights Division, Austin Office	Equal Employment Opportunity Commission, San Francisco Office Department of Fair Employment and Housing (DFEH)[a]
Workers' compensation	Texas Division of Insurance, Workers' Compensation Commission, Austin Office	Department of Industrial Relations, Workers' Compensation, Oakland Office
Active Alternative options (local)	Harris County Dispute Resolution Office Houston Police Department, Burglary and Theft Division (process "theft of service reports") Mayor's Office on Immigrant and Refugee Affairs	Santa Clara County Dispute Resolution Office Santa Clara County Office of Human Relations, Immigrant Relations and Integration Services

Source: Author's compilation.
[a] Unable to secure formal interview.

TABLE 4.4   *Overview of Interviews with Community Informants*

Houston (20)	San Jose (22)
• 5 - Immigrant rights groups • Interfaith group • Day labor center • Housing advocacy group • Faith-based advocacy group • Asian worker rights group • Leadership group	• 4 - Immigrant rights groups • Worker safety advocacy group • Social justice advocacy group • Environmental justice group • Day Labor center • Faith-based advocacy group • Leadership group
• AFL-CIO Central Labor Council • Manufacturing union • Retail industry union • 2 - Services industry unions • 2 - Construction industry unions	• AFL-CIO Central Labor Council • Retail industry union • 2 - Services industry unions • 3 - Construction industry unions
• 1 - Low-income legal services group	• 4 - Low-income legal services groups
• Consulado de México en Houston	• Consulado de México en San José

Source: Author's compilation.

FINDINGS

The research findings affirm previous conclusions that the political context and legal-administrative opportunity structure shape the need for, and feasibility of, collective action around labor and employment issues. Yet, I find that outside of the union context, this depends largely on the strategies that local governments and civil society organizations adopt in response to workplace conditions. In table 4.5, I outline the main mechanisms for protecting labor rights in each city. A puzzle emerges. In contrast to our initial assumptions that an open legal and administrative structure would encourage individual rights claims-making and foster collective organizing, I find that in spite of the more robust state guarantees in San Jose, there is less activism around basic labor rights than there is in Houston, where the political environment for immigrants is hostile and labor protections remain weak and decentralized.

I propose three main avenues through which this occurs:

• First, an open legal-administrative opportunity structure, like that in San Jose, encourages individual rights claims-making through formal state channels. Advocates recognize the limitations of using bureaucratic government structures to address workplace inequality, but generally see them as the best line of first defense for individual workers, and consequently refrain from collective action on the issue, in order to direct their resources to other issues.

TABLE 4.5   *Mechanisms for Protecting Labor Rights in Houston and San Jose*

Mechanism	Houston, Texas	San Jose, California
Strength of labor protections	Thin	Thick
History and power of labor unionism	Weak	Strong
Range of common labor abuses	Wider	More limited
Best avenues for contesting labor abuses	File formal claim with federal agency; active federal-local coalition of agencies, including alternative options such as the local police department, or dispute resolution center	File formal claim with state agency
Available community resources for workers filing formal claims	No active employment law clinics; hotline through mayor's office and Mexican consulate; direct action	At least two local university employment law clinics; more readily available legal counsel; accessible outreach for undocumented workers
Relationship between key actors	Coalition; focus on collective claims-making	Separated; focus on individual claims-making
Role of immigration in local politics	Several prominent immigrant rights organizations; strong "anti-immigrant" sentiment from local Republican elected officials and constituents	Several prominent immigrant rights organizations; though immigration per se is for the most part a political nonissue
General focus of labor movement	Basic labor protections, especially for immigrant workers, direct actions against abusive employers	Broader political demands for the "needs of working people" such as universal health care and transportation

Source: Author's compilation.

- Second, in places such as Houston, where state protections are weaker and the political context is more hostile toward immigrants, the range of abuses is indeed wider. However, the hostile political context and stark conditions also agitate workers and advocates. Meanwhile, the absence of strong state policies encourages civic coalition building with local government actors to fill this vacuum.

- Third, although unions have made great strides and become an established and recognized component of the local power structure in San Jose, they have in turn broadened their political focus, relying on the formal state structure to serve the more basic needs of nonunion immigrant workers. Where unions have not progressed this far, as in Houston, unions have maintained a more basic focus on workplace rights. As a result, the central labor council in Houston has remained a key partner to enforcing labor standards, in conjunction with the city government and Mexican consulate. The result is to increase the political weight of labor rights advocates.

These three mechanisms reflect a situation where, in San Jose, workplace concerns have been addressed through strong labor standards, which has in turn created a perception that there is no need for actors outside the state legal apparatus—such as local governments, unions, and other community-based organizations—to intervene. Meanwhile, their attention has shifted to broader concerns such as health care, housing, and transportation. Conversely, the weak labor protections in Texas have spurred the local government in Houston to address the needs of Latino immigrant workers, particularly those who are undocumented. The hostile political environment has provoked immigrant worker advocates outside of unions to take action at a collective level. Thus, what is good for individual rights and liberties does not necessarily seem to encourage creative coalitions and civic engagement.

An Open Legal-Administrative Opportunity Structure

In California, strong state labor standards and the presence of accessible legal resources seem to promote formal rights claims. Access to this thick structure of labor rights enforcement is also mediated by access to legal counsel and other advocates that can help workers navigate the system. I found more legal services willing to serve low-income, and in particular undocumented, immigrant workers in San Jose. This was comprised mainly of two major university law clinics, and a network of pro bono or low-cost attorneys willing to take on more complicated cases. The Mexican consulate in San Jose also provides limited legal counsel to its co-nationals.

Labor lawyers seem to be in shorter supply in Houston, and anxieties run high regarding serving undocumented workers (particularly for organizations funded by public and foundation support). As one lawyer in Houston explained, "labor law is simply not a profitable area to practice in terms of attorney's fees, especially if you are representing the worker." As a result, there are very few resources for low-wage workers who wish to pursue even basic employment or labor claims, be they an immigrant or not. One of the only legal aid societies in Houston has in fact stopped pursuing employment and labor claims due to a major defeat in a discrimination case several years ago. Following that, and on the strong advice of a board member (who also happened to be a partner at the defendant's law firm), the agency set an internal policy to no longer pursue employment cases of any kind. Despite suggestions to the contrary, calls to several other low-income legal service providers in Houston confirmed that no assistance was provided for employment and labor cases. The Harris County Dispute Resolution Center, which also handles many employment and labor cases, has also ceased their outreach to day laborers (common victims of wage theft) on the strong suggestion of the board of their fiscal agent, the Houston Bar Association. Thus, given this dearth of low-cost legal services, there are very few legal and administrative channels available for Latino workers in Houston, especially those who are low-wage or undocumented.

The relatively conservative court circuit in Texas is also a major deterrent for pursuing legal claims. The director for the Equal Employment Opportunity Commission (EEOC) in San Francisco, which has jurisdiction over San Jose, compares her experience in the Bay Area to that in Houston, where she served as director for more than twenty years, "The climate is much more liberal in California, compared to Texas, and there is much less resistance here. The ninth district is completely different; the fifth district is the worst! You also have more options for lawyers here [in the San Francisco district] than you do in Houston." Other attorneys in San Jose echoed this sentiment. Another legal clinic director explained, "I never go through the (federal) Department of Labor; state law is much better." As a result, formal channels to make claims on labor rights are seen as legitimate and accessible in San Jose. Community-based advocacy organizations regularly refer aggrieved workers to either the local law clinic or directly to the relevant state agency. Compared to federal agencies, which are also an option, state agencies are the preferred route because of their more robust protections, increased accessibility, and a lingering concern over potential information sharing between federal agencies and immigration authorities.

There is also a stark difference between California and Texas state labor standards enforcement agencies. In addition to having more robust provisions, a strong state structure is also important for buffering political swings at the federal level. Texas labor provisions generally replicate federal minimums, and most Texas state agencies are physically concentrated in Austin. For example, to file a wage claim with the Texas Workforce Commission (TWC), you must mail in a claim to the sole office in Austin. As a result, compared to workers in San Jose who are well served by the State of California, workers in Houston must rely mostly on federal agencies, and the help of local governments and mostly non-legal advocates who help them navigate these resources.

Nontraditional Collaborations: Local and Foreign Governments

The lack of a strong state presence for labor standards enforcement in Houston has created an opening for local initiatives, and paved the way for community organizations to garner political weight on the issue of labor rights. This shift has occurred largely through the creation of the Justice and Equality in the Workplace Partnership (JEWP). In 2001, JEWP was created primarily through the efforts of the Equal Employment Opportunity Commission and the Mexican consulate in Houston and, later, the U.S. Department of Labor (DOL) Wage and Hour Division. Member agencies signed an accord, to be renewed annually, which reiterated agency support for the project. The goal of this coalition was to address the large and growing issues of minimum wage enforcement, nonpayment of wages or overtime, and wage disparities between groups. According to the EEOC deputy director in Houston, the goal of JEWP was to "create many forms of outreach, including videos, town meetings, and public events, in order to show people how to file a complaint, and to raise awareness about their rights." The primary target audience was the Latino immigrant community, who these agencies felt were the most vulnerable and most underserved. Following these three initial signatory agencies, the Mexican American Legal Defense and Education Fund became involved, as did the city of Houston Mayor's Office of Immigrant and Refugee Affairs (MOIRA). MOIRA's involvement was key because it provided the coalition local political legitimacy, and also because, along with resources provided by the Mexican consulate, MOIRA staffed the JEWP hotline. Soon thereafter, the Occupational Safety and Health Administration also sent a liaison, as did several religious organizations, the Harris County AFL-CIO, and the consulates of Colombia, El Salvador, and Guatemala.[15] Several key immigrant-serving organizations have worked with JEWP informally, and provide referrals to the hotline, as well as promote outreach efforts. The mayor's support was fundamental to involving the Houston Police Department (HPD) in the coalition. Since its involvement, HPD has begun to enforce an internal memoranda that allows officers to pursue theft of service claims for individuals who are hired and not paid (a common dilemma for day laborers). The policy had long been in effect, but had laid dormant due to resistance from many officers, despite pressure from community organizations.

Early in its creation, JEWP launched a ¡No Se Deje! (Protect Yourself!) campaign that made use of public events, ethnic media, and billboard advertising to encourage workers to stand up for their rights and make use of the JEWP hotline. Staffs at member agencies were trained to refer callers to the appropriate agency, and claims were cross-filed with all signatories. Public appearances by the Mexican consul general and top enforcement agency officials were used to grant legitimacy to the labor rights enforcement process.

Before JEWP was established, MOIRA constantly received calls by workers needing assistance with labor claims. With no structure in place to help them, these individuals would simply be referred to Latino community-based advocacy agencies, who were minimally equipped to assist them. After JEWP, enforcement agencies, and the DOL Wage and Hour division in particular, saw a substantial increase in claims. Though discrimination and harassment issues—the primary purview of JEWP's founding partner, the EEOC—are no doubt a major concern in Latino immigrant communities, they come second in urgency to wage and hour violations. According to the director of MOIRA, "we were doing DOL a service, because this is their job, but they apparently don't have the resources to do it."[16]

MOIRA and the Mexican consulate were able to provide language capacity, and perhaps more importantly, a clearer sensibility and understanding about the immigrant community and the challenges that they face. As one union leader said, "Going to a federal agency is not really an undocumented worker's favorite thing to do!" Although MOIRA still represents a form of government, their explicit focus on the concerns of immigrants and refugees made them a more inviting venue for aggrieved immigrant workers. Furthermore, though distrust toward Mexican federales is a commonly held sentiment, here in the United States, they are considered a lesser evil. The Mexican consulate's liaison to JEWP explained: "Each agency attracts their own audience. For example, if the DOL holds a community meeting, no one will attend. [The community] sees the INS as government, and synonymous with all other government agencies. But if the Mexican consulate brokers the deal and hosts the event, there will be a better turnout." The consulate's mobile consulate program also proved to be a vital vehicle for getting the campaign out to more marginalized areas around Houston, which typically does not receive outreach on labor issues.[17]

The roles of MOIRA and the Mexican consulate in JEWP were key to the success of the project, but also rather innovative. Both agencies were stepping into legal territory over which neither had prior jurisdiction. Indeed, very rarely do local governments enact their own standards or intervene in the enforcement of state and federal standards.[18] MOIRA itself was a contested political maneuver on the part of Houston Mayor Bill White, and in 2003 his conservative opponent vowed to eliminate the office if elected. Yet, by backing the coalition, MOIRA has created a vital link between the federal agencies that mostly enforce labor rights in Houston, and community organizations that serve the workers most typically aggrieved. This has not only provided practical avenues for enforcement, but also lent political weight to immigrant-serving organizations such as the Harris County AFL-CIO and other partners who were largely marginalized in the anti-immigrant and anti-labor political environment.

The involvement of the Mexican consulate was also key to the success of JEWP. In fact, the consulate built on existing internal efforts through their Area of Protection, which is a national Mexican mandate that provides legal assistance to nationals living abroad. The director of the Mexican consulate's Area of Protection in Houston cited a 2004 memorandum from the Mexican Secretary of Foreign Relations Institute of Mexicans in the Exterior, which codified this relationship with American labor agencies. It stated, in translation:

The U.S. Department of Labor, local governments and community organizations, with the collaboration of Mexican consulates in Houston, Dallas, and

Colorado, launched the Justice and Equality in the Workplace Partnership. These initiatives are aimed at informing migrant workers about their rights and responsibilities, as well as offering mechanisms for those who do not speak English to report labor violations of laws administered by the Occupational Safety and Health Administration, the Wage and Hour Division, and the Office of Federal Contract Complicate of the U.S. Department of Labor. During 2004, considerations for launching similar initiatives in other regions of the United States are taking place (accessed at http://www.conapo.gob.mx/micros/infa vance/2004/17.pdf).

This formal agreement instilled a specific focus on protecting the labor rights of monolingual Spanish-speaking immigrants, many of whom are undocumented—the group of workers who are arguably the most exploited and underserved by traditional labor enforcement agencies. Though several other Latin American consulates also have signed onto to JEWP, it is the Mexican consulate that has had the biggest presence and influence. When asked about the role that the other three consulates play, I was told by other lead signatories that they simply do not have the same resources to support the initiative at a very involved level.

The creation of the Justice and Equality in the Workplace Partnership in Houston is significant because, although the EEOC (a federal agency) took a lead role at first, it was the mayor's office and the Mexican consulate that have invested the most resources and have been perhaps the most influential actors. Rather than necessarily squeeze out other community-based organizations, JEWP relies on community-based immigrant and labor rights organizations, as well as the ethnic media, to get the word out. In fact, these two agencies—the city of Houston and the Mexican consulate—are perfectly positioned to create avenues for local community groups to organize around labor rights. They are both closely connected to the pulse of the city and its Latino immigrant community, and the Mexican consulate is able to more efficiently direct resources to their constituency. These two agencies provide the resources that individual immigrant organizations were unable to gather and coordinate while granting these organizations with political legitimacy and voice in the area of immigrant labor rights.

There is no parallel coalition to JEWP in San Jose. Though the Mexican consulate has this same capacity in all of the cities it serves, its role is decidedly different in San Jose. There it has an outreach program, but the services are generally limited to legal referrals and collaborations with unions to give informational workshops. According to the Mexican consul in San Jose, "it is always important to have legal counsel, rather than going to administrative agencies alone." Thus, where in Houston the consulate has dedicated resources to staffing the JEWP hotline and promoting media outreach to the community, the consulate in San Jose focuses more on partnerships with individual labor unions, and providing legal counsel to aggrieved workers.

Federal agencies also have a less significant presence in California, because they are superseded by state statute, leaving alternative venues rather undeveloped. The San Francisco district office of the EEOC, which governs San Jose, has explicitly chosen not to adopt a more formal structure outreach structure. Unlike JEWP, collaborating agencies do not sign yearly accords, nor is there regular coordination of outreach activities. Coincidentally, the former EEOC director in Houston now directs the San Francisco district office. However, she admitted to not even knowing the current director of the DOL Wage and Hour Division. She explained the reason behind her decision not to replicate JEWP in the San Francisco district office, "we are not necessarily the best game in town." She went on to explain that unlike Texas, California provisions are much more stringent than the federal statute, and thus her agency is not always the preferred avenue to file a claim. Her main collaborative outreach focus is the California Department of Fair Employment and Housing.[19]

EEOC outreach to community organizations in the Latino immigrant community in San Jose has been targeted almost entirely to Latino agricultural workers. These efforts are mostly focused on raising public awareness around the issues agricultural workers face, and pursuing class-action litigation.[20] When asked about the overwhelming focus on agricultural Latino workers, despite the fast-growing service sector, the San Francisco EEOC district outreach manager simply explained that outreach in this sector is "a little trickier," and that labor unions are the main gatekeepers in these service industries. Although she has plans to begin collaborations with unions, she sees this as a delicate move, given that unions can also sometimes be "part of the problem." Additionally, agriculture has received much of the focus because this is where most of the class action cases have occurred. According to her, these successful cases are critical to profile in outreach campaigns and gain trust amongst workers, but such high-profile gains simply have not been made in sectors outside of agriculture.

Unlike those in Houston, local governments in San Jose, and Santa Clara County more broadly, play a very small role in the enforcement of labor rights. For example, although the San Jose Police Department has a strong policy of not carrying out immigration duties, it does not have a formal policy to pursue nonpayment of wages. Similarly, the Santa Clara County–sponsored Dispute Resolution Center does not typically handle workplace disputes. This is seen as a role fulfilled by state agencies, with little need for local intervention. The director of the Immigration Resources and Integration Services Program of the Santa Clara County Office of Human Relations confirmed that there are no city or county resources that he is aware of that serve workers who have labor claims, other than the local university-run workers rights clinic (the focus of which is teaching law students, and not necessarily service to clients, and the resources of which are limited to handling straightforward wage and workers compensation cases). The county-funded dispute resolution center in San Jose, unlike the one in Houston, also does not typically see any labor or employment cases. Overall, the state of California, rather than the federal or local government, is seen as the main actor in the labor rights enforcement process. Aside from negotiations over union contracts for city and county workers, local governments in San Jose have remained absent from a role in negotiating local labor relations.

Community organizations I spoke with have also largely evaded the area of labor rights issues. For example, the Santa Clara Committee on Safety in Health (SCCOSH) had a fleeting existence during the heyday of the electronic assembly industry. SCCOSH began during the late 1970s much as JEWP did, by setting up a hotline for workers to call in about chemical hazards, and offering medical and legal referrals. It joined in political efforts when in 1987 the conservative Governor Deukmejian eliminated the state OSHA agency; it was later resurrected under pressure two years later. SCCOSH focused primarily on issues facing immigrant workers in the electronic assembly, and positioned itself against the interests of the Semiconductor Industry Association and its member companies, which "placed the integrity of a chip above the safety of their workers," according to one of SCCOSH's former leaders. SCCOSH's main successes were achieved by framing the issue as an environmental and public health hazard facing residents (and not necessarily just workers) as a way to work with local governments. Over time, SCCOSH, which was founded by a group of lawyers, became focused on pursuing class action suits, rather than educating and organizing workers. According to a former employee, this focus on navigating the regulatory legal structure clashed with the goals of grassroots organizers. Coupled with the decline of the electronics industry, SCCOSH eventually disbanded in 2004. Safety and health issues, which are governed by Cal/OSHA, are now advocated at a state level by the statewide COSH group, WorkSafe!, which focuses on advocating for legislative changes at the state level. The dissolution of SCCOSH reflects a context in San Jose where strong state standards supersede the less relevant federal structure, leaving little room for local governments or other community groups to become involved.

The contrast between labor rights organizing in California and Texas hence reveals that different levels of government intervention can lead to either crowding out or coalition-building with community-based organizations. In both states, government agencies are important. However, in San Jose, where the state of California plays a stronger role than the federal government, the city and county have not played a direct role in addressing labor rights. Furthermore, unions hold a strong and legitimate position as the voice of workers, and hence other community-based organizations relegate labor issues to them. Conversely, in Texas, the lack of a strong state structure has led to reliance on federal standards and agencies. To bridge this gap in Houston, particularly for vulnerable Latino immigrant workers, local governments have stepped in to facilitate access to these agencies, as well as other local alternatives (such as small claims court, dispute resolution, and the city police). Federal agencies in Houston have actively sought partnerships with local governments, which in turn have relied on local community based organizations to facilitate outreach.

The involvement of local governments is significant because it provides immigrant organizations a proximate target to engage. Although the state of California has relied on local groups to help constituents file claims, the effort is limited mostly to legal clinics that act as service providers, rather than as community-based advocacy organizations per se. The provision of services is critical for immigrants, who need assistance in navigating the formal bureaucratic structure, but the process is inherently and necessarily individualized and,

I argue, ultimately inadequate to address structural issues that create the conditions for abuse.

The Role of Labor Unions: Setting the Agenda for Labor

Historically, the major proponent of improving labor standards at both the state and federal levels has been labor unions. All of the minimum labor standards now in place—such as the minimum wage, the forty-hour work week, equal employment protections, and so on—were achieved in large part due to the collective mobilization and political work of organized labor. In most cities, the collective voice of unions has typically been the AFL-CIO central labor council (CLC).[21] A central labor council is the local (typically county-wide) AFL-CIO body that represents all member union locals in the area. Despite the 2005 Change to Win (CTW) campaign that split the formerly consolidated union base in the AFL-CIO,[22] the central labor council in both San Jose (the South Bay Labor Council) and Houston (the Harris County AFL-CIO) remain among the strongest voices for working people. In both cases, several CTW unions have signed solidarity charters with the AFL-CIO.[23] Thus these central labor councils continue to play an important role in setting the political agenda for union workers, and work to advocate for particular policies and candidates. Most have in fact embraced immigrant rights as a central tenet of their political agenda.[24]

As argued, the legal-administrative opportunity structure and strong state involvement in labor rights in California, while perhaps good for individual workers, also squeezes out local governments and community organizations from organizing around these issues. Aggrieved workers rely on formal bureaucratic processes, largely through state agencies, to file claims. As a result, there is a common perception that these basic needs are taken care of through these channels, and consequently unions feel empowered to focus on broader political work. Although unions in San Jose engage Latino immigrant workers in their activities, they tend to do so strategically through their current membership, in targeted organizing drives, and in a broader political framework.

Conversely, in Houston, the Harris County AFL-CIO has adopted a model more focused on enforcing basic workplace protections through JEW and engaged in direct actions with other community partners (through initiatives such as the Justice Bus). The result of these divergent strategies is that though weaker protections in Houston jeopardize individual work experiences, they have spurred additional activism and coalition building, to which the Harris County AFL-CIO has been a key partner. Meanwhile, the South Bay Labor Council in San Jose has strategically relied on the robust standards proffered by state agencies in California to address basic labor rights needs, focusing their mobilization efforts on broader political efforts.

The South Bay Labor Council relies largely on local elected officials for political support. As an SBLC political director explained, "the union cannot do it alone, and needs the support of the city".[25] In a Democratic stronghold such as San Jose, this seems to be a very feasible goal. The SBLC political director identified six of the eleven San Jose city council members (including the vice mayor) as clear and constant allies, and only two adversaries (the current mayor and the current opponent contending against the vice mayor in the runoff for the mayor's seat). I also spoke with a thirty-year veteran of the labor movement, who attributed the success of the labor movement in Silicon Valley to the support of prominent elected officials in recent years, such as Susan Hammer, mayor of San Jose from 1990 to 1998. Though garnering such support is fought on an issue-by-issue basis, the labor movement veteran feels that labor is no longer a partisan issue in Silicon Valley—most all officials in the cities they work are Democrat, though not all are necessarily pro-union. Overall, organized labor is seen as a legitimate member at the political table, and a political and financial force to be reckoned with. In fact, a key criticism on the part of the newly elected San Jose mayor concerned the significant campaign donations his opponent received from the South Bay Labor Council.

Conversely, Texas labor advocates must fight a constant uphill battle to gain legitimacy and political weight. Although Houston is the fourth largest city in the nation and demographically diverse, the conservative political environment and weak state protections for labor make formal channels of labor rights enforcement less tenable. The director of one prominent community-based immigrant organizations could identify only three allies on the fourteen-member Houston city council. Although she described the Houston mayor as "a very pragmatic and moderate guy" who they can work with, many of the unions I spoke with reiterated the obstacle that the anti-labor political environment in Houston poses. As one of the Harris County AFL-CIO leaders stressed, "This is still Texas. Here, if you get hurt, somehow it is your fault. . . . there is no recourse for workers." He also cited the lack of a state OSHA agency, and the consolidated structure of the Texas Workforce Commission, as barriers for enforcing wage claims locally. He went on to explain that though he usually receives full support from Democratic officials, he doesn't even seek out Republican support because "I know how they vote, and I know who our friends are." The current president of the Houston Construction and Building Trades Department reiterated this sentiment, and bluntly described the political culture in Houston as one in which "local politicians can't even spell worker rights."

Coupled with the vastly different labor standards in California and Texas, these two distinct political contexts profoundly shape the way in which unions in each city engage workers and other community based organizations on the topic of labor rights. In Houston, the relationship between unions and community organizations is more focused on basic workplace conditions and labor practices. This focus is propelled by the growing low-wage immigrant population in the nonunionized sector. In fact, the Harris County AFL-CIO played a key role in the creation of the Justice and Equality in the Workplace Project. The Building Trades Council presented a white paper to the Equal Employment Opportunity Commission entitled "Houston's Dirty Little Secret," which detailed violations of the prevailing wage and documented that the majority of claimants were Latino. The EEOC subsequently spearheaded an initial task force and several labor representatives were invited to testify. This eventually lead to the creation of JEWP (Karson 2006).

In response to many high-profile workplace abuses, the Harris County AFL-CIO launched the Justice Bus, a self-professed Michael Moore-style campaign designed to either praise exemplary employers or, more often, shame abusive ones. The Justice Bus has targeted large employers such as Quiteflex, which was later the target of an employment discrimination case involving the disparate treatment of Hispanic workers. In this campaign, as with others, the bus is filled with community organizers, religious leaders, and local officials who confront the employer and pressure them to conform to fair labor practices.

Similarly, unlike the now-defunct Santa Clara Committee on Occupational Safety in Health group in San Jose, the Houston COSH group continues to be active, with the continued support of the Harris County AFL-CIO. Houston COSH's goal is to provide advocacy and education on safety and health issues particularly for vulnerable workers.[26] Houston COSH has also launched an initiative with the local NAACP to work primarily with African American women who are undergoing the welfare-to-work transition, as well as a program targeted at high school immigrant workers concentrated mostly in amusement parks, retail, and "greasy spoons." Houston COSH also works in partnership with the Mayor's Office on Immigration and Refugee Affairs (MOIRA) and several faith-based organizations.

The Harris County AFL-CIO has taken a decidedly broader approach to engaging community organizations and nonunionized workers than the South Bay Labor Council. Barbara Byrd and Nari Rhee (2006) described the SBLC approach as a three-tooled strategy of policy research and advocacy, community coalition building, and an aggressive political program. The overall focus of the SBLC, apart from coordinating support for union campaigns, has been the leadership development of potential elected officials and advocating for "issues of concern for working people." Unlike the Harris County AFL-CIO, which has been very involved in outreach campaigns for nonunion workers, such as JEWP and COSH, the SBLC has cast a more clearly political focus for its work. The SBLC has allied its efforts with its research and political arm, Working Partnerships USA (WPUSA). With WPUSA, the SBLC has focused on four main initiatives in recent months. Measure A, placed on the June 2006 ballot, would have instituted a half a cent tax to support local hospitals and the transportation agency; it ultimately failed. The Santa Clara County Children's Health Initiative is a county-based program that provides additional services to supplement state insurance programs that underserve workers who make too much to qualify, as well as undocumented workers. The Coyote Valley redevelopment plan is an urban reserve program that the SBLC wants to ensure employees' "smart growth with equity" while providing high-wage jobs and affordable housing. Last was an intense campaign in support of the vice mayor (and former political director of the SBLC) during the 2006 mayoral election, which she ultimately lost.

In reference to this agenda, an organizer for the SBLC emphatically explained that the SBLC "does not just advocate on behalf of union members, but rather of all workers."[27] Indeed, it has launched several initiatives such as these that are aimed at improving living conditions for all low-wage workers in Silicon Valley, unionized or not. Yet, I argue that an unintended consequence of this agenda is that it also crowds out community focus and resources to serve the immediate needs of nonunion workers who face labor rights violations. When I asked various community leaders what options were available in San Jose for workers who do not have union representation, the SBLC repeatedly emerged as a place where groups thought inquiring workers could go to seek help filing claims. In turn, when I asked SBLC leadership what resources or direct services they were able to offer workers who are not their members, they simply said that they would refer them to the California labor commissioner. As a result of the absent role of unions in San Jose on labor rights issues, as well as lack of involvement on the part of local governments, there is little community mobilization in the arena of basic labor protections.

There is no doubt that the political presence and weight of labor unions in San Jose is markedly stronger, compared to Houston. For example, although the UNITE-HERE! Local 19 can boast representation at twelve hotels in Silicon Valley (nine in San Jose alone), UNITE-HERE! represents only two hotels in the entire state of Texas, only one of which is in Houston. [28] Similarly, the representation of the Laborer's International Union (LUINA) Local 154 in Houston is so low, and staff resources spread so thin, that business meetings are held more than 250 miles away in Arlington. According to their business manager, there are usually no Houston members in attendance. This is a striking difference compared to the Laborer's Local 270 in San Jose which recently had more than fifty members in attendance at a monthly business meeting, and at least ten members represented at a weekend door-to-door drive in support of the favored mayoral candidate. [29]

Thus despite higher union density and strong labor standards, interviews with individual workers confirm that a gap that still exists between strong state provisions and the working reality of low-wage immigrant workers who are not represented by these unions. What are the implications of the broad political focus of labor unions such as the South Bay Labor Council? It seems that though the SBLC has the interests of all workers at heart, a strong state structure has enabled them to broaden the focus of their activities beyond the more mundane issues of labor abuse facing nonunion workers. Indeed, in the recent election season, several SBLC unions were actively pounding the pavement in support of their preferred mayoral candidate, and union halls hosted many candidates. Recent ballot measures have also relied on key support from the SBLC, which has in turn been very active in voter registration efforts.

This has given organized labor a front seat at the political table, and lent considerable political weight to labor unions in San Jose, but the shift has complicated the SBLC's ability and motivation to address the core needs of low-wage and immigrant nonunion workers, as well as their ability to empower other immigrant organizations to take up the cause of labor rights for their constituents. As the preeminent organization for labor issues, the SBLC has the power to set the political agenda regarding labor rights. Yet, it remains unclear whether broad initiatives such as transportation, redevelopment, and voting in political elections will have as direct appeal to workers whose immediate needs still focus on basic labor rights such as nonpayment of wages and unsafe work environments, and in particular for those who are noncitizens and unable to vote.

Furthermore, though the union movement in San Jose has gained increased political presence, there does not seem to be consensus in the immigrant community regarding their legitimacy. This tension was made manifest during the recent immigration marches, at which the leaders of established advocacy organizations (including the SBLC, prominent religious groups, and other immigrant advocates) clashed with the leaders of other more informal community-based groups. One group, which is allied with the SBLC, in particular objected to tactics it considered too informal and unsophisticated. This informal community group regularly holds forums at a popular shopping center, which was a previous target of an unsuccessful and bitter union campaign. March leaders and union supporters argued that the use of this plaza ran contrary to union efforts, but the leader of the informal community group argued that the focus should be practical convenience for the community. This leader referred to one major union in particular as corrupt and in opposition to the rights of the immigrants his group represented. Although tensions between community-based immigrant organizations and labor unions may be inevitable, such clashes illustrate a perceived disconnect between the labor movement and some in the immigrant community.

CONCLUSION

I have outlined how the thick state policy structure in San Jose has encouraged claims-making on formal legal grounds through bureaucratic proceedings and labor unionism. Community organizations in San Jose, though numerous, have generally relegated employment and labor rights issues to state agencies and labor unions. The local government, content to rely on the strong state apparatus, has played an almost nonexistent role in San Jose. Conversely, the relatively thin state policy structure in Houston has created an opening where the local government—in conjunction with community organizations and various Latin American consulates—has played a larger role in an arena where they typically do not have jurisdiction. The local government in Houston also relies closely on community leaders as liaisons to the immigrant community, who are aware of the antagonistic political context in which they operate, and employ a broad base of strategies to garner rights for immigrant workers.

In San Jose, a more open political context and robust legal-administrative opportunity structures has facilitated the ability of individuals to make claims on their legal rights, while legitimating the power and success of labor unions. This model of labor protections has privileged union members, legal services providers, and more policy-savvy advocate groups. Conversely, a more conservative political environment in Texas has inhibited the development of strong state provisions, and deterred unionization. Paradoxically, this has created an opening for local governments to bridge this gap, and simultaneously engage community organizations. Coalitions such as the Justice and Equality in the Workplace Partnership have garnered the resources of the federal government, as well as the local legitimacy and networks of local governments, to engage immigrant organizations on the issue of labor rights.

This contrast reveals that partnering with local government agencies can be helpful to enforcing labor rights protections on an individual level, but also for folding immigrant organizations into civic and political life. Labor rights represent an important avenue for this, given its core relevance to low-wage immigrant communities. Such local partnerships are beneficial to all low-wage workers, but particularly undocumented immigrants. Access to state and federal agencies are an intimidating prospect for undocumented immigrants, and to the extent to which local governments can reach out to these communities, the potentially better they are able to enforce the protection of their rights. Local governments have a long history of working with immigrant communities, through education, social services, and even law enforcement. State and federal governments have less history and rapport. When they collaborate with country-of-origin agencies such as the Mexican consulate, local governments are allowed a further measure of trust and access.

Yet if individual labor rights in San Jose are robust, why should we care about the absence of collective labor rights activism? I would argue that this is important, first, because the presence of robust standards and accessible administrative structures does not necessarily equate with the absence of basic violations, as interviews with workers in San Jose have revealed. These abuses remain commonplace, and often go unreported. Second, and perhaps more important, when immigrants stop organizing around basic labor rights, they remove a key point of access for future migrants who will be the next likely targets of such abuse. Labor rights are one of the primary ways to engage low-wage immigrant workers according to their self-interest, in the Alinsky tradition. Once involved, this can set the stage for civic involvement and coalition-building in other areas of their lives, including those currently championed by the South Bay Labor Council in San Jose. Losing that initial link to basic labor rights may jeopardize the long-term viability of the continued involvement of immigrants in these efforts. Furthermore, as Nelson Lichtenstein emphasized, the decline of the union movement has occurred because greater access to "rights conscious employment law" has become more attractive, and in many ways less cumbersome, than a union contract. Substituting this "rights-based model" to one based on the "collective advancement of mutual interests," overlooks the rights-based model's limited enforcement capabilities, dependence on a professional and government expertise, and an inability to attack structural crises at their core (1997, 71).

NOTES

1. The level of Latino unionization is 11.5 percent, compared to their white, black, and Asian counterparts (13.4, 16.5, and 12.2 percent respectively). Unionization rates in food and agriculture industries are 3 percent, compared to the overall 8.5 percent rate for the private sector.
2. The Federal Labor Standards Act (amended 1996) as of 2005 states that "covered nonexempt workers are entitled to a minimum wage of not less than $5.15 an hour." Effective January 1, 2002, under the California Industrial Welfare Commission

(IWC) orders, the minimum wage was $6.75 an hour, to be increased to $7.50 in January 2007 and to $8 by January 2008. California overtime provisions are stricter than the federal standard, requiring any time after eight hours in a day to be paid at a premium, compared to the forty hour per week federal minimum.

3. In addition to protection from employment discrimination based on race, color, religion, sex, or national origin, as well as several other statutes which prohibit discrimination on attributes such as age and disability, the state of California also provides protection from discrimination on the basis of sexual orientation.

4. The workers' compensation system provides a full range of benefits for the injured worker, including medical benefits and lost wages. This is a state-administered no-fault system in which the implicit agreement is that in exchange for these benefits, an employee cannot sue his or her employer if they are injured. If workers' compensation is not provided, employers are required to notify their employees and if a worker is injured, they have the option to sue their employer. However, a civil tort case such as this can be a lengthy and costly process that is likely prohibitive for most low-wage workers.

5. Based on charge data provided through a public records request to the Equal Employment Opportunity Commission.

6. Based on the WHISARD violation database, provided through a Freedom of Information Act request to the Department of Labor Wage and Hour Division.

7. Unlike the EEOC, which dual files all the charges at the federal and FEPA agencies, the U.S. Department of Labor does not keep track of claims filed to the state. Separate data requests to the state agencies in California and Texas reveal an additional 20,092 employees filing cases at the California Labor Commissioner, and 2,309 claims filed to the Texas Workforce Commission. However, because of differences in minimum standards and data collection strategies across states, I do not combine state and federal wage and hour violation data.

8. Several surveys suggest that underreporting of labor violations is an issue (McGrath 2005).

9. For example, Mark Ellis, a city councilmember and recent candidate for the Texas senate who opposes MOIRA, launched an initiative that would have reversed the policy of the Houston Police Department that prevents it from carrying out immigration enforcement functions. Though this initiative was eventually rejected, and has since been reversed, it was vehemently opposed by the AFL-CIO, several immigrant-rights organizations, and other community-based organizations.

10. George Bush received 55 percent of votes in Harris County in 2004, and the incumbent Republican candidate for governor, Rick Perry, received the majority 36 percent.

11. Although not the focus on this chapter, this analysis also draws on forty-three interviews I conducted with Latino immigrant restaurant workers in each city.

12. To establish a list of all nonprofits whose mission includes labor and employment issues, I used the premium search function provided by GuideStar, one of the leading organizations that compiles IRS database listings for charitable organizations (accessed at http://www.guidestar.org).

13. These included formal client-directed directories such as ImmigrantInfo.org—an online database or providers compiled by the Santa Clara County Immigrant Relations and Integration Services, the Houston Mayor's Office on Immigrant and Refugee Affairs (accessed at http://www.houstontx.gov/moira/index.html), as well as community partners mentioned by the central labor council, and federal and state labor standards enforcement agencies in each city.

14. Confidentiality restrictions do not permit me to disclose the exact names of the nongovernmental organizations and contacts who participated in this study. Interviews were semistructured and lasted about an hour on average. Most interviews were tape recorded and fully transcribed, then analyzed with the assistance of Atlas.ti.

15. According to MOIRA, efforts were made to sit down with the Texas Workforce Commission, but they received only a lukewarm response. Though the agency eventually sent a liaison, his presence was minimal, largely because all TWC functions are based in Austin, which is more than two hours from Houston. Efforts to involve the National Labor Relations Board also failed.

16. Involvement in JEWP is completely up to the discretion of agency directors, with no formal mandate from above. Although similar coalitions have been replicated in cities such as Dallas, Denver, and Los Angeles, all have involved significant support from local governments, the Mexican consulate, and community organizations.

17. The mobile consulate is a nationwide program that sends consular services out to surrounding communities that are too far away or otherwise isolated from central consulate offices.

18. A notable exception is wages. Several cities have passed living wage ordinances which exceed the state or federal minimums (see www.livingwagecampaign.org/index.php?id=1958).

19. In fact, as of 2006 the EEOC office in Oakland has plans to share office space with their state counterpart soon.

20. One of the most notable cases recently is that of Olivia Tamayo, who endured years of sexual harassment while employed at Harris Farms, before successfully suing the corporation in 2005, with the help of the EEOC and California Legal Rural Assistance.

21. For an excellent overview of the central labor councils in each city, see the Building Power Research Project, an initiative at Wayne State University undertaken to "document how local labor movements are developing systematic strategies for achieving regional power." Case studies have been completed for Los Angeles, San Jose, Denver, Houston, Cleveland, Seattle, and Buffalo. Reports for Atlanta, New York, North Carolina, and South Florida are forthcoming. My sincere thanks to Nari Rhee and Tom Karson, who authored the reports for San Jose and Houston, respectively, and who offered their time and conversation with me for this project.

22. The seven CTW affiliated unions include the International Brotherhood of Teamsters, the Laborers' International Union of North America, Service Employees International Union, the United Brotherhood of Carpenters and Joiners, the United Farm Workers of America, the United Food and Commercial Workers, and UNITE-HERE! (which represents hotel and restaurant workers).

23. According to the AFL-CIO website, "Change to Win local unions that are given Solidarity Charters will make per capita tax payments based on their membership to local and state AFL-CIO organizations at the rates applicable to other affiliated local unions. They will have the same rights and obligations as other affiliated local unions, including participation in governance and affairs of the state or local body, eligibility of their members to run for and hold office in the state or local body and the status and treatment of their members within the state and local body" (accessed at http://www.aflcio.org/aboutus/ns08262005.cfm).

24. See chapter 11, this volume, which discusses the role of immigrants' rights in the Change to Win split, and the evolution of the AFL-CIO's position on immigrant rights.

25. Interview with SBLC political director, April 20, 2006.

26. The group defines vulnerable workers as those who have limited proficiency in English (in Houston, particularly Hispanic and Vietnamese workers), day laborers, individuals working in risky occupations (such as residential construction, slaughterhouses, and poultry factories), health care workers, and new or returning workers.
27. Interview with SBLC organizer, March 20, 2006.
28. Based on information provided by UNITE-HERE! Local 19.
29. Despite the relative success of union organizing in key low-wage and immigrant industries, there still remains a tremendous incidence of labor rights violations. According to a 2005 U.S. Department of Labor report, the industry with the highest number of wage and hour claims is restaurants, which is also an industry that is underserved by unions. Hotel and motels follow close behind, and construction remains one of the most dangerous jobs in terms of health safety violations.

REFERENCES

AFL-CIO. 2007. "A Nation of Immigrants." Resolution 5. Accessed at http://www.aflcio.org/aboutus/thisistheaflcio/convention/2001/resolutions/upload/res5.pdf

Andersen, Ellen. 2005. *Out of the Closets and Into the Courts: Legal Opportunity Structures and Gay Rights Litigation.* Ann Arbor, Mich.: University of Michigan Press.

Bacon, David. 2000. "Immigrant Workers Ask Labor 'Which Side Are You On?'" *Working USA* 3(5): 7–18.

Byrd, Barbara, and Nari Rhee. 2006. "Building Power in the New Economy: The South Bay Labor Council." *Building Regional Power Research Project.* Detroit, Mich.: Wayne State University, Labor Studies Center. Accessed at http://www.laborstudies.wayne.edu/power/downloads/San_Jose.pdf.

Feagin, Joe. 1988. *Free Enterprise City: Houston in Political-Economic Perspective.* New Brunswick, N.J.: Rutgers University Press.

Fine, Janice. 2006. *Worker Centers: Organizing Communities at the Edge of the Dream.* Ithaca, N.Y.: Cornell University Press and the Economic Policy Institute.

Jayaraman, Sarumathi, and Immanuel Ness. 2005."Models of Worker Organizing." In *New Urban Immigrant Workforce: Innovative Models for Labor Organizing,* edited by Sarumathi Jayaraman and Immanuel Ness. Armonk, N.Y.: M.E. Sharpe.

Karson, Tom. 2006. "Confronting Houston's Demographic Shift: The Harris County AFL-CIO." Building Regional Power Research Project. Detroit, Mich.: Wayne State University, Labor Studies Center. Accessed at http://www.laborstudies.wayne.edu/power/downloads/Houston.pdf.

Lichtenstein, Nelson. 1997. *State of the Union: A Century of American Labor.* Princeton, N.J.: Princeton University Press.

McGrath, Siobhán. 2005. "A Survey of Literature Estimating the Prevalence of Employment and Labor Law Violations in the U.S." NYU School of Law Brennan Center for Justice. Accessed at http://www.brennancenter.org/dynamic/subpages/download_file_8418.pdf.

Milkman, Ruth, editor. 2000. *Organizing Immigrants: The Challenges for Unions in Contemporary California.* Ithaca, N.Y.: ILR/Cornell University Press.

———. 2006. *L.A. Story: Immigrant Workers and the Future of the U.S. Labor Movement.* New York: Russell Sage Foundation.

Rahsaan Maxwell

Chapter 5

Inclusion Versus Exclusion: Caribbeans in Britain and France

This chapter examines how national contexts influence migrant political organization dynamics. Its focus is on Caribbeans in Britain and France, who have similar migration histories as well as similar social and economic integration outcomes, but different patterns of national-level political organization. In many ways, some difference in political organization is to be expected, because there are many political, economic, and cultural differences between Britain and France likely to shape migrant organizational dynamics in the two countries. The different patterns of national-level political organization among Caribbeans in Britain and France pose an interesting puzzle, however, because they are the opposite of what one would expect.

Because British public policies are often cited as exaggerating racial and ethnic divisions, one might expect Caribbean national-level political organizations in Britain to focus on ethnic-specific and race-specific constituencies. Instead, they tend to be broadly defined and seek to represent all migrant groups. In comparison, French public policies are often cited as extremely resistant to political mobilization by ethnic and racial groups. However, it is in France that national-level political organizations have emerged among Caribbeans focusing on ethnic-specific Caribbean or race-specific black constituents.

To explain these outcomes, I analyze variation across key indicators of political presence and political weight as defined in this volume. French Caribbeans, I argue, cannot obtain significant visibility and recognition among government officials, affiliations with elected and appointed officials, involvement in governance, or the capacity to have their interests represented in public policy either as individual citizens or through existing broad-based migrant political organizations. As a result, Caribbean activists have decided to politically mobilize along ethnic and racial lines as a way of addressing the issues important to them. In comparison, Caribbeans in Britain have enjoyed more political presence and greater political weight through broad-based migrant coalitions. Therefore, Caribbeans in Britain have fewer incentives to mobilize politically along racial and ethnic lines.

CASE SELECTION PROCESS

Britain and France are useful for studying migrant political organization dynamics because they share fundamental similarities in their migration histories. At the end of World War II, Britain and France both suffered severe labor shortages as a result of wartime deaths and the need to rebuild and expand industrial capacity, which created a need for foreign labor. Thus, the large waves of postcolonial migration to Britain and France occurred at the same time during the 1950s, 1960s, and 1970s as employers in both countries actively recruited these migrants, who enjoyed special visa privileges because they were from former colonies or from territories still under colonial rule (Nanton 1999).

The composition of the migrant populations in Britain and France was also similar, heavily influenced by these colonial-era ties and special migration privileges. As Britain and France were the two largest European global imperial powers in the nineteenth and twentieth centuries, they received a diverse range of colonial and postcolonial ethnic minority migrants from the Caribbean, Africa, and Asia (Noiriel 1988; Spencer 1997). Many of the migrants who arrived in Britain and France had similar emigration incentives because they came from societies that were experiencing rapid population growth, high unemployment, and at times political instability (Castles and Miller 2003). In addition, Caribbean migrants came from societies that had been long exposed to European culture, due to more than 300 years of colonialism dating to the early 1600s.

That both Britain and France received migrants under similar conditions makes a comparison of migrant political organizations feasible. This chapter, though, explores the important differences in how Britain and France have politically incorporated migrants, which I argue can account for the variation in Caribbean national-level political organization dynamics across the two countries.

In addition to similar migration histories, Caribbeans in Britain and France share a number of common contemporary social and economic integration outcomes. The long exposure to European culture during 300 years of colonialism has meant that Caribbean migrants in Britain and France are more likely to be fluent in the host country language and to intermarry with the host country population in comparison to other migrant groups, which received minimal exposure to European culture during colonialism. Furthermore, Caribbeans in both Britain and France are less likely to engage in unfamiliar cultural and religious practices, less likely to live in ethnically segregated neighborhoods and less likely to be stigmatized as inassimilable outsiders in comparison to other migrant groups (Anselin 1990; Hiro 1991; Maxwell 2008). Economically, a significant percentage of first-generation Caribbeans in both countries has enjoyed upward mobility over time and the benefits of middle class status. However, second-generation Caribbeans in Britain and France suffer from a number of socioeconomic difficulties, including some of the highest unemployment rates in each country (Maxwell 2008). Therefore, although Caribbeans are socially integrated in comparison to other migrant groups, their economic difficulties have been an important motivation for political mobilization in both countries.

It is important to note that, despite these similarities, Caribbean migrants in Britain and France do not come from the same islands. Caribbeans in Britain come from Antigua and Barbuda, Bahamas, Barbados, Grenada, Guyana, Jamaica, St. Kitts and Nevis, St. Lucia, St. Vincent and the Grenades, and Trinidad and Tobago, whereas Caribbeans in France come from Guiana, Guadeloupe, and Martinique. Furthermore, another key difference is that while Caribbeans in Britain come from foreign countries, Caribbeans in France are domestic migrants given that Guiana, Guadeloupe, and Martinique have been French departments since 1948.[1] Nevertheless, despite these different geographical origins, the historical as well as the contemporary social and economic integration similarities among Caribbean migrants in Britain and France allow me to control for group-level variables and focus on the role of national-level contexts for shaping political organization dynamics.

RECENT POLITICAL ORGANIZATION DYNAMICS

First, it is important to define a few key terms. My definition of a political organization is one that is politically engaged, that is, involved in activities related to the formal political system, often with the intention of influencing government policies and practices. National-level organizations may also engage local governments, but to be considered a national organization they must not focus on any one local or regional territory.[2]

The first step in data collection was to identify the relevant national-level migrant political organizations in both countries. To accomplish this, I conducted more than 200 elite interviews in Britain and France.[3] I asked my subjects to name the national-level migrant political organizations in their respective countries with the most civic presence as defined in this volume: high visibility and recognition among the general population and mainstream media. There was a high level of agreement among interview subjects on which organizations had a significant civic presence. Tables 5.1 and 5.2 present the full list of national-level migrant political organizations in both countries, excluding government agencies that handle migrant issues and organizations that focus primarily on refugees and asylum seekers, along with a brief description of their activities.

These tables show a number of national-level organizations that represent Caribbean and black constituents in France but only one in Britain. In France, we find fifteen, eight of which are dedicated either to ethnic-specific Caribbean or race-specific black constituents. The Association of Metropolitan Politicians from the Caribbean (AMEDOM) is a network of elected officials that primarily offers personal and emotional support to fellow Caribbean elected officials, but is also involved in several political campaigns. CIFORDOM promotes awareness of Caribbean culture and history, participates in anti-discrimination campaigns, and sponsors social welfare programs. The Collective of DOM Citizens (CD) was founded to lobby for reduced airfares between metropolitan France and the Caribbean but has since pressured the government to better finance social services in the Caribbean, to improve access to public sector employee privileges for Caribbeans, and a number of other issues of concern to Caribbeans such as police brutality and labor market discrimination. The Committee for the March of May 23, 1998 (CM98) lobbies the government on various issues related to Caribbean history, including the passage of a law declaring slavery a crime against humanity and the inauguration of a holiday to commemorate the abolition of slavery. The Committee for the Memory of Slavery (CPME) produces reports and participates in campaigns on the commemoration of the history of slavery in France's Caribbean territories, often working with CM98. The National Federation for Overseas Migrants (FADOM) traditionally organized events to commemorate Caribbean culture and heritage but recently has been increasingly active with other Caribbean organizations to lobby the government on various issues of interest to the Caribbean community.

The two race-specific black organizations are Africagora and the Council Representing Black Associations (CRAN). Africagora was initially a business network of entrepreneurs and professionals from Africa and the Caribbean although in recent years it has also campaigned for more ethnic minority political candidates.[4] The Council Representing Black Associations (CRAN) is a recently formed organization whose aim is to become an organized interlocutor between blacks (Caribbeans and Sub-Saharan Africans) and the French government.

In addition to ethnic-specific Caribbean and race-specific political organizations, table 5.1 lists a number of broad-based organizations that seek to represent all migrant groups. The Collective Association for Liberty, Equality, Fraternity, Together, United (AC Le Feu) was founded after the urban unrest of the autumn of 2005 and is dedicated to increasing political participation and improving access to policy makers for ethnic minority migrant residents of socioeconomically disadvantaged neighborhoods across the country. The Collective of Rights and Memory (CDM) was recently founded to increase public awareness of the history of ethnic minority migrants in France and lobby the government for better treatment of ethnic minority migrant groups in contemporary society. The Indigenous People of the Republic (LI) organize public debates and events aimed at influencing public and political debate with a critical perspective on French oppression and discrimination against ethnic minority migrant groups. The International League Against Racism and Anti-Semitism (LICRA) has participated in various campaigns and supported a wide range of cases concerning discrimination since the 1930s. The Movement Against Racism and for Friendship Among People (MRAP) was created in 1949 to combat racism and discrimination and has participated in various campaigns and supported a wide range of cases concerning diverse ethnic minority migrant groups. Neither Prostitutes Nor Submissive (NPNS) is technically dedicated to combating sexism, but has primarily been led by Maghrebian women, has been closely allied with the antiracist organization SOS Racisme, and therefore has also been associated with ethnic minority migrant issues. Finally, SOS Racisme organized a number of

TABLE 5.1   *National Level Migrant Political Organizations in France, 2004*
            to 2007

Organization	Brief Description
The Collective Association for Liberty, Equality, Fraternity, Together, United (AC Le Feu)	A grassroots organization founded after the urban unrest of fall 2005 dedicated to increasing political participation and improving access to policy makers for ethnic minority migrant residents of socio-economically disadvantaged neighborhoods across the country.
Africagora	A club of entrepreneurs, professionals, and elected officials from Africa, the Caribbean, and the Pacific founded in 1999. The initial goal was to form an economic network although in recent years Africagora has also promoted its own list of political candidates and lobbied political parties to increase ethnic minority candidates.
The Association of Maghrebian Workers in France (ATMF)	Founded in 1982 to support issues of concern to Maghrebian workers, such as racism, working conditions, living conditions, immigration status, as well as political developments in the Maghreb.
Association of Metropolitan Politicians from the Caribbean (AMEDOM)	A network of elected officials that primarily offers support and advice on how to serve as a Caribbean elected official in metropolitan France, but at times also supports campaigns such as the recent debate over a new holiday to commemorate the abolition of slavery.
CIFORDOM	Founded in 1982 to promote awareness of Caribbean culture and history, to participate in anti-discrimination campaigns, and to conduct social welfare programs.
Collective of DOM Citizens (CD)	Founded in 2003 to lobby for reduced airfares between metropolitan France and the Caribbean. CD pressures the government to better finance social services in the Caribbean, to improve access to public sector employee privileges for Caribbeans, and a number of other issues such as police brutality and labor market discrimination.
Collective of Rights and Memory (CDM)	A grassroots organization recently founded to increase public awareness of the history of ethnic minority migrants in France and lobby the government for better treatment of ethnic minority migrant groups in contemporary society.

TABLE 5.1   *Continued*

Organization	Brief Description
Committee for the March of May 23, 1998 (CM98)	Founded after the Paris march of May 23, 1998 in which 40,000 Caribbeans protested discrimination. CM98 then lobbied the government on various issues, including the 2001 Taubira Law declaring slavery a crime against humanity and the new holiday to commemorate the abolition of slavery.
Committee for the Memory of Slavery (CPME)	Formed to analyze and participate in campaigns on the commemoration of the history of slavery in France's Caribbean territories.
Council of French Muslims (CFCM)	Since the 1980s there have been a number of organizations attempting to manage issues of concern to Muslims in France, the latest of which is the CFCM, for which the French government and a number of prominent Muslim leaders have been negotiating since 2002. The CFCM is now an interlocutor between Muslims and the French government for issues concerning the practice of Islam.
Council Representing Black Associations (CRAN)	Formed in 2005 with the aim of becoming an organized interlocutor between blacks (Caribbeans and Sub-Saharan Africans) and the French government.
National Federation of Overseas Migrants (FADOM)	Grassroots organization that organizes events to commemorate Caribbean culture and heritage. Recently, has been increasingly active with other Caribbean organizations to lobby the government on various issues of interest to the Caribbean community.
The Indigenous People of the Republic (LI)	Formed in 2005 by circulating a polemical text criticizing French society for being colonialist and oppressive, attracting signatures from numerous activists and sympathizers, as well as media attention. LI has also held a number of public events aimed at making French political discourse more critical of its discriminatory tendencies.
The International League Against Racism and Anti-Semitism (LICRA)	Since the 1930s LICRA has fought discrimination in France and abroad by participating in various campaigns and supporting a wide range of cases.

TABLE 5.1   *Continued*

Organization	Brief Description
The Movement Against Racism and for Friendship Among People (MRAP)	Created in 1949 to combat racism and discrimination and has participated in various campaigns and supported a wide range of cases concerning diverse ethnic and religious minorities.
Neither Prostitutes Nor Submissive (NPNS)	Created in 2002 after a Paris march protesting sexism in French society. Technically dedicated to combating sexism, but it has primarily been led by Maghrebian women, has been closely allied with the anti-racist organization SOS Racisme, and therefore has also been associated with ethnic minority issues.
SOS Racisme	Founded in 1984 after the "Beur March" of 1983 in which young French Maghrebians (beurs) and other ethnic minorities marched from Marseille to Paris to protest discrimination. SOS organized a number of prominent anti-racist events in the 1980s, continues to pursue anti-discrimination campaigns, and has been an important starting point for ethnic minority activists to enter mainstream politics.

Source: Authors' compilation.

prominent antiracist events in the 1980s, it continues to pursue anti-discrimination campaigns, and it has been an important starting point for ethnic minority activists to enter mainstream politics.

Table 5.1 also lists an ethnic-specific political organization for Maghrebian migrants and a religious-specific organization for Muslim migrants. The Association of Maghrebian Workers in France (ATMF) is involved in various issues of concern to Maghrebian workers, such as racism, working conditions, living conditions, immigration status, as well as political developments in the Maghreb. The recently formed Council of French Muslims (CFCM) is an interlocutor between Muslims and the French government for issues concerning the practice of Islam.

Table 5.2 presents information for fourteen national-level migrant political organizations in Britain and shows a sharp contrast to France in that there is only one organization dedicated to ethnic-specific Caribbean or race-specific black constituents, the West Indian Standing Conference (WISC). WISC was in part a response to violence during the summer of 1958 when Caribbeans in Nottingham and the Notting Hill section of London were attacked by groups of white men who resented their presence in Britain (Wickenden 1958, 23–35). These at-

TABLE 5.2   *National-Level Migrant Political Organizations in Britain, 2004 to 2007*

Organization	Brief Description
1990 Trust	Founded in 1990 to engage in research, policy development, government consultation, and to articulate the needs of people of African, Asian, and Caribbean descent.
Campaign Against Racism and Fascism (CARF)	Primarily a magazine documenting resistance against racism, but CARF also works with other organizations to publicize a variety of campaigns on police brutality, racial violence, and the plight of asylum seekers.
Confederation of Indian Organisations (CIO)	Established by the High Commissioner of India in 1975 to provide support services, advice, and consultancy to the numerous local South Asian organizations in the country. In addition, the CIO has worked with various government agencies to manage funding schemes for the smaller organizations.
Hindu Forum of Britain (HFB)	An umbrella organization for numerous smaller Hindu organizations. HFB conducts public policy analysis, facilitates community consultation with government bodies, assists Hindu organizations in developing capacity, and promotes activities with other religious communities.
Indian Workers Association (IWA)	The first IWA was established in Coventry in 1938 to support the Indian independence movement and was followed by numerous others across the country. In 1958 the local associations were federated into a national IWA, which now primarily focuses on labor issues, discrimination, and social, welfare, and cultural activities.
Institute of Race Relations (IRR)	Established in 1958 to conduct policy-oriented research on international race relations for the British government. In 1972 the IRR no longer focused on how racial diversity impacted the government and instead became an antiracist think tank dedicated to fighting discrimination and responding to the needs of ethnic minorities.
Islamic Human Rights Commission (IHRC)	A research and advocacy organization that focuses on religious discrimination and issues of relevance to Muslims.

TABLE 5.2 *Continued*

Organization	Brief Description
The Monitoring Group (MG)	Runs a twenty-four-hour helpline for victims of racial violence, police misconduct, and domestic violence. Also offers legal and logistical assistance for the victims while pursuing their cases. MG also trains local organizations to better assist their clients.
The Muslim Council of Britain (MCB)	An umbrella organization that coordinates activities for more than 250 smaller Muslim organizations and fights discrimination against Muslims. In recent years, MCB has become a prominent—if contested—interlocutor between Muslims and the British government.
The Muslim Parliament (TMP)	Founded in 1992 as a forum for Muslims to debate issues concerning life in Britain. TMP also lobbies the government and supports campaigns for various issues affecting Muslims in Britain and across the world.
National Assembly Against Racism (NAAR)	Formed during a 1994 campaign against a right wing British National Party political candidate. The activists from antiracist organizations, trade unions, and religious organizations then formed NAAR as a national federation of their respective constituencies to pursue antiracist campaigns and to consult the government on how public policy impacts ethnic minorities.
Operation Black Vote (OBV)	Founded in 1996 to improve the political voice of Africans, Asians, and Caribbeans in Britain. OBV registers voters, conducts policy analysis, and consults with the government on how policies will impact ethnic minorities.
Runnymede Trust (RT)	Founded in 1968 as a think tank dedicated to issues of concern for ethnic minorities.
West Indian Standing Conference (WISC)	Founded in 1958 as an umbrella organization for smaller Caribbean organizations to lobby the government on issues of concern for Caribbeans and to provide logistical support for the smaller organizations.

Source: Author's compilation.

tacks highlighted the vulnerability of Caribbean migrants and inspired a number of local and national organizations, of which WISC was one, to work toward strengthening political and legal protection for migrants in Britain. WISC became a prominent government interlocutor and lobbied for antidiscrimination legislation that was passed in the 1960s and 1970s (Sewell 1993). However, since the late 1970s, WISC has become less important both for the British government and the Caribbean population because other broad-based migrant organizations and various government agencies are seen as more effective intermediaries (Goulbourne 1990, 104). In addition, WISC's membership has dwindled as Caribbean activists are now more likely to participate in broad-based migrant political organizations. According to a director of WISC,

> once the CRE was established the government consulted less with us . . . they felt they had their one body so there was no need to consult with the community . . . in general, we have fewer resources now than we used to, cannot do the things we used to . . . in the past there was more of a mission, the first generation was more unified . . . we have a hard time attracting younger people.[5]

Although table 5.2 presents only one ethnic-specific Caribbean organization, it lists seven broad-based activist organizations that seek to represent all migrant groups. The 1990 Trust consults with the government and conducts research and analysis on how public policy will impact ethnic minority migrant groups. The Campaign Against Racism and Fascism (CARF) is a magazine about contemporary antiracist developments and works with a number of campaigns on police brutality, racial violence, and the plight of asylum seekers. The Institute of Race Relations (IRR) is an antiracist think tank conducting research of relevance to ethnic minority migrant groups. The Monitoring Group (MG) primarily runs a twenty-four-hour helpline for victims of police brutality or racial and domestic violence, but it also works with victims to pursue legal cases and lobbies the government on their behalf. The National Assembly Against Racism (NAAR) supports a wide range of anti-racist and anti-fascist campaigns and consults with the government on how policy impacts ethnic minority migrant groups. Operation Black Vote (OBV) conducts voter registration drives, policy analysis, and consults with the government on how policies will impact ethnic minority migrant groups.[6] The Runnymede Trust (RT) is a think tank dedicated to issues of concern for ethnic minority migrant groups.

Table 5.2 also lists two ethnic-specific organizations for South Asian migrants and four religious-specific organizations. The Confederation of Indian Organisations (CIO) supports smaller South Asian organizations across the country and assists them with accessing government funding. The Indian Workers Association (IWA) historically focused on labor issues and immigration rights, but is now involved in a number of campaigns related to discrimination as well as social, welfare, and cultural activities. The Islamic Human Rights Commission (IHRC) conducts research and advocacy activities for issues of relevance to British Muslims. The Muslim Council of Britain (MCB) coordinates activities for smaller Muslim organizations across the country and has become the public voice of Muslims in Britain. The Muslim Parliament (TMP) was founded as a forum to debate issues of relevance to Muslims, but also supports a number of campaigns relating to religious discrimination. For Hindus, the Hindu Forum (HFB) of Britain supports smaller Hindu organizations across the country, assists them with accessing government funding, and performs lobbying functions of its own as well.

To summarize, in Britain the only national-level ethnic minority migrant political organization (WISC) that caters to a Caribbean constituency was most prominent in the 1960s and has been relatively inactive since the mid-1970s. In comparison, eight organizations in France are dedicated either to ethnic-specific Caribbean or race-specific black constituents. Before developing my argument about levels of political presence and political weight, I first turn to academic literature on the role of identity in political organizations and show that it cannot account for outcomes among Caribbeans in Britain and France.

LOOKING FOR EXPLANATIONS: THE CURRENT LITERATURE

There is a long tradition of social science research on the conditions under which ethnic and racial identities are more or less likely to be politically mobilized. This literature can be grouped into three main arguments on the composition of ethnic and racial groups, the degree of competition for scarce resources, and the political opportunity structure.

Such research argues that similar languages, traditions, symbols, and cultural activities create common interests and meaningful bonds that facilitate political cooperation (Anderson 1991; Gellner 1983; Rabushka and Shepsle 1972). According to these arguments, we should expect ethnic-specific and race-specific political organization among migrant groups who are more likely to have practices that distinguish them from the mainstream population. However, generally speaking, Caribbeans in Britain and France are socially integrated in comparison to other migrant groups and are not likely to have substantial linguistic or cultural differentiation from the mainstream population (Anselin 1990; Hiro 1991; Maxwell 2008). Furthermore, Caribbeans in France are even less likely to retain traditional symbolic practices than their counterparts in Britain. Although Caribbeans in Britain migrated from islands that have now declared their independence, Caribbeans in metropolitan France come from territories that remain part of France. In fact, Caribbeans in France have traditionally emphasized their legal, cultural, and historical assimilation and tried to avoid being classified as an ethnic minority migrant group (Giraud 2004; Nanton 1999). Yet it is precisely among Caribbeans in France that ethnic- and race-specific political organizations have emerged. Therefore, arguments about the composition of racial and ethnic groups cannot account for the different national-level political organization dynamics among Caribbeans in the two countries.

Another strand of literature claims that ethnic- and race-specific political mobilization is more likely to emerge in situations of conflict over scarce resources. According to this logic when there are limited numbers of jobs, social welfare benefits, or access to political elites, individuals will be more likely to feel that they are in direct competition with other groups and become more likely to emphasize ethnic and racial identities in political mobilization (Fearon and Laitin 2003; Olzak 1992). These arguments are potentially persuasive because Caribbeans in both countries suffer from high unemployment rates, discrimination, and other socioeconomic difficulties that could serve as the basis for ethnic- and race-specific political organizations. However, there is no reason to believe that this competition for scarce resources is more intense in France than in Britain. For example, recent data suggest that second generation Caribbean unemployment levels range from 20 to 30 percent in both Britain and France, which is two to three times as high as the national average for young people in each country (see Maxwell 2008 for detailed data on recent socioeconomic outcomes among Caribbeans in Britain and France). Therefore, this argument about scarce resources offers minimal analytical leverage to distinguish between the different national-level political organizational dynamics among Caribbeans in Britain and France.

The third group of arguments focuses on political opportunity structures and claims that ethnic and racial categories are most likely to become politically relevant when national institutions, policies, or discourses structure social, economic, and political outcomes along ethnic lines. When applied to Britain and France this literature has traditionally argued that Britain's multicultural political opportunity structure is characterized by relatively few restrictions on ethnic minority religious and cultural practices and various public policies that explicitly use ethnic and racial categories. In comparison, France's republican political opportunity structure is characterized by the fact that ethnic and other subnational categories are considered illegitimate bases for claims in the public sphere, and government policies refuse to recognize such categories in an attempt to reduce their salience (Schnapper 1991, 1992; Soysal 1994). However, these arguments are unable to account for political organization dynamics among Caribbeans in Britain and France because according to their logic, ethnic- and race-specific political organization should be more likely to develop in Britain than in France, whereas the reverse has occurred for Caribbeans. Moreover, recent research suggests that the sharp dichotomy between multicultural Britain and republican France has been overstated and in practice both countries' political opportunity structures contain elements of each ideal type (Favell 2001; Garbaye 2005; Joppke 1999).

In summary, academic literature generally focuses on the composition of ethnic and racial groups, the degree of competition for scarce resources, or the political opportunity structure to explain the conditions under which ethnic and racial identities are more or less likely to be politically mobilized. Although each of these arguments may explain particular cases of ethnic and racial mobilization, none can account for variation among Caribbean national-level political organization dynamics in Britain and France. Therefore, I claim that an additional explanation for the role of identity in migrant political organization is necessary.

In the rest of the chapter, I develop an argument about the importance of political presence and political weight. As such, I claim that because French Caribbeans are unable to obtain enough visibility and recognition among government officials, affiliations with elected and appointed officials, involvement in governance, or the capacity to have their interests represented in public policy either as individual citizens or through existing broad-based migrant political organizations, they have decided to mobilize politically along ethnic and racial lines as a way of addressing issues. In comparison, Caribbeans in Britain have enjoyed more political presence and greater political weight through broad-based migrant coalitions. Therefore, Caribbeans in Britain have fewer incentives to politically mobilize by racial or ethnic identity.

FRANCE: A LACK OF POLITICAL PRESENCE AND WEIGHT FOR CARIBBEANS

Most national-level political organizations in France that represent ethnic-specific Caribbean or race-specific black constituents were formed in the late 1990s and early 2000s by activists who were frustrated at the inability of Caribbeans to obtain political presence and political weight either as assimilated citizens or through existing broad-based migrant organizations.

During the 1950s, 1960s, 1970s, and 1980s, many Caribbeans tried to access political influence as individual citizens of the French republic. Caribbeans were encouraged to pursue this strategy because French public discourse discourages ethnic and racial mobilization and Caribbeans' status as assimilated citizens distinguished them from other ethnic minority migrants who were discriminated against as inassimilable foreigners. In addition, Caribbeans' status as citizens granted them the rights to freely work and travel in metropolitan France, whereas foreign immigrants were often subject to bureaucratic procedures that consumed significant amounts of time, money, and energy to obtain the necessary visas. Caribbeans were also qualified for public sector jobs that were unavailable for immigrant foreigners. Furthermore, Caribbeans' eligibility to vote gave them formal access to political institutions that did not exist for immigrant foreigners. Therefore, in many respects, Caribbeans had reason to believe that it would be possible for them to assimilate in French public life as individual citizens.

Moreover, to the degree Caribbeans faced difficulties with migration and integration in metropolitan France a number of government agencies were established to assist them, which further reduced the incentive to form their own ethnic- and race-specific political organizations during the 1950s, 1960s, and 1970s. In fact, these government agencies assisted Caribbeans from the earliest stages of the migration process as the Bureau for the Migration from Overseas Departments (BUMIDOM) arranged transportation to metropolitan France, housing, job training, and job placement for French citizens from the overseas departments and territories. In addition, The National Agency for the Promotion of

Overseas Workers (ANT), the Association for Caribbean and Guyanese Workers in France (AMITAG), the Center for Aid to Overseas Citizens (CNARM), the Municipal Center for Welcome and Information for Citizens of Overseas Departments in Paris (CMAI DOM-TOM), and the General Delegate for Overseas Citizens in Paris were all government agencies that supported Caribbean integration into metropolitan French society, by offering job training and career counseling to promoting Caribbean cultural events and facilitating the development of local Caribbean cultural associations (Domenach and Picouet 1992, 86–88). All of these agencies were based on the premise that Caribbeans were eligible for government assistance as a result of their status as French citizens.

However, by the 1980s, it became clear that government agencies designed to assist Caribbean migrants would not be sufficient for promoting successful integration, especially for the second generation. Most first-generation migrants had found jobs in the 1950s and 1960s because of the strong French economy, but with the recession of the 1970s job opportunities for second-generation Caribbeans dwindled and many in the first generation began to worry about job prospects for their children.[7] Early Caribbean migrants had used their French citizenship and assimilation to avoid many of the indignities suffered by foreign immigrants. But, with the recession and increasingly competitive labor market ethnic minority migrants were particularly vulnerable to discrimination on the basis of their skin color, regardless of their citizenship status or cultural practices.[8] As a result, in the late 1970s and 1980s, a number of new Caribbean civic organizations emerged. These organizations provided recreational activities that offered young people constructive alternatives to delinquency and sponsored events that improved awareness of Caribbean culture (Beriss 2004). In addition, Caribbean political activists increasingly acknowledged that their status as assimilated citizens was not sufficient to provide political influence that could address issues of concern in the Caribbean community. However, in many respects Caribbeans were trapped because focusing on their insider status reduced their ability to claim political rights as a racial or ethnic minority even though they suffered from racial and ethnic discrimination. Longtime Caribbean activist Freddy Loyson explained how Caribbeans' assimilation actually hindered mobilization efforts: "The key to understanding Caribbean political difficulties is this, they will always tell you that you are French so you should have no problems, while in reality there are problems, and we do need help."[9]

In addition to their lack of political presence and political weight as individual citizens, Caribbean activists were also frustrated by their inability to access significant influence via the broad-based migrant organizations. In fact, a number of broad-based migrant organizations achieved a degree of political presence and political weight during the 1980s and 1990s but they were largely dominated by Maghrebians. Maghrebians have been one of the most stigmatized and economically disadvantaged ethnic minority migrants in France during the post-World War II period and as a result have been among the leading political activists for ethnic minority migrant rights. In the early 1980s, Maghrebian youth organized a series of sit-ins, hunger strikes, and demonstrations to protest the fact that they were often harassed by native whites and treated like second-class citizens despite having been born and raised in France. Maghrebian youth were then the primary organizers for the March against Racism and for Equal Rights which started with a few dozen people marching from Marseille to Paris with a series of stops for rallies in certain cities along the route. By the time the march reached Paris, the crowd had grown to over 100,000 and had attracted considerable media attention. The national media quickly labeled it the Beur March and the subsequent increase in civic activity among ethnic minority migrants became known as the Beur Movement, in reference to the term *Beur* that was becoming a slang term for second-generation Maghrebians (Bouamama 1994; Jazouli 1986).[10]

A number of broad-based national political organizations such as Convergence 84, SOS Racisme and France-Plus emerged out of the Beur Movement and fought for the rights of all ethnic minority migrant groups. However, Maghrebians tended to be the most prominent activists in these organizations. Over time, these broad-based organizations have had a number of prominent Caribbean and African leaders, but Maghrebians have been more likely to dominate the agenda. Therefore, when these organizations established connections with government officials to access funds for local development projects, the money was often dispersed to associations and projects with the goal of stabilizing young Maghrebians (Moore 2002). In addition, when the organizations developed connections with political parties and advocated for ethnic minority migrant candidates, it was more often than not Maghrebians who were supported (Garbaye 2005; Wihtol de Wenden and Leveau 2001). In fact, recent research shows that though Caribbeans and Maghrebians are both severely underrepresented among elected officials at the national, departmental, and regional levels, Maghrebians are two to three times more likely than Caribbeans to be proportionately represented among local councilors relative to their percentage of the local population (Maxwell 2008).

Frustration at their inability to access political presence and political weight either as individual citizens or through broad-based migrant organizations eventually led Caribbean activists to pursue race- and ethnic-specific organizations that could directly address the issues of the French Caribbean community. A key event that led to the formation of many of these organizations was the 1998 celebration of the 150th anniversary of the abolition of slavery in France's Caribbean colonies. The French government marked the occasion with a series of public celebrations and coordinated an interministerial commission to plan the events. However, many Caribbean activists were unhappy with the government's excessive focus on the actions of the French republic in freeing the slaves and wanted more attention on the lives of slaves themselves. Therefore, more than 200 local Caribbean organizations across the country formed the Unified Committee to Commemorate the 150th Anniversary of the Abolition of Slavery in French colonies and organized a silent march in Paris on May 23, 1998. The march was intended to highlight the needs of Caribbeans and the decision to march in silence accentuated the fact that many Caribbeans felt they had no voice in French public policy. The march was generally considered to be a success as there were approximately 40,000 participants and it generated significant publicity. After the march, organizers of the Unified Committee formed CM98 as a permanent organization which would organize an annual march on May 23 along with a week-long series of events to further increase public and government awareness of Caribbean issues.[11]

CPME was also founded in the aftermath of the 1998 march as part of the government's attempt to increase consultation with Caribbean activists creating a holiday to commemorate the abolition of slavery in France's overseas territories. The government initially proposed to celebrate on April 27 to commemorate the day in 1848 on which the law abolishing slavery was signed in metropolitan France. However, Caribbean activists argued that by the time the law was actually applied in the Caribbean colonies the slaves had already rebelled and liberated themselves from the white plantation owners. Therefore, activists wanted a date for the holiday that would better honor the memory of the slaves. CPME's role was to liaise between the government and the Caribbean community and create visibility and recognition for Caribbean political organizations that previously had not existed at the national level (Comité pour la mémoire de l'esclavage 2005).[12]

CIFORDOM and FADOM were formed before the 1998 celebration of the 150th anniversary of the abolition of slavery, but gained new civic presence and new levels of grassroots support with the emergence of CD, CM98, CPME, and the larger debate about commemorating slavery. According to one parliamentary assistant, "Caribbeans have done a magnificent job with this issue of commemorating slavery, before you never heard anything about these issues, but they have really pushed it—and their organizations—into the mainstream."[13] CM98, CPME, CIFORDOM, and FADOM are thus a direct response to the fact that Caribbean activists were frustrated with their lack of visibility and recognition among government officials, their inability to develop significant affiliations with elected and appointed officials, and their inability to have their interests represented during public policy decisions. They believed that mobilization along ethnic-specific lines would better advance their concerns.

Caribbean activists were also inspired by the ability of other groups to obtain political presence and political weight through aggressive demonstrations and prominence in the broad-based migrant organizations. In fact, the Caribbean march of 1998 was in many ways modeled on the Beur march fifteen years earlier. According to one of the organizers, "the march of May 23, 1998 was supposed to be our Beur march, it was supposed to bring us the same amount of attention and show that we needed help too."[14] The founder of CD was directly inspired by the ability of Maghrebians to obtain visibility and recognition among government officials as well as affiliations and connections with elected and appointed officials in the broad-based migrant organizations. He concluded that if Caribbeans wanted to achieve the same results they needed ethnic-specific political organizations that would be more strident about their issues: "There are more Maghrebian politicians because political parties realize they need to put Maghrebians on their lists, but people from the DOM-TOM Caribbean have not been recognized . . . people are more afraid of Maghrebians, they are more ethnically organized . . . and they are easier to organize . . . but the Caribbeans really need to make more noise."[15] The founder of CD was recently appointed Minister of Equal Opportunities for Overseas French Citizens by the François Fillon government, which is evidence that his new mobilization strategies are working.

Similarly, Africagora and CRAN were formed to increase the political presence and political weight for black people in France as the organizers felt blacks had a weak role in governance and a limited capacity to have their interests represented in public policy either as individual citizens or through the broad-based migrant organizations. The leaders of CRAN have been explicit about their goal of creating an official organization to represent the interests of black people in negotiations with the French government. For some people, these goals are radical and threaten the universal values of the French republic that view citizens first and foremost as individuals, not as members of ethnic and racial groups. However, the organizers of CRAN respond that they have resorted to racial political organization because the current mainstream institutions have failed black people in France: "This is the birth of the French black community . . . we need this because lack of organization and fragmentation was always the big problem holding back political influence . . . but CRAN is not social, we're not focused on parties, CRAN is purely political, to fight discrimination and to advance the place of blacks in France . . . there is a growing energy, the issues are becoming more public, discrimination will be less and less possible."[16]

The founder of Africagora has a similar response to critiques that his organization seeks a role in public policy solely because of the race of their members. "The parties tell me that they will not be pressured into quotas for minority candidates, but I tell them we don't want quotas. They already have a quota of zero! We just want our issues to be heard but in the end it is impossible without enough force, votes, people . . . so we have formed our own list, registration drives, it's the only way to make people aware of our issues."[17]

In summary, Caribbeans in France have been encouraged to form ethnic and race-specific national political organizations because they were unable to access visibility and recognition among government officials, affiliation with elected and appointed officials, a role in governance, or the capacity to have their interests represented in public policy either as assimilated citizens or through broad-based migrant organizations. So, as race and ethnicity have become sources of political disadvantage for Caribbeans in France, those identities have become more likely to be mobilized by national political organizations.

BRITAIN: POLITICAL PRESENCE AND WEIGHT IN BROAD-BASED MIGRANT COALITIONS

Caribbeans have incentives to participate in broad-based national-level political organizations in Britain, the result of more than forty years of mobilization by a variety of migrant pressure groups that have produced both the institutions and the precedent to access significant political presence and political weight.

During their first years after arriving, in the late 1940s and 1950s, many migrants in Britain were focused on finding lodgings and stable employment. At that time, the main form of migrant organization was local and focused on social welfare assistance or cultural activities (Hiro 1991). Migrant political organizations that engaged national level politics emerged a bit later, in the late 1950s and early 1960s, and largely in response to two key issues. The first was racial violence and the sense that British authorities would not adequately protect migrants. After various scattered incidents of racial violence during the late 1940s and early 1950s, the issue received broader national attention during the summer of 1958, when groups of white men attacked Caribbean migrants in London and Nottingham. Then, in 1959, Caribbean migrant Kelso Cochrane was killed in a racially motivated attack for which the far right Union Movement organization claimed responsibility, though no arrests were ever made (Ken Gardner, "Britain's Biggest Bully Unmasked." *Sunday People*, September 24, 1961). The second issue was the 1962 Commonwealth Immigrants Act, which restricted travel and work access to Britain for migrants from the Commonwealth by requiring them to obtain a visa. Together, the highly publicized racial violence and the increasingly strict immigration legislation inspired migrant activists to become more involved in national politics to ensure that their interests were better represented (Shukra 1998).

As a result, several ethnic-specific and broad-based migrant political organizations emerged in British national politics during the 1960s. The two largest were Caribbeans and South Asians. For Caribbeans, WISC was the most prominent national-level political organization. For South Asians, it was IWA. In addition, a broad-based coalition of activists formed the Campaign Against Racial Discrimination (CARD) in 1964 in an attempt to lobby the government as one unified ethnic minority migrant lobby. Together WISC, IWA, and CARD were all active in lobbying the government on antidiscrimination legislation, including the initial Race Relations Act in 1965 (Shukra 1998, 10–25). Shortly after that legislation, CARD was officially disbanded due to internal divisions. Many of its activists, however, remained involved in WISC, IWA, and other organizations and were consulted by the government during debates for the following Race Relations Acts of 1968 and 1976. The 1976 act was especially important because it established a broad definition of discrimination as receiving unfavorable treatment on the basis of racial difference regardless of intention. This definition gave significant powers to the courts to punish discrimination offenders. The 1976 act also developed local race relations councils that served as intermediaries between migrant groups and local government. Finally, it established the Commission for Racial Equality (CRE), which had a broad mandate to work toward reducing discrimination, to issue codes of good practice for training employers, and to investigate complaints of discrimination with the power to eventually bring them to court (Bleich 2003; Goulbourne 1998). Migrant political organizations were not necessarily the most important lobby during the formulation of this legislation, given that the debates were largely conducted internally among members of the government (Spencer 1997). However, the process did establish a precedent of government consultation with migrant activists, an important political presence and weight for the nascent organizations. In addition, after the passage of these three acts, there was an important legal framework to exploit in the upcoming years and decades.

One area in which the race relations acts and the race relations councils had an immediate impact was local politics. The acts and the race relations councils gave migrant activists new tools to mobilize for better schools, access to better quality public housing, more rights in the workplace, and access to special provisions for their religious practices, all of which were often directly relevant for local politics. The councils were also an important point of entry for many ethnic minority migrant activists, who leveraged their involvement in those race relations councils to be elected as local councilors in the late 1970s and early 1980s (Garbaye 2005; Maxwell 2008). Furthermore, in the 1970s, ethnic minority migrants began to vote in greater numbers and become more involved in political parties, especially the Labour Party, which meant that it was increasingly important for white candidates to at least pay lip service to the needs of ethnic minority migrant communities.

However, despite the increase in local level political presence, many migrant activists felt they lacked substantial power and influence in mainstream political decisions. Therefore, in the early 1980s, a group of activists in the Labour Party decided to campaign for an autonomous section within the party that would be known as the Labour Party Black Section (LPBS). The struggle to form the LPBS faced a number of difficulties, both among the migrant activists themselves and in obtaining official recognition from the central Labour Party leadership. The main goal for LPBS activists was to pressure the party into supporting more ethnic minority migrant candidates (Layton-Henry 1985). Ethnic minority migrant activists disagreed, however, about the best way to achieve their goals and whether they needed complete freedom and autonomy in determining candidate short lists or should be willing to cede authority to the central party leadership in exchange for official recognition (Shukra 1998, 71–73). The LPBS was never officially recognized but some of the ethnic minority migrants who actively campaigned for it were elected local councilors in the 1980s, which helped increase the political resources available to migrant activists. During the 1987 general election, LPBS activists successfully lobbied for the party to support a number of ethnic minority migrant MP candidates, four of whom were elected as the first nonwhite ethnic minority MPs (two Caribbean, one Indian, and one African) in the post–World War II era.

The 1987 general election was an important example of success for the LPBS and ethnic minority migrant political organization in general, but because of internal divisions it also led to the end of the LPBS. Although LPBS activists had been able to increase the number of ethnic minority migrant candidates chosen by the Labour Party, there were allegations that the candidates were pressured by the party leadership to distance themselves from the LPBS once the campaign began. In addition, a Caribbean Labour candidate for Nottingham East was deselected by the party leadership after she publicly described the Labour Party as racist. Furthermore, several prominent members of the LPBS, including three of the candidates who would then be elected MP, released a public statement saying that LPBS should show loyalty to the party and accept its decision to deselect the Nottingham East candidate (Shukra 1998, 73–74). LPBS decline continued after the election as the central Labour Party leadership used its power to remove ethnic minority migrant candidates chosen by local LPBS activists in 1988 and 1989 parliamentary by-elections and replace them with white candidates. Moreover, the new ethnic minority migrant MPs and other LPBS moderates increasingly stressed loyalty to the party and publicly disagreed with the more radical members of the LPBS (Shukra 1998, 75–76).

However, although the LPBS was never officially recognized by the Labour Party and its activist engagement dwindled after the 1987 election, it still played an important role in opening the door for ethnic minority migrants to become elected at the national level. Since that election, all mainstream political parties have increasingly supported ethnic minority migrant candidates for office. After the by-election of 2007 there were fifteen Caribbean, South Asian, and African MPs. That meant that Caribbeans had 67 percent of the number of MPs they would need to be proportionately represented and that South Asians had 43 percent. These numbers indicate that though ethnic minority migrant groups in Britain are still underrepresented among MPs, they have nonetheless been more successful than in France, where Caribbeans have 33 percent and Maghrebians have 0 percent of the deputies they would need to be proportionately represented (Maxwell 2008). Furthermore, on the local level, ethnic minority migrant groups in Britain have been even more successful. Research has shown that Caribbeans, and especially South Asians, are increasingly likely to be proportionally represented or overrepresented on local councils in municipalities with large ethnic minority communities (Le Lohé 1998, 86–88; Maxwell 2008).

This increase in ethnic minority migrant elected officials is the result of numerous factors, including an increase in ethnic minority political participation through voting and various local ethnic-specific, race-specific, religion-specific, and broad-based migrant pressure groups. However, the LPBS was the high-profile political organization that contributed to the first breakthrough among national-level elected officials. Its broad-based ethnic minority migrant coalition set an important precedent. Although the word *black* was included in its name and might appear to be a race-specific term to contemporary readers, in Britain during the 1980s, *black* was a generic political term used to refer to all nonwhite ethnic minorities.[18] LPBS lobbied for diverse ethnic minority candidates (as evidenced by the Caribbean, South Asian, and African MPs elected in 1987), and in many ways that broad-based coalition set the tone for national-level ethnic minority migrant political organizations in the 1990s and beyond. Additionally, the success of LPBS in promoting ethnic minority migrant candidates helped facilitate the rising levels of political presence and political weight for migrant political organizations.

A number of the contemporary broad-based migrant organizations listed in table 5.2 (NAAR, 1990 Trust, OBV, Runnymede Trust) are both active in lobbying the government and regularly consulted by government officials on how potential policy changes will (or might) affect ethnic minority communities. They therefore have a significant amount of political presence and political weight in contemporary Britain. This political presence and political weight builds on the previous decades of political mobilization by LPBS, CARD, and others. In some respects this influence is the result of the institutional legacy established by the

Race Relations Acts of 1965, 1968, 1976, and the 2000 Amendment Act, which enables ethnic minority organizations to file official complaints against people who discriminate, complaints that can lead to a CRE investigation or a lawsuit. The 2000 Amendment Act also bolstered Britain's antidiscrimination legislation by requiring public authorities to actively monitor their racial equality progress by producing race equality statements and schemes.[19] An activist for OBV in London explains how this legal protection is an important source of power for his organization: "the Race Relations Act Amendment gives us legal backing and means that people have to be responsive. We wouldn't be able to do what we do without it."[20]

In addition, it is important to note that Labour governments have offered critical support for ethnic minority migrant activists over the years. Most elected ethnic minority officials are with the Labour Party and it was Labour that passed key legislation such as the 2000 Race Relations Act Amendment. According to an OBV activist, "since Labour returned, equalities have been mainstreamed by Jack Straw as home secretary, and it's gotten to the point that even if the Conservatives return to power they won't be able to take us away from the action, all the systems are in place thanks to Labour."[21]

However, in addition to the institutional legacy and the support of the Labour Party, the political presence and political weight enjoyed by contemporary national ethnic minority migrant organizations is reinforced by their capacity to maintain broad-based coalitions of supporters. Many—such as NAAR, 1990 Trust, and OBV—were started by individuals who were politically active in organizations like the LPBS during the 1980s, but now have the political savvy as well as the connections to establish independent organizations capable of engaging mainstream policy networks (Shukra et al. 2004). In addition, leaders of the new generation of organizations (established since the 1990s) consciously focus on maintaining a broad base of support—ethnic, racial, religious, ideological, and other—to avoid the internal divisions that plagued CARD in the 1960s and LPBS in the 1980s. As grassroots organizations with limited funding these organizations realize that their best hope of maintaining political presence and political weight is to demonstrate that they represent a large constituency of ethnic minority migrant voters. According to the president of the 1990 Trust, "we are a UK-wide alliance and we want to change the discourse around race . . . the government only responds if they think you have massive public behind you, so we have been up and down the country, organizing demonstrations, connecting with communities, letting people know what's been happening in their name. . . . NGO's influence is in numbers, but we do have an influence, even if it's a slow drip process."[22]

Similarly, the coordinator of NAAR explains that although ethnic minority migrant organizations have made tremendous strides in their visibility and influence, a broad base of support is necessary to maintain and increase their level of political weight: "It can be difficult, but we try to be as broad, comprehensive, and as wide-reaching as possible, because that is how you attract the attention of politicians. . . . Labour is helpful because we no longer need to get in the street and we can meet directly with Labour MPs to discuss our issues, but they still have to be convinced that you have the support of lots of people."[23]

Thus ethnic minority migrant organizations in Britain now enjoy visibility and recognition among government officials, organizational affiliations with elected and appointed officials, a legitimate role in governance, and the ability to have their interests represented in public policy decisions. This is the result of more than forty years of political mobilization and legal support from a number of institutions. It is reinforced by the ability of political activists to maintain broad-based coalitions. Because of all this, Caribbeans in Britain have ample incentive to avoid the ethnic- or race-specific mobilization that has emerged in France, where Caribbeans feel excluded from mainstream politics. It also helps explain why WISC has found it difficult to engage Caribbean activists: the access and influence of the organizations make them more attractive than WISC.

It is important to note that broad-based ethnic minority migrant political coalitions in Britain are not always easy to maintain. Further, in recent years, increasing evidence has indicated that Muslims in Britain feel the need to form religion-specific political organizations because of religious discrimination and religious issues that are not adequately addressed by the more general ethnic minority migrant political organizations (Modood 2005; Statham 1999). Nonetheless, it appears that the lack of Caribbean ethnic- or race-specific national political organizations is best explained by their ability to access political presence and political weight through broad-based coalitions of ethnic minority migrant groups.

CONCLUSION

In exploring the importance of national contexts for ethnic minority migrant political organization dynamics, then, we see that Caribbeans in France are unable to secure visibility and recognition among government officials, affiliations with elected and appointed officials, a role in governance, and the capacity to have their interests represented in public policy, either as individual citizens or through broad-based migrant organizations. As a result, they have decided to politically mobilize along ethnic and racial lines to address issues of concern. In comparison, their counterparts in Britain have enjoyed more political presence and greater political weight through broad-based migrant coalitions. The capability of these coalitions to do so is rooted in institutional support and several decades of national and local ethnic minority migrant mobilization, both ethnic- and race-specific and broad-based. However, this success leaves Caribbeans in contemporary Britain with fewer political incentives to mobilize racially and ethnically.

This analysis has several implications for our understanding of migrant political organizations. It shows that national contexts can be important in shaping the dynamics of migrant political organization, which suggests that further cross-national research should be conducted. It also suggests that national institutions are important not only for the form they take but also for their level of performance. This focus on institutional performance is in line with recent research on ethnic mobilization more generally, which shows that there is less violent protest in countries that offer more political rights to racial and ethnic minorities (Olzak 2006, 9–10). Similarly, my analysis complements that in chapter 6 of this volume, which shows that government policies about migrant cultural rights in the Netherlands and Germany have important ramifications for organizations dynamics among Turkish migrants in both countries.

Last, this chapter also has implications for understanding ethnic minority political organization in the United States. African American political organizations gained rising levels of political presence and political weight in the decades following the civil rights struggle. It remains to be seen, however, as the number of Asians and Latinos increases in the upcoming decades, whether broad-based coalitions can emerge or whether more narrow ethnic- and race-specific mobilization will dominate. In the end, much is likely to depend on which option provides the greatest political presence and political weight.

The research for this chapter was made possible through funding from the Chateaubriand Fellowship awarded by the Embassy of France in the United States, the Graduate Division of the University of California, Berkeley, and the NSF/UC Diversity Initiative for Graduate Study in the Social Sciences (UC-DIGSSS). The author would like to thank Neil Abrams, Matthew Kroenig, two anonymous reviewers, and the editors and other contributors to this volume for comments on earlier versions of the chapter.

NOTES

1. An additional source of Caribbean migrants in France is Haiti. However, Haitians are not included in this analysis because of significant differences in their historical relationship with France in comparison to migrants from Guiana, Guadeloupe, and Martinique. Most notably, Haitians rebelled against French colonial rule in 1791 and became an independent nation in 1804, and Guiana, Guadeloupe, and Martinique remain part of the French republic.
2. This chapter does not claim to be an exhaustive study of migrant organizations in Britain and France. It focuses on national political organizations despite the numerous local migrant political organizations in each country. Local organizations are important for a comprehensive understanding of migrant politics, but are beyond the scope of this chapter. There are also numerous migrant civic organizations in each country that provide community services such as cultural, sporting, and social activities. They too are beyond the scope of this chapter.
3. I conducted 224 interviews in Britain and France between September 2004 and July 2007 with politicians (14 percent), bureaucrats (14 percent), activists and community workers (58 percent), professors, journalists, and other experts (9 percent), and an assortment of individuals including business people and young people (5 percent). The subjects were chosen through purposive snowball sampling aimed at finding people involved in ethnic minority migrant politics.
4. Technically, Africagora also reaches out to migrants from the Pacific, although they are primarily black migrants from the South Pacific.

5. William Trant, director of West Indian Standing Conference (London), interview, September 15, 2005.
6. It is important to note that the word *black* is often used in Britain to refer to all non-white ethnic minority migrant groups while in France it refers to racial groups descended from the Caribbean and Sub-Saharan Africa. Therefore, though the British organization Operation Black Vote may use the word *black* in its name, the intended consistency includes all nonwhite ethnic minority migrant groups.
7. Recent data suggest that the unemployment gap across Caribbean generations remains significant. According to the 1999 census, the unemployment rate for native whites was 11.5 percent, and for first-generation Caribbeans it was 10.6 percent. However, for second-generation Caribbeans, it was 32.5 percent (1999 Population Census; INSEE 2003).
8. For example, a Caribbean entrepreneur in his forties explains how he became increasingly aware of the salience of his skin color: "before people thought France was better than other places, the country of human rights and all, but now we realize that is not the case . . . it is difficult if you have a foreign sounding name, or if you have a darker skin color, you are not judged by your capacities, doesn't matter if you are French, Caribbean, African, or Arab, all they see is the skin color" (Jocelyn Moradel, entrepreneur in Sarcelles, interview, June 19, 2006). In addition, recent research presents evidence of white French employers who openly admit that skin color is an important criterion in their hiring decisions (SOS Racisme 2005, 7–10).
9. Freddy Loyson, interview, August 3, 2006.
10. A number of theories explain the origins of the term Beur to refer to second-generation Maghrebians in France but the most common is that it is an inversion of the French word Arabe (Arab).
11. Tony Mango, member of CM98, interview, March 2005.
12. Choosing a date for the holiday turned out to be a complicated process because Caribbean activists themselves were divided on what date would be best for honoring the slaves. Some argued for May 23 in honor of the day on which the first slaves were free in Martinique and the day of the annual CM98 march. Others advocated either May 27, the day slaves were free in Guadeloupe, or August 10, the day slaves were free in Guiana. The French government eventually chose May 10, the day on which the 2001 law declaring slavery to be a crime against humanity was passed, as a compromise and a concession to pressure from CD, CPME, CIFORDOM, CM98, FADOM and various local groups (Béatrice Gurrey and Jean-Baptiste de Montvalon, "M. Chirac invite la France à assumer toute son histoire" ["Mr. Chirac Invites France to Assume All of its History"], *Le Monde*, January 31, 2006).
13. Eros Sana, parliamentary assistant to Alima Boumediene-Thiery, interview, June 20, 2006.
14. Tony Mango, member of CM98, interview, March 2005.
15. Patrick Karam, founder of CD, interview, January 31, 2005.
16. Pap N'Diaye, organizer of CRAN, interview, February 25, 2005.
17. Dogad Dogui, president and founder of Africagora, interview, July 18, 2005.
18. It is important to note that though the LPBS was a broad-based political organization that lobbied for issues relating to all ethnic minority migrant groups, at times some South Asian members did voice concern that they were not adequately represented within the LPBS and would benefit from political organization more explicitly focused on South Asian concerns (Sewell 1993, 113–15).
19. More on the acts is available online at http://www.opsi.gov.uk/ACTS/acts2000/

20000034.htm and, for the 2003 changes, at http://www.opsi.gov.uk/si/si2003/20031626.htm.
20. Mohammed Kebbay, policy coordinator for Black Londoners Forum, a subdivision of Operation Black Vote, interview, August 11, 2005.
21. Ashok Viswanatham, co-founder of Operation Black Vote, interview, September 22, 2005.
22. Karen Chouhon, president of 1990 Trust, interview, September 8, 2005.
23. Milena Buynum, coordinator of NAAR, interview, September 2, 2005.

REFERENCES

Anderson, Benedict. 1991. *Imagined Communities*. London: Verso.
Anselin, Alain. 1990. *L'émigration antillaise en France: La troisième île* [*Caribbean Emigration to France: The Third Island*]. Paris: Éditions Karthala.
Beriss, David. 2004. *Black Skins, French Voices: Caribbean Ethnicity and Activism in Urban France*. Boulder, Colo.: Westview Press.
Bleich, Erik. 2003. *Race Politics in Britain and France: Ideas and Policymaking since the 1960s*. New York: Cambridge University Press.
Bouamama, Saïd. 1994. *Dix ans de marche des Beurs* [*Ten Years of the Beur March*]. Paris: Desclée de Brouwer.
Castles, Stephen, and Mark Miller. 2003. *The Age of Migration: International Population Movement in the Modern World*. New York: Guilford Press.
Comité pour la mémoire de l'esclavage. 2005. *Mémoires de la traite négrière, de l'esclavage et de leurs abolitions: Rapport à Monsieur le Premier Ministre* [*Memories of the Slave Trade, Slavery, and its Abolition: Report to the Prime Minister*]. Paris: Editions La Découverte.
Domenach, Hervé, and Michel Picouet. 1992. *La dimension migratoire des Antilles* [*The Migratory Dimension of the Caribbean*]. Paris: Economica.
Favell, Adrian. 2001. "Integration policy and integration research in Europe: a review and critique." In *Citizenship Today: Global Perspectives and Practices*, edited by T. Alexander Aleinikoff and Doug Klusmeyer. Washington: Brookings Institute and the Carnegie Endowment for International Peace.
Fearon, James and David Laitin. 2003. "Ethnicity, Insurgency, and Civil War." *American Political Science Review* 97(1): 75–90.
Garbaye, Romain. 2005. *Getting Into Local Power: The Politics of Ethnic Minorities in British and French Cities*. Malden, Mass.: Blackwell Publishing.
Gellner, Ernest. 1983. *Nations and Nationalism*. Ithaca, N.Y.: Cornell University Press.
Giraud, Michel. 2004. "The Antillese in France: Trends and Prospects." *Ethnic and Racial Studies* 27(4): 622–40.
Goulbourne, Harry. 1990. "The Contribution of West Indian Groups to British Politics." In *Black Politics in Britain*, edited by Harry Goulbourne. Aldershot, Hampshire, UK: Avesbury.
———. 1998. *Race Relations in Britain Since 1945*. New York: St. Martin's Press.
Hiro, Dilip. 1991. *Black British, White British: A History of Race Relations in Britain*. London: Grafton Books.
Institut National de la Statistique et des Études Économiques (INSEE). 2003. Longitudinal Demographic Study. Paris: INSEE.
Jazouli, Adil. 1986. *L'Action collective des jeunes maghrébins de France* [*Collective Action by Young Maghrebians in France*]. Paris: L'Harmattan.

Joppke, Christian. 1999. *Immigration and the Nation-state: The United States, Germany, and Great Britain.* Oxford: Oxford University Press.

Layton-Henry, Zig. 1985. "The Labour Party and 'Black Sections'." *New Community,* 12(1): 173–78.

Le Lohé, Michel. 1998. "Ethnic Minority Participation and Representation in the British Electoral System." In *Race and British Electoral Politics,* edited by Shamit Saggar. London: University College Press.

Maxwell, Rahsaan. 2008. "Tensions and Tradeoffs: Ethnic Minority Integration in Britain and France." Ph.D. dissertation, University of California, Berkeley.

Modood, Tariq. 2005. *Multicultural Politics: Racism, Ethnicity, and Muslims in Britain.* Minneapolis, Minn.: University of Minnesota Press.

Moore, Damian. 2002. *Ethnicité et politique de la ville en France et en Grande-Bretagne* [*Ethnicity and Urban Regeneration Policy in France and Great Britain*]. Paris: L'Harmattan.

Nanton, Philip. 1999. "Migration Dynamics: Great Britain and the Caribbean." *Review* 22(4): 449–70.

Noiriel, Gérard. 1988. *Le creuset français: Histoire de l'immigration XIXe-XXe siècles* [*The French Crucible: The History of Immigration in the 19th and 20th Centuries*]. Paris: Éditions de Seuil.

Olzak, Susan. 1992. *The Dynamics of Ethnic Competition and Conflict.* Stanford, Calif.: Stanford University Press.

———. 2006. *The Global Dynamics of Ethnic and Racial Mobilization.* Stanford, Calif.: Stanford University Press.

Rabushka, Alvin, and Kenneth Shepsle. 1972. *Politics in Plural Societies: A Theory of Democratic Instability.* Columbus, Ohio: Charles Merrill.

Schnapper, Dominique. 1991. *La France de l'intégration: sociologie de la nation en 1990* [*The France of Integration: The Nation's Sociology in 1990*]. Paris: Gallimard.

———. 1992. *L'Europe des immigrés* [*Immigrant Europe*]. Paris: François Bourin.

Sewell, Terri. 1993. *Black Tribunes: Black Political Participation in Britain.* London: Lawrence and Wishart.

Shukra, Kalbir. 1998. *The Changing Pattern of Black Politics in Britain.* London: Pluto Press.

Shukra, Kalbir, Les Back, Azra Khan, Michael Keith, and John Solomos. 2004. "Black Politics and the Web of Joined-up Governance: Compromise, Ethnic Minority Mobilization, and the Transitional Public Sphere." *Social Movement Studies* 3(1): 31–50.

SOS Racisme. 2005. *Rapport d'analyse des affaires récentes de discriminations à l'embauche poursuivies par SOS Racisme* [*Analytical Report of the Recent Incidents of Discrimination in Hiring Pursued by SOS Racisme*]. Paris: SOS Racisme.

Soysal, Yasemin. 1994. *Limits of Citizenship: Migrants and Post-National Membership in Europe.* Chicago, Ill.: Chicago University Press.

Spencer, Ian. 1997. *British Immigration Policy Since 1939: The Making of Multi-racial Britain.* London: Routledge.

Statham, Paul. 1999. "Political Mobilization by Minorities in Britain: Negative Feedback of 'Race Relations'?" *Journal of Ethnic and Migration Studies* 25(4): 597–626.

Wickenden, James. 1958. *Colour in Britain.* London: Oxford University Press for the Institute of Race Relations.

Wihtol de Wenden, Catherine, and Rémy Leveau. 2001. *La beurgeoisie. Les trois âges de la vie associative issue de l'immigration* [*The Beur-geoisie: Three Generations of Immigration Community Organizations*]. Paris: CNRS Editions.

Floris Vermeulen and Maria Berger

Chapter 6

Civic Networks and Political Behavior: Turks in Amsterdam and Berlin

Immigrant organizations play a central role in the political behavior of immigrants in host societies. Local organizations often serve as a bridge between local authorities and immigrant constituencies, providing authorities with access to the immigrant communities and representing collective interests of immigrants. The organizing process of immigrants is therefore of particular importance to understanding the political behavior and political positions of immigrant communities.

Meindert Fennema and Jean Tillie (1999, 2001; Fennema 2004; Tillie 2004) have suggested that immigrant groups with a relatively high number of ethnic organizations, which are well connected through a dense network, can be characterized as more civic than those with fewer organizations and fewer networks. Networks among immigrant organizations are critical to a civic community, primarily because they create channels for communication. This process of community building is based on an accumulation of trust among organizations, achieved through the communication channels and an exchange of norms and values (Fennema and Tillie 2001). Fennema and Tillie also assumed that social trust among ethnic communities is carried over into a sense of trust in local political institutions, but only if immigrant community leaders in the ethnic elite are adequately integrated in the local political system.

The basic idea here is that the greater the number of interconnected organizations an immigrant group has, the more this group can be considered civic. A subsequent question is whether, within more civic immigrant groups, immigrants will also prove to be more politically active on the individual level. Fennema and Tillie's study of immigrant groups in Amsterdam seemed to suggest this relationship: of all the city's immigrant groups, Turks have established the densest and most extended network of organizations and have proved the most politically active group of immigrants (Fennema and Tillie 1999, 2001).

This chapter takes on these ideas by looking at the influence of the host state on the immigrant organizing process, and seeks to learn how immigrant organizing affects the political behavior of individual immigrants. The focus here is on Turkish organizations in Amsterdam and Berlin from 1970 to 2000. This was the period during which a Turkish organizational structure first emerged in both cities and simultaneously developed, albeit in different ways. In the early 1980s, the Netherlands implemented a multicultural regime that was meant to integrate the growing immigrant population: newcomers could obtain Dutch citizenship with relative ease and ethnic minorities' right to maintain their cultural identities was recognized. By contrast, Germany's approach could be characterized as one of exclusion: by making naturalization difficult, immigrants and their descendants were denied access to the political community and, in general, little appreciation was shown for cultural diversity (Koopmans and Statham 2000). After 2000, the political environment for the Turkish communities in both cities changed significantly. Amsterdam witnessed a multicultural backlash, as did the rest of the Netherlands. In Berlin, multicultural practices slowly became institutionalized in local integration policies (Vermeulen and Stotijn 2007).[1] This analysis will also examine the relationship between degrees of group civicness and the political behavior of individual Turkish immigrants in Amsterdam and in Berlin.

We first analyze the impact of different policies and institutional environments on the Turkish organizing process in Amsterdam and in Berlin. We find that Turks in Amsterdam have established a relatively high number of organizations compared with those in Berlin. Amsterdam's Turks have also established a more civic associational community: the network structure of Turkish organizations in Amsterdam is characterized by numerous horizontal ties, as measured by interlocking directorates among board members. By contrast, Berlin's organizational structure is more ideologically polarized and hierarchical: few powerful organizations are included and extreme ideological organizations are excluded. In other words, different host state environments have produced divergent Turkish organizational landscapes.

We then examine whether differences in organizational networks affect political participation and political influence, demonstrating how Turkish organizations in Amsterdam have had more opportunities to influence policy making and how they seem to be better incorporated in the local political system. One example is that many Amsterdam politicians of Turkish descent have been active board members in at least one of the many local Turkish organizations.

Our research also shows that, at the individual level, membership in Turkish organizations has a positive influence on the degree of political participation by individual Turks in their host societies. This is true in both cities. Turks who are active in Turkish organizations are more likely to respond proactively to political issues at the national level.[2] However, in contrast to our expectations going into this project, and those of the literature, we did not find a necessary relationship between the degree of group civicness and individual political activity. Although Amsterdam has a more civic Turkish community than Berlin does, based on the number and ties of Turkish organizations, Turks in Amsterdam prove less politically active on an individual basis. It seems that a higher degree of group inclusion in Amsterdam relieves the city's Turkish organizations from a duty to mobilize their ethnic constituency. Turks' inclusion came not as the result of ethnic mobilization, but as a by-product of Dutch institutions and policies. Indeed, perhaps because their organizations and leaders are more incorporated in the political system than their counterparts in Berlin, Amsterdam's Turkish immigrants have had fewer incentives as individuals to become politically active.

Turkish immigrants in Berlin have had, perhaps, more reasons to be politically active. They, along with their organizations, have had to face a greater struggle to become politically incorporated than their counterparts in Amsterdam. Because Berlin's Turkish organizations do not have access to the local political system, there is greater demand for a politically active community that will work to provide them with additional tools for access. We show that more Turks in Berlin are members of Turkish organizations than Turks in Amsterdam, and that it is the hierarchical network of organizations in Berlin that seems to enhance ethnic mobilization.

Still, it is worth noting that Amsterdam's Turks seemed more inclined to trust the political system than those in Berlin, which is also what Fennema and Tillie's research would anticipate. Our research endeavors to provide an answer for these different patterns of political participation and political trust by pointing to the relatively high degree of Turkish organizations that are incorporated in Amsterdam's political system. In Berlin, Turkish organizations contend with being more detached from the policy makers in their host state, a distance that enables them to act with greater independence and autonomy, but also a distance that encourages Berlin's Turks and their organizations to be more distrustful toward their city politicians. This analysis evokes Rahsaan Maxwell's findings (chapter 5, this volume) from his study of ethnic Caribbean political organizations in Britain and France: the inclusion or the exclusion of immigrant organizations in the political system plays a large role in motivating their strategies. Seeking to understand the political behavior of immigrants at the local level, this comparative study demonstrates the utility of measuring an immigrant group's civicness, both in terms of the number of organizations that belong to its network and its structure.

THE EMERGENCE OF TURKISH CIVIC COMMUNITY IN AMSTERDAM AND BERLIN

Similar reasons propelled Turkish migration to both Amsterdam and Berlin. Economic motives were the most important ever since the start of Turkish immigration during the early 1960s, when Turks began arriving in Western Europe, predominantly as guest workers. Later on, political motives for migration would gain importance, especially after Turkey's military coup in 1980, though economic factors continued to dominate. The influx of guest workers officially came to a halt in 1973 during Western Europe's economic recession, when the Dutch government, much like the German, imposed an immigration ban targeting all guest worker countries. However, guest workers who were already in the Netherlands and Germany were entitled to bring, or send for, their families, and many of the Turkish workers did. Family unification transformed the Turks into a sizable migrant population in Western Europe and modified the group's demographic composition as more and more Turkish women and children began to arrive in the 1970s and early 1980s.

The arrival of Turks to Berlin began relatively late compared to the rest of Germany. This is an advantage in our comparison, because Turkish migration to Berlin occurred during the same period as Turkish immigrants began arriving in Amsterdam: between 1964 and 1968. In terms of numbers, Amsterdam's Turkish population was significantly smaller than Berlin's for the entire period of the study. The percentage of women among Berlin's Turkish population was high. Throughout the 1970s, 28 percent of guest workers in all of Germany were women, but in Berlin more than 40 percent were. This was a direct result of the favorable economic structure (Schwarz 1992, 123). Until the end of the decade, relatively more Turkish women were present in Berlin than in Amsterdam, though the distinction is not as great as that between Berlin and other German cities. As the process of family reunification unfolded, the percentage of women among Amsterdam's Turkish population also increased, creating greater similarities between the demographic compositions in both cities. In fact, by the end of the 1990s, the numbers were nearly even (Vermeulen 2006).

Because individuals from urban areas are assumed to have higher educational and occupational skills than those from rural areas, we need to know from which regions in Turkey the immigrants came. A lack of reliable data makes it difficult to provide a precise comparison between the Turkish populations in the Netherlands and in Germany, but it is generally assumed that Germany recruited Turkish immigrants with higher educational backgrounds and occupational skills than the Netherlands did (Böcker and Thränhardt 2003, 37). Research in Berlin during the early 1970s showed that 15 percent of Turkish immigrants had been employed in the civil service sector before their departure, primarily as schoolteachers. In addition, a relatively high percentage of Turkish students were found studying at one of Berlin's numerous universities and an above-average percentage of Turkish immigrants had more than nine years of schooling. By the 1980s, the percentage of low-skilled workers would increase considerably with the arrival of immigrants from rural Turkey coming to join their families (Gitmez and Wilpert 1987, 90–92). Once again, this influx created more points of parity between Turkish communities in Amsterdam and in Berlin. Overall, size was the only major difference; otherwise, the Turkish populations in Amsterdam and Berlin between 1970 and 2000 were not notably different (Vermeulen 2006).

Turkish Ideological Movements in Western Europe

Founded between the late 1960s and early 1970s, the first Turkish immigrant organizations in Western Europe were mostly leftist and rightist political workers organizations. Their focus was overwhelmingly on their homeland and on each other. A wide array of political and religious movements jockeyed for power in

Western Europe's ever-growing Turkish communities. The left-right political polarization was imported from Turkey, a country that suffered serious political upheaval during this period. The major polarities were the radical left versus the radical right, Turkish versus Kurdish, Sunnis versus Alevis, and religious versus secular. The Turkish state founded and supported pro-state organizations, and opposition movements established groups of their own (Østergaard-Nielsen 2003, 63–66). Such ideological rivalries had a dramatic impact on the establishment of new Turkish organizations in Western Europe. No group could afford to stay behind. The number of new Turkish organizations hence exploded. Both Germany and the Netherlands witnessed the development of left wing and right wing political movements, Islamic movements (some of which even banned in Turkey), as well as Islamic organizations that were supported by the Turkish government.

Then, as now, Islam was the greatest and strongest common denominator across Turkish immigrant organizations in Western Europe (Doomernik 1995; Vermeulen 2006). Most Turkish immigrants are affiliated with one of the main Islamic Sunni denominations: the Diyanet movement, the oppositional Milli Görüş movement, and the more spiritually guided Süleymancilar movement. Both socially and politically, these religious groups have organized separately because they each support different political parties in Turkey. The Diyanet movement, naming itself after Turkey's Presidency for Religious Affairs, was established by advocates of a state-controlled, fairly moderate, yet nationalistic form of Islam. The Milli Görüş movement proved one of the most important oppositional forces against the influence of the Diyanet throughout the 1980s and 1990s. The Süleymancilar movement shuns being linked to Turkish politics and rejects state control over the Islamic faith (Østergaard-Nielsen 2003). Islamic denominations sought to improve their standing in Amsterdam's and Berlin's Turkish communities by establishing as many organizations as possible. This resulted in the registration of many small Islamic prayer sites among different Turkish neighborhoods throughout the 1980s. Each site was affiliated with a particular Islamic denomination.

Turkish oppositional leftist groups have historically comprised both radical and more liberal secular groups. The radical side includes numerous communist splinter groups, some of which were related to the Turkish Communist Party (TKP) and some that were influenced by other forms of communism. The right wing organizations can be further classified into moderate and radical wings, most of them directly related to Islamic movements or having their own religious purpose. The moderate groups are categorized as Hür-Türk organizations and the extreme right wing organizations are better known as Grey Wolves organizations. The Grey Wolves movement strongly opposes organizations that are of a Turkish leftist vein or come from Kurdish background.

The Kurdish-Turkish conflict has had a long history in Turkey, and ever since its increased level of violence in the 1980s has been a major factor in the organizing process of Turkish and Kurdish immigrants in Western Europe. One of the main demands of Kurdish organizations is the recognition of the Kurdish people as an independent nation. Apart from this clear political agenda, Kurdish organizations are also engaged in celebrating Kurdish cultural events and studying the Kurdish language.

Two Opportunity Structures: Policies in Amsterdam and Berlin

Many immigration studies argue that the behavior of immigrants in a host society is shaped not only by the characteristics of the group and its immigration history, but also, and to a large extent, by the opportunities the host society offers. For instance, the local labor market's structure may be more significant in carving out work opportunities for newcomers in destination cities than an individual's skills or previous professional experience (Waldinger 1996; Morawska 1996; Lucassen 2002).

In a similar fashion, scholars have stressed the fact that host states often act as a catalyst for ethnic mobilization and that they provide opportunities and constraints for immigrants' ability to organize themselves. State policies may unintentionally stimulate ethnic mobilization by triggering a resurgence of ethnic markers or by assigning a status to immigrant groups (Olzak 1983). To a large extent, the state defines who the legitimate actors within the field of organizations are, and therefore has the power to provide legitimacy to certain immigrant groups or specific immigrant organizations (Kasinitz 1992).

A number of these studies have drawn on recent social movement literature, which stresses the importance of political opportunities for levels of social protest. Because the factors relevant to social protest vary across issues and constituencies, it is important to distinguish those elements of the political environment most relevant for immigrant mobilization. When it comes to collective immigrant action, the literature identifies citizenship regimes and integration policies as the main factors at play in political opportunity structures (Koopmans and Statham 2000; Koopmans et al. 2005; Odmalm 2005). It is useful to conceptualize the different citizenship regimes and integration approaches in a two-dimensional space (Koopmans and Statham 2000). The first dimension concerns the degree to which full and equal citizenship is accessible to individual migrants. The second deals with granting immigrants rights as a recognized cultural group. Although there are reasons to expect that organizational dynamics would differ from other collective behavior, researchers tend to employ similar models of explanation to both processes (Meyer and Minkoff 2004; Fennema and Tillie 2004).

Turkish organizers arriving in Amsterdam and in Berlin encountered distinct political opportunity structures, despite the fact that they are in neighboring countries. First, these differences might be attributed to different national citizenship regimes. The Netherlands' citizenship regime for Turks was characterized as relatively open and tolerant. For example, Dutch citizenship and attaining dual nationality were easily accessible. By contrast, the German regime, at least until 2000, tended to be closed to Turkish newcomers. The acquisition of German citizenship through naturalization was relatively difficult and uncommon for Turks and, compared with Amsterdam, Berlin demonstrated less cultural and religious tolerance (Koopmans and Statham 2000; Koopmans et al. 2005).

Amsterdam   The Dutch citizenship regime, especially in terms of group rights, cannot be understood without referring to the traditional Dutch system of pillarization (verzuiling). Originally developed to cope with the country's traditional religious minorities, pillarization was based on the idea that each social or cultural group should provide its own organizational services, such as hospitals, schools, newspapers, broadcasting networks, trade unions, and voluntary associations. Cooperation existed, though primarily at the level of Dutch society's political elites (Lijphart 1968). Traces of the pillarization system can still be found in Dutch immigration policy at almost every level. It has been observed that Muslims, in particular, use legal structures that originated in the heyday of pillarization, and it is because of this specific structure that very few Islamic claims have been categorically denied by Dutch authorities (Rath et al. 2001). This tendency away from a routinely dismissive policy is illustrated, for example, by the fact that every religion in the Netherlands is entitled to establish its own school with full financing by the national government (Duyvené de Wit and Koopmans 2001).

In line with the system of pillarization, the Dutch government of the early 1980s introduced a multicultural policy designed to integrate the growing immigrant population. It officially classified the main immigrant groups as minority target groups whose socioeconomic positions needed improvement. The minority policy had two principal objectives for immigrant groups. First, their social and economic conditions were to be improved through the enactment of active public interventions in the labor market and the education system, thus ensuring equal access for all groups. Second, the Netherlands was to become a tolerant, multicultural society in which every immigrant culture would be accepted, respected, and valued (Lucassen and Penninx 1994, 148).

Rooted in the idea of the welfare state, the first objective became the focal point of Dutch minority policy and, consequently, was visibly manifested in actual practice. The second objective proved equally evident in attitudes toward immigrant organizations in the Netherlands and, in particular, Amsterdam. Such an outlook fostered the sense that immigrants could integrate into Dutch society yet retain their cultural identity. Politicians have long argued that group-specific services would be needed to accomplish the establishment of a tolerant multicultural society. The basic idea was that organizations run by immigrants themselves would provide enough opportunities to "maintain and develop their own ethnic immigrant culture and identity" (Lucassen and Penninx 1994, 148).

Amsterdam authorities complied with this new national policy development and, in 1981, introduced a multicultural policy for immigrant groups. This meant, among many other things, that from 1981 onward, different minority target groups (including Turks) would become eligible for direct operational subsidies for establishing and developing their own organizations. The city council envisaged three primary tasks for such organizations: to promote and preserve cultural identities, to emancipate their constituencies, and to represent community interests. In principle, political and religious organizations were not entitled to subsidy funding. Nevertheless, Amsterdam authorities insisted that all segments of guest worker communities be included, so as not to isolate certain groups or associations. The authorities explicitly called on religious organizations to found additional sociocultural organizations for the city to be able to support these groups financially (Vermeulen 2006).

By 1985, in a further attempt at political incorporation into Dutch society, resident aliens had been granted the right to vote at the municipal level (Tillie 2000). The same year, Amsterdam's city government decided to establish several minority advisory councils to guide local authorities on new integration policies, in addition to evaluating existing ones. The council for the Turkish community represented a broad range of Turkish organizations, including the left wing, the right wing, and the religious. The advisory council worked to enhance the structural collaborations among Turkish groups that were previously engaged in virulent struggles over funding, constituencies, and influence, yet were now obliged to collaborate on many issues (Vermeulen 2006).

In the 1990s, Dutch integration policy entered a new phase. Both politicians and the public had been disappointed by the previous ten years' worth of results in multicultural policy. Social and economic deprivation among immigrants seemed to have only increased, despite the fact that so much money and policy making had been directed to changing the situation. Politicians argued that the higher unemployment rates among immigrants deserved more attention, and that emancipation and cultural expression merited less. The most salient point of the new integration policy, therefore, was not to focus on cultural diversity, but rather to emphasize the participation of immigrants in the educational system and the labor market. Government programs became less multicultural and more integrative (Thränhardt 2000, 172). In Amsterdam during this period, the focus of the policy also shifted away from cultural diversity and toward social and economic integration.

Berlin   Berlin began formulating its integration policy in the early 1970s as the city experienced an overall increase in its number of Turkish guest workers and immigrants through family reunion and asylum seeking. The early policy attempted to address contemporary social problems among the immigrant groups, including segregation, racial violence, unemployment, and housing challenges (Schwarz 1992, 125–26). This policy of the 1970s—one of cautious integration—became to be seen as totally inadequate as the political significance of immigration and integration issues increased, leading to political crises over these issues (Schwarz 2001, 129–30).

The Christian Democrats (CDU) won the 1981 local elections, proposing highly restrictive and occasionally even xenophobic measures for the growing immigrant population in Berlin (Hunger and Thränhardt 2001, 109). After the election, a new policy was introduced that was supposed to prevent further growth of the immigrant population while, at the same time, furthering integration of those immigrants already living in Berlin. The slogan used to sum up the policy program was "integration or departure" (Schwarz 2001, 131), which had a very different resonance than Amsterdam's "integration while retaining ethnic identity."

Berlin's motto well illustrates the two sides of integration policy during the 1980s. On the one hand, there was an emphasis on restrictive measures meant to ensure that the number of immigrants in the city decreased. On the other, focus fell on a more integrative regime meant to incorporate newcomers into the host society, thus taking care not to leave them behind. The policy's restrictive side was formulated and subsequently implemented by several conservative CDU senators, of whom Heinrich Lummer (1981 to 1986) is the most renowned (Gesemann 2001, 16). The policy's integration side was to be implemented by the Ausländerbeauftragte, a new bureaucratic institution established in 1981 by a coalition of the CDU and the liberal Free Democratic Party (FDP).

Barbara John, a moderate CDU politician, founded the Ausländerbeauftragte, held her position for more than twenty years, and was undoubtedly the principal actor in the field of integration in Berlin throughout the 1980s and 1990s. Several similarities could be drawn between John's stance and Amsterdam's policies. Very different from German national policy, the Ausländerbeauftragte emphasized naturalization, around which it launched a successful 1981 campaign that focused particularly on second- and third-generation Turks. To this day, naturalization rates in Berlin are much higher than those in other German states (Böcker and Thränhardt 2003, 123). A second component was clearcut support for immigrant organizations. The support may not have been as straightforward or structural as in Amsterdam, but proved critical to the development of Turkish organizations in Berlin.

A comparison of the subsidy policy for immigrant organizations in Berlin and in Amsterdam reveals differences reflecting the extent to which the two opportunity structures varied. In Amsterdam, the subsidy for Turkish and other immigrant organizations was integrated into the city's minority policy. The municipal government explicitly stated in reports that Turkish organizations would be helpful to the emancipation of the Turkish population and should therefore receive state money. In Berlin, the integrational aspects of the Ausländerbeauftragte and its accompanying support for Turkish organizations were not completely structured into local immigration policies. Ausländerbeauftragte policy was limited by both the exclusion approach at the federal level and restrictive measures created by the conservative wing of the local CDU (Gesemann 2001, 16).

Subsidy policy for Turkish organizations was therefore less straightforward in Berlin than in Amsterdam. For example, many organizations receiving financial support within the framework of self-help groups were not actually founded by Turks, but rather were created for Turkish people, which often had German board members. The Ausländerbeauftragte did, however, manage to fund several ethnic Turkish organizations. This was less a political decision than a practical strategy to sustain the position of the Ausländerbeauftragte within the local political field. Funding organizations would improve relationships with immigrant communities, which, in turn, would ensure the political legitimacy of the Ausländerbeauftragte over a longer period. Turkish organizations in Berlin were thus not so much supported for the sake of their activities as they were for pragmatic reasons. According to Barbara John, too many Turkish organizations in the city would jeopardize the Turkish population's integration (Schwarz 2001).

The third difference between the two subsidy policies is that Amsterdam's was often operational or foundational and, in general, continued over a long period.[3] In Berlin, subsidies were normally devoted to individual projects and operational or general financial support for Turkish organizations proved rare.

To complete the comparison between the two policies, it is worth examining the position of Turkish religious organizations in Berlin. The political environment for these organizations has very much been influenced by the ambiguous status of Islam in Germany. Because Islam is not recognized as an official religion in Germany, it has been very difficult for Turkish religious organizations to participate in the local political system. In contrast to their counterparts in Amsterdam, where Islamic organizations have received subsidies and participated on advisory councils, Berlin's Turkish Islamic organizations are basically ignored or not recognized as partners by local authorities. Neither do they receive financial support or have official contact with politicians. The financial support given to religious Turkish organizations in Amsterdam would be unthinkable in the context of Berlin or, for that matter, throughout greater Germany (Gesemann and Kapphan 2001, 412–13; Jonker 2005).

Hypothesizing the Effects   What distinct outcomes can be expected for the numbers of Turkish organizations and the networks between them, two central elements of a civic immigrant community? The political opportunity model predicts that mobilization, which includes the founding of organizations, is likely to occur when changes in the external political climate make collective action more conducive to success. Changes within mainstream political institutions work to facilitate certain groups, demands, and forms of action and to constrain others. Such a transformation will affect people's expectations regarding the success or failure of their collective behavior and, ultimately, their collective action (McAdam 1982; Tarrow 1998). One of the main differences between the two cities is that Amsterdam's citizenship regime was extended to include specific group rights for immigrants. This multicultural policy acknowledged Turks as an official minority entitled to particular rights as an immigrant group. Turkish organizations were seen as a product of the ethnic community, thereby receiving state funding and being given an official role within the local political system as a way to emancipate and integrate the Turkish community into Dutch society. Amsterdam authorities, moreover, attempted to target the entire Turkish community, which included both Islamic movements and more conservative ones. Some attempts to reach out to the community were also visible in Berlin, yet Turks received no special policy status, nor were the city's Turkish organizations seen as an important product of the group's collective identity. Instead, local politicians focused on using such organizations as a way to access the Turkish population.

The existing literature on opportunity structures would suggest that as resources become more available, organizations are not only better able, but also more inclined, to express their ideological distinctiveness and look for formal collaboration with similar organizations (Knoke 1990, 79). If the opportunity structure is less open, organizations will be more hesitant to express their ideology and remain, at least at the formal level, independent or isolated. We would thus expect, after 1980, more Turkish organizations to begin appearing in Amsterdam than in Berlin. In terms of the number of Turkish interlocks in the city, we would expect more overlapping Turkish board memberships in Amsterdam than in Berlin.

There are further reasons to expect that the hospitable opportunity structure in Amsterdam would encourage the number of Turkish interlocks. The Dutch political system of pillarization has always stimulated interlocking directorates among the political elite and civil society (Lijphart 1968). In other words, in the Dutch context, it makes sense to establish a formal elite network through which immigrant groups adapt to the Dutch political system. Amsterdam policy is also conducive to having a more direct influence on Turkish interlocks. The formation of immigrant advisory councils has essentially forced Turkish organizations to establish formal contacts and to collaborate with one another, which, in turn, may have encouraged the array of Turkish interorganizational relationships that exist in Amsterdam. In addition, providing state subsidy for immigrant organizations in itself can influence the emergence of interlocks. Subsidized organizations attract other organizations seeking collaborations that can help increase their resources. This results in more interlocks and, simultaneously, a centralized network (Tillie and Fennema 1998, 234).

DATA AND RESEARCH ON INTERLOCKING DIRECTORATES

Following in the footsteps of Fennema and Tillie (Fennema and Tillie 1999, 200; Fennema 2004; Tillie 2004), this study gathered information on immigrant organizations from the archives of the Chamber of Commerce in Amsterdam (Kamer van Koophandel Amsterdam) and the Registration of Associations in Berlin (Vereinsregister Berlin Amtsgericht Charlottenburg). These archives hold data indicating the year an immigrant organization was founded and dissolved, as well as other details such as the organization's mission statement. The Amsterdam archives also provided personal information about board members and founders, including their names and dates and places of birth. In Berlin, only the nationalities of board members and founders are specified. Board member data are used to determine an organization's ethnic composition and to assess whether it is an authentic immigrant organization. An immigrant organization is defined as a formal, officially registered nonprofit organization of which at least half the board members are first- or second-generation descendants of a single immigrant group. Every formal nonprofit organization founded by members of a single immigrant group is included in the database, regardless of the organization's mission statement or the ethnic composition of its members (Fennema 2004).

Data from the chamber of commerce and the registration of associations provide interesting research possibilities for analyzing Turkish interorganizational relationships. Key to this analysis is the overlapping board membership that occurs when a person affiliated with one Turkish organization simultaneously sits on the board of another organization, thereby creating a link between the two. These links allow for a network of formal relations among Turkish organizations in both cities to be mapped and analyzed, and help to demonstrate how these relations evolve over time. By gathering the names of all Turkish board members in Amsterdam and in Berlin, spanning the period from 1960 through 2000, this study surveys overlapping board memberships at different points in time. Research on overlapping board membership, also referred to as interlocking directorates, is a method often used to study interorganizational relationships and elite networks (Mizruchi 1996; Fennema and Tillie 2001; Fennema 2004). This type of analysis, however, has not been used extensively to study interorganizational relationships among immigrant organizations over time.

We also use longitudinal analysis to identify the nature of Turkish interorganizational relationships. Longitudinal interlocking directorates occur when a person is active on the board of more than one voluntary organization for more than one year. The person need not necessarily be simultaneously active in more than one organization, but can instead be active in different organizations sequentially over certain periods (for example, five, ten, or thirty years). Because networks among Turkish organizations tend to be volatile, longitudinal network analyses help provide a subtler understanding. Further, these analyses reveal links between organizations that are otherwise often difficult to detect (Vermeulen 2006).[4]

This study also draws on survey data to examine the political behavior of individual Turkish immigrants. For the Amsterdam statistics, we rely on an annual municipal survey, *Burgermonitor*, in which citizens from all major ethnic groups are questioned about issues related to social and political participation. The 2001 survey produced a total of 2,171 Dutch interviewees and 167 Turkish interviewees (Bosveld et al. 2003). We rely on the Netherlands' official definition for classifying members of an ethnic group, which includes those who were born in a foreign country or whose parents were born in that country.

In Germany, there are considerable limitations to existing surveys. Few, for example, use mother-tongue interviewers, and samples of so-called immigrants, usually exclude those who hold German nationality (Berger, Galonska, and Koopmans 2004). To overcome these problems, this study conducted its own survey, which was carried out in collaboration with the Center for Studies on Turkey (Zentrum für Türkeistudien) in November 2001 and January 2002. The objective was to gain information on the degree of political participation at the individual level by Berlin's Turks.

The study opted to employ a sampling technique based on a sampling frame of Turkish names. This was facilitated by the fact that immigrant households can be identified by first names and family names. To first locate names, a CD-ROM database query of telephone registers was accessed.[5] This was particularly advantageous because it produced an unbiased sample based on names alone, rather than on legal status or subjective affiliations.[6] The interviews were conducted over the telephone by bilingual interviewers who used a standardized bilingual questionnaire for each migrant group. A quota plan was used to prevent problems related to gender (for example, women might dispense with a telephone directory entry for fear of being harassed) and age (for example, older migrants tended to exit Germany without deregistering at the registry office). Following this method thus, 306 Germans and 317 Turks were interviewed (Berger, Galonska, and Koopmans 2004; Berger forthcoming).

THE NUMBER OF TURKISH ORGANIZATIONS

Figure 6.1 displays the organizational activity of Turkish immigrants in Amsterdam and in Berlin between 1970 and 2000. The number of Turkish organizations is shown per 1,000 Turks in both cities. We see how, in the 1970s, relatively few organizations existed in either Berlin or Amsterdam. Nevertheless, it is evident that this decade marks the beginning of the Turkish organizing process in both cities. After 1974, Amsterdam and Berlin experienced an increase in their number of Turkish organizations. Until 1980, patterns in both cities look almost identical, mainly due to the associational activities of similar ideological movements. After 1980, however, there is rapid change in the relative number of Turkish organizations in each city: Turks in Amsterdam display more associational activities than Turks in Berlin. In 1985, there are two-and-a-half times more Turkish organizations in Amsterdam than in Berlin, and by 1995, the statistic quadruples. The implementation of multicultural policy clearly augmented Turkish associational activities in Amsterdam, as would be anticipated by the opportunity structure model. The largest increase in the number of Turkish organizations per 1,000 Turks came at the beginning of the 1980s, in parallel emergence to the Dutch minority policy and the introduction of organizational or administrative subsidies for Turkish organizations in Amsterdam. The second half of the 1980s does not show such impressive growth, though around 1985, two important policy measures were taken: granting local voting rights to immigrants and the establishment of a Turkish advisory council.

Despite the less hospitable situation in Berlin, especially as compared to Amsterdam, we do see some opportunity structure effects in Berlin. The Ausländerbeauftragte's establishment appears to have affected the city's number of Turkish organizations: Berlin's statistics steadily increase throughout the first half of the 1980s, producing in 1986 almost one Turkish organization for every 1,000 Turks.

In figure 6.2, we see, in both Amsterdam and Berlin, that the number of new Turkish organizations greatly increased by the end of the 1970s. The pattern of founding rates in both cities is almost identical to that of the 1980s: similar peak years can be seen in 1982 to 1983 and 1986, and similar drops in 1984 and 1988.

FIGURE 6.1 *Ethnic Organizations per 1,000 Turks in Berlin and Amsterdam*

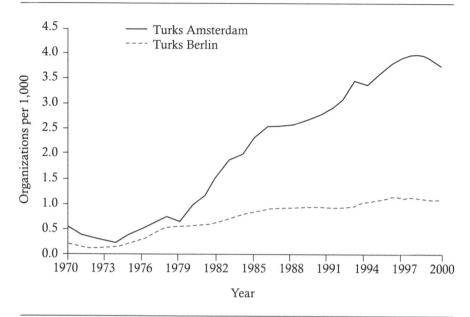

Source: Amsterdam Chamber of Commerce; Berlin Registration of Associations.

FIGURE 6.2 *Number and Density of Newly Founded Turkish Organizations in Amsterdam and Berlin*

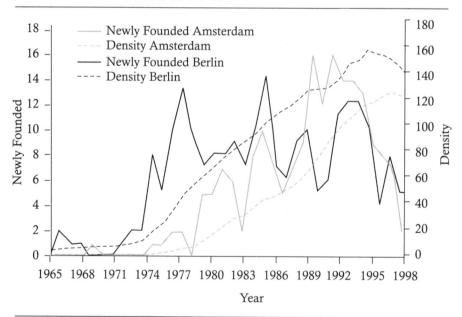

Sources: Amsterdam Chamber of Commerce; Berlin Registration of Associations.

This parity may be attributed to a comparable sequence of successive political and religious Turkish movements. Such a pattern indicates the strong influence of transnational political influences from Turkey on the Turkish organizing process in both cities during this decade. In other words, the Turkish organizing process patterns in Amsterdam and Berlin do not differ so much. Turks in Amsterdam, however, used opportunities to establish and maintain a relatively greater number of organizations.

These results argue against the idea that state intervention crowds out immigrant associational activities. Much as Irene Bloemraad (2005) revealed for Toronto, the Amsterdam case illustrates how a government support of immigrant organizations can play an important role in building organizational capacity among immigrant communities. However, the influence of the host state is not neutral. It influences the organizational capacity not only of an immigrant group, but also of a certain constituency within the group. Vermeulen (2007) shows how, in Amsterdam, religious and conservative Turkish organizations hold a significant position, whereas left wing secular organizations hold the equivalent position in Berlin. This distinction may be explained by the fact that Amsterdam extended an equal opportunity to organize to the whole Turkish ideological spectrum, and even the most powerful transnational movements (Islamic and right wing) were able to exploit the opportunity. In Berlin, strong ideological movements tended to be hindered in their organizational activities, and politicians relied on contact with left wing Turkish organizations to gain access to the Turkish community. As a result, these left wing organizations became more influential than those representing other ideologies. This result seems to correspond with the conclusion that the Dutch political institutional environment, at least in comparison to the German, has produced a form of immigrant mobilization highly focused on religious identities (Duyvené de Wit and Koopmans 2005). There is also some indication that Amsterdam's funding policy has been especially supportive of Turkish social-cultural associations operating at the neighborhood level, the occurrence of which are in fact more numerous in Amsterdam than in Berlin (Vermeulen 2006).

INTERNAL NETWORK TURKISH ORGANIZATIONS

Until 1980, there were few formal contacts among the Turkish organizations in Amsterdam and in Berlin. The Turkish networks in both cities during the 1980s could be characterized by high degrees of isolation and polarization. Violent competition between left wing and extreme right wing organizations dominated the strategies of all Turkish organizational leaders, whose main goal was to establish organizational structures for their own political or religious movement. Most leaders concerned themselves with only one organization and no formal networks emerged (Vermeulen 2006).

During the 1980s, both cities saw a change as many interorganizational relationships began to form. Surprisingly, this decade's development in the two cities is fairly similar, even despite their completely different opportunity structures. Both cities demonstrated a relatively large left wing network and a separate Islamic network whereby different Islamic denominations actively collaborate. Religious leaders in both cities simultaneously held positions in other types of Islamic organizations to support the establishment of a greater Turkish religious organizational structure. The Islamic network in both cities connected the more liberal Diyanet organizations with the more fundamentalist and controversial Islamic organizations such as the Grey Wolves Mosque ULU Camii in Amsterdam and the Milli Görüş Mevlana Mosque in Berlin. Yet, in both cities, collaboration between local Islamic leaders came to an end in the second half of the 1980s. By then, the Turkish religious organizational structure was firmly established and, due to increasing competition, old religious dividing lines reappeared (Vermeulen 2006).

By the 1990s, however, behavior among local Turkish organizers in Amsterdam and in Berlin became very different, primarily as the result of the cities' different opportunity structures. In Amsterdam, there was more collaboration between left wing and religious and conservative groups. One of the main goals of the Amsterdam policy was to encourage internal cooperation among Turkish organizations. Although Amsterdam authorities were apprehensive to include the entire span of the Turkish political and religious spectrum in their programs, they did so. Moreover, they provided subsidies for all groups (including more extreme organizations that were commonly banned in Berlin) and established advisory councils welcoming almost all movements.

Figure 6.3 shows the main interlocks of the extended and inclusive networks of Turkish organizations in Amsterdam during the 1990s. The network consists of 113 Turkish organizations and 255 interlocking directorates, which means that 65 percent of the existing Turkish organizations from this period are accounted for in this one network. Displayed here are two paths that lead from the Grey Wolves organizations to the left wing organizations, indicating a high degree of convergence among Turkish organizations in Amsterdam during this period. Three nonpolitical foundations operating at the city district level provide the connection from left to right: Stichting Turks Volkshuis Osdorp, Stichting Turks Platform Bos & Lommer en de Baarsjes, and Stichting Turkse Algemene Belangengroep Amsterdam-Noord.

Turkish organizational leaders from the various movements came to meet in more neutral organizations and created a communication network that included all the parties from their community. It took nearly a decade for city policy and the activities of Turkish leaders to become visible within the structure of Amsterdam's Turkish interlocks. During the 1990s, Turkish leaders across the various movements collaborated on the boards of neutral, nonaligned Turkish organizations, which operated at the city district level. Together, they engaged in welfare programs for youth and the protection of Turkish interests within a particular neighborhood. These organizations have also profited the most from the structural state funding programs of Amsterdam's city council (and city districts). Because the more extreme Turkish organizations were incorporated in integration

FIGURE 6.3 *Longitudinal Interlocking Directorates Among Turkish Organizations in Amsterdam in the 1990s*

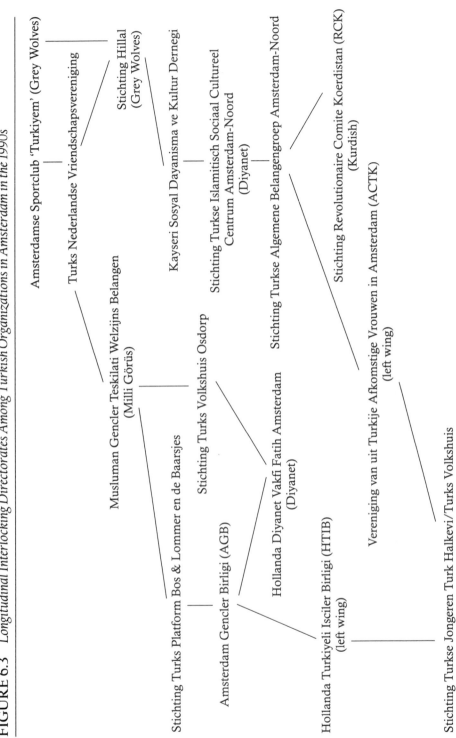

programs and advisory councils, it became acceptable for others to collaborate with them as well. Kurdish leaders established interlocks with left wing leaders; left wing leaders established links with the Islamic leaders of the Diyanet; and the Diyanet leaders were in close contact with more conservative religious groups such as Milli Görüş and Grey Wolves mosques.

The Turkish interlocks in Berlin during the 1990s paint a completely different picture from those of Amsterdam. Here, authorities were hardly inclined to include all aspects of the Turkish community. Rather, the city's Turkish organizational process was controlled by two new Turkish umbrella organizations, the Türkischer Bund Berlin-Brandenburg (TBB) and the more conservative Türkische Gemeinde zu Berlin (TGB). The TBB's left wing leaders came mostly from the left wing student organization Berlin Türk Bilim ve Teknoloji Merkezi (BTBTM), which was Berlin's most influential Turkish left wing organization in the 1980s. The TBB established strong relationships with numerous other leftist Turkish groups, and the leaders of the TGB commonly emerged from religious Diyanet organizations and made ties with the more conservative groups. The TBB is characterized as a classic top-down intellectual interest organization, whereas the TGB is a typical grass roots organization, originally founded by local Turkish businessmen. The TGB tends to appeal to a larger group of Turkish people than the TBB (Yurdakul 2006). This study's survey shows that 82 percent of Turks in Berlin are familiar with the TGB, and that just 53 percent are with the TBB. Moreover, Turks in Berlin have greater actual contact with the TGB (calculated at 19 percent) than with the TBB (8 percent). The most renowned Turkish organization among Berlin's Turks, however, is the soccer club Türkiyemspor (91 percent). Overall, Turks in Berlin show a rather low level of confidence in Turkish organizations: only 18 percent say they trust the TGB to do a good job in representing their interest and only 15 percent, the TBB (Berger forthcoming).

Figure 6.4 displays the main interlocks in Berlin during the 1990s and illustrates how the TBB and the TGB came to dominate this city's interorganizational relationships. The complete network consists of forty-four organizations (22 percent of all existing Turkish organizations during decade) and is produced by fifty-seven interlocks. In addition, there are four other smaller networks, not displayed in figure 6.3: two Milli Görüs groups (by now separated from the Diyanet organizations), one Kurdish component, and one Grey Wolves network. The more extreme movements in Berlin such as the Grey Wolves, Kurds, and the Milli Görüs are isolated as separate entities.

The major network of Turkish interorganizational relationships reveals several interesting elements. First is the central position of the TDU (Türkisch-Deutsche Unternehmervereinigung in Berlin-Brandenburg), an organization for Turkish entrepreneurs that played a vital role in combining the secular left wing Turkish umbrella organization TBB with the conservative and religious organizations of the conservative umbrella organization TGB. The link between the TBB and the TGB was created by two Turkish leaders: Hüsnü Özkanli, a TGB and TDU founder, and Bahattin Kaya, a TDU founder, TBB board member from 1996 until 1999, and founder and president of the Vereini-

FIGURE 6.4 *Interlocking Directorates Among Turkish Organizations in Berlin in the 1990s*

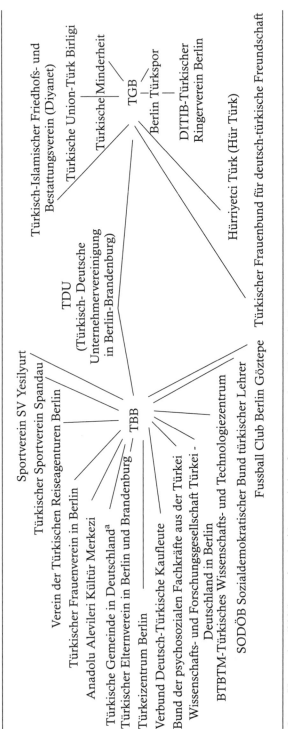

Source: Vermeulen (2006), reprinted with permission from Amsterdam University Press.
[a] It is interesting to note that the TGB's national organization has not established an interlocking directorate with the TGB, but rather with the TBB.

gung Türkischer Reiseagenturen Berlin (BETÜSAB), an organization for Turkish travel agencies.

It is worth noting that the link between the extremes within the community was not due to Berlin's opportunity structure, but rather came from the Turkish community itself. Not a state-sponsored association, the TDU is an organization of Berlin's remarkably more successful Turkish immigrants. However, the fact that the TBB and the TGB came to play such a central role in this network did indeed come as a direct result of Berlin's opportunity structure. The Ausländerbeauftragte provided financial support to both umbrella organizations in an endeavor to gain a better foothold in the Turkish community.

The emergence of two new Turkish umbrella organizations could easily have resulted in polarizing left wing and religious sides. However, this did not happen, thanks to collaboration by the leaders of both blocks in founding the TDU, a Turkish association for entrepreneurs. This organization provided Berlin's Turkish elite a means to become connected and subsequently establish a communication network. Nevertheless, several important movements and organizations were not incorporated in this large network, which did lead to other forms of polarization in Berlin's Turkish community of the 1990s. Milli Görüs, the Grey Wolves, and a number of Kurds established their own networks of interlocks that were completely separate from all other Turkish organizations. During this decade, the number of Turkish organizations that established no interlocks also increased. Polarization within the network is also apparent at the individual level. More so than other ethnic groups, Turks in Berlin are considered very well aware of their community's most prominent organizations. Still, a high level of distrust toward these organizations exists, significantly more than is observed among Berlin's other ethnic groups (Berger forthcoming).

This overview of the number of Turkish organizations and their networks in Amsterdam and in Berlin proves consistent with the belief that different opportunity structures influence their communities. In Amsterdam, Turks have relatively more organizations and are well connected through a dense network of interlocks. In other words, they have created a more civic and less polarized organizational network than their counterparts in Berlin. It is important to note that Amsterdam's opportunity structure has had its greatest effect on precisely the two elements of the Turkish organizing process we are examining—the number of organizations and the number of internal networks. The political opportunity structure's effect is less apparent, however, on other elements, for example, types of organizations and founding rates (Vermeulen 2006).

FROM CIVIC ORGANIZATIONS TO POLITICAL PRESENCE AND PARTICIPATION

A subsequent question is the extent to which differences in Turkish organizational structures affect the political presence of Turkish organizations and the political behavior of individual Turks. Here we deal with the political weight of Turkish organizations. Are Turkish organizations politically more influential in Amsterdam, seeing as they are greater in number, better connected with one another, and have received more opportunities to participate in city life? At the individual level, do Turks in Berlin behave differently than Turks in Amsterdam, and to what extent can we attribute possible variation to different organizational structures? Does the Turkish community in Amsterdam, being characterized as more civic, facilitate participation in local politics more than in Berlin?

Political Presence of Turkish Organizations

Most studies on immigrant organizations that deal specifically with Turks (as well as with immigrants in general) in Germany and the Netherlands ascribe a low political relevance to Turkish organizations (Rijkschroeff and Duyvendak 2004; Weiss and Thränhardt 2005; Schrover and Vermeulen 2005; Pfaff and Gill 2006). Steven Pfaff and Anthony Gill (2006) said that Muslims have yet to become an organized force in European politics, despite the fact that there are so many salient political issues pertaining to them. Turkish organizations in Amsterdam and in Berlin are, first and foremost, providers of religious, cultural, and social services. Only subsequently does interest representation become relevant (Vermeulen 2006). Other studies on civic participation among Turks in Germany come to similar conclusions. One study (Cyrus 2005) found that religion is most important for Turkish organizations (29 percent), followed by sports (28 percent), cultural activities (17 percent), educational activities (14 percent), and representation of professional interest (11 percent). Interest representation only accounts for 5.6 percent of Germany's Turkish civic participation.

Explanations given for a lack of political influence by Turkish organizations are varied. They include the decentralized organizational structure of Turkish Islamic immigrants, which provides ample opportunity for a small faction to undermine broad-based immigrant collective action (Pfaff and Gill 2006), preoccupation with homeland politics (Østergaard-Nielsen 2003), and other associational priorities (Rijkschroeff and Duyvendak 2004; Vermeulen 2006). Among Turkish organizations in Amsterdam and in Berlin, there seems to be a strong tendency toward narrow interest articulation on a local level. On the national level, political relevance of these Turkish organizations is even lower. Most interaction between host state authorities and Turkish organizations relates to practical issues such as finding accommodations or securing a permit to conduct activities, especially those pertaining to religious organizations (Van Heelsum 2004; Maussen 2006).

Turkish organizations in Amsterdam have always complained about their lack of influence on the process of policy making (Vermeulen 2005). The main opportunity proved to be in the Turkish advisory council, established in 1986 to advise Amsterdam authorities on policy topics related to immigrants and integration. The official status of this advisory council worked to enhance the sociopolitical legitimacy of appointed Turkish organizations. Research on the development of Amsterdam minority policy during the 1990s indicates that when it came to the formulation of minority policy, the advisory council played a small role, in fact much greater than that of any individual Turkish organization (Berveling 1994, 279). However, the council's political influence, relevance, and performance were often questioned in policy reports by local authorities, as well as by Turkish organizations. In 2003, Amsterdam authorities abolished the council, arguably without ever having been able to prove its political significance.

The atmosphere in which Turkish organization in Berlin could influence local politics was indeed less favorable than that of Amsterdam. Even the main official institution involving Turkish organizations, the Ausländerbeauftragter, did not formulate integration policy. Until 2003, there were no immigrant advisory councils in Berlin, and the city's senate did not issue its first official integration policy report until 2006. Local politicians would occasionally hear out Turkish organizers regarding their opinions on certain topics, though, in general, there were few opportunities for Turkish organizations in Berlin to influence the policy-making process. Islamic organizations, in particular, had few opportunities to come into contact with local authorities in Berlin (Vermeulen 2006).

Nevertheless, there were other ways to influence policy makers and to make contact with political parties. For instance, the individual linkages were made between Turkish organizations and local politicians. Both cities have had a number of active local Turkish politicians, many of whom once served as board members for one or more local Turkish organizations. It proved doubly advantageous for political parties to incorporate Turkish representatives with ethnic civic experience: they were familiar with local political issues, and, more important, they brought potential voters into the party who would eventually become the rank and file of the organizations. Maria Berger and her colleagues (2001) found that local immigrant politicians in the Netherlands gained their primary civic experience while sitting on the boards of secular interest organizations. At the same time, a significant fraction (nearly one-fifth) had been active on the boards of Islamic organizations. The great majority of the immigrant politicians said that they were frequently contacted by immigrant organizations to request that their interests or their constituency be represented. This indicates that organizations rely on personal linkages to augment their political weight. Laure Michon and Floris Vermeulen (2007) found that 70 percent of Amsterdam's Turkish city councilors and almost 60 percent of the Turkish city district councilors were board members of a local Turkish organization (for the period 1990 to 2006). This clearly illustrates the central position that local Turkish organizations have in recruiting local immigrant Turkish politicians.

This same mechanism seems to work in Berlin, with the important caveat that fewer Turkish politicians were recruited in Berlin than in Amsterdam. Of notable significance seems to be the personal linkages between the TBB as an umbrella organization with Berlin's Social Democratic Party (SPD). The TBB's former director is chair of the SPD working group that specializes in immigrant issues and presents reports to the party's authorities and is married to an SPD member on the Berlin senate. The TBB's treasurer is a member of the SPD in the women's commission (Yurdakul 2006).

Table 6.1 illustrates the number of local Turkish politicians in both cities, in-

TABLE 6.1   *Number of Turkish Representatives*

	Amsterdam	Berlin
2002 City Council	4 (8.9%)	—
2002 City Districts	16 (5.0%)	—
2002 share Turks in population	5.0%	—
2006 City Council	3 (6.6%)	6 (4.0%)
2006 City Districts	22 (6.8%)	—
2006 share Turks in population	5.2%	+/~ 5.5%

Source: Authors' compilation from Michon and Tillie (2003).
Note: Percentage of total in brackets.

dicating possible access points of influence for Turkish organizations. It shows that Turks in Amsterdam have a better position in the local political system than their counterparts in Berlin. The percentage of Turkish people who serve as representatives in the city council (as well as in city district councils) is higher than the percentage of those Turkish civilians who comprise Amsterdam's population, a sign of overrepresentation. For example, in 2006 almost 7 percent of members of the city council and city district councils were Turkish, whereas just over 5 percent of the city population was Turkish. In Berlin, Turks are politically under-represented: 4 percent of representatives in the Berlin senate are of Turkish background, whereas the Turkish community constitutes about 5.5 percent of the city population.

The discrepancy between the proportion of Turkish politicians in the two cities is easily explained by the fact that many more Turks have the right to vote in Amsterdam, thanks to the Netherlands' 1985 provision of local voting rights for immigrants. Political parties in Amsterdam have more to gain in terms of possible voters if they have a Turkish representative on their candidacy list, especially given that Turks have shown much higher turn-out rates over the last four local elections than other immigrant groups (Van Heelsum and Tillie 2006). Hansje Galesloot (2004) found Amsterdam's situation as particularly interesting, when compared to other Dutch cities, because of the unusually high number of female immigrant politicians, almost 40 percent between 2002 and 2006. In addition, at both the city district and the city levels, Amsterdam has had several immigrant aldermen, many of whom have been active on the board of immigrant associations.

The number of local Turkish politicians, which is high in Amsterdam and increasingly so in Berlin, would suggest the possibility that Turkish organizations have the opportunity to augment their political weight. Yet numbers notwithstanding, immigrant politicians usually have a very difficult position within political parties and many fail to become successful politicians (Berger et al. 2001; Michon and Vermeulen 2007). Amsterdam's immigrant aldermen have, so far, proven to be more an exception to the rule; furthermore, none of them is of Turkish origin. Berlin demonstrates the same scenario. Despite strong links between the TBB and the SPD, the influence of the former over the latter's integration policies seems rather limited (Yurdakul 2006).

Overall, until now the political weight of Turkish organizations has been relatively low. Some umbrella groups, such as Berlin's TBB and TGB, are more visible than others and have more contacts with local politicians, but even these do not seem to have a clear political influence. Nonetheless, the degree of inclusion of Turkish organizations into the local political system is much higher in Amsterdam than in Berlin. Amsterdam has had a Turkish advisory council for almost twenty years, as well as witnessed the election of many more local Turkish politicians, a large majority of whom once served as members of a local Turkish organization.

Individual Political Participation

What is the degree of political participation of Turks in Amsterdam and Berlin? Table 6.2 presents scores on political participation for Turks in both cities, as well as for the nonimmigrant German and Dutch populations. The results show that 62 percent of Germans had undertaken at least one political activity within the last year, but only 29 percent of the Dutch had done so.

Furthermore, and perhaps surprisingly, Berlin's Turks are also more politically active than those in Amsterdam. One could perhaps expect Turks in Amsterdam to be more politically active than those in Berlin. There are more Turkish organizations in Amsterdam, and research shows that membership in Turkish organizations enhances the degree of political participation among individual Turks in both cities (Tillie 2004; Berger forthcoming). Yet table 6.2 suggests the opposite is true. Among Turks in Berlin, 45 percent took up one or more political activity during the last year, whereas only 14 percent did so in Amsterdam. In line with a higher level of political activity, the expressed intention to vote at the next election also proved much higher in Berlin (83 percent) than in Amsterdam. The Dutch proved to be far less inclined to vote, and Turks in Amsterdam demonstrated even lower interest: only 30 percent said they would vote at the next local election, which was precisely the percentage of Turks who showed up at the 2002 local elections (see table 6.3).

What explains these counterintuitive findings? More Turkish organizations may not always mean more active members. Interviews and survey data from the larger project on which this chapter draws gave the impression that, in Berlin, more Turks are members of a Turkish organization (Berger forthcoming; Berger and Koopmans 2004). Table 6.2 shows how, in general, Turks have a similar degree of associational membership in nonethnic organizations in Amsterdam and in Berlin: 41 percent in Berlin and 45 percent in Amsterdam are members of a nonethnic organization. However, the number of Turks who are members of ethnic organizations is significantly higher in Berlin. The incentive is probably lower in Amsterdam, where Turkish organizations and leaders are more incorporated in the political system than their counterparts in Berlin. This means that there is less demand for a politically active community to provide ethnic organizations with additional tools for access.

TABLE 6.2　*Political Behavior and Association Membership*

	Berlin		Amsterdam	
	Germans	Turks	Dutch	Turks
Political participation (1)	62	45	29	14
Political trust (2)	59	25	59	42
Intention to vote	86	83	66	30
Membership association (3)	62	41	62	45
Membership ethnic organization (3)	—	23	—	11
N	306	317	2171	167

Source: Berger (forthcoming); Bosveld et al. (2002); Tillie (2004); Amsterdam Bureau of Research and Statistics (2005).

Notes: (1) Percentage of respondents who participated in at least one political activity within the last twelve months. In Amsterdam, the following question was posed: "Have you, alone or together with someone else, engaged in any activity that concerns public life in your neighborhood or city? Could you please indicate whether you have engaged in any of the following activities listed (for example, contact with politicians, a demonstration)?" In Berlin, the following question was posed: "Have you, within the last twelve months, engaged in any activity that concerns public life in Berlin or Germany? Could you please indicate whether you have engaged in any of the following activities listed (for example, contact with politicians, a demonstration)?"

(2) Percentage of respondents who disagreed with at least one of the following statements: "Political parties are only interested in my vote, not in my opinion;" "Berlin/Amsterdam civil servants are only interested in rules and forms;" "Representatives do not care about people like me."

(3) Amsterdam membership data on Dutch: Raat (2005); data on Turks: Tillie (2004). In Amsterdam, the following question was posed: "Are you active in any of these organizations or are you associated with them (for example, a sports association, cultural association, or a national or ethnic organization)?" In Berlin, the following question was posed: "Could you please indicate if you are a member of any organization on this list and whether it could be considered an ethnic organization (for example, a sports association, cultural association, political organization)?"

TABLE 6.3　*Turnout Rates of Turkish Voters at Local Elections*

	Amsterdam	Berlin
1994	67	—
1998	39	—
2002	30	—
2006	44	—

Source: Michon and Tillie (2003); Van Heelsum and Tillie (2006).

In addition, it should be noted that more organizations and greater interorganizational linkages do not necessarily yield a better functioning network. The Berlin network of Turkish organizations may function more effectively as a mobilizing network than Amsterdam's. It is not hard to imagine how much more effective Berlin's hierarchical network of Turkish organizations—depicted as a star-shaped diagram revealing three main organizations in the middle—is for mobilizing people than the inclusive, albeit more extended, network found in Amsterdam. Furthermore, Amsterdam's network seems to be strongly influenced by a city policy that is particularly inclined to support small and localized Turkish interest organizations, which connect leaders of different ideological backgrounds. In contrast, Berlin's organizational network originated from within the Turkish community, independent of city authorities, while leaders from the main umbrella organizations together established an organization for successful Turkish businessmen. This likely led to Berlin's having a stronger and more effective mobilizing network than Amsterdam.

Another important factor possibly at stake is the relationship between the ethnic elite and the rest of the community. This study suggests that the distance between the organization's elite (the organizers who constitute the network) and its members can be influenced by state policies. The cases of Amsterdam and Berlin produce the conclusion that a higher number of state policies, as manifested in subsidies, could increase the sense of detachment between board members and their constituency. Or, as one of the presidents of a large Turkish organization said during an interview when asked for his opinion regarding the lack of state subsidy for his organization: "Da wir keine finanzielle Unterstützung bekommen sind wir unabhängiger [Because we do not receive financial support we are more independent]" (Berger forthcoming).

Table 6.2 indicates, furthermore, that Turks in Berlin are participating almost as much as nonimmigrant Germans when it comes to political activities, intention to vote, and associational membership. However, Turks show only half as much trust in the German political system as Germans do. Considering the policies of Germany and, in particular, Berlin, this distrust is not very remarkable. In comparison, in Amsterdam, where there has been greater outreach to immigrants and minorities, Turks express much greater political trust.

CONCLUSION: POLICIES, CIVIC NETWORKS, AND POLITICAL BEHAVIOR

We have looked into the possible relationships between a host state's political opportunity structure and an immigrant group's organizational structure, and between the immigrant group's organizational structure, along with the political weight of its organizations, and the level of political activity among its individuals. We anticipated findings in which a stimulating host state environment would work to promote the number of existing immigrant organizations and the networks between them. We also expected that more organizations and more networks would produce a more civic community in which organizations gain greater political influence and their members become more politically active, as well as place greater trust in the political system.

The study's first expectation was met. Indeed, on comparing the Turkish organizing processes of Amsterdam and Berlin, Amsterdam's policies and the city's institutional environment resulted in relatively more Turkish organizations and a more connected network of interlocks between them. The organizations and networks also proved to be better incorporated in Amsterdam's political system than in Berlin's. Examples such as the Turkish advisory council and the number of existing Turkish representatives illustrate that Turkish organizations in Amsterdam have played a more central role in the local political system than those in Berlin. At the same time, it must be noted that Turkish organizations in both Amsterdam and Berlin hold relatively little political weight.

The study's second expectation, however, was not completely met. Despite the fact that there are more Turkish organizations in Amsterdam, with a greater extended and inclusive network among them, survey results revealed that Turks in Berlin are much more politically engaged when it comes to their activities and electoral participation as expressed in intentions to vote. An explanation for this unexpected result is, first, that Turkish immigrants in Amsterdam have less incentive to participate in local politics than their counterparts in Berlin because the former city's organizations and leaders are already more politically incorporated. Second, in Amsterdam, fewer Turkish immigrants are members of a Turkish organization. Third, the distance between board members and their constituencies is greater in Amsterdam, which would mean that, though the Turkish elite are better incorporated in the city's local political system, it is more difficult for them to mobilize their ethnic constituency. Finally, Amsterdam's extended and inclusive interorganizational network of Turkish organizations may have less mobilizing potential than Berlin's hierarchical grass roots network. At the same time, Turks in Amsterdam report greater political trust than their counterparts in Berlin.

What, then, is the importance of place in this study on Turkish organizations in Amsterdam and in Berlin? The answer is twofold. First, as this chapter illustrates, the host city can have a significant influence on key characteristics that shape the organizing process. Consider, for instance, the role that small local Turkish interest organizations play for the entire network of Turkish organizations in Amsterdam. These organizations, which are strongly supported by state subsidies, have lessened ideological polarization among Turkish organizations by functioning as a nexus between different Turkish ideological movements. The fact that this network of Turkish organizations was, to a certain degree, incorporated into the local political system explains why Turkish immigrants in Amsterdam show few tendencies for political participation yet exhibit substantial confidence in the political system. Because, at the individual level, Turks trust their leaders and organizations to represent their interests, personal political activity is deemed less necessary. In Berlin, the opposite proves true. Turkish organizations are politically excluded, but individual Turks display high levels of political participation and low levels of political trust. An active but distrustful Turkish community is thus necessary to pressure Berlin politicians to provide more opportunities for participation by Turkish organizations. This explanation closely resembles Rahsaan Maxwell's findings in chapter 5 of this volume. He shows that Caribbean activists in France have been especially motivated to pursue ethnic-specific political mobilization in response to a lack of Caribbean-elected representatives who can respond to the specific needs of the Caribbean community, especially compared to their more incorporated and less ethnically focused counterparts in the United Kingdom.

At the same time, however, the direct political influence of Turkish organizations in Amsterdam is weak and their political position is vulnerable, despite better political incorporation. Since 2000, Dutch society has experienced a multicultural backlash and the situation for immigrant organizations in the Netherlands has changed drastically. An important reason for the backlash can probably be attributed to an unwillingness by Dutch politicians to openly discuss multicultural issues, ignoring the feelings and interest of other groups. Many consider the integration of immigrant groups in Dutch society a failure. One of the main causes is attributed to immigrant groups' reluctance to denounce old cultural ways. Immigrant organizations and, in particular, Turkish organizations are often accused of serving only to enhance ethnic identities and preventing successful integration.

Although this backlash has been less severe in Amsterdam than in other parts of the Netherlands, the political climate for Turkish organizations has clearly worsened. Subsidies for ethnic-specific organizations have disappeared, the Turkish advisory council has been shut down, and the political position of immigrant ethnic organizations has been strongly criticized. Within just a few years, the inclusion of Turkish organizations into the Amsterdam political system diminished, illustrating both the intensity of the backlash and how politically powerless immigrant organizations actually are, despite their former incorporation in the system. Turkish organizations have not been able to circumvent these developments. They have also failed to successfully mobilize their ethnic constituency to protest the increasing exclusion from the political system. This is probably related to a weak relationship between the constituency and its leaders.

In Berlin, opposite developments come to the fore. In 2006, in line with national political developments, the city transformed its approach toward immigrant groups into a more accommodative stance. Since then, Berlin has seen the establishment of immigrant organization advisory councils, an official integration policy framework, and an appointed senator for integration affairs. These measures have all worked to increase the degree of political incorporation of Turkish organizations into Berlin's political system. We expect that such incorporation will eventually lead to a decreased level of political activity among individual Turks in Berlin and, conversely, increase their trust in the local political system. However, looking at recent developments in Amsterdam, a lack of individual political participation may leave Turkish organizations in a vulnerable position, because their link with the ethnic constituency is in many ways their most powerful political asset.

NOTES

1. Here we focus on the period before 2000, but in the conclusion we return briefly to the striking policy developments early in the twenty-first century.
2. This also holds after controlling for socioeconomic background variables (for Amsterdam, see Tillie 2004; for Berlin, see Berger forthcoming).
3. Only in the second half of the 1990s was more emphasis placed on subsidies for individual projects in Amsterdam.
4. One of the disadvantages of focusing on longitudinal interlocking directorates is that it can produce interlocks between organizations that are mainly coincidental. If, for instance, an individual sits on the board of a certain Berlin Turkish organization between 1976 and 1981 and then serves as a board member of another Berlin Turkish organization between 1989 and 1991, the longitudinal network analysis will display a longitudinal interlocking directorate between these two organizations for the 1980s. It is, however, possible that this individual has had a complete change in ideology between 1981 and 1989. In such a case, the interlock in question could not be considered a genuine ideological interorganizational relationship. Nevertheless, the individual does carry into the second organization the skills and knowledge gained in the previous organization. The interlock is thus not totally without meaning.
5. Among non-German households, 90 percent have telephones, the equivalent to the percentage possessed by German households.
6. Such controls were set to minimize potential biases in favor of migrants who might be more integrated linguistically and, often as a result, culturally and politically.

REFERENCES

Amsterdam Bureau of Research and Statistics. 2005. "De Staat van de Stad III" ["State of the City III"]. Amsterdam: O + S: Amsterdam Bureau for Research and Statistics. Accessed at http://www.amsterdam.nl/custom/pdf/StaatvandeStadAmsterdam III.pdf.

Berger, Maria. Forthcoming. *Politiek Burgerschap van Migranten in Berlijn: De Weerbarstige Effecten van Sociaal Kapitaal op de Integratie van Turken, Italianen, Russische Joden en Aussiedler* [*Political Citizenship of Immigrants in Berlin: The Unruly Effects of Social Capital on the Integration of Turks, Italians, Russian Jews, and Ethnic Germans*]. Unpublished Ph.D. dissertation, University of Amsterdam.

Berger, Maria, and Ruud Koopmans. 2004. "Bürgerschaft, Ethnische Netzwerke und die Politische Integration von Türken in Amsterdam und Berlin" ["Citizenship, Ethnic Networks, and the Political Integration of Turks in Amsterdam and Berlin"]. *Forschungs Journal neue Soziale Bewegungen* 1(1): 70–79.

Berger, Maria, Christian Galonska, and Ruud Koopmans. 2004. "Political Integration by Detour: Ethnic Communities and Social Capital of Migrants in Berlin." *Journal of Ethnic and Migration Studies* 30(3): 491–507.

Berger, Maria, Meindert Fennema, Anja van Heelsum, Jean Tillie, and Rick Wolff. 2001.

Politieke Participatie van Etnische Minderheden in vier Steden [*Political Integration of Ethnic Minorities in Four Cities*]. Amsterdam: IMES.

Berveling, Jaco. 1994. *Het Stempel op de Besluitvorming: Macht, Invloed en Besluitvorming op Twee Amsterdamse Beleidsterreinen* [*The Mark on Decision Making: Power, Influence, and Decision Making in Two Policy Fields in Amsterdam*]. Amsterdam: Thesis Publishers.

Bloemraad, Irene. 2005. "The Limits of de Tocqueville: How Government Facilitates Organisational Capacity in Newcomer Communities." *Journal of Ethnic and Migration Studies* 31(5): 865–87.

Böcker, Anita, and Dietrich Thränhardt. 2003. "Einbürgerung und Mehrstaatigkeit in Deutschland und den Niederlanden" ["Naturalization and Double Nationality in Germany and Netherlands"]. In *Migration im Spannungsfeld von Globalisierung und Nationalstaat* [*Immigration in an Area of Conflict of Globalization and the Nation State*], edited by Dietrich Thränhardt and Uwe Hunger. Wiesbaden, Germany: Westdeutscher Verlag.

Bosveld, Willem, Ellen Lindeman, Karin Klein Wolt, and Suzanne Oosterwijk. 2003. *De Amsterdamse Burgermonitor 2002* [*The Amsterdam Citizen Monitor 2002*]. Amsterdam: O + S, Amsterdam Bureau for Research and Statistics. Accessed at http://www.amsterdam.nl/?ActItmIdt=3919.

Cyrus, Norbert. 2005. "Active Civic Participation of Immigrants in Germany." Country report prepared for research project POLITIS. Oldenburg, Germany: University of Oldenburg.

Doomernik, Jeroen. 1995. "The Institutionalization of Turkish Islam in Germany and the Netherlands: A Comparison." *Ethnic and Racial Studies* 18(1): 46–63.

Duyvené de Wit, Thom, and Ruud Koopmans. 2001. "Die Politisch-Kulturelle Integration Ethnischer Minderheiten in den Niederlanden und Deutschland" ["The Political Cultural Integration of Ethnic Minorities in the Netherlands and Germany"]. *Forschungsjournal Neue Soziale Bewegungen* 14(1): 26–41.

———. 2005. "A Comparison of the Integration of Ethnic Minorities into the Political Culture of the Netherlands, Germany and Great Britain." *Acta Politica: Tijdschrift voor Politicologie* 40(1): 50–73.

Fennema, Meindert. 2004. "The Concept and Measurement of Ethnic Community." *Journal of Ethnic and Migration Studies* 30(3): 429–47.

Fennema, Meindert, and Jean Tillie. 1999. "Political Participation and Political Trust in Amsterdam: Civic Communities and Ethnic Networks." *Journal of Ethnic and Migration Studies* 25(4): 703–26.

———. 2001. "Civic Community, Political Participation and Political Trust of Ethnic Groups." *Connections* 24(1): 26-41.

———. 2004. "Do Immigrant Policies Matter? Ethnic Civic Communities and Immigrant Policies in Amsterdam, Liège and Zurich." In *Citizenship in European Cities. Immigrants, Local Politics and Integration Policies*, edited by Rinus Penninx, Karen Kraal, Marco Martiniello, and Steven Vertovec. Aldershot, Hampshire, UK: Ashgate Publishing.

Galesloot, Hansje. 2004. *De Wereld in Huis. Allochtonen in Amsterdamse Raden en Besturen* [*The World at Home: Immigrants in Councils and Boards in Amsterdam*]. Amsterdam: Instituut voor Publiek e n Politiek.

Gesemann, Frank. 2001. "Einleitung: Migration und Integration in Berlin" ["Introduction: Immigration and Integration in Berlin"]. In *Migration und Integration in Berlin. Wissenschaftliche Analysen und Politische Perspektiven* [*Immigration and Integration in Berlin. Scientific Analyses and Political Perspectives*], edited by Frank Gesemann. Opladen, Germany: Leske + Budrich.

Gesemann, Frank, and Andreas Kapphan. 2001. "Lokale Gefechte eines globalen Kulturkonfliktes? Probleme der Anerkennung des Islam in Berlin" ["A Local Fight Over a Global Conflict? Problems with the Acceptance of Islam in Berlin"]. In *Migration und Integration in Berlin. Wissenschaftliche Analysen und Politische Perspektiven* [*Immigration and Integration in Berlin: Scientific Analyses and Political Perspectives*], edited by Frank Gesemann. Opladen, Germany: Leske + Budrich.

Gitmez, Ali, and Czarina Wilpert. 1987. "A Micro-Society or an Ethnic Community? Social Organization and Ethnicity Amongst Turkish Migrants in Berlin." In *Immigrant Associations in Europe*, edited by John Rex, Daniele Joly, and Czarina Wilpert. Aldershot, Hampshire: Gower Publishing.

Hunger, Uwe, and Dietrich Thränhardt. 2001. "Die Berliner Integrationspolitik im Vergleich de Bundesländer" ["The Berlin Integration Politics in Comparison to the Other German States"]. In *Migration und Integration in Berlin. Wissenschaftliche Analysen und Politische Perspektiven* [*Immigration and Integration in Berlin: Scientific Analyses and Political Perspectives*], edited by Frank Gesemann. Opladen, Germany: Leske + Budrich.

Jonker, Gerdien. 2005. "The Mevlana Mosque in Berlin-Kreuzberg: An Unsolved Conflict." *Journal of Ethnic and Migration Studies* 31(6): 1067–82.

Kasinitz, Phillip. 1992. *Caribbean New York: Black Immigrants and the Politics of Race.* Ithaca, N.Y.: Cornell University Press.

Knoke, David. 1990. *Political Networks: The Structural Perspective.* Cambridge: Cambridge University Press.

Koopmans, Ruud, and Paul Statham. 2000. "Migration and Ethnic Relations as a Field of Political Contention: An Opportunity Structure Approach." In *Challenging Immigration and Ethnic Relations Politics: Comparative European Perspectives*, edited by Ruud Koopmans and Paul Statham. Oxford: Oxford University Press.

Koopmans, Ruud, Paul Statham, Marco Giugni, and Florence Passy. 2005. *Contested Citizenship: Immigration and Cultural Diversity in Europe.* Minneapolis, Minn.: University of Minnesota Press.

Lijphart, Arend. 1968. *Verzuiling, pacificatie en kentering in de Nederlandse politiek* [*The Politics of Accommodation: Pluralism and Democracy in the Netherlands*]. Haarlem, Netherlands: H.J.W. Becht.

Lucassen, Jan, and Rinus Penninx. 1994. *Nieuwkomers, Nakomelingen, Nederlanders. Immigranten in Nederland 1550–1993* [*Newcomers: Immigrants and Their Descendants in the Netherlands, 1550–1993*]. Amsterdam: Het Spinhuis.

Lucassen, Leo. 2002. "Bringing Structure Back In: Economic and Political Determinants of Immigration in Dutch Cities, 1920–1940." *Social Science History* 26(3): 503–29.

Maussen, Marcel. 2006. *Ruimte voor de Islam? Stedelijk Beleid, Voorzieningen, Organisaties* [*Space for Islam? Urban Policy, Facilities, Organizations*]. Apeldoorn, Netherlands: Het Spinhuis.

McAdam, Doug. 1982. *Political Process and the Development of Black Insurgency, 1930–1970.* Chicago, Ill.: University of Chicago Press.

Meyer, David, and Debra Minkoff. 2004. "Conceptualizing Political Opportunity." *Social Forces* 82(4): 1457–92.

Michon, Laure, and Jean Tillie. 2003. *Amsterdamse Polyfonie. Opkomst en Stemgedrag van Allochtone Amsterdammers bij de Gemeenteraads- en Deelraadsverkiezingen van 6 Maart 2002* [*The Amsterdam Polyphony. Turnout and Voting Behavior of Immigrant Amsterdammers at the City Council and the City District Elections of March 6, 2002*]. Amsterdam: IMES.

Michon, Laure, and Floris Vermeulen. 2007. "Turkish Councillors and Their Ties with Turkish Organisations in Amsterdam." Paper for Dag van de Sociologie. Erasmus University Rotterdam.

Mizruchi, Mark. 1996. "What Do Interlocks Do? An Analysis, Critique, and Assessment of Research on Interlocking Directorates." *Annual Review of Sociology* 22(1): 271–98.

Morawska, Ewa. 1996. *Insecure Prosperity. Small-Town Jews in Industrial America, 1890–1940*. Princeton, N.J.: Princeton University Press.

Odmalm, Pontus. 2005. *Migration Policies and Political Participation: Inclusion or Intrusion in Western Europe?* Houndmills, Hampshire, UK: Palgrave Macmillan.

Olzak, Susan. 1983. "Contemporary Ethnic Mobilization." *Annual Review of Sociology* 9: 355–74.

Østergaard-Nielsen, Eva. 2003. *Transnational Politics. Turks and Kurds in Germany*. London and New York: Routledge.

Pfaff, Steven, and Anthony Gill. 2006. "Will a Million Muslims March? Muslim Interest Organizations and Political Integration in Europe." *Comparative Political Studies* 39(7): 803–28.

Rath, Jan, Rinus Penninx, Kees Groenendijk, and Astrid Meyer. 2001. *Western Europe and its Islam*. Leiden, Netherlands: Brill.

Rijkschroeff, Rally, and Jan Willem Duyvendak. 2004. "De Omstreden Betekenis van Zelforganisaties" ["The Contested Meaning of Self-Organizations"]. *Sociologische Gids* 51(1):18–35.

Schrover, Marlou, and Floris Vermeulen. 2005. "Immigrant Organizations." *Journal of Ethnic and Migration Studies* 31(5): 823–32.

Schwarz, Thomas. 1992. *Zuwanderer im Netz des Wohlfahrtsstaats. Türkische Jugendliche und die Berliner Kommunalpolitik [Immigrants in the Net of the Welfare State: Turkish Youth and the Local Politics in Berlin]*. Berlin: Edition Parabolis.

———. 2001. "Integrationspolitik als Beauftragtenpolitik: Die Ausländerbeauftragte des Berliner Senat" ["Integration Politics as Commissaries Politics: The Commissary for Foreigners of the Berlin Senate"]. In *Migration und Integration in Berlin. Wissenschaftliche Analysen und Politische Perspektiven [Immigration and Integration in Berlin. Scientific Analyses and Political Perspectives]*, edited by Frank Gesemann. Opladen, Germany: Leske + Budrich.

Tarrow, Sidney. 1998. *Power in Movements: Social Movements and Contentious Politics*. Cambridge: Cambridge University Press.

Thränhardt, Dietrich. 2000. "Conflict, Consensus, and Policy Outcomes: Immigration and Integration in Germany and the Netherlands." In *Challenging Immigration and Ethnic Relations Politics: Comparative European Perspectives*, edited by Ruud Koopmans and Paul Statham. Oxford: Oxford University Press.

Tillie, Jean. 2000. *De Etnische Stem. Opkomst en Stemgedrag van Migranten Tijdens Gemeenteraadsverkiezingen (1986–1998) [The Ethnic Vote: Turnout and Voting Behavior of Immigrants at Municipal Elections (1986–1998)]*. Utrecht: FORUM.

———. 2004. "Social Capital of Organizations and Their Members: Explaining the Political Integration of Immigrants in Amsterdam." *Journal of Ethnic and Migration Studies* 30(3): 529–41.

Tillie, Jean, and Meindert Fennema. 1998. "De Turkse Gemeenschap in Amsterdam. Een Netwerkanalyse" ["The Turkish Community in Amsterdam: A Network Analysis"]. In *Uit de Zevende: Vijftig Jaar Politieke en Sociaal-Culturele Wetenschappen aan de University of Amsterdam [Since the Seventh: Fifty Years of Political and Sociocultural Sciences at the University or Amsterdam]*, edited by Anne Gevers. Amsterdam: Het Spinhuis.

Van Heelsum, Anja. 2004. *Migrantenorganisaties in Nederland (Deel 2). Het Functioneren van de Organisaties [Immigrant Organizations in the Netherlands (Part 2)]*. Utrecht: FORUM.

Van Heelsum, Anja, and Jean Tillie. 2006. *Opkomst en Partijvoorkeur van Migranten Bij de gemeenteraadsverkiezingen van 7 Maart 2006* [*Turnout and Party Preference of Immigrants at the Municipal Elections of March 7, 2006*]. Amsterdam: IMES.

Vermeulen, Floris. 2005. "Organizational Patterns: Surinamese and Turkish Associations in Amsterdam, 1960–1990." *Journal of Ethnic and Migration Studies* 31(5): 951–73.

———. 2006. *The Immigrant Organising Process. Turkish Organisations in Amsterdam and Berlin and Surinamese Organisations in Amsterdam, 1960–2000.* Amsterdam: Amsterdam University Press.

——— 2007. "Competing Ideologies: Turkish Immigrant Organizations in Amsterdam and Berlin, 1965–2000." Paper presented at the ASA Annual meeting, New York, August 13, 2007.

Vermeulen, Floris, and Rosanne Stotijn. 2007. "Local Policies Toward Unemployment Among Immigrant Youth: The Example of Amsterdam and Berlin." Paper for IMISCOE Conference—The Multilevel Governance of Immigrant and Immigration Policies, Turin, Italy, May 10, 2007.

Waldinger, Roger. 1996. *Still the Promised City? African-Americans and New Immigrants in Postindustrial New York.* Cambridge, Mass.: Harvard University Press.

Weiss, Karin, and Dietrich Thränhardt, editors. 2005. *SelbstHilfe. Wie Migranten Netzwerke Knüpfen und Soziales Kapital Schaffen* [*Self Help. How Immigrants Tie their Networks and Create Social Capital*]. Freiburg, Germany: Lambertus.

Yurdakul, Gökçe. 2006. "State, Political Parties and Immigrant Elites: Turkish Immigrant Association in Berlin." *Journal of Ethnic and Migration Studies* 32(3): 435–53.

Part II

Variations Across
Ethnic Groups

Caroline B. Brettell and Deborah Reed-Danahay

Chapter 7
"Communities of Practice" for Civic and Political Engagement: Asian Indian and Vietnamese Immigrant Organizations in a Southwest Metropolis

The voluntary immigrant associations that provide the context for the events described in the vignettes that follow are important to processes of political incorporation and good citizenship because it is often through such organizations that immigrants become aware of the problems and possibilities of American civic life and participation in the public sphere—that is, the realm between the private and that of governmental institutions (Habermas 1989).

VIGNETTE #1

On April 21, 2006, the Irving DFW Indian Lion's Club held its annual fundraising banquet. About 300 people, the majority of them Asian Indians, were in attendance. The formal part of the evening, with a Hispanic woman from one of the local television stations serving as the Master of Ceremonies, began with the pledge of allegiance and the singing of both the American and Indian national anthems. Several local dignitaries were recognized—a judge from one of the juvenile courts, the mayor of Flower Mound (a Dallas-Fort Worth area suburb), and city council members from several other communities in the area. The president addressed the audience by describing the mission of the club, founded eleven years earlier—"Vision without action is merely a dream; vision with action can change the world." He suggested that the club, through its actions, including the primary care clinic in Lewisville and the Grace home for the handicapped in India, had grown in stature and impact. During the evening, a citizen of the year award was given to the founder (an Anglo) of Thanksgiving Square, an interfaith center in downtown Dallas. Also honored were a nurse of the year (of Indian origin) and a policewoman (an Anglo) who won the community award. Four high school students of various ethnic backgrounds were given $500 college scholarships and a social worker (Indian origin) was recognized as the Lion of the Year. The president also enumerated the financial contributions made by the club to various charity activities over the past year—$20,000 to the primary care clinic; $10,000 to the Sight Foundation; and $500 to the American Diabetes Foundation. A live auction raised additional funds, as did the evening raffle. Following some cultural entertainment, Carole Keeton Strayhorn, Texas state comptroller and an independent candidate in the 2006 Texas gubernatorial race addressed the crowd through video. She had been scheduled to appear in person, but an emergency session of the Texas legislature prohibited her from attending. After recognizing the generosity of Lions serving the DFW community, Ms. Strayhorn delivered a campaign speech. The surprise guest of the evening was Kinky Friedman, another independent gubernatorial candidate. He enraptured the audience with his own, highly entertaining campaign speech.

VIGNETTE #2

On April 15, 2006, the Vietnamese American Community (VAC) of Tarrant County held the grand opening of its new community center. On this sunny Saturday afternoon, the official proceedings began with a ribbon cutting outside, in front of the main door to the center. Flanked by American and South Vietnam flags (the latter often referred to as the Freedom and Heritage flag), Vietnamese leaders were joined by the Filipino president of the Asian American Chamber of Commerce, the chairman of the Dallas VAC, and local politicians—including the mayor pro tem of Arlington, Texas, a city council member, and political candidates for state office. There were several brief speeches by these male leaders, celebrating the VAC and its presence in this region of north Texas. Attending this event were at least 200 Vietnamese Americans of various ages, but primarily both older and middle-aged adults and their children (who ranged from college age to infants and toddlers). The local politicians and an anthropologist were among the handful of non-Vietnamese in attendance. Various rooms were set up inside the community center for viewing, including the new computer room where instruction in the Internet is being offered especially to older people, and a room where ESL classes are taught. A dedication ceremony was held in an assembly hall decorated with an altar to the ancestors (a Vietnamese cultural symbol that can be shared by both Buddhist and Catholic participants) displaying objects of symbolic cultural meaning to the Vietnamese. This altar was, like the front door, flanked by United States and South Vietnamese flags. The new logo for the VAC was also on display at the community center, with its map of Vietnam as a backdrop to a group of multiracial characters spreading between Vietnam and the United States, symbolizing a bridge between the two peoples. During the formal dedication ceremony, an elder in traditional dress "blessed" the center, and awards were given to various supporters of the VAC, including individuals and businesses. As the day continued, intensification of links to the wider community in which the center is located, symbolized by the ribbon cutting and presence of dignitaries, gave way to intensification of bonds between

VAC members, as language use switched primarily to Vietnamese and the atmosphere turned more informal.

IMMIGRANT ASSOCIATIONS AS
COMMUNITIES OF PRACTICE

It is through such organizations that immigrants learn ways of practicing citizenship, broadly defined, in the United States. The editors of the volume invoke this idea of the public sphere in defining civic engagement as the involvement in communal activities that have some purpose or benefit beyond a single individual or family's self-interest. They then define political engagement as involvement in activities related to the formal political system, often with the intention of influencing government policies and practices. In our view, civic and political engagement are closely allied and are put into practice in the context of organizations, such as the DFW Irving Indian Lion's Club and the Vietnamese American Community of Greater Tarrant County, that develop within immigrant communities.

Although several European scholars have begun to examine the role of organizations in the civic and political integration of immigrants in Europe (Berger, Galonska, and Koopmans 2004; Bousquet 1991; Dorais 1998; Fennema and Tillie 1999; Hamidi 2003; Jacobs and Tillie 2004; Odmalm 2004; Tillie 2004), less attention has been paid to this issue in relation to post-1965 immigrants to the United States, looking particularly at how such organizations foster individual and collective practices of civic engagement.[1] We argue here that it is at the local level, in the neighborhoods, churches and temples, and cultural and business associations, that one finds the kinds of grassroots civic engagement that lay the foundation for political incorporation. An important element in understanding the process of civic and political engagement is the question of how immigrants acquire knowledge about and modes of participation in American civic and political life. In what ways do associations enhance this learning process as a form of social practice?

The study of voluntary associations and their role in civic engagement has primarily focused on the modes of social capital—shared values, social networks, collaboration, and mutual trust—developed through participation in associations (Putnam 2000, 2007; Maloney, Smith, and Stoker 2000) and on the civic skills acquired through participation in various organizations (Verba, Schlozman, and Brady 1995). Research on the political socialization of youth through voluntary associations (Hanks 1981; McFarland and Thomas 2006) has found correlations between adolescent participation in associations and adult political participation. Although these approaches underscore the crucial links between associations and civic engagement, they do not focus adequately on the processes through which individuals acquire knowledge about forms of participation. Instead, they tend to focus on the results of participation (that is, having high or low social capital, having civic skills, and so on), and hence the individual resources and relationships that are accrued and that assist in achieving specific ends. As Michael Aguilera and Douglas Massey suggested, people "gain access to social capital through membership in networks and institutions and then convert it into other forms of capital to improve or maintain their positions in society" (2003, 673). This is certainly an important aspect of the relationship between immigrants and organizations, but the emphasis on social capital tends to overlook processual questions about the specific social contexts in which knowledge and social practice, particularly the practice of civic engagement, are developed. Equally neglected in an emphasis on social capital alone is the role of social agency in civic and political engagement.

To focus attention on the process of what people do (as well as on what they have in terms of resources), we use the notion of communities of practice (Lave and Wenger 1991). This heuristic concept draws the focus of attention to the ways in which participation in associations may affect and effect other forms of participation in the public sphere among immigrants. Although not a new concept, the idea of a community of practice has not yet been used in the context of immigration. As articulated by Jean Lave and Etienne Wenger, the concept can shed light on the role of associations for immigrant civic and political engagement through its attention to the incorporation of newcomers into established communities of practice.[2] A community of practice implies "participation in an activity system in which participants share understandings about what they are doing and what that means in their lives and for their communities" (Lave and Wenger 1991, 98). Newcomers start from a position of peripheral participation in such communities, and then participate "as a way of learning—of both absorbing and being absorbed in—the 'culture of practice'" of the community of practice (95). Communities of practice may be located at various levels of sociality, so that an immigrant association may be viewed as a community of practice, but so also may larger units. For example, elected politicians such as Hubert Vo (a Vietnamese-American Texas state representative from the Houston area) or Bobby Jindal (an Indian American former congressman and recently elected governor of Louisiana), have moved from a peripheral position as newcomers and immigrants to full participation in the community of practice of the American political system.

By adopting this framework for the study of immigrant incorporation, we posit that American civic life itself is a large community of practice, that may nor may not be receptive to newcomers in various ways, and that more localized or specialized ethnic or other civic associations can be seen as other communities of practice that articulate with each other and with the wider civic sphere. Each individual participates in multiple communities of practice. Etienne Wenger (2006) suggested that an organization is made up of several interconnected communities of practice through its members, and that such communities serve as homes for identities (2006, 5). He outlined three aspects—the domain, the community, and the practice. First, the identity of the community of practice derives from a shared domain of interest (a joint enterprise) and those involved are committed to this domain. Second, to pursue these interests, members of the community of practice engage in joint activities and learn together—in other words, there is mutual engagement that binds people together. Third, members of a community of practice develop a shared practice. M. K. Smith added that a community of practice "needs to develop various resources such as tools, documents, routines, vocabulary and symbols that in some way carry the accumulated knowledge of the community" (2003, 3). Lave and Wenger pointed out, however, that a community of practice does not necessarily require "co-presence, a well-defined identifiable group, or socially visible boundaries" to be identified as such (1991, 98). Rather, the emphasis is placed on shared understandings (for full participants) about the meaning of activities in which members engage.

In this chapter, which is based on ethnographic fieldwork among Asian Indian and Vietnamese immigrants in the Dallas–Fort Worth metropolitan area (DFW), we explore how associations, as communities of practice where situated learning takes place, foster civic and political engagement and thereby "make citizens." Our research methods have included four major approaches: participant-observation research among these two populations at both formal and informal events (from family dinners to association meetings to community festivals to fundraising events); semi-structured and open-ended interviews with community leaders (religious, ethnic, and mainstream) and parents of high school and college-aged youth; focus groups with college students from the two immigrant communities; and content analysis of print media (Internet, newspapers, magazines, and so on). Our study includes research participants from a variety of age groups (first, 1.5, and second generation) and both males and females. The investigation of the role played by associations in civic engagement, reported here, is just one part of the larger project on how immigrants learn to participate in the public sphere. Although we share a common set of research questions and methods aimed at enhancing the comparative approach we seek, we are each working with one population (Brettell with Asian Indians, and Reed-Danahay with Vietnamese).

After a brief demographic overview of Asian Indian and Vietnamese immigrants in the DFW area, we turn to our two populations—first the Asian Indians and then the Vietnamese. For each group, we briefly describe the range of associational activity to provide context for our subsequent discussion of two specific organizations chosen to illustrate communities of practice within each group and their role in making citizens. Participation in a community of practice is a process of learning but also of creating meanings. Through these four case studies, we argue for a focus on the diverse contexts in which immigrants learn to become civically engaged as well as for an analysis that emphasizes both structure and agency. Our focus is not primarily on differences or similarities in the ways that Asian Indians and Vietnamese participate in the public sphere in the United States, but, rather, on the similar processes members of both populations experience and shape as participants in communities of practice. Our overall questions are, thus, how do associations foster individual practices of civic and political engagement and, alternatively, how do the social practices of individuals shape and influence associational activities? These questions, we suggest, are fundamental to the broader topic with which this volume is concerned—the civic and political presence and weight of immigrant populations and the associations they form.

DEMOGRAPHIC AND ASSOCIATIONAL OVERVIEW

During the 1990s, the foreign-born population in the DFW region almost doubled and demographic data indicate that these growth trends have continued into the first decade of the twenty-first century. The 2000 census counted 36,522 foreign-born Vietnamese in the four counties (Collin, Dallas, Denton and Tarrant) of the DFW region and 30,030 foreign-born Indians. The numbers were higher for the broader Dallas-Fort Worth CMSA—with 49,669 Asian Indians and 47,090 Vietnamese. After the Mexicans these are the second and third largest foreign-born population in the area, though they represent only 0.95 and 0.90 percent of the total CMSA population respectively. Both populations are spread across the metropolitan area, but the Vietnamese have two nodes of concentrated settlement—in the cities of Garland (Dallas County) to the northeast of the city of Dallas, and Arlington (Tarrant County), in the mid-cities area between Dallas and Fort Worth. The Indians are characterized by a more dispersed pattern of settlement in an arc-like pattern north of Dallas, and particularly in Collin County, one of the fastest growing suburban counties in the United States during the 1990s (Brettell 2008).

These two groups differ in their auspices of immigration, the level of education and English-language skills, and in the culture, including political culture, they bring with them to the United States. Indians have come voluntarily as economic migrants from a democratic country, and most of the Vietnamese as refugees from a communist regime. Asian Indians have entered the United States largely on student visas, as H1-B workers, with green cards (for example, women who come to pursue nursing careers), or as dependents or sponsored relatives. Among the Vietnamese, even those who have arrived most recently, visa status is often tied to the aftermath of the Vietnam War—either due to imprisonment, Amerasian status, or sponsorship by relatives who were able to gain refugee status. A growing number of Vietnamese are now arriving as international students, but they often plan to return home after their education. Indians are generally characterized by high levels of education and income, and they have the advantage of speaking English. First-generation Vietnamese nationwide have lower income levels and are at a linguistic disadvantage. Even when they did receive secondary or higher education in Vietnam, their degrees do not translate well in the American system. Stories of former generals working as janitors are common among Vietnamese refugee populations.

Table 7.1, which includes county-level data drawn from the 2000 U.S. Census, illustrates further differences between these two populations. Household ownership is higher among the Vietnamese, but house values are higher among Indians. Vietnamese have lower per capita income overall and lower household incomes in two of the three counties profiled.[3] Although there are far fewer Vietnamese living in Collin County, which is more affluent than either Dallas or Tarrant counties, those who live there have higher levels of education and income. Despite the differences between these two populations, both are racialized ethnic

TABLE 7.1 Selected Demographic Characteristics in Three Counties of the Dallas-Fort Worth Region

	Dallas		Collin		Tarrant	
	Indians	Vietnamese	Indians	Vietnamese	Indians	Vietnamese
Total population	23,752	21,355	9,673	3,390	9,821	19,396
Median age	29	30	30	30	29	29
Average household size	3	4	3	3	3	4
Average family size	3	4	3	4	3	4
Percentage of owner-occupied housing units	34.2	50.5	55.4	74.8	40.5	60.0
Percentage of population twenty-five years and older with BA or higher	60.8	19.6	83.3	52.4	65.2	16.0
Percentage foreign-born	78.2	72.4	69.6	74.1	74.2	73.7
Percentage of population five years and older speak language other than English at home	85.7	88.1	76.7	97.6	82.4	94.5
Median household income in 1999 (dollars)	56,759	46,061	80,446	85,269	59,167	49,337
Per capita income in 1999	24,880	16,534	34,466	27,758	25,506	14,921
Median values of single-family owner-occupied homes	123,500	93,400	199,800	173,800	143,900	86,700

Source: U.S. Census Bureau (2000).

minority groups in the United States and, as a consequence, may face barriers to political incorporation. What do all these characteristics, both the major differences as well as the similarities, mean for associational life, civic engagement, and political incorporation?

In the DFW region, members of Asian migrant populations are involved in pan-Asian associations, associations based on shared national identity (Indian or Vietnamese, for example), and mainstream organizations. Many organizations are directed to activities at the local level; others are linked to national level organizations. Still others are focused on transnational activities, linking Indian and Vietnamese immigrants, respectively, to home. Table 7.2 presents examples of the range of associations that we have found in the DFW area. This is by no means an exhaustive list, but it does identify the universe of opportunities for civic and political engagement available to Asian migrants in general, and Indian and Vietnamese migrants more specifically.

We focus only on associations based on shared nation of origin because we have found that it is within these communities of practice that newcomers begin their associative life and practice the situated learning that is essential to civic and political engagement. However, we also recognize that individuals are often involved in multiple communities of practice simultaneously and may equally participate in an organization based on shared ethnicity or national origin as they do in a pan-Asian or mainstream organization. We have found that immigrant participation in civic and political behaviors is a fluid and dynamic process, and that the role played by national origin in the types of activities engaged in may vary across Asian populations. For instance, due to language barriers and also to the strongly anticommunist sentiment of many Vietnamese who arrived as refugees, which causes them to be heavily involved in homeland politics, this group is, overall, less involved with mainstream associative life than are Indian immigrants. We have also found that Indian and Vietnamese immigrants are often less involved in the pan-Asian organizations than East Asians are. Indeed the Asian and Asian American identity categories are often problematic for these two populations—either they see them as ascriptors applied to them from outside, often on census and other forms, or, for Indians in particular, they view Asian as a term that applies to Orientals (a racialized category) and do not therefore include themselves. This emic understanding of Asian influences their organizational affiliations and participation, and the organizations through which they operate to seek political presence and political weight.

ASIAN INDIANS

In the major metropolitan areas where Asian Indians have settled, they have founded a large number of cultural, regional, religious, professional, and charitable organizations (Bacon 1996; Dhingra 2007; Khandelwal 2002; Leonard 1997; Lessinger 1995; Rangaswamy 2000). In the DFW area, there is no precise list of all such organizations but estimates from various sources run between eighty and 100. The majority are religious (for example, the Hindu, Jain, Sikh and SwamiNarayan temples, various Christian Churches, and mosques that gather Indian Muslims with Muslims of other national origins) or regional (Gujarati, Punjabi, Kerala, Telugu, Bengali Associations, for example).[4] But, as table 7.2 indicates, there are many others as well, including professional associations, cultural arts organizations, and transnational organizations that focus on supporting projects in India. Many are gathered under the broad umbrella of the India Association of North Texas, the oldest organization (1962) and one that is widely known within the Indian community. This organization sponsors two community-wide events each year, the Anand Bazaar in August to commemorate Indian Independence Day and India Nite in January to celebrate Indian Republic Day (Brettell 2005). The India Association also hosts a visit every other month from the Indian consul in Houston to address passport and visa issues for the entire community. At one of these consular days, in the fall of 2004, officers of the association were handing out voter registration cards. At least once each year, the India Association, which was recognized in the fall of 2006 for its contributions to the Dallas area by the Greater Dallas Asian American Chamber of Commerce, holds a meeting for all the Indian organizations in the city, with the goal of facilitating joint activities and promoting common goals. The India Association of North Texas has civic presence and civic weight in DFW; its leaders are often called upon by local media as spokespeople on pertinent issues and its events are covered by the press.

Many Indians in the DFW area belong to multiple organizations and are active in several of them, others are active primarily in a religious organization and little else, and still others are not active in any organization. The religious organizations are important for the preservation of cultural traditions and identity (Leonard 2006). But they are equally important for fostering civic engagement in the form of activities whereby individuals can give back to the community, whether the community is defined in relation to India or as the wider American community—both are operative and important. For Hindus, this attitude is rooted in the concept of seva, which means help or service and encompasses the idea that service to humanity is service to God. For Muslims, civic engagement and volunteerism are closely allied to Zakat, the third of the Five Pillars of Islam that requires spending a fixed portion of one's wealth for the poor and needy. When asked if zakat was part of being a good citizen, a leader at one of the area Mosques insisted that Islam does not separate who you are from your belief in God, nor civic duty from your duty to God. Indian Christians attribute these same actions to Christian values. As one member of a local Marthomite congregation stated, the mission of his church is to "lead people to Christ, and some of the way we execute that is by serving other people."[5]

Whatever their faith, Asian Indians in the DFW area who are connected to a religious organization have been involved in taking food to food banks, serving the homeless at a shelter at Thanksgiving, or raising money for a host of worthy causes. Most of the Asian Indian religious organizations were active in the aftermath of Hurricane Katrina. Children at the Jain Temple, for example, filled knapsacks with school supplies for evacuated children who found themselves in Dallas area schools. These are forms of social citizenship learned in the context

TABLE 7.2   *Types of Organizations Among Immigrants in Dallas-Fort Worth Area*

	Asian Indians	Vietnamese[a]
Regional or hometown	North Texas Bengali Association Gujarati Society Punjabi Cultural Association	Hue Association
Religious	DFW Hindu Temple MarThoma Church Chinmaya Mission American Federation of Muslims of Indian Origin (local chapter)	Lien Hoa Temple Phap Quang Temple Vietnamese Martyrs Catholic Church Our Lady of Fatima Vietnamese Church Vietnamese Baptist Church
Cultural, arts, and sports	International Hindi Association Indian Classical Music Circle Academy of Indian Arts, Plano Plano Cricket Club	Vietnamese Science and Culture Association (DFW Chapter) Vovinam Martial Arts Vietnamese Golf Association (DFW) Tram Huong Poet Society
Professional	Indian American Nurses Association Network of Indian Professionals DFW Indian Pharmacist Association Texas Indo-American Physicians Association	Vietnamese Professionals Society (Dallas chapter) Vietnamese Health Professionals Association of North Texas DFW Vietnamese Air Force Association Former Cadets of the National Military Academy
Pan-ethnic group	India Association of North Texas Greater Dallas Indo-American Chamber of Commerce	Vietnamese American Community of Greater Tarrant County Vietnamese American Community of Dallas
Political or lobbying	Indian American Friendship Council (local chapter) Freedom and Justice Foundation (Muslim)	Amerasian Citizenship Initiative Vietnamese American Public Affairs Committee (VPAC)

TABLE 7.2   *Continued*

	Asian Indians	Vietnamese[a]
Educational	Alumni of Baroda University India Institute of Technology Alumni Association Indian Students Association (various campuses)	Vietnamese Student Association (various campuses) Alumni of Trung Vuong
Women's	Chetna (domestic violence) Muslim Women's Society	
Ethnic youth	SEVA (Students Engaged in Volunteer Activities) Youth League of St. Mary's Orthodox Church India, Dallas	Vietnamese Scout Association Viet Soul Kids Helping Kids Buddhist Youth Association Eucharistic Youth Association (Roman Catholic)
Mainstream-related	Irving DFW Indian Lions Club Dallas Indian Lions Club	VietScouting (various troops in DFW)
Pan-Asian[b]	Greater Dallas Asian American Chamber of Commerce Tarrant County Asian American Chamber of Commerce Dallas-Fort Worth Asian American Citizen Council Asian American Charity Ball Voice of Asian Americans Asian American Journalists Association (DFW chapter) Asian Professional Exchange (Dallas) APEX Dallas Asian American Bar Association	
Pan-immigrant[b]	DFW International	

Source: Authors' compilation.
[a] Many of the organizations listed for the Vietnamese are English translations of organizations with Vietnamese names.
[b] The level of participation in pan-Asian and pan-immigrant groups varies. Several of these are more dominated by Chinese and other East Asian immigrants and Indians and Vietnamese are less involved although often there are individuals who represent their respective communities on the board. This table is by no means exhaustive. It simply suggests the larger organizational universe.

of a religious community of practice and adapted to the circumstances of living in the United States. Yet, these are not organizations that actively seek or receive either civic presence or political presence, as this is accorded by those external to the organization.[6]

If much of associational life for Asian Indians in the United States and in DFW revolves around religious institutions that define civic engagement as part of their social and religious responsibility, there are still a number of other associations with which first-generation immigrants are involved that foster civic and political engagement, that focus on attaining a level of civic or political presence either locally, nationally, or transnationally, and that may even carry some civic and political weight. Two that will be discussed here are the Irving DFW Indian Lions Club and the Indian American Friendship Council. Both bridge to the American mainstream community but the interest (domain) of the first is decidedly civic and that of the second is decidedly political.

Local Civic Engagement: The Irving DFW Indian Lions Club

There are several Indian Lions Club chapters in the DFW area, and most recently a Dallas Women's Lions Club, whose members are primarily women of Indian origin, was established in the fall of 2005. One of the more active is the Irving DFW Indian Lions Club mentioned earlier. All Lion's Clubs, including those formed within in Indian community are part of the district convention and representatives are expected to attend both local and national conventions. Most take on one annual eye clinic service project because this is the charitable cause of Lions globally. But, beyond this obligation, they can define their own activities and projects. They are therefore simultaneously connected and independent and their civic presence must be understood with this in mind.

Many Indians who come to the United States are already familiar with Lions International but they view Lions Clubs as operating differently in the United States. The current president of the Irving DFW Indian Lions Club, who initially had no interest in becoming a member, observed that in India only the rich or upper class are members. The friend who was trying to recruit him claimed that in the United States the clubs were about service not status. He attended a meeting and decided to apply for membership.

The motto of the DFW Irving Indian Lions Club, which has thirty-three members of all faiths but primarily from the state of Kerala in India, is "we serve."[7] The president described this as a higher calling, "higher than those who are called to service only themselves, and not their community." When asked what he meant by community, he noted that there are two communities, the geographical community of those in the DFW area and the greater Indian community, including people in India. Another individual noted that, by establishing an Indian Lions Club, it was possible to support charitable causes in India as well as in the United States. The former would not be of much interest to a mainstream Lion's Club. About 40 percent of the funds raised (largely through the annual banquet described) by the Irving DFW Indians Lions Club supports service projects in India and 60 percent is spent in the United States on projects such as Habitat for Humanity and a sports extravaganza for the physically challenged.

When asked about the role that serving plays in good citizenship, the current president responded that "serving goes hand in hand with being a good citizen, especially here in America. I feel it is a citizen's duty to give back." He underscored the learning process that goes on within an organization like the Lions Club when he observed that citizenly duty is not connected with service in India but that Indians in the United States make the connection. "I think it's the environment that influences us. It's not a change of values because I would like to think that I still hold the same values toward mankind, however, those values are worn more on America's shirt sleeves. They are acted out in a bolder way."

The median age of members of the Irving DFW Indian Lions Club is sixty [the president noted that in India the average age would be in the mid-thirties], reinforcing an analysis that is frequently offered for the life course of civic engagement and service by Indian informants. One informant suggested that community participation is itself a process. People first are involved in their religious organizations. Then they get involved in the Indian community organizations. Then they move to the next level outside the community with chambers, school boards, mainstream organizations. "One is a stepping-stone to the next," she observed. Embedded in this informant's characterization is an understanding that, as the individual branches out, he or she is becoming involved with organizations with greater civic and political presence or weight. Further, all these communities of practice provide the opportunity to develop leadership skills. Leadership of the Irving DFW Indian Lions Club rotates each year to fulfill a very explicit goal of leadership development.

One of the major accomplishments of this club is the support of a clinic for the uninsured in the general population. This clinic, which serves an average of 4,000 people a year, is located in the suburb of Lewisville to the northwest of the city of Dallas. It is open every Saturday morning and is staffed by volunteers from the club and volunteer physicians and nurses of different backgrounds. The fee for all visits is $30 and for lab work a nominal charge of $8 to $10. If a patient needs specialty services, the clinic has prearranged referral agreements with other physicians in the Indian community, again for a nominal fee for service. Patients are 40 percent Anglo, 40 percent Hispanic, 10 percent Asian, 5 percent African American, and 5 percent Indian (mostly Indians who are visiting from overseas and do not have insurance). It is important to emphasize that several other local Indian organizations sponsor health clinics—for example the India Association of North Texas and the SwamiNarayan Temple, as well as an Indian Physicians Network—but in these cases the patients are largely Indians. It is certainly possible that the well-known aegis of Lions enhances the recognition, and hence civic presence of the DFW Irving Indians Lions Club, and therefore makes the broader reach of its clinic possible.

The commitment to and support of this clinic reflects the concerns that the Irving DFW Indian Lions Club has about the rising cost of health care and declining coverage—their shared domain of mutual interest. In acting upon this shared domain, the members of this club have become civically engaged. For them, citizenship follows a rule of reciprocity. They have become citizens of the United States and it is their duty to serve. But equally, by serving they learn to be and can be recognized as good citizens.

Although participants in these ethnic-based Lions Clubs are largely focused on civic engagement, and hence on the broader meaning of citizenship that is central to our discussion of the learning that takes place in communities of practice, the brief description of the annual banquet presented earlier suggests that the members use their club to build civic and political presence. They do so by inviting local political officials, by recognizing mainstream individuals for their service, and by making monetary donations to mainstream charities. Their ability to attract two candidates for governor of Texas to their event demonstrates that politicians themselves have become aware of this particular immigrant population, their monetary resources, their ability to vote, and the fact that they generally exercise that right. The Lions affiliation may enhance the visibility and legitimacy of this particular organization in the eyes of politicians and the community at large, but given that other Indian organizations, including the India Association of North Texas, which has attracted state and nationwide non-Indian senators to its events (Brettell 2005), it is clearly not a necessary condition for establishing civic and political presence.

National Political Engagement: The Indian American Friendship Council

The Irving DFW Irving Indian Lions Club is largely a civic organization. Other organizations more forthrightly define their mission as political. One example is the Texas state chapter of the Indian American Friendship Council (IAFC), which was founded in 1990 by a physician of Indian origin living in California. Its mission is ambitious: "to create political awareness among Indian Americans, and maintain an ongoing dialogue with local, national and international policy makers as well as to educate, encourage, and involve Asian Indian Americans with voter registration, volunteerism, community service and youth leadership training, better the ties between USA and India, protect the interests of the Indian-American community, promote global democracy, and support the developing countries" (IAFC, Texas Chapter, Banquet Program, March 11, 2006). The IAFC was launched nationwide in 1996 and the Texas state chapter was established in Dallas in 2003 by a past president of the India Association of North Texas—a good example of overlapping membership and the multiple communities of practice with which individuals are engaged.

The IAFC logo shows an arm draped in an American flag shaking the hand of an arm draped in an Indian flag. This logo clearly symbolizes the key goal of shaping and influencing the relationship between India and the United States, and building the visibility, and hence political presence, of the Indian American community in Washington. The latter goal is largely achieved at the annual national convention, where members of the organization nationwide gather with power brokers in Washington, D.C. One of the major IAFC goals is to secure India a seat on the UN National Security Council. Another issue that preoccupied the organization was the backlash against outsourcing. Most recently, the focus has been on the nuclear arms agreement between the United States and India. This agreement has galvanized many individuals in the Indian community. It was debated for several weeks on the pages of *India Abroad*, a New York-based publication to which many DFW Indians subscribe, and provided the theme for the third annual banquet of the Texas state chapter of the IAFC— "Strategy, Stability, and Security."

The activities of the Texas state chapter are largely focused on these annual banquets through which funds are raised to support congressmen and senators who take an interest in their causes. Clearly, members of this organization have learned that money leads to influence in the American political process. The IAFC aims to amass political weight that is more than symbolic and beyond the local. Further, the localized banquets also offer an arena where the political accomplishments of Indian Americans nationwide can be highlighted. The evening opens with the same kind of patriotic symbolism as the Lions Club banquets—singing both national anthems, displaying both flags and, with a similar strategy to establish its civic presence, announcing monetary contributions to important American charity organizations such as the Boy Scouts, or Meals on Wheels, the American Cancer Society, or the American Red Cross. At the 2006 banquet the tables were dressed with napkins of green, white, and gold (the colors of the Indian flag) and the centerpieces were an array of American, Indian, and Texas flags.

The IAFC founder attended the first three banquets in Dallas, and in 2006 suggested that members of Congress were now beginning to pay attention to India and the India community. He described India and the United States as the two largest democracies in the world—a phrase that many Indian respondents have brought up as a point of reference for talking about their two homes as well as a way to frame for themselves and others their political standing in the United States.

The theme of connection was already present at the first annual banquet of the Texas state chapter. That year, 2004, not only was Texas Congresswoman Eddie Bernice Johnson in attendance, but also mayors from various local communities in the DFW area. The 2005 theme was more apparently political— "Democracy Leads to Freedom and Freedom leads to Opportunity"—but it also evoked visibility and shared values, both important foundations for developing the civic and political presence necessary for political influence. In 2004, the roster of speakers also included New Jersey State Assemblyman Upendra Chivukulu and an Indian-born member of the Iowa House of Representatives, Swati Dandekar. In 2005, South Carolina State Representative Nikki Randhawa Haley and Democratic State Senator from Minnesota Satveer Chaudhary were featured speakers.[8] These individuals, who related their individual paths to political office, are role models for others in the Indian American community who might have political aspirations. Being able to call on these human resources is evidence of the weight of this organization within the nationwide Indian community as well as in the broader mainstream community.

At the third annual banquet in the spring of 2006, President George W. Bush's trip to India and the nuclear arms accord were of central interest. The editor of *India Abroad,* Aziz Haniffa, an individual well connected in the halls of power in Washington and able to secure important interviews for his newspaper, received an award. He was also one of the featured speakers. His speech emphasized the growing pro-India stance of the U.S. government, but it also called on Indians in the United States to use their economic weight to help bring about social change in India by adopting and developing local communities. The other featured speaker was then-Congressman Bobby Jindal (Rep-LA), a second-generation Indian American, and right now an embodied symbol of the political success of Indians in the United States. After thanking the Indian American Community in Texas and the state as a whole for the support extended to Katrina and Rita victims, Jindal moved on to a discussion of Indian American identity, expressing discomfort with a form of essentializing whereby he was always called on to explain "what the Indian American community thinks about some issue." "Everyone knows," he said, "that if you get two Indians together you have three opinions and four organizations. There is no single voice." He then observed that when people ask him where he is from he says "Baton Rouge" and then they look at him and ask, "where are you really from" and what they mean by this is where are your parents from. This is an observation that has also been raised in interviews with first-generation Indians in the Dallas area who are naturalized citizens, suggesting that a sense of belonging and identity are constructed by outsiders as much as by immigrants. But it also offers one explanation for why the situated learning of citizenship and political engagement generally takes place first in these peripheral locations of associative life; that is in national-origin organizations.

As a community of practice, the IAFC links Indians together locally as well as nationally. It involves them in the shared enterprise of strengthening their profile in the national political arena, including shaping the way that the United States and India interact. The banquets and conventions provide the venues for the joint activities of the organization and for the exchange of critical information about political participation as well as about national and international issues of importance. They also provide a context for learning how other Indians across the country have achieved success in the political arena. Perhaps most revealing as evidence of how effective the IAFC has been as a venue for the political incorporation of Indian immigrants and how quickly they have learned about how political influence is mustered in the United States, is an event that brought Texas Senator John Cornyn to Dallas in the fall of 2006 to meet with some twenty to twenty-five IAFC members by invitation only. The cost to attend the community dinner reception was upwards of $1,000—clearly a donation to Senator Cornyn's coffers. Cornyn was billed as the chairman of the immigration, border security, and citizenship subcommittee and as a "dedicated defender of free markets, traditional values, and individual liberty."

VIETNAMESE AMERICANS

There is no comparable umbrella association for the Vietnamese that plays the same role as the India Association. Rather, there are multiple associations and

organizations that represent various groups and sometimes overlap in membership—at least 100 with chapters in the DFW region, according to informants,
many of which advertise their activities and meetings in Vietnamese print media
or on the Vietnamese radio stations. Few are known to those outside of the ethnic community. This seems typical of Vietnamese diaspora communities. Among
the Vietnamese in Montreal, Louis-Jacques Dorais (1992) similarly counted a
high number of associations—at least sixty associations in 1989 among a population of 11,500. He also points out that this continues a tradition from Vietnam,
in both rural and urban settings, of multiple voluntary associations (1992, 79).
Bloemraad (2006, 164) likewise found a high number of organizations among
Vietnamese Americans in Boston. In her earlier, pioneering work on Vietnamese
Americans in the Philadelphia region over twenty years ago, Nazli Kibria (1993)
pointed to the factionalized nature of Vietnamese refugee associational life. She
noted the "absence of a strong and cohesive Vietnamese community organization in the area" despite the fact that "there were numerous competing Vietnamese ethnic associations in the city that claimed to represent the community"
(26).

In the DFW region of Texas today, one could also argue that there is faction-
alism and that there are numerous Vietnamese ethnic associations. Some of the
associations reflect continued ties to the past for those who came as refugees—
such as groups for the first generation of Vietnamese who arrived and are composed of military veterans from various branches and ranks of service, or those
based on city or region of origin in Vietnam. There are also groups within large
corporations among younger adults that group Vietnamese with other Asians in
interest groups primarily for social activities, there are medical associations like
the Vietnamese Health Professionals Association, and there are politically explicit groups—such as the Vietnamese-American Public Affairs Committee.
Groups among youth also exist—such as Vietnamese American student organizations at colleges and universities in the region, martial arts groups focused on
Vovinam (a Vietnamese form of martial art), Doan Thanh Hon Viet (Vietsoul
Youth Organization), a group of young adults who aim to keep Vietnamese culture and tradition strong, and a performance group called Kids Helping Kids
that performs at charity events and raises money for both domestic and Vietnamese charities. There are also a large number of religious institutions based on
ethnicity—Vietnamese Catholic parishes, Buddhist temples, Protestant denominations, and other smaller religious sects, such as Cao Dai.

Despite the large number of associations, there is a range of participation.
Many research participants interviewed belonged to none of these groups, and
others were actively involved in several of them. Between these two extremes,
however, one finds that the older generation, in particular, is heavily involved in
associations related to Vietnam—either military veterans groups, hometown associations, or alumni associations for schools in Vietnamese cities. Participation in associations that interact more with mainstream society is associated
with higher education and income levels, and with generation (1.5 or second
generation).

As with Asian Indian immigrants, religious institutions play an important role
in civic engagement, particularly through volunteer work, for the Vietnamese.

These groups—in the context of Vietnamese Buddhist temples, Catholic churches, and Evangelical Protestant churches—assist immigrants and refugees initially with help in settling in the new surroundings, and outreach to new arrivals continues after that. Several people interviewed mentioned that they were unexpectedly met at the airport when they arrived by church groups who offered to help them get settled and arranged their initial lodgings, jobs, and so on. For those arriving since 1990, these groups are often composed of Vietnamese Americans, though earlier refugees were sponsored by churches with more mainstream members. There is a strong sense among many of the Vietnamese who have moved to the United States as political refugees that they should help out those left behind in Vietnam. Explicit political engagement in the context of religion, however, is discouraged by religious leaders interviewed—both Catholic and Buddhist. One priest remarked that "the church should not be involved in politics. . . . Some community leaders had wanted the church to get involved in some political things and I refused, and said it is important to keep religion and politics apart."

Volunteer work and mutual aid are important aspects of participation in religious organizations, however, reflecting another aspect of citizenship. One informant, who arrived in 1989 at the age of forty-six and has only one year of formal schooling, told me that she is not particularly active in community service, but helps out with cooking and cleaning at her temple "for a good feeling. I volunteer and meet people and this makes me happy." A Buddhist monk explained this in terms of the notion of loving kindness connected to the teachings of Buddhism, a practice that can enhance one's karma and lead to enlightenment, thereby helping to reinforce charity work. The temples and churches have raised funds for victims of Katrina and Rita, and for Vietnamese orphanages, hospitals, and other charities in Vietnam. The two nonreligious associations described below cross-cut religious affiliation, and their leadership teams include Buddhists, Catholics, and more recent Evangelical Christian converts who work together. They form communities of practice through which large groups come together as Vietnamese Americans to make their political presence and weight felt in the DFW region.

The Vietnamese American Community (VAC)

The Vietnamese American Community of Tarrant County is a highly visible symbol of the Vietnamese population in the western part of the DFW region, and has many functions. Since the 1990s, nonprofit organizations with official names translated to versions of The Vietnamese American Community of X (fill in the blank) have formed in many cities across the United States. There are two Vietnamese American communities, established as nonprofits, in the Dallas-Fort Worth region. The VAC of Greater Tarrant County, which is also known but generally only in Vietnamese as the Vietnamese Nationals Community of Greater Fort Worth, was founded in 1985 and became incorporated as a nonprofit in 1997. The VAC of Greater Dallas was founded in 1983. Other major groups in Texas include the Vietnamese American Community of Austin and the Vietnamese Community of Houston and Vicinity.

The VAC of Greater Tarrant County draws primarily from people living in the cities of Fort Worth, Arlington, and Grand Prairie—all to the immediate west of Dallas. It recently took an active role in efforts to raise money for Katrina relief. Although it was not the only organization active in this effort, its leaders have become the spokespeople in mainstream media for such efforts. The VAC also organizes a major festival to celebrate the New Year (Tet) each winter, and is a major participant in the Egg Roll Festival and Health Fair each spring (organized by the Tarrant County Asian American Chamber of Commerce), and the annual commemoration each April of the fall of Saigon (known as Black April among Vietnamese Americans). Another organization, The Vietnamese Science and Culture Association, organizes the Moon Festival each fall in this region, though members of the VAC attend and participate. The Tet and Moon festivals gather hundreds of Vietnamese families and individuals to watch performances of song and dance, rituals that reinforce ethnic identity among the youth and reaffirm it among the elders. The VAC recently started to offer ESL classes on a regular basis, is organizing computer skills classes, and rents out smaller office space to a few other organizations (such as the association of elders, a hometown association, and a veterans group). The VAC also participates in a local 4th of July festival each year by entering a float and, for this, it won the mayor's award in 2006.

In addition to its various public events and outreach through its classes and other activities, the VAC is known among the Vietnamese population as a political organization, one that lobbies primarily on behalf of Vietnamese issues in the United States and back home in Vietnam. Many of its members are concerned about homeland politics, and distribute frequent emails to each other about events connected to Vietnam. This group mobilizes protests of various sorts. For instance, it sends delegations to protest visits by Vietnamese officials to Washington. It is also, however, active in local politics. Local politicians take note of the VAC's role in mobilizing voters to support various candidates, so that many regularly appear at community events, such as the grand opening of the community center described in the second vignette early in this chapter. Local officials, as well as Texas legislative candidates, also attend and campaign at the Tet festival each year. The Vietnamese population in this region of Texas has a high rate of naturalization and a high rate of voter turnout, mainly as a consequence of the efforts of leaders of the VAC and other organizations to mobilize the community to vote. A large voter registration drive, Viet Vote, was conducted during the presidential elections in 2004, during which there was also a referendum to approve the construction of a new Dallas Cowboys stadium in Arlington. Then member of the Cowboys' team Dat Nguyen, who is Vietnamese American, helped rally support among this population.

Members of the VAC try to influence politicians on issues such as citizenship and other rights for Amerasians, human trafficking in Vietnam, and pressure on the Vietnamese government to increase religious freedom and freedom of speech. They also work to get financial support at the local level for the community center and its activities. In summer 2006, leaders of the VAC who are also connected to the Amerasian Citizenship Initiative organized a town hall meeting with representatives of the office of Congresswoman Kay Granger on the issue of citizenship for Amerasians, held at a Vietnamese restaurant in Fort Worth. The VAC also recently mobilized its networks to protest the display of the official Vietnamese flag at a large public university in the north Texas region. This flag was raised in the context of an International Student Festival, to celebrate Vietnamese international students who are studying at the university. The action provoked protest by a vocal group of Vietnamese American students at the university, supported by the Vietnamese American Community of Greater Tarrant County as well as other VACs both in Texas and in other states who rallied their support. The activists argued that the only Vietnamese flag displayed should be that representing the Vietnamese American population, the so-called Freedom and Heritage flag, not the flag representing the regime in Vietnam from which they fled. A protest rally at the university gathered thousands of supporters, including people coming from as far as California and Washington, D.C. In this effort, the VAC was following in the footsteps of other Vietnamese groups in various American cities who have protested the display of the official flag of the Socialist Republic of Vietnam (Ong and Meyer 2004).[9]

As a community of practice, the VAC includes insiders and those more peripheral to its activities. All who attend the Tet festival, however, are eligible to vote for the leadership of the VAC, and it is at this festival that the ballot boxes are available. Although this makes membership somewhat loosely defined, there are membership fees and forms to fill out to become an official member of the VAC. Efforts have been made to make this more formal, including a fundraising event for the VAC in fall of 2006, and a membership drive that encourages different levels and benefits of membership, including some corporate sponsorship. The VAC has old-timers (those who helped establish the organization) and tries to recruit newcomers among the younger generation. Active members range from retired generals who arrived in 1975 and first started the group as one for Vietnamese Nationals, a group with limited English-language skills, to business owners who arrived in the United States as children and interact regularly with mainstream clients. Some Vietnamese American college students who are getting involved in the VAC, drawn into this group initially through the controversy over the Vietnamese flag on their campus, are actively engaged in situated learning in the VAC. They are observing how elders influence American politicians, what has been successful and what is less successful. As a community of practice, the VAC provides a context for social learning about ways to engage in civic activities and to practice citizenship. The VAC is the Vietnamese association in this region of Texas with the most political presence and political weight. It gets the attention of the media, of local mainstream politicians, and of the public. For many non-Vietnamese in this region, it represents the public face of the Vietnamese.

Vietnamese Professionals Society (VPS)

Less well known in the mainstream, yet highly active and with a large membership, the Dallas chapter of the Vietnamese Professionals Society is part of an international network of twenty-five chapters in North America, Europe, Australia, and Asia, and one of nine chapters in the United States. The English version of the VPS website (http://www.vps.org) states as its mission to "increase the knowledge and understanding of the social and economic conditions in Vietnam, to promote the welfare of the Vietnamese people and, through international cooperative effort, to apply science, technology, and humanity to the renovation of Vietnam." Its goals are both civic and political. Membership is based on having a university-level degree and being of Vietnamese descent, though the latter can be waived in certain cases. In this, it differs from the VAC, whose membership is not restricted to any level of education and whose most active adult members tend to be small business owners or working class employees, rather than professionals, though some members do have professional jobs.

The Dallas chapter serves as a social network for its members as much as it does a community of practice for civic and political engagement. Although many members of VAC are first-generation Vietnamese who arrived as adults, the majority of members in VPS are of the 1.5 generation or even increasingly of the second generation. In contrast to the current chairman of the VAC, who is a 1.5 generation leader and arrived in the United States as a youth, the current president of VPS arrived in the early 1960s as a young adult and so is a first-generation immigrant. The leader of VPS is, however, younger than the leader of the VAC. The VPS organizes parties and other get-togethers among its members as part of its social activities. But it is also very active in community and volunteer events. The VPS arranged a work party to the Gulf region in summer 2006, in response to a call by Vietnamese there to go to the New Orleans region to help with continued problems related to Hurricane Katrina. It organizes a health fair, an academic challenge event for Vietnamese youth, a Vietnamese film festival, and other events throughout the year. It has raised money for Katrina. Some of its members also travel to Vietnam to undertake charity work there. One leader in the VPS Dallas chapter who was interviewed identified the major goals as, first, professional networking. He then added that it also had a role as an advocate for the Vietnamese community, and, as an example, cited human trafficking (in which Vietnamese children are sold as brides) and that VPS helps lobby the U.S. State Department on such issues. He also mentioned the lack of religious freedom in Vietnam as being important.

The two major events organized by VPS are the Vietnamese Film Festival and the Academic Challenge. The first is a day-long event held in the auditorium of a major public university in the region, and showcases films made by Vietnamese American filmmakers, including feature-length films, documentaries, shorts, and music videos. Some of the films are in Vietnamese with English subtitles, but some are in English. The festival also brings some directors and actors to Texas for the event, and Q&A sessions with them are held after screenings. One of the goals of this, as expressed by an organizer, is to both help form a broader audience for Vietnamese American films and to educate local Vietnamese youth about possible careers in the arts. A dinner is held after the event for VPS members, those involved in the films as directors, producers, or actors, and audience members who wish to attend. In 2005 there was a gala fundraiser for Katrina after the festival. The second event, the Academic Challenge, is targeted to children under sixteen and held at a local community college. This event features teams from churches, temples, and other groups that instruct Vietnamese children in the language and culture of Vietnam. They are quizzed on their knowledge of the language and culture. Although the film festival is primarily enveloped in an English-language environment, with occasional cross-translation between Vietnamese and English, the academic challenge is exclusively conducted in Vietnamese. Gifts are given to the winning teams, but all children receive gift packages for participating. A lunch is also served to participants.

Neither of these events is explicitly political, of course, but there are members of the Dallas VPS who are also active in political associations. The current president is active in Texas party politics and works on political campaigns, as do other members. As a community of practice, VPS involves the three elements that Wenger (2006) identifies as critical—domain, community, and practice. Members are committed to the domain of the mission of the society, which is to promote and enhance Vietnamese culture and the interests of the Vietnamese community. As written in the VPS March 2006 newsletter, which is published in both English and Vietnamese, the organizers of the academic challenge, for instance, hope that participating students "will find in themselves the pride of their roots, and would realize that they too have a harmonious and sacred relationship with Vietnam the culture and Vietnam the origin." Members of VPS also participate jointly in organizing activities and learn together, and they have a shared practice. As a cohort of mostly under-forty professionals, most of whom arrived in the United States as children, the VPS is a community of practice that provides a context for situated learning about American civic and political engagement for its members and by extension to those other, younger, Vietnamese who attend its events. In contrast to the VAC, which has political weight and presence, VPS is a group with ties primarily within the ethnic community of Vietnamese Americans. It is also, however, a site for the making of citizens, because through their networking, their charity and volunteer work, and their learning to organize events that help socialize the younger generations in the United States about their Vietnamese heritage, members of VPS are active in many forms of civic engagement.

CONCLUSION

We have argued here that conceptualizing immigrant organizations as communities of practice adds a new dimension to the literature on voluntary associations as sites for the development of civic and political skills because it draws attention to how individuals acquire knowledge about forms of participation and hence how they become agents in their own process of civic and political incorporation. By viewing voluntary associations not only as venues for acquiring and enhancing social capital, but also as sites of learning, we can better grasp the ways in which newcomers develop a set of shared understandings, as well as a shared set of behaviors (both civic and political) with various goals, modes of operating, and styles of meaning and communication. Immigrant groups, such as the Indian and Vietnamese populations described here, create a host of organizations at the local level that offer opportunities for engaging in community service and other activities, for learning about the political process and for acting politically. Smith (2003, 4) has argued that "learning is not seen as the acquisition of knowledge by individuals so much as a process of social participation." We suggest that in fact both occur and that both are important to citizenship and political incorporation.

The members of the Indian American Friendship Council who make a significant donation in order to rub shoulders with a U.S. senator at an exclusive dinner have certainly learned what it takes to be at the influence-buying epicenter of the political process in the United States. The members of the Vietnamese American Community who can effectively mobilize a protest against the display of a flag that they do not feel represents them, and who can also mobilize votes for local political candidates who they feel will represent their interests, have clearly learned about grassroots political action that can produce outcomes. The members of the DFW Indian Lions Club who recognize the community service of outsiders to their organizations, who make donations to mainstream organizations, who rally their membership to collect goods and money for the victims of natural disasters in America or to engage in charity work in the home country, are communicating their understanding of what it means to be a good citizen. Members of the Vietnamese Professionals Society who, like those in the Indian Lions Club, organize to help victims of natural disasters and engage in charity work in their home country, are civically engaged in similar ways. The VPS runs an event for Vietnamese children and their parents aimed at preserving and respecting Vietnamese culture, but it also organizes events like the film festival aimed at broadening the audience for Vietnamese cultural production to the mainstream. Indians and Vietnamese who are involved in these organizations may be engaged in varied activities, but what they share is the process of learning how to participate in the public sphere in the context of these different communities of practice. To become civically and politically engaged, immigrant newcomers must start somewhere, and the most accessible place is within organizations like those discussed here.

Communities of practice are also homes for identities. In the contexts of the organizations we have described, Indian and Vietnamese immigrants are constructing dual or multiple identities and engaging multiple communities. First-generation Indians speak about the community (Indian) and the community at large. One articulated the relationship this way: "We live in one community (Indian) and engage the other (American)." When members of Indian organizations display two flags, recite the pledge of allegiance, and sing two national anthems at their events, they enact a dual identity as well as a form of emergent patriotism. When the Vietnamese organizations do the same, there is an added layer of meaning, however—that of anticommunism and South Vietnamese nationalism. By displaying the flag of South Vietnam and singing its national anthem in the same context with the American flag and anthem, these immigrants make a political statement of resistance to the current government of Vietnam.

Organizations such as those we have described here bind people together into a common purpose, as defined by the organization, and allow them to express themselves not only as Indians or Vietnamese, but also as Americans. In this expression, they exercise their own agency as both social and political citizens. Further, the activities fostered by these organizations suggest that immigrant populations can be both inward and outward focused at the same time and that formal political participation often develops in the context of informal civic engagement in multiple communities of practice. The particular organizations we have described have different degrees of civic and political presence and weight that to some extent are shaped by their respective domains of interest. A voice that is loud enough to have a flag removed from a display on a state university campus certainly carries political weight. An organization that can attract gubernatorial candidates to speak at its annual banquet certainly manifests political presence. These actions and outcomes represent varying dimensions of power, but they are equally important to the process of political incorporation. Further, if we only emphasize political return, or the social capital possessed by immigrants, we overlook the more fundamental processes by which citizens are made. This occurs in the context of charitable and other activities such as those of the Vietnamese Professional Society and the DFW Indian Lions Club that have been described here.

Finally, though we have emphasized here similarities in the processes by which Vietnamese and Indian immigrants learn about and practice citizenship and political participation in the context of the organizations they build within their communities, there are also some important differences. These differences are framed by the political cultures that each group brings to the table. Indians are well aware that they come from a big country and an important global democracy. The IAFC draws on this to leverage its political impact within the halls of power in Washington, D.C. Many of the Vietnamese focus instead on the anticommunist values of the American political process. The VAC, in particular, draws on these values to organize its activities and political voice.

The authors are grateful to the Russell Sage Foundation for supporting the research on which this paper is based. They would also like to thank their graduate research assistants for their help with this project: Faith Nibbs, who has worked with Caroline Brettell on research among Asian Indians; and Marylyn Koble, who worked with Deborah Reed-Danahay on research among Vietnamese Americans.

NOTES

1. Exceptions, at least in the Vietnamese case, would be discussions of Vietnamese associations and political engagement by Hien Duc Do (1999), Steven Gold (1992), and Jeremy Hein (1995). These authors mention generational differences and those among different waves of Vietnamese refugees, and all note that political engage-

ment with homeland politics has been an important part of Vietnamese American associative life. Hein (1995, 96) mentions that Vietnamese associations are sites for generational conflict between traditional and Americanized leaders. Reed-Dana-hay's research shows that this continues to be an issue. In the Indian case, there are general discussions of organizations in the chapters of some monographs (see, for example, Rangaswamy 2000; Khandelwal 2002; Dhingra 2007). In our recent edited volume (Reed-Danahay and Brettell 2008), several cases of civic engagement among immigrants in the United States and in Europe were presented to bridge the gap between research conducted in these two contexts.

2. Juliet Merrifield (2002) provides a useful model for using the concept of situated learning in terms of citizenship and civic education, but does not make specific reference to immigrant groups.

3. The differences in rate of home ownership probably have to do with the auspices of immigration (H1B workers, for example, are more likely to rent) as well as length of time in the country—more Indians are more recent arrivals.

4. Caste does not appear to be relevant to the formation of organizations in DFW but it is certainly still relevant in other aspects of associative life, particularly in relation to dating and marriage. Padma Rangaswamy (2000) came to a similar conclusion in her study of Indians in Chicago, and Madhulika Khandelwal (2002) identified some caste-based (jati) groups in the New York area where the Indian community is larger.

5. Marthomites are Indian Christians, the majority of whom live in or come from the state of Kerala in South India. The Mar Thoma Syrian Church is an offshoot of the Syrian Orthodox Church. It is one of several groups of St. Thomas Christians, who trace their origins to the arrival of St. Thomas (Mar Thoma) on the shores of India in the first century CE. The Mar Thoma churches are among several Indian Christian churches in the DFW area. Others include the Indian Pentecostal Church of God, the Church of South India, and a Calvary Chapel that is an American church with a largely Indian membership.

6. An exception, in recent years, would be the main Mosque in Richardson, to which some Indians belong, and some of the other mosques (the Plano Mosque, for example) that have been called upon for programs of interfaith dialogue and commentary on international events in the aftermath of 9/11.

7. This is clearly an example of the importance of networks in the formation of some of these associations, or at least in the critical mass of members. The Dallas Women's Lions Club is largely composed of Indian women who knew one another previously and came together into a club—indeed, several of the members are of Indian descent but born in Africa, especially Zambia.

8. On the front page of the issue of *India Abroad* published immediately after the November 2006 election, the photographs of all of these individuals appeared. They had all been reelected to office. Indeed two issues were devoted to the success of Indian origin candidates in the fall 2006 election.

9. Although Ong and Meyer (2004) usefully pointed to the role of protest in Vietnamese American political mobilization, they see this as focused primarily on homeland political issues and not having much potential for domestic action. In the case of some protests observed in this research, Reed-Danahay would conclude that, from a more transnational perspective, homeland and domestic issues are not easily separable (for a more detailed analysis of the flag protest and also more discussion of Vietnamese American civic engagement and communities of practice, see Reed-Danahay 2008).

REFERENCES

Aguilera, Michael B., and Douglas S. Massey. 2003. "Social Capital and the Wages of Mexican Migrants; New Hypotheses and Tests." *Social Forces* 82(2): 671–701.

Bacon, Jean. 1996. *Life Lines: Community, Family, and Assimilation Among Asian Indian Immigrants.* New York: Oxford University Press.

Berger, Maria, Christian Galonska, and Ruud Koopmans. 2004. "Political Integration by a Detour? Ethnic Communities and Social Capital of Migrants in Berlin." *Journal of Ethnic and Migration Studies* 30(3): 491–507.

Bloemraad, Irene. 2006. *Becoming a Citizen: Incorporating Immigrants and Refugees in the United States and Canada.* Berkeley, Calif.: University of California Press.

Bousquet, Gisèle L. 1991. *Behind the Bamboo Hedge: The Impact of Homeland Politics in the Parisian Vietnamese Community.* Ann Arbor, Mich.: University of Michigan Press.

Brettell, Caroline B. 2005. "Voluntary Organizations, Social Capital, and the Social Incorporation of Asian Indian Immigrants in the Dallas-Fort Worth Metroplex." *Anthropological Quarterly* 78(4): 853–83.

——. 2008. "Big D: Incorporating Immigrants in a Sunbelt Metropolis," In *Twenty-First Century Gateways: Immigrant Incorporation in Suburban America*, edited by Audrey Singer, Susan Hardwick, and Caroline Brettell. Washington: The Brookings Institution.

Dhingra, Pawan. 2007. *Managing Multicultural Lives: Asian American Professionals and the Challenge of Multiple Identities.* Stanford, Calif.: Stanford University Press.

Do, Hien Duc. 1999. *The Vietnamese Americans.* Westport, Conn.: Greenwood Press.

Dorais, Louis-Jacques. 1992. "Les Associations Vietnamiennes à Montréal" ["The Vietnamese Associations of Montréal"]. *Canadian Ethnic Studies* 24(1): 79–95.

——. 1998. "Vietnamese Communities in Canada, France, and Denmark." *Journal of Refugee Studies* 11(2): 107–25.

Fennema, Meindert, and Jean Tillie. 1999. "Political Participation and Political Trust in Amsterdam: Civic Communities and Ethnic Networks." *Journal of Ethnic and Migration Studies* 25(4): 703–26.

Gold, Steven J. 1992. *Refugee Communities: A Comparative Field Study.* Newbury Park, Calif.: Sage Publications.

Habermas, Jurgen. 1989. *The Structural Transformation of the Public Sphere.* Cambridge, Mass.: MIT Press.

Hamidi, Camille. 2003. "Voluntary Associations of Migrants and Politics: The Case of North African Immigrants in France." *Immigrants and Minorities* 22(2/3): 317–32.

Hanks, Michael. 1981. "Youth, Voluntary Associations and Political Socialization." *Social Forces* 60(1): 211–23.

Hein, Jeremy. 1995. *From Vietnam, Laos, and Cambodia: Refugee Experience in the United States.* New York: Twayne Publishers.

Jacobs, Dirk, and Jean Tillie. 2004. "Introduction: Social Capital and Political Integration of Migrants." *Journal of Ethnic and Migration Studies* 30(3): 419–27.

Khandelwal, Madhulika S. 2002. *Becoming American, Being Indian: An Immigrant Community in New York City.* Ithaca, N.Y.: Cornell University Press.

Kibria, Nazli. 1993. *Family Tightrope: The Changing Lives of Vietnamese Americans.* Princeton, N.J.: Princeton University Press.

Lave, Jean, and Etienne Wenger. 1991. *Situated Learning: Legitimate Peripheral Participation.* Cambridge: Cambridge University Press

Leonard, Karen. 2006. "South Asian Religions in the United States: New Contexts and

Configurations," In *New Cosmopolitanisms: South Asians in the US*, edited by Gita Rajan and Shailja Sharma. Stanford, Calif.: Stanford University Press.

Leonard, Karen Isaksen. 1997. *The South Asian Americans*. Westport, Conn.: The Greenwood Press.

Lessinger, Johanna. 1995. *From the Ganges to the Hudson: Indian Immigrants in New York City*. Boston, Mass.: Allyn and Bacon.

Maloney, William A., Graham Smith, and Gerry Stoker. 2000. "Social Capital and Associational Life," In *Social Capital: Critical Perspectives*, edited by Stephen Baron, John Fiueld, and Tom Schuller. Oxford: Oxford University Press.

McFarland, Daniel A., and Reuben J. Thomas. 2006. "Bowling Young: How Youth Voluntary Associations Influence Adult Political Participation." *American Sociological Review* 71(3): 401–25.

Merrifield, Juliet. 2002. "Learning Citizenship." *IDS Working Paper* 158. Brighton, Surrey: Institute of Development Studies.

Odmalm, Pontus. 2004. "Civil Society, Migrant Organizations and Political Parties: Theoretical Linkages and Applications to the Swedish Context." *Journal of Ethnic and Migration Studies* 30(3): 471–89.

Ong, Nhu-Ngoc T., and David S. Meyer. 2004. *Protest and Political Incorporation: Vietnamese American Protests, 1975–2001*. Irvine: University of California, Center for the Study of Democracy. Accessed at http://repositories.cdlib.org/csd/04-08.

Putnam, Robert D. 2000. *Bowling Alone: The Collapse and Revival of American Community*. New York: Simon & Schuster.

———. 2007. "E Pluribus Unum: Diversity and Community in the Twenty-first Century." The 2006 Johan Skytte Prize Lecture. *Scandinavian Political Studies* 30(2): 137–74.

Rangaswamy, Padma. 2000. *Namasté America: Indian Immigrants in an American Metroplis*. University Park, Pa.: Pennsylvania State University Press.

Reed-Danahay, Deborah. 2008. "From the 'Imagined Community' to 'Communities of Practice': Immigrant Belonging Among Vietnamese Americans." In *Citizenship, Political Engagement, and Belonging: Immigrants in Europe and the United States*, edited by Deborah Reed-Danahay and Caroline B. Brettell. Piscataway, N.J.: Rutgers University Press.

Reed-Danahay, Deborah and Caroline B. Brettell, editors. 2008. *Citizenship, Political Engagement, and Belonging: Immigrants in Europe and the United States*. Piscataway, N.J.: Rutgers University Press.

Smith, M. K. 2003. "Communities of Practice." *The Encyclopedia of Informal Education*. Accessed at http://www.infed.org/biblio/communities_of_practice.htm.

Tillie, Jean. 2004. "Social Capital of Organizations and Their Members: Explaining the Political Integration of Immigrants in Amsterdam." *Journal of Ethnic and Migration Studies* 30(3): 529–41.

U.S. Census Bureau. 2000. Census of Population, Summary Files. Accessed at http://www.factfinder.gov.

Verba, Sidney, Kay Lehman Schlozman, and Henry E. Brady. 1995. *Voice and Equality: Civic Voluntarism in American Politics*. Cambridge, Mass.: Harvard University Press.

Wenger, Etienne. 2006. "Communities of Practice: A Brief Introduction." Accessed at http://www.ewenger.com/theory.

Sofya Aptekar

Chapter 8

Highly Skilled but Unwelcome in Politics: Asian Indians and Chinese in a New Jersey Suburb

Declining civic participation is decried in academic and popular media alike as endangering American democracy. Meanwhile, like native-born Americans, immigrants start clubs, leagues, and societies. In this chapter, I consider the role of civic organizations in the political incorporation of immigrants in one suburban community in New Jersey. These highly skilled immigrants have educational and material resources that rival those of native-born white residents and yet, as I show, their organizations are largely excluded from the local power circles. This happens despite greater potential openness and flexibility that exists in smaller municipalities compared to large cities. I analyze the local organizational field and assess factors implicated in the ability of immigrant organizations to leverage influence in local politics.

Most studies of immigrant adaptation focus on low skilled immigrants in urban areas. I extend this tradition by considering highly skilled Asian Indian and Chinese immigrants in a suburban setting.

HISTORICAL AND DEMOGRAPHIC CONTEXT

Thirty years ago, Edison was a sprawling suburban town populated by descendants of European immigrants. A few hailed from the early Dutch settlers while many others were children of immigrants from Eastern and Southern Europe. The parents of these Irish, Polish, and Italian Americans first came to the immigrant cities of New Jersey, across the Hudson River from New York City. A generation later, their children and grandchildren moved to Edison during the dramatic wave of suburbanization (Shaw 1994). In the 1950s, Edison's Camp Kilmer became home to refugees from the Hungarian revolution. Added to the mix were a small number of African Americans and Latinos (Karasik 1986).

White ethnics—overwhelmingly Democrat—hold most of the local elected offices and they dominate local municipal and county committees, having overwhelmed the older rural Republican political machine earlier in the century

(Karasik 1986; Moakley and Pomper 1979). Edison has a mayor-council form of government, in which the mayor has the executive power and appoints department heads with council's approval, prepares the budget, and has some veto powers over ordinances passed by the council. The council is elected at-large in partisan elections (Egenton 1992). Today, as has been the case for the last thirty years, political party competition is largely absent.

Through the 1970s, many Edison residents were employed in the thriving local industrial economy, working in factories of companies such as Ford, Lockheed Martin, Revlon, and Westinghouse (Salmore and Salmore 1993).[1] Then, deindustrialization deprived blue collar workers of stable livelihoods, delegating them to the low-paid service sector with few prospects for advancement, as happened throughout the country. Although the Ford plant hung on until 2004, most of the factory jobs left in the 1980s. Many neighborhoods saw small businesses shut down and some became blighted. But, unlike towns and cities in the inner ring of New York suburbs, Edison's population actually grew. As employment in the industrial sector declined, people were attracted by Edison's new informatics, finance, and pharmaceutical jobs. Others were drawn by its excellent public schools, reasonable distance to New York, and confluence of several major highways. Today, this town of 100,000—the sixth largest municipality in the state—has low unemployment and higher than average household incomes and home values (U.S. Census Bureau 2006a).

In addition to fast-paced growth in employment, office space, and jobs, the 1980s also brought a flood of immigrants. Half of the new Edison residents in the 1980s were Asian, settling mostly in the northern part of the town.[2] The Asian population in Edison sextupled between 1980 and 1990; by 2005, more than 35,000 residents of Edison were of Asian origin.[3] Edison now has the highest concentration of Asian Indians in United States, as well as the state's largest Chinese population.[4]

Asian residents are by far the wealthiest group in Edison. Their median household income is $16,000 higher than that of non-Hispanic whites. Asians are also highly educated; an astounding 43 percent of Asian men and a quarter of Asian women in Edison hold a graduate or professional degree, compared to only 13 percent of white men and 8 percent of white women. In fact, whites in Edison are most likely to be high school graduates who have completed no additional degrees (Ruggles et al. 2004). High levels of education among Asians are consistent with their immigration trajectories as professionals and advanced students. The resources that Asian groups possess, in the form of income and social ties through professional employment, may aid their political incorporation.

Asian Indians and Chinese are comparable in terms of socioeconomic status, but Asian Indians can be expected to be more effectively incorporated into the local politics, for two reasons. First, many are fluent English speakers.[5] Although most Chinese immigrants are professionals who have some mastery of the English language, the leaders of Chinese organizations whom I interviewed mentioned their difficulties with fluency and a more halting control over their speech. Second, Asian Indians come from the largest democracy in the world and are likely to find some elements of American politics familiar. The Chinese, on the other hand, have had various levels of exposure to democratic forms of governance depending on their country of origin.

The sheer size of the growing Asian Indian community in Edison makes us expect more political influence and weight among them than among the Chinese. However, both groups are primarily first-generation immigrants (71 percent) and most adults are not American citizens (U.S. Census 2000; see figure 8.1). Inability to vote may allow local officials to ignore this population despite its size. Furthermore, many Asian immigrants now migrate directly to Edison rather than moving from a large immigrant city like New York. Their newness makes them unfamiliar with the local political situation.

Today, Edison has both a Little India and a Chinatown (see figure 8.2). Little India has hundreds of businesses providing a range of services and drawing visitors from the entire northeast. Starting in the 1990s, Oak Tree Road became a thriving business district bringing considerable tax revenue (Trivedi 1997). The hub of ethnic stores and services draws Asian Indian immigrants not just to visit but to settle as well. The transition from an economically moribund white area to a booming Little India has not occurred without vandalism, name calling, and complaints of foreign invasion (interviews).[6] The Chinatown area is far less developed and concentrated than Little India. There are many Chinese businesses

FIGURE 8.1   *Asian Foreign-Born Population in Edison by Year of Entry to the United States*

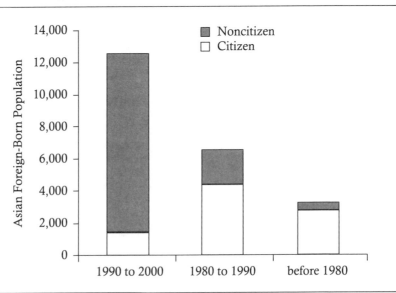

Source: U.S. Census Bureau (2000).

FIGURE 8.2   *Map of Edison, New Jersey*

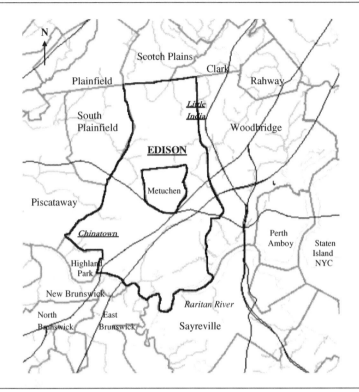

Source: U.S. Census Bureau (2006b).

along a stretch of Route 27 in the southern section of Edison, but there is nowhere close to the shopping frenzy one sees in Little India, and the Chinese businesses do not have as much of a regional draw.

In sum, in just a few decades, Edison was transformed from a manufacturing suburb of white ethnics to a center for research and finance with a large new minority group, and more polarized ethnic relations. Wealthy and educated, the new immigrants in Edison are unlike their white predecessors.

POLITICAL CONTEXT

The political structure in Edison features a strong municipal government and a de facto one party system. As a result of a long tradition of home rule in New Jersey, the county governing body—the board of freeholders—has limited jurisdiction (Connors and Dunham 1993). The county party organizations, on the other hand, have traditionally dominated politics. Although much weaker after new legislation in the 1970s, county party organizations continue to control the electoral process at the local level (Moakley 1986; Salmore 1986). Lack of challenge to the Democratic Party in Middlesex County has resulted in fragmentation and intraparty factions (Moakley and Pomper 1979). Elections are candidate centered and media-advertisement driven (Salmore and Salmore 1993; Worton 1997).

The influence of the county party organization in Middlesex County was seemingly undermined in 2005, when a political novice from the lowest stratum of the party broke ranks, ran in the Democratic mayoral primary in Edison, and defeated a party-backed, three-term incumbent Italian American mayor. The political candidacy of Jun Choi, a child of Korean immigrants, made national headlines when local shock jocks on NJ 101.5 FM referred to Asian Americans as "damn Orientals and Indians," spoke in a stereotypically East Asian accent, and said: "I don't care if the Chinese population in Edison has quadrupled in the last year, Chinese should never dictate the outcome of an election, Americans should. In Edison, this is just another example of us losing our own country. Ray and I represent the average guy in NJ, blue collar white people."[7]

The racist comments gave Choi instantaneous visibility and strong support base. Choi started out with sizable donations from friends and family across the country,[8] but soon garnered attention of national progressive organizations like Howard Dean's Democracy for America and MoveOn.org, due to his platform against cronyism and Wal-Mart (Green and Stoller 2006). After becoming the only party outsider to ever win a local primary, Choi went on to narrowly defeat a formidable Democrat-turned-Independent opponent. Late in the process, Choi was finally endorsed by the county party organization which ended up contributing heavily to his campaign. Upon election, Choi pledged to work from within the party, confirming Maureen Moakley's assertion that in New Jersey, "integration into the organization is considered essential" (1986, 60). This can also be taken as evidence in support of Clarence Stone's (1993) argument about urban regimes and the difficulty of dislodging them from power. Thus, despite progressive promises, Choi had to embrace the local party organization in the end. Upon assuming office in 2006, the maverick politician was faced with a dire financial deficit and a community rife with ethnic tensions.

Beyond the mayoral election, police and the Asian Indian community have had a tense relationship for as long as there have been Asian Indians in Edison. Business owners in Little India complain of harassment and some may have paid bribes to avoid it.[9] However, the past two years saw an escalation of the conflict with two allegations of police brutality. On India Day in 2005, two Asian Indian men claimed to have been beaten by police officers, who also allegedly spat on the Indian flag.[10] The two men were charged with obstructing justice and resisting arrest. An internal investigation cleared the officers and charges against the men were dropped.[11]

A year later, one of the officers involved in the India Day incident was accused of beating an Asian Indian man during 4th of July celebrations. A public meeting was organized to discuss the incident with the Asian Indian community but Mayor Choi pulled out of it at the last minute and held his own press conference with the police. This precipitated a demonstration of Asian Indians and a counter demonstration by police supporters. Tipped off by Edison police, immigration officers apprehended the alleged victim on an outstanding deportation order at the protest. The mayor and the chief of police launched an investigation into the breach in the chain of command, leading the Police Benevolent Association to call for the mayor's resignation. The officer accused of the beating was cleared in an internal investigation. When the mayor attempted to address the Asian Indian community at a heavily Indian apartment complex, he was ignored and jeered. Some Asian Indians circulated a petition and demonstrated against Mayor Choi's participation in the subsequent India Day parade. Choi formed a new community relations advisory committee but the police representative withdrew after only a month.[12]

Thus tensions between whites and Asian Indians have escalated in Edison. Within his first year in office, the Asian mayor was strongly criticized by both parties. Notably, the rancor and unease in intergroup relations seems to have bypassed the Chinese residents of the township.

POLITICAL OPPORTUNITY STRUCTURE AND POLITICAL CONTEXTS OF RECEPTION

I draw on two related strands of literature—the literature on political incorporation and the literature on immigrant adaptation—to understand political incorporation of Asian immigrants in Edison. The focus of this chapter is not on individual Edison residents, but on local voluntary and civic organizations. The salience of civil society to the political realm in the United States has been written about as long ago as de Tocqueville (1835/2001), recently capturing public attention through the work of Robert Putnam (2000). Civic organizations, even those having nothing to do with politics, have been shown to provide resources and impart skills relevant to their members' political involvement (Verba, Schlozman, and Brady 1995).

The pluralist tradition in political science also stresses the role of various organizations, parties, groups, associations, clubs, and committees. People with similar interests come together in these groups and work to influence government policy. In his classic study of New Haven, Robert Dahl (1961) argues that this political stratum is an open and inclusive structure, representing various local interests. Even people who are not active in organized activities have an indirect influence on policy making because the political stratum tends to reflect the goals and values of the entire community.

Many scholars do not see political incorporation as a pluralist process. In their study of urban politics, Rufus Browning, Dale Marshall, and David Tabb (1984) point out that it is not enough for minorities to protest and make demands to get the local government to respond. Instead, it is electoral mobilization that ultimately matters, because political elites respond to votes. Stone (1993), on the other hand, stresses that powerful local regimes cannot be dislodged through electoral mobilization alone. These regimes are long-term partnerships of interdependence between the government and private groups that provide it with a resource support base. Those outside the regime face a daunting task in trying to gain power: they have to establish a monopoly over decision making and essential resources in the community. Local political party organizations also play a role in political incorporation. Michael Jones-Correa (1998) found that the lack of party competition in New York City provided few incentives for outreach to immigrant voters.

To gain insight into political incorporation of immigrants, I turn to literature on immigrant adaptation. Straight-line assimilation theory (Alba and Nee 2003; Gordon 1964) predicts that immigrants and their descendants become incorporated into the dominant society's organizations and political processes. Alejandro Portes and Rubén Rumbaut (2001) have challenged this view and emphasize the segmented nature of assimilation, in which contexts of reception are crucial in understanding the experiences of immigrants. In terms of local political context, it is important to look at the reaction of the host community to immigrant groups. This reaction hinges on many factors, including the socioeconomic status, size and density, and cultural aspects of the immigrants, and can determine the relationship between the immigrant groups and the local office holders. Hostility on the part of the host community can lead to formation of reactive ethnicity and creation of ethnic organizations that defend the rights of the group.

In this chapter, I examine the degree of civic and political stratification among Asian immigrant and white mainstream organizations in Edison. In the process, I consider the applicability of pluralism and straight-line assimilation theories in this particular context. I compare the organizations in my sample based on the type and amount of civic and political resources, measure their presence in the civic and political realm, and attempt to determine their civic and political weight in the township. I then look at whether civic weight is translated into political weight and the mechanisms that facilitate or retard the process.

When referring to organizations, the concepts of civic and political stratification can be defined as stratification in organizational presence and weight. Civic or political presence of an organization includes its visibility, resources, and legitimacy. More specifically, civic presence refers to the visibility of an organization among the general population and mainstream media, its network of connections with other organizations, its longevity, and its nonprofit status. Political presence, on the other hand, describes the visibility of an organization among government officials, its network with officials, its network with other organizations in specifically political activities, and its perceived role in the local government. The concept of weight refers to actual activities of organizations rather than to any perception of them. Thus, civic and political weight are used to describe the ability of organizations to advance their interests in the civic and political realms. An organization with civic weight can influence resource flows to other organizations and lead collaborative projects. An organization with political weight has its interests represented in the local government and can influence the flow of power (not just resources) to other organizations.[13]

DATA AND METHODS

I arrived at a population of organizations using several methods. I attempted to interview leaders of the fourteen Asian Indian and eight Chinese nonprofits registered in electronic directories of nonprofits under Edison zip codes. Other organizations in my sample were not based in Edison but in the neighboring communities and included a large proportion of Edison residents. These organizations were identified though snowball sampling, interviews with informants, and internet and newspaper searches. The data on political visibility and weight were obtained through informant interviews with elected and appointed officials in the township and county (nine interviews). In all, there were twenty-three interviews with Asian organizations, six interviews with white mainstream organizations and one interview with an African American organization (see table 8.1).[14]

The respondents and informants were told that the study focuses on civic participation in general and questions concerning immigration were placed toward the end of the interview to reduce social desirability bias. Interviews with government officials were used to gauge the political presence and weight of organizations as well as organizational dynamics in the political sphere. Consistent with other research sites studied as part of the Immigrant Civic Engagement Project, discussed in chapter 2, informants were asked to name prominent local organizations in fifteen categories, to describe participation levels of Asian Indian and Chinese residents and their organizations in the town, and to comment on involvement of immigrants in general and change in involvement over time, on immigration as a local political issue, and on racial and ethnic tensions.

Further information on civic and political presence and weight was obtained from leaders of organizations. Interviews with them helped determine the resources available to the organizations—including resources devoted to political activities—and their degree of isolation or connections to other organizations in civic and political activities. A series of multifaceted questions explored relationships between organizations and government officials, supplementing the data on political presence and weight of the organizations obtained from government officials. Leaders were also asked about challenges facing their organizations in various dimensions of organizational activity. This information was helpful in understanding the ability of the organizations to further their civic or political interests.

ASIAN INDIAN ORGANIZATIONS

Asian Indians have formed many nonprofit organizations in the Edison area. The majority are cultural or religious. For instance, there is a large and resource-

TABLE 8.1   *Sample of Organizations and Officials Interviewed*

Mainstream Organizations	Asian Indian Organizations	Chinese Organizations	Officials
Catholic Charities	Indo-American Cultural Society	Hua Xia Chinese School	mayor
Edison Arts Society	BAPS Temple	Chinese Chorus	two councilmemb (town)
Edison Wetlands Association	Indian Business Association	Chinese American Chamber of Commerce	member of Board Education
Edison Greenways	Asian Indian Chamber of Commerce	Wang Da Chung Hand Puppet Group	director of Depart ment of Health a Human Services (town)
Rotary Club	South Asian American Leaders of Tomorrow (SAALT)	Organization of Chinese Americans	administrator of Adult Protective Services (county)
Keep Middlesex Moving	Cricket Club	Chinese Computer Professionals Association	two freeholders (county)
Edison Community Association	Jain Vishwa Bharati Temple	Chinese-American Cultural Association	coordinator of Cu tural and Heritag Commission (county)
NAACP (African American)	Carnatic Music Association Association of Indian Pharmaceutical Scientists South Asian Women's Shelter[a] Art of Living Balabharati Cultural Center Central Jersey Indian Cultural Association Asian American Retailers Association	Asian Cultural Center Chinese American Dance Ensemble	

Source: Author's compilation.
[a] Name of organization disguised at the request of the leader interviewed.

rich temple of a Hindu sect that serves as a community center and engages in charitable activity in India and in Edison. There is also a range of smaller temples, culture schools, and arts organizations. A nascent cricket team competes in a large state league. Due to the high number of entrepreneurs and business owners, there are three business organizations: two focused on the state—one for small retailers and one for larger company owners—and a third representing local entrepreneurs in Little India. There are also organizations that represent Asian Indian professionals, such as pharmaceutical scientists.

Finally, there are a few advocacy organizations. South Asian American Leaders of Tomorrow is a national South Asian advocacy group only beginning outreach in Edison; another organization is a beleaguered domestic violence group battling hostility from the community; and a third is the Indo-American Cultural Society, which has an explicit advocacy mission in Edison. In the early 1990s, the latter—originally a cultural organization—encountered discriminatory regulation of an enormous festival it was running and it successfully sued the township over violation of constitutional rights. The leader of this group, Pradip Kothari, calls himself the Al Sharpton of the Asian Indians. He is at the forefront in confronting the township over alleged cases of discrimination and violence against Asian Indians: "I am a follower of Mahatma Gandhi, of Martin Luther King, of Nelson Mandela, who all stood up for the rights of minorities."[15]

Although some Asian Indian organizations have civic presence and even weight, few have political presence and even fewer carry political weight. The large Hindu temple described earlier is recognizable to most Edison residents due to its colorful building and large sign. This organization is even able to channel resources from other organizations in disaster-relief efforts. Government officials are quick to mention it as a source of volunteers, as an example of charitable work, or as an exotic religious site. The temple, however, explicitly avoids political involvement. For four years, it had a direct connection to the township in the person of Parag Patel, the sole Asian councilman and eventually a council vice president and president.[16] The former mayor, an Italian American, conducted voter registration drives at the temple and visited during religious functions. However, Parag Patel, whom some pegged as a possible future mayor, was the only incumbent not to be re-elected on Choi's ticket in 2006.[17] With this loss of connections, the temple's political weight in the township is diminished but still rivals most other Asian organizations.

The Indo-American Cultural Society, headed by the activist Kothari, also carries civic presence and weight, albeit only within the Asian Indian community. Government officials are certainly aware of the activism of its vocal leadership. When it comes to power, however, the organization is in an adversarial stance with the township, and it has alienated the white mainstream and many Asian Indians alike. In 2001, Kothari ran for county freeholder as a Republican after becoming frustrated with the Democratic party organization, which he accused of shutting out Asian Indians. Kothari was shut out despite his close relationship to James McGreevey, the mayor of neighboring Woodbridge who went on to become a controversial governor. Republicans reinstated Kothari after he lost the primary but, predictably, he came in last in the freeholder race in a county that is a Democratic stronghold (Kalita 2003). Since then, it has become less likely that the party would embrace Kothari and his organization, and their relationship with the township grew increasingly confrontational.[18]

In a less confrontational stance, the Indian Business Association, representing merchants of Little India, is able to maintain regular contact with the mayor to discuss the needs of its members. It has a good measure of civic presence and weight within the Asian Indian community—sponsoring cultural events, for instance—and some political presence in the township. It also has some weight with town officials, who have put its president on a community relations board following the latest police brutality scandal and who have acted on traffic concerns. The business leaders get the ear of the local government partly by avoiding confrontation: "We come here to make our life, build our career, educate our kids, make some money, and have a good life. We don't come here to fight. We want to keep that goal and try to work around the situation to make sure we don't create more enemies than necessary."[19]

The Central Jersey Indian Cultural Association is another large local cultural organization that organizes a myriad of activities, from parties to trips to dance competitions. Its only dealings with the township and county governments have to do with finding space for its large events and inviting officials to them. Although the leaders of this organization felt that they were the largest, most visible group around, none of the officials interviewed even mentioned them. The rest of the organizations have negligible civic or political presence and weight on the local level, but a few have some effect on the state or even national level.[20] Some of this may be due to shying away from all things political. It is important to note, however, that leaders of several organizations are actively trying to have their needs met by the township, with limited results. The cricket team, for instance, has been trying to get a field, an amenity enjoyed by cricket teams in many other New Jersey towns. Similarly, the leader of the Balabharati Cultural Center has made an unsuccessful bid for a seat on the board of education after the existing board rejected his concerns. To stay involved, he attends the township council meetings or watches them on public access television.

CHINESE ORGANIZATIONS

There are far fewer Chinese in Edison than Asian Indians, and fewer and less diverse Chinese organizations. The central organization of the Chinese community in Edison is the Hua Xia Chinese School. With close to a thousand students, this organization takes over the local high school every weekend. The many cultural activities of the school have spun off into smaller affiliated organizations, such as the Chinese Chorus. Thus, the school has significant civic weight in the Chinese community, controlling the resources of other organizations. Edison also has a nascent Chinese business organization and a statewide computer professionals' organization that includes many local Chinese residents. A state branch of the Organization of Chinese Americans, a national advocacy group, works with second and higher generations and is distant from the life of the immigrant community.

Although the influence of Asian Indian organizations on the township is not extensive, the Chinese organizations have even less political weight. The Hua Xia Chinese School is the only Chinese organization town officials are able to name. The chairman of the school recently completed his second term on the township school board, deciding not to run for re-election.[21] Through him, the Hua Xia Chinese school was able to influence school district policy. Its broader political weight in the township, however, was limited because the board of education is a largely autonomous body and has few ties to the council or the mayor. Nevertheless, the Chinese board member—previously the sole Asian on the board, which now has none—was highly visible to officials and served as a liaison between the township and the Chinese community. With the completion of his term on the board of education, the already limited political weight of the Chinese school is likely to decline.

The other Chinese organizations have almost no political presence and weight in Edison. Despite the fact that Edison has the largest Chinese population of any community in New Jersey, Chinese organizations are largely invisible to government officials. One could say that the Chinese themselves are invisible—a county freeholder told me that there are not many Chinese in the county at all. Those who did recognize the significant Chinese population saw it as more insular than the Asian Indian and as uninvolved in civic activities outside of education. This perception is not entirely accurate and reflects bias and lack of outreach on the part of white officials. Although much of the more obvious political activity is done by second generation Chinese and Asian organizations, even the immigrant organizations with seemingly insular focus encourage dialog and engagement with the mainstream in the form of voting or communication with officials.

OTHER ORGANIZATIONS

So far we have seen that, for the most part, civic participation among Asian immigrants in Edison is disconnected from the political life of the township. The few visible ethnic organizations, with some exceptions in the Asian Indian group, are inwardly oriented and not significant players in the policy-making arena. The rest are small and largely invisible. Government officials may, when asked about prominent local organizations, mention a few Asian organizations but most often describe mainstream groups. Here I look at some of these in an attempt to account for the higher visibility and political power of these groups in comparison with Asian groups. In addition, it is important to gauge the extent to which the mainstream organizations are integrating immigrants into their ranks. I also consider a branch of a national African American advocacy organization.

New Jersey is a site of environmental devastation and thus it is not surprising that one of the most politically visible organizations there is environmentalist. Edison Wetlands has a large independent source of funding and has much civic and political weight in the community and the state. By the nature of its work, the focus of this organization is rarely local. The Edison Art Society, on the other hand, is locally focused and plugged into the local government and the county party organization. It has significant political presence and weight but struggles to attract volunteers. Neither organization is close to having a representative number of Asians. Although the Art Society has a severe volunteer shortfall, it does not reach out to Asian residents, nor do any of the other white mainstream organizations. A leader of the Rotary Club put it this way: "I don't know whether they have their own civic organizations where, you know, they have that identity together and do their own service projects that way."

The local branch of the National Association for the Advancement of Colored People (NAACP) has recently seen an influx of Asians as clients in its legal clinics and has been partnering with the activist Kothari. The organization is a sleeping giant in the sense that it confines its role to negotiating intergroup issues when they come up in Edison but has the enormous power of the national organization behind it if the need arises. Aside from playing a role in mediating tense ethnically charged situations, such as police brutality scandals, the NAACP deals with Asian store owners who feel that they have been unfairly targeted by local health inspectors and with South Asian drivers experiencing racial profiling. However, the NAACP does not reach out to Asians as potential members, dealing with them primarily as clients and, strikingly, the NAACP was not mentioned by any government officials as an important local organization.

In all, non-Asian organizations seem to have more political visibility and power in the local government and remain controlled by white ethnics (even NAACP's legal volunteers are all white), with little outreach to Asian immigrants.

WHAT ACCOUNTS FOR CIVIC AND POLITICAL STRATIFICATION?

We have seen that, despite having a fair number of organizations, the Chinese residents of Edison have little political presence and though Asian Indians have some political weight, neither group has much of either. Their organizations are hardly valuable partners in town and county governance, nor have they yet turned into sites of recruitment to political office. In all, the Asian residents of Edison and their civic realm appear to be shut out of the local politics.

It is true that many Asian organizations have an insular focus, with mostly cultural and transnational activities. The fact that politics is something many of these organizations stay away from certainly plays a role. "It's a personal thing. People don't discuss it and it's not on our agenda," a leader of a large Asian Indian religious organization said. However, even organizations that would like to stay out of politics still need to interact with the local government. Cultural organizations need permits for their parades, enrichment schools rent space from the township, and religious organizations negotiate parking regulations. It is noteworthy that some of the confrontations between the Asian Indian community and the township took place precisely at such intersections between ethic cultural activity and local governance. For instance, the Asian Indian men who accused white police officers of brutality were putting up Indian and American flags in preparation for India Day Parade. The Navrati festival was almost shut down by the township government and resulted in a prolonged fight in court.

Another reason insular orientation is inadequate in explaining lack of political weight among Asian organizations in Edison is that not all Asian organizations have an insular focus. A few are more oriented to advocacy for their ethnic community and try to influence the local government. However, even these have little political weight. Thus there is little evidence for the pluralism thesis in Edison. The lack of political power and visibility among Asian organizations is puzzling in part because there are so many Asians in Edison—though it is also true that the majority cannot vote—and they are much better off than whites in terms of socioeconomic status. The material resources and connections they might have at work should increase the effectiveness of their organizations in having their needs met.

The political opportunity structure is part of the explanation for the lack of political power and visibility among Asian Indian and Chinese organizations in Edison. Similar to the situation in New York City that Jones-Correa (1998) described, the entrenchment of the Democratic Party in Edison allows it to be largely indifferent to immigrants without a threat to its stability, even when the proportion of immigrants among the general population is high. Only 7 percent of the county Democratic steering committee for Edison have Asian Indian surnames, and only one of 156 committee members is Chinese. The steering committee is the first step for any political hopeful in the county. Traditionally, county parties in New Jersey are powerful organizations, and in Middlesex County the dominant Democratic organization does largely determine who will hold office by controlling the nomination process. The party can incorporate immigrants at whatever pace it desires—or perhaps not at all—because it faces few challengers. Its internal wrangling, on the other hand, may become beneficial for Asians because, in the struggle for dominance, a faction of the party might reach out to them. This is what happened in 2001, when the Italian American mayor was suddenly facing a defection of two council members on his re-election ticket to a third councilman now running against him. Parag Patel, a thirty-one-year-old American-born lawyer[22] and member of the local Democratic organization with experience in McGreevey's gubernatorial campaign, was drafted to fill the void. Four years later, despite a meteoric rise within the council itself, Patel was not re-elected.

What about the Asian mayor of Edison? How can there be such a degree of political stratification between Asian and white mainstream organizations when the person running the township is Asian? Isn't Choi's election evidence that local political elites have opened their arms to Asian minority groups and, at the same time, a sign that Asian organizations should expect to see their political weight grow? Not necessarily.

First, Choi initially ran in defiance of the Democratic Party organization. Party bosses wanted him to aim lower—a school board election, perhaps—or wait. Possibly precisely because he defied the party, Choi was able to win the primary among residents tired of the old politics of nontransparency and catering to developers. Choi garnered additional supporters from his stance against Wal-Mart by drawing a connection between big box development and the squeezed middle class and disappearing open space (Green and Stoller 2006).[23] After the primary, however, the party threw its support behind Choi and helped him win a 270 vote margin over a Democrat-turned-Independent openly feuding with the party organization. The four Democratic councilmen who ran against him in the primary were now on Choi's ticket. Thus, Choi may have started outside the urban regime but had to work from within it to succeed (Stone 1993).

Choi's election was also not necessarily a sign that the local government reached out to Asians in Edison because there are reasons for white residents to have not grouped him with the visible Asian Indian population. Choi is a second-generation Korean immigrant, does not speak the language of his homeland, and stresses his Edison upbringing and his American-ness. He uses assimilationist language and looks to the future when second-generation immigrants like himself will comprise a greater portion of the Asian community in Edison: "The kids are mixing well, the parents are not," he said of immigrant participation in the civic sphere. "The both so-called community leaders in the Indian community, and in my parents' generation, are more comfortable with ethnic politics, but only because they haven't lived the full American experience."[24] On issues, Choi was indistinguishable from his opponent in the mayoral election and was endorsed by whites who were drawn to his impressive credentials (MIT and Columbia degrees) and technological savvy, hoping that he would make Edison an outpost of Silicon Valley with his Edison Project.[25] Thus, though Choi was undoubtedly perceived as an Asian candidate, the political elites quickly accepted his appeal to middle class white suburbanites and threw their resources behind him, probably ensuring his extremely close victory. It seems unlikely that a first-generation Asian Indian leader, speaking the language of civil rights and unabashedly Indian in identity—such as the activist Kothari—would have met the same reception at the hands of white political elite.

At the same time, Choi is not exactly evidence of mainstream outreach given that many in the Asian community did not see him as one of their own. For example, a large group of Chinese leaders, including the Chinese American Chamber of Commerce, endorsed Choi's opponent, emphasizing that Choi's Asian identity made no difference for them.[26] Asian Indians and Chinese immigrants, especially recent arrivals, hardly self-identify as Asians. Asian Indians are a diverse group from a multicultural and multilingual nation, and Chinese come from Taiwan, Hong Kong, and mainland China. In interviews with Asian Indian leaders, I heard few references to common interests with the Chinese, and vice versa. In fact, most did not mention the other group at all. And both groups see hardly any commonalities with the few Koreans in Edison. Perhaps to offset the resentment of some white blue collar residents about the visible wealth of new Asian immigrants, Choi emphasizes that he is a son of laundry workers.

Although exit poll data indicated that 97 percent of Asians voted for Choi in the mayoral election, and the voter registration drives at the heavily Asian Indian

Hilltop Apartments alone could have provided the 270 vote margin for Choi's win, Asians are nowhere close to establishing a monopoly over decision making that Stone (1993) believed is necessary for the government to pay attention to them.[27] The influence of county party machines over nominations remains strong at the county and local levels though it has waned on the state level.[28] The political opportunity structure in Edison is such that the party machines that continue to control politics on the local level have few incentives to respond to the needs of Asian residents or to partner with their organizations. Electoral mobilization of Asian voters does not seem to have made a difference.

At the same time, we have seen that Asian Indian organizations have relatively more political presence and weight than their Chinese counterparts, and Asian Indians have been more represented in elected offices. The Asian Indians and Chinese in Edison are not very different in terms of socioeconomic status, stability of legal status, citizenship rates, or recency of immigration. What accounts for the difference between these two groups?

First, there are more Asian Indians, so we might expect more of their organizations to make political inroads. Language and experience with democracy probably also play a role. Asian Indians enjoy a higher level of fluency in English and come from a democratic nation. Comfort with the dominant language clearly makes political engagement more accessible—from voting to attending the council or board of education meetings to running for office. That Edison is hostile to non-English speakers became increasingly obvious during the last election, during which Department of Justice monitors found flagrant violations of language minorities' rights at the polls and white residents explained their vote as a choice for someone who speaks English.[29] Experience with democracy is relevant as well. For instance, some Asian Indian leaders spoke of having parents who had been involved in the local government in India.

The lower profile of Chinese immigrants is not due to their individual or group characteristics alone but also the behavior of the political elites. Chinese residents were widely perceived by the officials I interviewed as insular and more interested in education than politics. This view of Chinese immigrants is consistent with their model minority status, a label that affects the way mainstream groups perceive Asian Americans at the same time as it impacts their own identities (Wong et al. 1998). The influence of the model minority myth makes Asian American organizations that deal with civil rights, mental health, and poverty invisible because these issues are dissonant with dominant perceptions of model minorities. It is telling that the one Chinese immigrant who was recruited to vie for an elected office ran for the school board and represented an educational organization. The model minority label attached to the Chinese can make their political efforts invisible or anomalous and stifles outreach to them by political leadership.

Are Asian Indians not a model minority as well? Here the local context of reception matters. In Edison, Asian Indians are seen as invaders and foreigners rather than as a model minority. The distinctive character, high concentration, and busy bustle of Little India are far more visible to white residents than the more placid stretch of Route 27 Chinatown. The political elites may respond to

feelings of tension and discomfort among its electorate toward the rapidly growing, visible, and conspicuously wealthy immigrant group by attempting to distance themselves from the Asian Indians. A defeated mayoral candidate (Democrat turned Independent), William Stephens, gave a voice to this sentiment
during his campaign: "We are losing a sense of Edison"[30] and, more recently, "I
think there's a little thought of 'they're taking over and I'm being pushed out of
my community.'"[31] At the same time, however, political elites are much less
likely to ignore activism or engagement with the mainstream among the Asian
Indians. The themes of racial discrimination and civil rights that emerged during
the confrontations with the police strike a deep chord of discomfort in the hearts
of these Democrats. The racial politics of Edison are about the Asian Indians
and they are in a state of disconcerting flux that forces the political elites to engage with them. As Kothari explained in an interview, "any time the police officers . . . talk to mainstream American people, including African American and
Latinos, they show some respect to them. To their leaders, because of their
stance or whatever . . . They fear bad publicity. But we are not African Americans and we are not Latinos, we are *in between*" [emphasis added].

CONCLUSION

Immigrant civic engagement in Edison is not, then, being converted into political weight. There is also little evidence of pluralism. Asian Indian and Chinese
organizations focus on cultural, educational, religious, and business issues and
are unable to influence policy or to affect the power of other organizations because the political opportunity structure—with powerful county party organizations and the entrenchment of the Democratic Party—effectively marginalizes
Asian residents. The party opposition comes primarily from members who de-
fected to run as Independents and thus has no need to mobilize immigrant voters. In fact, it may see danger in upsetting long-time white supporters if it were
to do much outreach to Asian organizations. The result is a stratified political
field that electoral mobilization of Asian residents has not been able to level.
      When it comes to political incorporation, there is, at this early point in the
adaptation of these recent immigrants, some evidence against straight-line assimilation theories. Asian Indians and Chinese may be better off economically
than the mainstream but they have thus far not incorporated into the dominant
society's organizations and political processes. At the same time, Asian Indians
seem to have made more inroads into local politics than the Chinese have. The
local context of reception encountered by these otherwise economically similar
groups results in differential reception of them on the part of political elites. The
model minority myth that makes the Chinese and their organizations less visible
politically is not, in Edison, as applicable to Asian Indians. As a result, local political elites are more likely to grapple with Asian Indian demands and needs.
      Examination of small cities with large skilled immigrant populations is an
important addition to the study of immigrant adaptation. With most work done
on civic and political participation in large cities among working class immigrants, professional immigrants are often ignored. And many of these Asian

computer programmers, pharmacists, and doctors are moving directly to smaller cities like Edison. Meanwhile, attention to precisely such contexts can enrich our theories on immigrant adaptation and identify the conditions for political incorporation or exclusion. Smaller cities have a potential for accessibility and responsiveness that large cities do not. It also takes a smaller immigrant population to tip the power scale in a small city. Immigrants with educational and material resources can construct inroads to power more easily than working class immigrants. Despite these advantages, a number of factors conspire to create a stratified civic and political realm in Edison, with the highly skilled Asian Indian and Chinese immigrants not yet reaping the benefits of their resources or the potential for inclusion inherent in the small city.

I thank Christopher Wildeman for help with logistics, Karthick Ramakrishnan for guidance, Sharon Bzostek for editing, and David Potere for help with maps.

NOTES

1. See also Kevin Coyne, "Even After Race Is Won, Race Is Still the Issue," *New York Times*, August 13, 2006, 1.
2. Robert Hanley, "In Edison, a Crossroads of Diversity," *New York Times*, April 17, 1991, B2.
3. Tara Fehr, "Town Snapshot: Edison," *Star-Ledger*. [Newark, N.J.], July 13, 2006, 2.
4. Daniel Shorter, "Asian Indian Communities, Based on U.S. Census 2000," ePodunk.com, 2005; Michelle Sahn, "Commercial Takes Aim at Prejudice: Police Produce TV Ad That Shows Kids the Diversity of Their World," *Home News Tribune* [East Brunswick, N.J.], October 20, 2004, accessed at http://docs.newsbank.com/openurl?ctx_ver=z39.88-2004&rft_id=info:sid/iw.newsbank.com:AWNB:EBTB&rft_val_format=info:ofi/fmt:kev:mtx:ctx&rft_dat=10611005DF920D66&svc_dat=InfoWeb:aggregated5&req_dat=0D0CB55F0325556A.
5. It is nevertheless erroneous to assume that all Asian Indians are fluent English speakers. In 2005, exit polls in Edison indicated that 31 percent of Asian Indian voters were Gujarati speaking and had limited English proficiency (Shaw 2006).
6. Rick Harrison, "Changes in Iselin Bemoaned," *Home News Tribune* [East Brunswick, N.J.], July 2, 2006, accessed at http://docs.newsbank.com/openurl?ctx_ver=z39.882004&rft_id=info:sid/iw.newsbank.com:AWNB:EBTB&rft_val_format=info:ofi/fmt:kev:mtx:ctx&rft_dat=116A50A624665430&svc_dat=InfoWeb:aggregated5&req_dat=0D0CB55F0325556A.
7. Jay Bodas and Patricia Miller, "Many Condemn Radio Remarks about Asians," *Edison-Metuchen Sentinel* [N.J.], May 7, 2005, accessed at http://ems.gmnews.com/news/2005/0503/Front_Page/001.html.
8. Diane C. Walsh, "Political Novice Plans to Run for Edison Mayor," *Star-Ledger* [Newark, N.J.], March 30, 2005, accessed at http://docs.newsbank.com/openurl?ctx_ver=z39.88-2004&rft_id=info:sid/iw.newsbank.com:AWNB:STLB&rft_val_format=info:ofi/fmt:kev:mtx:ctx&rft_dat=1092BECC510C3C75&svc_dat=InfoWeb:aggregated5&req_dat=0D0CB55F0325556A.
9. "New Jersey Businesses Claim Harassment," *News India-Times* [New York], May

16, 1997, accessed at http://proquest.umi.com/pqdweb?did=468012961&sid=16 &Fmt=3&clientId=17210&RQT=309&VName=PQ.

10. Jerry Barca, "India Day Boondoggle: Mixed Reactions in Edison," *Home News Tribune* [East Brunswick, N.J.], August 24, 2005, accessed at http://docs.newsbank .com/openurl?ctx_ver=z39.88-2004&rft_id=info:sid/iw.newsbank.com: AWNB:EBTB&rft_val_format=info:ofi/fmt:kev:mtx:ctx&rft_dat=10C44173D7F6 FAB0&svc_dat=InfoWeb:aggregated5&req_dat=0D0CB55F0325556A.

11. Suleman Din, "In Edison, Asian-Indians Face Off with Police Allies: Rally Held in Protest of Alleged Brutality," *Star-Ledger* [Newark, N.J.], August 3, 2006, accessed at http://docs.newsbank.com/openurl?ctx_ver=z39.88-2004&rft_id =info:sid/iw.newsbank.com:AWNB:STLB&rft_val_format=info:ofi/fmt:kev: mtx:ctx&rft_dat=11348BDA713A8618&svc_dat=InfoWeb:aggregated5&req_dat= 0D0CB55F0325556A.

12. Jay Bodas, "Cop Cleared in Brutality Claim by Indian Activist," *Edison-Metuchen Sentinel* [N.J.], August 9, 2006, accessed at http://ws.gmnews.com/news/2006/ 0809/Front_Page/008.html; "PBA Backs out of Community Committee," *Edison-Metuchen Sentinel* [N.J.], October 11, 2006, accessed at http://ws.gmnews.com/ news/2006/1011/Front_Page/048.html; Suleman Din, "Tensions Grow Over Incident in Edison—Choi Trades Words with Asian-Indian," *Star-Ledger* [Newark, N.J.], August 16, 2006, accessed at http://docs.newsbank.com/openurl?ctx_ver =z39.88-2004&rft_id=info:sid/iw.newsbank.com:AWNB:STLB&rft _val_format=info:ofi/fmt:kev:mtx:ctx&rft_dat=112DF5309EFCA1E8svc _dat=InfoWeb:aggregated5&req_dat=0D0CB55F0325556A; Tom Haydon, "Asian Man Planning Suit Against Edison," *The Star Ledger*, August 16, 2006, accessed at http://docs.newsbank.com/openurl?ctx_ver=z39.88-2004&rft_id=info: sid/iw.newsbank.com:AWNB:STLB&rft_val_format=info:ofi/fmt:kev:mtx:ctx&rft _dat=1138D44C56F3DAC0&svc_dat=InfoWeb:aggregated5&req_dat=0D0CB55 F0325556A.

13. For a detailed treatment of these terms, see chapter 1.

14. In addition, four hybrid organizations were interviewed. These were Asian branches of mainstream organizations and an employee organization within a large company. They are excluded due to their focus on internal organizational politics rather than local township or county politics. The research in Edison was conducted as part of the Immigrant Civic Engagement Project, thus the sampling methodology mirrors that of other places in ICEP, as outlined in chapter 2.

15. Suleman Din, "High-Profile Spat Dominates Politics in Edison: Mayor and Asian-American Leader Not on Same Page," *Star-Ledger* [Newark, N.J.], July 23, 2006, accessed at http://docs.newsbank.com/openurl?ctx_ver=z39.882004&rft_id=info: sid/iw.newsbank.com:AWNB:STLB&rft_val_format=info:ofi/fmt:kev:mtx:ctx&rft _dat=1130F046E4074440&svc_dat=InfoWeb:aggregated5&req_dat=0D0CB55F0 325556A.

16. Dina Guirguis, "Patel to Lead Edison Council," *Home News Tribune* [East Brunswick, N.J.], January 11, 2005, accessed at http://docs.newsbank.com/ openurl?ctx_ver=z39.88-2004&rft_id=info:sid/iw.newsbank.com:AWNB :EBTB&rft_val_format=info:ofi/fmt:kev:mtx:ctx&rft_dat=107BF593CEC740B0& svc_dat=InfoWeb:aggregated5&req_dat=0D0CB55F0325556A.

17. Jerry Barca, "Patel Likely to Lead Edison," *Home News Tribune* [East Brunswick, N.J.], January 10, 2005, accessed at http://docs.newsbank.com/openurl?ctx _ver=z39.88-2004&rft_id=info:sid/iw.newsbank.com:AWNB:EBTB&rft _val_format=info:ofi/fmt:kev:mtx:ctx&rft_dat=107B4D351390E8A9&svc_dat=In

foWeb:aggregated5&req_dat=0D0CB55F0325556A; Suleman Din, "Rival Claims Choi Played 'Race Card' to Win in Edison," *Star-Ledger* [Newark, N.J.], November 10, 2005, accessed at http://docs.newsbank.com/openurl?ctx_ver=z39.88-2004 &rft_id=info:sid/iw.newsbank.com:AWNB:STLB&rft_val_format=info:ofi/fmt: kev:mtx:ctx&rft_dat=10DCEA7119A287D0&svc_dat=InfoWeb:aggregated5&req _dat=0D0CB55F0325556A.

18. Suleman Din, "Asian-Indian Protest Planned in Edison," *Star-Ledger* [Newark, N.J.], August 2, 2006, 21.

19. Interview with leader of business association, December 12, 2006.

20. For instance, the Asian Indian Chamber of Commerce lobbies in defense of out-sourcing to India. Its president is the Ratepayer Advocate of New Jersey. Although based in Edison, the focus of this group is the state and the country.

21. John Dunphy, "Twelve File to Run in School Board Race," *Edison-Metuchen Sentinel* [N.J.], March 15, 2006, accessed at http://ems.gmnews.com/news/2006/0315/ Front_Page/005.html.

22. There are some parallels between Jun Choi and Parag Patel. Both are young and children of immigrants. However, Parag Patel was always more explicit in identify-ing himself as an Asian Indian, speaks fluent Gujurati, is married to an Asian In-dian, and travels to India once a year.

23. The anti-Wal-Mart stance brought Choi the endorsement of several labor unions that have traditionally remained neutral in the local elections (Green and Stoller 2006).

24. Suleman Din, "Edison's Novice Mayor Caught in a Racial Divide," *Star-Ledger* [Newark, N.J.], August 29, 2006, 9.

25. Patricia A. Miller and Rochelle Lauren Gerszberg, "Choi Pledges End to 'Old-style Politics,'" *Edison-Metuchen Sentinel*, October 26, 2005, accessed at http://ws.gm news.com/news/2005/1026/Front_Page/022.html; "Edison at Critical Turning Point, Stephens Says: Focus on Qualifications and Experience, Former Councilman Says," *Edison-Metuchen Sentinel* [N.J.], October 26, 2005, accessed at http://ws.gm-news.com/news/2005/1026/Front_Page/011.html; "Choi for Edison Mayor," *The Star Ledger* [Newark, N.J.], October 21, 2005, accessed at http://docs.newsbank .com/openurl?ctx_ver=z39.88-2004&rft_id=info:sid/iw.newsbank.com:AWNB :EBTB&rft_val_format=info:ofi/fmt:kev:mtx:ctx&rft_dat=10E1875733BAD7F8& svc_dat=InfoWeb:aggregated5&req_dat=0D0CB55F0325556A.

26. Jerry Barca, "Mayor Won't Be Called Chicken: Campaign Stunt Gets Spadoro to Debate," *Home News Tribune* [East Brunswick, N.J.], May 18, 2005, accessed at http://docs.newsbank.com/openurl?ctx_ver=z39.88-2004&rft_id=info:sid/ iw.newsbank.com:AWNB:EBTB&rft_val_format=info:ofi/fmt:kev:mtx:ctx&rft_da t=10A630FF120B5364&svc_dat=InfoWeb:aggregated5&req_dat=0D0CB55F0325 556A; Elaine Van Develde, "Asian Leaders Back Spadoro in Primary," *Edison-Metuchen Sentinel* [N.J.], May 24, 2005, accessed at http://ems.gmnews.com/ news/2005/0524/Front_Page/005.html.

27. Exit poll conducted by Asian American Legal Defense and Education Fund (see also Green and Stoller 2006).

28. State district boundaries are redrawn and do not coincide with county boundaries. In this way, district 18 includes some of Middlesex County as well as neighboring Somerset County. The county party machines have much less control over state elec-tions than local elections. The state assemblyman from the district is an Asian In-dian immigrant, Upendra Chivukula (D), a former councilman and mayor of a De-mocratic township within a Republican-dominated Somerset County, who won the

year district boundaries were re-drawn. He is the highest placed Asian Indian in office in the state.

29. The Department of Justice monitored only fifteen other communities in the United States that year. Eric Holland, the department spokesperson, stated in a public letter that "poll workers across Edison Township expressed hostility toward and even interfered with Asian American citizens receiving assistance from persons of their choice. . . . [One poll worker] stated that when a Gujarati or Hindi-speaking voter appeared at the polls, she would send them to the nearest gas station." Few poll workers spoke Gujarati or Chinese (Patrica A. Miller, "Poll Workers Under Scrutiny During Election," *Edison-Metuchen Sentinel* [N.J.], 2005, accessed at http://ems.gmnews.com/news/2005/1109/Front_Page/001.html).

30. Patricia A. Miller, "Poll Workers Under Scrutiny During Election," *Edison-Metuchen Sentinel* [N.J.], November 9, 2005, accessed at http://ems.gmnews.com/news/2005/1109/Front_Page/001.html.

31. Jonathan Miller, "Edison Works to Cope With Simmering Ethnic Tensions," *New York Times*, October 10, 2006, accessed at http://www.nytimes.com/2006/10/10/nyregion/10edison.html?scp=2&sq=jonathan+miller+edison&st=nyt.

REFERENCES

Alba, Richard D., and Victor Nee. 2003. *Remaking the American Mainstream: Assimilation and Contemporary Immigration*. Cambridge, Mass.: Harvard University Press.

Browning, Rufus P., Dale Rogers Marshall, and David H. Tabb. 1984. *Protest Is Not Enough: The Struggle of Blacks and Hispanics for Equality in Urban Politics*. Berkeley, Calif.: University of California Press.

Connors, Richard J., and William J. Dunham. 1993. *The Government of New Jersey: An Introduction*. Lanham, Md.: University Press of America.

Dahl, Robert Alan. 1961. *Who Governs? Democracy and Power in an American City*. New Haven, Conn.: Yale University Press.

De Tocqueville, Alexis. 1835/2001. *Democracy in America*. New York: New American Library.

Egenton, Michael A. 1992. "Modern Forms of Municipal Government." Trenton, N.J.: New Jersey State Commission on County and Municipal Government.

Gordon, Milton M. 1964. *Assimilation in American Life: The Role of Race, Religion, and National Origins*. New York: Oxford University Press.

Green, Adam, and Matt Stoller. 2006. "Jersey Boy: The Election of a Korean-American Mayor in Edison, New Jersey May Offer a Blueprint for Democrats Nationwide in 2006." *The American Prospect*. Accessed at http://www.prospect.org/cs/articles?article=jersey_boy.

Jones-Correa, Michael. 1998. *Between Two Nations: The Political Predicament of Latinos in New York City*. Ithaca, N.Y.: Cornell University Press.

Kalita, S. Mitra. 2003. *Suburban Sahibs: Three Immigrant Families and Their Passage from India to America*. New Brunswick, N.J.: Rutgers University Press.

Karasik, Gary. 1986. *New Brunswick and Middlesex County, The Hub and the Wheel: An Illustrated History*. Northridge, Calif.: Windor Publications.

Moakley, Maureen W. 1986. "Political Parties." In *The Political State of New Jersey*, edited by Gerald M. Pomper. New Brunswick, N.J.: Rutgers University Press.

Moakley, Maureen, and Gerald Pomper. 1979. "Party Organizations." In *Politics in New*

Jersey, edited by Richard Lehne and Alan Rosenthal. New Brunswick, N.J.: Rutgers University, The Eagleton Institute of Politics.

Portes, Alejandro, and Rubén Rumbaut. 2001. *Legacies: The Story of the Immigrant Second Generation*. Berkeley, Calif.: University of California Press.

Putnam, Robert D. 2000. *Bowling Alone: The Collapse and Revival of American Community*. New York: Simon & Schuster.

Ruggles, Steven, Matthew Sobek, Trent Alexander, Catherine A. Fitch, Ronald Goeken, Patricia Kelly Hall, Miriam King, and Chad Ronnander. 2004. Integrated Public Use Microdata Series: Version 3.0 [machine-readable database]. Minneapolis, Minn.: Population Center.

Salmore, Barbara G., and Stephen A. Salmore. 1993. *New Jersey Politics and Government*. Lincoln, Neb.: University of Nebraska Press.

Salmore, Stephen A. 1986. "Voting, Elections, and Campaigns." In *The Political State of New Jersey*, edited by Gerald M. Pomper. New Brunswick, N.J.: Rutgers University Press.

Shaw, Douglas V. 1994. *Immigration and Ethnicity in New Jersey History*. Trenton, N.J.: New Jersey Historical Commission.

———. 2006. "Solid Asian Bloc Voted for Choi." *Asian Week*, June 16–22, 2006.

Stone, Clarence N. 1993. "Urban Regimes and the Capacity to Govern: A Political Economy Approach." *Journal of Urban Affairs* 15(1): 1–28.

Trivedi, Niraj. 1997. "Indo-American Cultural Society: Launched in a Fight, It Struggles On." *India in New York* 1(16): 17.

U.S. Census Bureau. 2000. "Census 2000 Summary File 3, Edison CDP." Accessed February 21, 2008 at http://factfinder.census.gov.

———. 2006a. "American Community Survey Fact Sheet: Edison Township, Middlesex County, New Jersey." Accessed February 21, 2008 at http://factfinder.census.gov.

———. 2006b. Reference maps. 2006 Cities and Towns, generated using http://factfinder.census.gov.

Verba, Sidney, Kay Lehman Schlozman, and Henry E. Brady. 1995. *Voice and Equality: Civic Voluntarism in American Politics*. Cambridge, Mass.: Harvard University Press.

Wong, Paul, Chienping Faith Laid, Richard Nagasawa, and Tieming Lin. 1998. "Asian Americans as a Model Minority: Self-Perceptions and Perceptions by Other Racial Groups." *Sociological Perspectives* 41(1): 95–118.

Worton, Stanley N. 1997. *Reshaping New Jersey: A History of its Government and Politics*. Trenton: Department of State, New Jersey Historical Commission.

Laurencio Sanguino

Chapter 9

Selective Service: Indians, Poles, and Mexicans in Chicago

Immigration and immigrant participation have been among the hallmark features of civic and political life in Chicago for more than a century, from the era of Irish-dominated machines and central European migration in the early twentieth century to the contemporary period, with a weaker and more diverse political machine and immigrants from Mexico, Poland, India, and several other Asian and Latin American countries. Just as in the rest of the United States, immigration to Illinois and the Chicago area grew considerably in the last two decades of the twentieth century. Between 1990 and 2000, the number of foreign-born residents in Illinois grew from about 950,000 to 1.5 million, and continued growing to nearly 1.8 million by 2006. During this period, nearly 94 percent of the workers who entered Chicago's regional workforce were immigrants, and accounted for 23 percent of workers in manufacturing, 12 percent in transportation, and at least 12 percent in agriculture (Paral and Norkewicz 2003; Paral and Lewis 2001). According to the 2000 census, at least 574,000 Mexican, 138,570 Polish, and 79,000 Indian immigrants currently reside in the Chicago metropolitan area. As the three largest and some of the fastest growing immigrant groups in the state of Illinois, they account for 56 percent of all immigrants in Cook, DuPage, Kane, Lake, McHenry, and Will counties (Paral and Norkewicz 2003).

In this chapter I describe how Chicago's post-1965 Indian, Polish, and Mexican immigrant communities were formed, how they were affected by subsequent immigration acts and practices, and how particular factors (such as immigration history, economic standing, and political interest) have played a role in the selective development of social service organizations committed to assisting, organizing, and advocating on behalf of immigrants. As reference points, these factors will allow us to better analyze civic and political involvement among Indian, Polish, and Mexican immigrants and the effects they have on gaining political presence (visibility among public officials) and political weight (recognition as a politically significant group and interests are taken into account or formally represented). They will also help us understand the following:

- why the Indian immigrant community, without question the best socioeconomically situated of the three groups to be discussed, has struggled to gain political presence and weight among Chicago's government officials and policy makers;

- why the Polish immigrant community, a community with a long history of receiving immigrants, has struggled to develop a network of social service organizations to meet the needs of and advocate on behalf of recent immigrants; and

- how Mexican immigrants, as the least likely to have a socioeconomically secure position (in terms of status, fluency in English, education, occupation, and income) have successfully captured the attention of city and county officials and managed to advance, albeit as part of a larger Mexican or Latino agenda, their own sociopolitical agenda in Chicago.

This chapter is based on research conducted for the Immigrant Civic Engagement Project (ICEP), a study examining the circumstances in which immigrant groups and their respective organizations acquire political visibility and influence.[1] A significant part of this study involved collecting information on particular immigrant communities (those described as having the first, second, and third highest concentration of Indian, Polish, or Mexican immigrants, respectively, by the 2000 census) and conducting interviews with city and county government representatives, school officials, individuals at immigrant rights organizations, workers at community-based organizations, and community activists throughout the city.[2] What follows is an analysis of civic and political involvement among Indian, Polish, and Mexican immigrants in Chicago.[3] In the end, information collected on civic and political activity among these groups will be used to explore questions regarding the role of immigrant organizations in political mobilization and to suggest that the development of social service organization and the creation of alliances between immigrants and their native-born ethnic counterparts play important roles in shaping the political relevance of community organizations, and perhaps a greater role than factors such as economic resources and racial privilege.

SETTING THE CONTEXT: INDIAN, MEXICAN, AND POLISH IMMIGRANTS IN CHICAGO

Although Mexican, Polish, and Indian immigrants comprise the largest Latin American, European, and Asian immigrant groups in Chicago, they vary considerably in age, education, occupation, and income (table 9.1). For example, 25 percent of Mexican immigrants are under twenty-five, compared to more than 50 percent of Polish immigrants, who are forty-five or older (Paral and Lewis 2001). In terms of education, 62 percent of the immigrants that arrived in

Chicago between 1990 and 2000 reported that they had at least a high school diploma—88 percent of Indians, 69 percent of Poles, and only 34 percent of Mexicans. Approximately 66 percent of Indian and 16 percent of Polish immigrants were college graduates, but only 3 percent of their Mexican counterparts were (Paral and Lewis 2001). As one might expect, disparities in education among immigrant groups readily translate into disparities in occupation and income. Some 57 percent of Indian immigrants hold managerial or professional positions, compared to 16 percent of Polish immigrants, and an additional 28 percent hold skilled and semi-skilled positions in construction, extraction, and maintenance. Although these positions are not among the highest paid in Chicago, they do pay significantly more than the semi- and unskilled positions held by an overwhelming number of Mexican immigrants (43 percent) in the production and transportation sectors, which, along with the service sector, are considered the lowest paying industries in Chicago (Paral and Lewis 2001). Another significant difference relates to income. The average household income for Chicago's immigrant community was $46,000 a year in 2000. Indian immigrants, who, as a group, enjoy one of the highest levels of educational attainment (even when compared to the larger, white population), earned $65,000 a year, Polish immigrants earned $44,000, and Mexican immigrants $42,000.[4]

Places of Settlement

When I speak of the Indian, Polish, or Mexican immigrant communities in Chicago, I am not referring to all individuals, immigrant and ethnic alike, throughout the Chicago Metropolitan area that can be broadly conceived of as being Indian, Polish, or Mexican. Instead, I am making reference to the three community areas described by the 2000 census as having the highest concentration of foreign-born Indians, Poles, and Mexicans. Although these communities may also be those with the highest concentration of people of Indian, Polish, or Mexican descent (foreign- and native-born), it does not necessarily follow that they are, in fact, the largest Indian, Polish, and Mexican communities in the Chicago metropolitan area. The names of the communities, their community area numbers (used to situate a particular community geographically in figure 9.1), and descriptions of their respective boundaries follow.

Indian Immigrant Communities   West Ridge (Community Area 2) is located on the north side of Chicago. It is bordered on the north by Howard, on the east by Ridge, Western, and Ravenswood, on the south by Bryn Mawr (5600 North), and on the west by Kedzie (3200 West) and the north shore of the Chicago River.

Albany Park (Community Area 14) is located on the northwest side of Chicago. It is bordered by Foster (5000 North) and the West branch of the Chicago River on the north, the North Branch of the Chicago River on the east, Montrose (3600 North) on the south, and Elston on the southwest.

The Near West Side (Community Area 28) is adjacent to the central business district in downtown Chicago (the Loop). It is bordered by Chicago (800 North) on the north, Halsted (800 West) on the east, 18th Street (1800 South) on the south, and Western (2400 West) on the west.

Polish Immigrant Communities   Portage Park (Community Area 15) is located on the northwest side of Chicago in Jefferson Township. It is bordered by Lawrence (4800 North) on the north, Pulaski (4000 West) on the east, Belmont (3200 North) on the south, and Narragansett (6400 West) on the west.

Dunning (Community Area 17) is located on the northwest side of Chicago. It is bordered by Addison (4200 North) on the north, Laramie (5200 West) on the east, Belmont (3200 North) on the south, and Pacific (8000 West) on the west.

Belmont Cragin (Community Area 19) is located on the northwest side of Chicago. It is bordered by Belmont (3200 North) on the north, Pulaski (4000 West) on the east, Diversey (2000 North) on the south, and Austin (6000 West) on the west.

Mexican Immigrant Communities   South Lawndale (Community Area 30) is located on the west side of Chicago. It is bordered by 16th Street (1600 South) on the north, Western (2400 West) on the east, Pershing (3900 South) and the South Branch of the Chicago River on the south, and Cicero (4800 West) on the west.

The Lower West Side (Community Area 31) is located on the west side of Chicago. It is bordered by 16th Street (1600 South) on the north, Canal (500 West) on the east, 31st Street (3100 South) on the south, and Western (2400 West) on the west.

Brighton Park (Community Area 58) is located on the southwest side of Chicago. It is bordered by the Chicago Sanitary and Ship Canal on the north, Western (2400 West) on the east, 51st Street (5100 South) on the south, and Central Park (3500 West) and the Corwith Yards on the west.

INSTITUTIONAL CONTEXT: IMMIGRANTS AND THE EMERGENCE OF MACHINE POLITICS

Political machines emerged as powerful political institutions in the late nineteenth and early twentieth centuries. Maintaining power by mobilizing voters and through patronage, political machines appealed to voters' needs and ambitions—providing services, employment, and party standing—instead of traditional class or group loyalties. During the formative years of patronage politics, machines supported several mutual benefit programs, including labor legislation passed during the Progressive era, social welfare legislation introduced by the New Deal, and the social programs of the Great Society, strategically working with ethnic and minority groups to increase visibility and solidify power (Erie 1988).

In the early decades of the twentieth century, Irish ethnics who were, in de-

TABLE 9.1 *Select Characteristics of Immigrants in Metropolitan Chicago*

	1980			2000		
Characteristics	Indian	Polish	Mexican	Indian	Polish	Mexican
Demographic						
Number	21,360	63,140	165,320	79,210	138,570	573,627
Share of total population	0.3%	0.9%	2.3%	1.0%	1.7%	7.0%
Share of foreign born population	2.90	8.50	22.20	5.60	9.70	40.30
Number entered in last ten years	17,640	14,880	111,000	40,914	67,878	282,815
Percent entered in last ten years	82.6	23.6	67.1	51.7	49.0	49.3
Proportion citizens	21.2	60.9	19.9	43.6	40.0	24.5
Male	54.6	47.1	56.4	53.9	47.8	56.2
Female	45.4	52.9	43.6	46.1	52.2	43.8
Less than eighteen years of age	13.6	3.3	21.2	6.8	8.8	12.7
Eighteen to sixty-four years of age	85.2	63.3	75.4	85.2	78.0	84.5
Sixty-five years of age or older	1.2	33.4	3.4	7.9	13.2	2.8

Education and language proficiency						
High school graduate or higher	87.5	37.3	21.8	87.5	69.3	46.9
Bachelor's degree or higher	63.5	7.7	2.9	65.8	16.0	33.5
Speak English well or very well	92.8	71.5	49.0	90.2	70.0	49.6
Workforce participation and occupation						
Sixteen years of age or older in labor force	79.6	57.1	72.1	65.5	63.3	62.5
Management-professional	55.5	12.8	4.6	57.2	15.8	6.7
Service	6.2	17.9	16.1	5.4	20.7	23.9
Sales and office	17.4	14.4	11.0	22.8	19.0	13.9
Farming-forestry-fishing	0.1	0.4	1.7	0.0	0.0	0.8
Construction-maintenance	1.7	8.3	7.5	0.8	16.6	12.0
Production-transportation	19.0	46.2	59.1	13.7	27.9	42.7
Poverty and homeownership						
Receiving public assistance	0.4	2.8	3.3	0.8	0.9	1.6
Below poverty line	4.8	8.4	18.9	5.0	6.5	16.1
200 percent or more above poverty line	86.3	77.4	52.4	84.7	80.2	52.8
Homeowners	56.6	65.2	32.4	58.1	70.5	52.3

Source: Author's compilation from U.S. Census Bureau 2000, accessed at http://factfinder.census.gov/servlet/DatasetMainPage Servlet?_program-DEC&_submenuId-datasets_1&_lang-en.

FIGURE 9.1   *Community Areas in Chicago with Highest Concentrations of Immigrants*

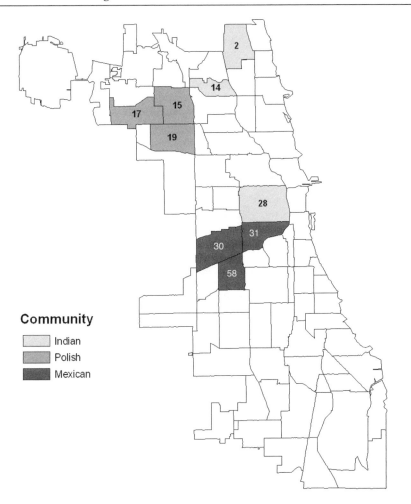

Community

    Indian
    Polish
    Mexican

Source: Author's compilation with the assistance of the University of Chicago Map Collection.

mographic and political terms, the most important actors in the development and maintenance of political machines, withheld access to political office from other ethnic groups in American cities. In *Rainbow's End* Steven Erie suggested that the Irish had little need to share power and jobs with the non-Irish (1988). Although many ethnic groups in the 1910s and 1920s were aware of the Irish's unwillingness to share political power, there was very little they could do given their relative smaller numbers. However, this would change beginning in the 1930s, when Southern and Eastern Europeans began voting in record numbers and reformers began mobilizing recent immigrants and disillusioned ethnics in hopes of undermining political machines throughout the country (Erie 1988).

Afraid that Irish party leaders would acquire the votes of Southern and Eastern European immigrants and undermine GOP control of the state and federal government, Republicans instituted a series of laws making it more difficult for recent immigrants to gain citizenship. The Naturalization Law of 1906 passed by the Republican majority, for example, introduced a literacy test, and required proof of lawful entry and at least five years of residency in the United States. As a result, the number of applicants who were denied citizenship increased from 3 to 15 percent. The law also extended the application process considerably, from an average of five years before 1906 to an average of eleven afterward (Erie 1988). In Chicago, Republicans and Democrats engaged in what would later be called the Great Naturalization Wars, with parties on either side conducting aggressive citizenship drives. According to Harold Gosnell, at least 70 percent of Democratic precinct captains in 1928 reported assisting their constituents with the naturalization process (1969). Such was the drive to increase party numbers among recent immigrants that by 1930 almost 67 percent of the city's foreign-born had petitioned for and successfully secured American citizenship (Erie 1988).

In Chicago, the number of Polish immigrants increased from about 24,000 in 1890 to more than 400,000 in 1930, accounting for 12 percent of the city's population (Erie 1988). During this period, Polish leaders, confronting an Irish monopoly on public office, began a recognition drive, or a concerted effort to increase the political visibility and importance of Chicago's Polish community. In response, the Irish extended (albeit hesitantly) patronage to Chicago's Polish community, often in the form of economic goods, such as public sector employment or monetary support, as opposed to political advancement, such as ward leadership and committee membership. Even those Poles who did manage to secure political office in the 1920s and 1930s found their influence confined, almost exclusively, to local affairs (Kantowicz 1975). Although there were several reasons why Polish politicians were not able to secure important posts within the Democratic Party in Chicago during the period, perhaps the most significant had to do with the fact that they were never considered a significant threat to the machine leadership (Kantowicz 1975). Had Polish political leaders mounted a serious attack on the Chicago machine and demanded that Irish party leaders take the needs and interests of Polish voters seriously it is likely that they would have enjoyed a greater deal of respect and recognition from the political machine.

The Chicago Political Machine, 1930s to the Present

Today the Cook County Democratic Organization, often referred to as the Daley Machine, is considered by many to be one of the last formidable political machines in the United States. Relying on a dense network of aldermen, ward bosses, and precinct captains, the Cook County Democratic Organization dominated city and county politics uninterrupted from 1931 to 1976. Aside from a complex structure of patronage, the Chicago Machine's political reign has depended, in large part, on the integration of the city's prominent ethnic groups. In the 1930s, for example, Anton Cermak (a Czech) sought, and eventually secured, political support from Poles and Italians—groups that had historically been excluded from the predominantly Irish-ethnic Democratic Organization. By creating a broader support base, Cermak effectively extended the party's reach and won the 1931 mayoral election.

In the 1950s, Richard J. Daley further solidified the party's hold on local politics by successfully incorporating African American voters and community leaders. However, it was not until the 1950s that Daley consolidated his power by securing a municipal real estate tax exemption for Chicago (under the Illinois constitution, the state legislature, not the mayor or city council, had the power to set municipal real-estate taxes), eliminating the budget-making power of the city's aldermen, and forming intergovernmental (city-county-state) alliances (Erie 1988). Daley used his newfound decision-making power to raise city taxes and increase the number of city employees. By 1963, taxes and the number of city employees had increased by 100 and 33 percent, respectively. Homeowners were affected disproportionately by the mayor's measures and they protested publicly to their city and ward officials. Polish Americans were particularly vocal, having long been excluded by the predominantly Irish ethnic machine from city and county office (Erie 1988).

When Daley died in 1976, the party struggled to find a formidable replacement. Michael Bilandic, Daley's successor, did not have nearly as much political power or influence as the former mayor and thus lost the primary to Jane Byrne, who went on to win the 1979 election. In 1983, Richard M. Daley, the deceased mayor's son, ran against Byrne in a three-way primary that included African American candidate Harold Washington. Although Washington ultimately won both the primary and mayoral election, his time in office set back the operations of the Chicago Machine, if only briefly. In 1987, when Washington died unexpectedly, the Chicago Machine began courting white liberal and Latino voters, many of whom supported Harold Washington's antimachine campaigns in 1983 and 1986. In 1989, Richard M. Daley was elected mayor, a position he has held ever since.

As the presiding mayor, Richard M. Daley's current political machine relies heavily on incorporating former opponents, city council support, maintaining historically Democratic wards, and courting large ethnic and minority groups (particularly African American and Latino voters) who seek political representation, as did the groups that preceded them, at the neighborhood, ward, city, and county level.

IMMIGRATION TO CHICAGO AFTER 1965

Immigration to the United States, which immigrant exclusion acts and the quota system had curtailed in the early to mid-twentieth century, increased significantly after 1965. The Immigration Act of 1965 not only allowed more people to enter the country by raising admission to 290,000 people a year, but also provided that parents and extended family members of American citizens could migrate as nonquota immigrants—a welcome addition to a section that previously limited sponsorship to marital partners and dependent children. Under the new act, admission was more equally divided, reserving 170,000 slots for countries in the eastern hemisphere (Europe, Asia, and Africa) and an additional 120,000 for the western. In the case of Europe, Asia, and Africa, admission was to be granted based on family reunification (80 percent) and occupational or professional demand (20 percent), providing that no country send more than 20,000 migrants a year. Similar conditions, however, were not placed on migration from the western hemisphere (Ngai 2004). Between 1955 and 1965, Asian immigration accounted for no more than 7.7 percent of the total number of people entering the United States. In the next ten years, however, 1 million Asian immigrants entered the United States, increasing their contribution threefold, to 26 percent. By 1988, the figure would grow even higher, accounting for 44 percent of all lawful immigration to the United States (Liu 1992). During this period, the Indian immigrant community in Chicago went from 600 to 79,210 residents. Similarly, the Mexican immigrant community increased from 24,000 in 1960 to 582,000 in 2000, albeit for different reasons (Paral and Norkewicz 2003).

Indian Immigrants

The economies of several Asian countries were characterized by political instability and limited professional mobility in the 1960s and 1970s. Consequently, a growing number of the professional class was inclined to migrate. Indians who migrated to the United States after 1965 belonged overwhelmingly to this class of young, middle and upper middle class professionals (Rangaswamy 2000). As early as 1969, 45 percent of Indian immigrants were admitted under the occupational-professional demand clause (Ngai 2004). As mentioned earlier, Asians were more likely to take advantage of the family reunification clause than other immigrant groups. Indian immigrants were no different. Aside from bringing their marital partners and children, immigrants also sponsored parents and less-educated siblings, who may not have qualified for entry under the occupational-professional demand provision. The practice of bringing nonquota immigrants to the United States was so prevalent in Chicago's Indian community that between 1980 and 1990 anywhere from 76 to 86 percent of all Indian immigrants arriving in the metropolitan area were sponsored by relatives (Rangaswamy 2000). Because family reunification allowed immigrants to bring their family members to the United States, regardless of education and occupation, sponsored immigrants did not always occupy the same socioeconomic position as their sponsors, who worked, almost exclusively, in engineering, medicine, science, and research. Many entered the small business sector, running local shops, grocery stores, and restaurants (Rangaswamy 2000).

As an increasingly middle and upper middle class community the Indian immigrant community in Chicago did not experience the same level of socioeconomic hardship as other immigrant groups. In the 1970s and 1980s, members of the Indian immigrant community, were convinced that "Indians had no real problems." Rangaswamy's observation illustrates this point:"Long after the Indian community in Chicago had changed from an elite, highly skilled and affluent group to a more [sic] motley crowd that included non-English-speaking, unskilled and often destitute immigrants, the community itself did not recognize the growing need for social services among its members. "Problems" were equated with "failure" and the early warning signs of trouble in paradise were often greeted with denial" (2000, 306).

As a group that enjoyed a certain level of financial security, many believed "they had no need to fight political battles," maintaining that "only the poor or dispossessed or those on the fringes of society need to get politically organized" (Rangaswamy 2000, 296). As a result, Indian immigrants did not think it necessary or in their best interest to build a social service sector in the Indian community. Quite naturally, the first service organizations that emerged were organized around economic and educational development in India. This would change in the 1980s, when the Indian community, who had enjoyed a great deal of economic security since 1965, was subject (like most of the country) to mass layoffs and unemployment. Skilled and unskilled workers alike were dislocated by the local economy's shift from a manufacturing to a service-oriented economy. In 1990, the census revealed that 10 percent of Indians lived below the poverty line. Those who entered between 1980 and 1990 suffered most, with an estimated 14 percent well below the poverty line, compared to only 5 percent of those who migrated before 1980 (Rangaswamy 2000).

Polish Immigrants

In the late 1960s, economic and political conditions in Poland deteriorated. Dissatisfied with the socialist state, a growing number of Poles left the country to reunite with family abroad, demonstrate their growing animosity toward the national government, and, in some cases, to avoid political persecution. As refugees, the decision to migrate was economic and political. Like Indians who migrated to Chicago during this period, Polish immigrants in the 1960s were highly educated and occupied managerial and professional positions prior to migrating (Erdmans 1998). Unlike Indians, who also belonged to the eastern hemisphere category under the Immigration Act of 1965, Poles did not benefit as much from occupational-professional demand or family reunification provisions. In the five years before the act was passed, 7,000 Poles entered the United States, a number reduced significantly by the national-origin quotas of 1924 and 1952. After it was introduced, even fewer Poles were admitted. What had led to an increase in Asian migration—the elimination of national-origin quotas and the reservation of 170,000 slots for the eastern hemisphere—had the unanticipated consequence of interrupting European migration.

Whatever benefits Polish immigrants may have derived from the act, and at least 75 percent of those who migrated during this period did so under the family reunification provision, they paled in comparison to those derived by Indian immigrants—82 percent under family reunification and 45 percent under occupational-professional demand. It would not be until 1990, when Congress introduced the diversity visa provision, that Chicago's Polish immigrant community would make the most of the 1965 act. In the meantime, Polish nationals dissatisfied with socioeconomic conditions in Poland began applying for temporary visas in increasing numbers in the 1960s. As nonimmigrants, temporary visitors were not granted residence and were prevented from being gainfully employed while in the United States. The exception was those who arrived with work visas. In the 1960s, about 12,000 Poles entered the country as temporary visitors a year. The number would double in the ten years that followed. Many of these visitors, as Mary Patrice Erdmans has demonstrated, remained in the United States long after their visas expired. In the 1980s, 80 percent of the 450,000 Poles who arrived in the United States as nonquota immigrants did so with temporary visas. An estimated one-third overstayed their visas each year, amounting to 250,000 people by 1991—of which 50,000 to 100,000 lived in Chicago (Erdmans 1998).

Chicago's post-1965 Polish immigrant community, which had slowly been growing with the arrival of immigrants and visitors in 1960s and 1970s saw a noticeable increase during the 1980s and 1990s. This current was driven by three distinct, yet not entirely unrelated factors—the 1980 Refugee Act, declaration of martial law in Poland, and the creation of diversity visas (Immigration and Naturalization Act of 1990).

In 1980, Congress passed the Refugee Act, adopting the designation used by international law, defining refugees as persons unable or unwilling to return to their native country because of persecution or a well-founded fear of persecution. The act became increasingly important for Polish nationals, who were placed under martial law in 1981. By 1985, two years after martial law had been lifted, at least 1,000 Polish refugees settled in Chicago. In the following months, a considerable number of refugees who had originally migrated to other parts of the country began relocating to Chicago (Erdmans 1998). The numbers coming as refugees, however, was smaller than the subsequent numbers who came under the diversity visa provisions of the 1990 Immigration and Naturalization Act. Polish immigrants readily took advantage of the program, making Polish immigration the largest legal, migratory current to Chicago in the 1990s. Thus, of the 138,570 individuals who made up Chicago's Polish immigrant community in 2000, at least 49 percent (67,878) arrived after the Immigration and Naturalization Act of 1990 (Paral 2004).

Post-1965 migration from Poland, under the auspices of the Immigration Act of 1965, the Immigration Act of 1980, and the Immigration and Naturalization Act of 1990, had several noticeable effects on Chicago's Polish immigrant community. Not only did the current revitalize the Polish immigrant community, which had formerly suffered under national-origin quotas, it also increased the need for social service organizations in the newer Polish immigrant community. With respect to the newer Polish immigrant and Polish American communities, Mary Patrice Erdmans makes an important distinction in her book between the needs of Polish immigrants and Polish Americans:

> A difference between later-generation Polish Americans and new Polish immigrants was related to the fact that the former were ethnics and as such were established members of American society, while the latter were immigrants and

therefore, newcomers. Each group had different needs, resources, and networks. Comparatively, the immigrants had weaker ties in the United States and the ethnics had weaker connections to Poland. The immigrants needed networks that gave them information about housing, schools, jobs, and public transportation. In contrast, ethnic needs were linked to their generational distance from the ancestral homeland. Consequently, immigrants were not attracted to Polish American organizations, which were organized to satisfy ethnic, rather than social needs. Immigrants wanted these organizations to help them find jobs; the ethnic organizations preferred to spend their money on cultural programs and anti-defamation initiatives. (1998, 11)

A growing number of Polish immigrants who migrated to Chicago by 1990 began turning to previous immigrants and the more established Polish American community for assistance. Much to their surprise, a network of organizations to facilitate settlement in the Polish immigrant community did not exist, forcing those in need to turn increasingly to friends, family members, and the Catholic Church for support.

Mexican Immigrants

Observers have noted that Mexican immigration to Chicago has grown considerably since 1965. The 1980 census reported that 165,320 Mexicans had migrated to Chicago in the previous decade. By 1990, the figure had increased to 268,293. By 2000, it had reached 573,627, accounting for 7 percent of the total population and 40.3 percent of the foreign-born. Of the total, 49.3 percent, or 282,815 had lived in the United States for fewer than ten years (Paral and Norkewicz 2003). This dramatic increase was driven by, among other things, Mexico's underdeveloped economy, its inability to absorb new workers, its low wages, and its proximity to the United States.

Illegal immigration from Mexico did not begin with the Immigration Act of 1965. During World War II, Mexicans began entering the United States without papers. In 1965, a year after the Bracero Program was terminated and migration from the western hemisphere was reduced through the introduction of continental quotas (120,000 a year, regardless of country) in the Immigration Act of 1965, undocumented immigration increased significantly. One of the clearest indications of this shift is the number of people detained or deported, which increased by 40 percent between 1980 and 1990. In 2000, the U.S. Bureau of Citizenship and Immigration Services, formerly the U.S. Immigration and Naturalization Service (INS), maintained that 1.8 million undocumented immigrants were deported from the United States every year and that that figure was growing by an estimated 275,000 a year (Ngai 2004). That year also, the U.S. Bureau of Citizenship and Immigration Services reported that at least 432,000 undocumented immigrants lived in Illinois, making the state the fourth largest in that ranking (Mehta and Theodore 2002).

In 1971, an Illinois legislative investigative commission formed by senators and congressmen based in Chicago published a report on Mexican immigration to Illinois titled *The Illegal Mexican Alien Problem.*[5] In it they asserted that figures regarding apprehension rates provided an accurate picture of the broader phenomenon of undocumented immigration, pointing out that 85 percent of the 8,728 individuals apprehended by the INS that year were Mexican. In 1992, when the INS released its report of the national origins of illegal immigrants, it estimated that Mexicans accounted for 44 percent of all undocumented immigrants in the state of Illinois. This, however, had little effect on the way illegal immigration was perceived in the city of Chicago, where, as late as 1997, 96 percent of the total number of undocumented immigrants apprehended in the metropolitan area were Mexican nationals (De Genova 2005).

According to Nicholas De Genova, the commission's report and perceptions of Mexican migration after 1965 had two distinct effects in Chicago: it made notions of illegality synonymous with Mexicans and mobilized the Mexican immigrant–Mexican American community (2005). Mounting hostilities toward Mexicans posed by Chicago's larger, white community and the INS, which regularly carried out raids in factories, parks, grocery stores, and movie theaters in Latino neighborhoods, led to protests in 1974 and 1976 and culminated in the creation of civil rights and community-based organizations in Pilsen (Near West Side) and Little Village (South Lawndale), the two largest Mexican neighborhoods in the city. Social service workers, who witnessed the mistreatment of Mexicans, also took note and began extending their services by hiring Latino organizers, incorporating programs for immigrants, and in some cases creating organizations to better serve the needs of the Mexican community. Even the INS felt compelled to address the grievances of Mexicans, establishing a community relations committee in Chicago.

Given the linked fates of Mexican immigrants and Mexican Americans, community-based organizations eschewed distinctions based on nativity and pushed for a broader Mexican community interest—a decision that more often than not would work in the favor of Mexican immigrants. Since the 1970s, Mexican immigrants also gained access to a larger network of (non-Latino specific) service organizations in Chicago. As a result, the resources available to Mexican immigrants have grown considerably, as has their political visibility. This stands in contrast to Indian immigrants, who initially did not think it was in their best interest to form such organizations (they were better off than the larger, immigrant, and American population, and saw no point in bringing attention to problems that were marginal to the community), and to Polish immigrants, whose interests were not integrated into existing Polish American organizations (Erdmans 1998).

VARIATIONS IN COMMUNITY ORGANIZATIONS

Although social service organizations throughout the city assist Indian, Polish, and Mexican immigrants, the number of immigrant- or community-based organizations catering specifically to each group varies considerably. This is particularly true for Indian and Polish immigrants. The lack of geographical concentration and greater socioeconomic mobility of Indian immigrants, for example, has had a significant effect on the number and size of Indian and South Asian community organizations in Chicago. Polish immigrants, who live primarily in areas with a dense concentration of Polish immigrants and Polish Americans, on the other hand, have struggled to get the attention of existing community organizations and create new organizations of their own.

Indian

Chicago's Indian immigrant community is home to several cultural and professional organizations. They vary according to interest, region, language, and religion, as well as education and profession and are supported by different members of the Indian community. Among the types of organizations those that are cultural occupy a central position. According to one organization leader, the Indian community's preference in cultural organizations is apparent in the prominence of language and history classes in the community and the plethora of hometown, regional, and national organizations or dance, music, and performance ensembles throughout the metropolitan area.

City representatives noted that Indian immigrants were very involved in the Chicago Public Schools (CPS), stating that they regularly attended school functions, volunteered, and sat on local PTAs. Indian immigrants also participated in CPS's larger, citywide initiatives. Despite their interest in and presence in local schools, officials noted that such activism was lacking in other aspects of local governance. Although most respondents were not sure why this was the case, some believed it had something to do with the Indian immigrant community's overwhelming interest in cultural and educational programs and activities.

Members of the larger service community noted that though the number of organizations addressing the needs of the Indian immigrant community is small, the work they do is recognized and held in high regard by the larger service community. They also noticed that, in recent years, the number of individuals representing and advocating on behalf of the Indian community has grown. Although some of this increased visibility may have something to do with the increase in the size of the Indian community, it also has a lot to do with the work of Indian American and Indian immigrant activists, who have brought attention to the distinct needs of recent immigrants by cultivating intergroup relationships, participating in pan-Asian organizational drives, and by actively serving in immigrant and interracial coalitions.

As recently as the 1980s, many in the Indian community believed that their numbers were not significant enough to have a noticeable effect on local decision making. The problem is complicated further by the fact that members of the Indian community, unlike other ethnic-racial groups in the city, do not necessarily share political beliefs or policy priorities, making it increasingly difficult to form coalitions as a means to compensate for demographic shortcomings. Political apathy is another concern often cited by organization leaders within the Indian immigrant community. In *Namasté America: Indian Immigrants in an American Metropolis*, Padma Rangaswamy notes that "for years, activists in the Indian community of Chicago have tried to get Indians interested in political issues to no avail" (2000, 294). A founding member of the Indo American Democratic Organization (IADO) told Rangaswamy that "Indians are only keen to on cultural extravaganzas, they are not interested in issues-oriented politics," adding, "in fact, to most Indians here, politics is a dirty word" (2000, 294). A current member of the IADO supported the claim, maintaining that despite the growing number of nonprofit organizations serving the Indian community and greater visibility outside the Indian community, most organizations struggle to secure resources and support from prominent residents, who give to cultural and national organizations with greater frequency.[6]

Although more people have realized the importance of community-based organizations in the last few years, and many are in a position to lend economic support to their initiatives, a significant proportion of the Indian community remains indifferent. This indifference continues to be based, in large part, on the belief that Indians in Chicago are an educated, relatively well-off group that does not need to court city and county officials or policy makers as heavily as lower-income immigrant and minority groups. An increasingly vocal faction in the Indian immigrant community, however, is contesting the assumption, bringing attention to the growing number of Indian immigrants at or below the poverty line; the needs of abused children, women, and the elderly; and local and national anti-Indian hostilities, particularly with respect to employment, racial, and religious discrimination.

Nevertheless, the number of organizations serving the needs of the Indian immigrant community, at least in part, remains small. In hesitating to support service initiatives, failing to cultivate working relationships with other immigrant communities, and underestimating the importance of city and county officials and policy makers, the Indian immigrant community has enjoyed little political presence or weight in Chicago. When asked which Indian organizations were considered prominent in the Indian immigrant and Indian American communities, most city and county government officials and representatives named very few if any (none to three), and noted that Indians (immigrants and Americans) were noticeably absent from most of the mayor's special committees and did not occupy any city, county, or state-appointed seats. One respondent maintained that, even though Indians participated in local and educational organizations and have begun taking part in coalitions, they have yet to successfully capture the attention of the larger, nonimmigrant community or local officials. Consequently, people occupying important organizational or government positions have yet to address the distinct needs of Asians, particularly those of Indian immigrants.[7]

Polish

There are several hometown, fraternal, and cultural organizations in the Polish community. Recent immigrants often form close relationships with individuals who migrated from the same town, city, or region or with those who share an interest in Polish nationalism and politics. Some families place their children in Polish Saturday schools to learn or retain language skills and history and may also belong and regularly contribute to one of the dozens of Polish regional and national organizations. A member of the Polish immigrant community declared that interest in religious, cultural, and educational activities within the Polish immigrant community is very high, adding that such organizations are far more numerous than any other type and engage the most immigrants in Chicago's Polish communities.

City representatives and officials noted that Polish immigrants, though involved in CPS at the local level, were not visible at the city level or in local government. In addition, they could not recall Polish immigrants participating in citywide community awareness campaigns or name prominent Polish immigrant organizations. If anything, most respondents assured us, the involvement of Polish immigrants in local government was limited to activity at the ward level. According to a CPS official, Polish immigrant involvement is confined, almost exclusively, to local school and cultural activities.[8] They do not appear to be as concerned with the issues that affect the larger, immigrant community, like immigrant rights. If they do, in fact, play an active role outside the Polish community, he argued, they are not as vocal or visible as other immigrant groups.

Members of the larger, service community stated that Polish immigrants, even though they were active in their own communities, rarely participated in or helped organize their events or organizational drives. As far as they could tell, Polish immigrant efforts concentrated on cultural (Saturday schools), educational (English language), and religious activities. They were noticeably absent on coalitions, committees, and boards. City representatives did not know how Polish immigrants, as a group, were organized. Some believed they were organized, but could not comment on the extent to which they were organized or provide the names of prominent individuals or organizations. The director of a division at the city's Commission on Human Relations stated that Polish immigrants did not approach them as often as Indian or Mexican immigrants, limiting that office's familiarity and relationship with activity in Chicago's Polish immigrant community considerably.

It is difficult to isolate one particular cause for the absence of Polish immigrants in the larger, organizational and political arena. One informant believed it had something to do with the immigrants' interest in getting situated, stating that "recent immigrants do not have much time to get involved in local or community-based organizations." The same informant maintained that, "working and spending time with family is more of a priority than volunteering." If anything, he said, recent immigrants may take English as a second language (ESL) classes or place their children in Saturday schools to learn Polish history and retain language skills.[9]

A leader in the Polish immigrant community believed that Polish immigrants did not participate in noncultural organizational and political activities for several reasons, most of them having to do with the disorganization of the

Polish immigrant community, the absence of a strong network of immigrant organizations that could facilitate Polish involvement, and the general distaste among recent Polish immigrants for political involvement. The lack of community-based and social service organizations was echoed by other respondents. For instance, one observer noted that it was particularly difficult to get Polish immigrants involved in existing organizations to increase their political influence, let alone create new ones, because many in the Polish immigrant community were disinterested in politics. This was particularly true for those families who had fled Poland as refugees.

To date, only one organization in Chicago is committed exclusively to serving the needs of the Polish immigrant community, the Polish American Association. Founded in 1922, the Polish American Association (PAA) is the only bilingual-bicultural English-Polish social service organization in the United States. In 2005, the organization assisted more than 12,000 immigrants from the Chicago metropolitan area (Paral 2004). The organization offers more than thirty programs and services to the Polish immigrant community—including advocacy, education, employment, economic, housing, immigration, and vocational training programs and services. However, as the only Polish social service organization in Chicago, it is increasingly difficult for the organization to meet the needs of Chicago's growing Polish immigrant community. According to the PAA's executive director, very few Poles solicit assistance or services from community-based organizations or larger, immigrant-serving social service organizations. The most likely causes were a lack of familiarity with the types of programs and services offered or uncertainty over whether these organizations would be able to accommodate immigrants with limited English proficiency. Some Polish immigrants had approached Polish American organizations, convinced that they have culturally competent staff and provide the types of programs and services they are interested in (education, employment, immigration, housing, and vocational training), only to be told that organizations are cultural and educational, and consequently do not help situate recent immigrants. Many Polish immigrants therefore turn to friends and family members for assistance, with the Catholic Church as the only other organizational source of support.[10]

Thus, the network of community-based and social service organizations in the Polish immigrant community is underdeveloped. Served, almost exclusively, by the Polish American Association, the number of organizations that could serve as potential advocates for the needs and interests of Polish immigrants in Chicago is limited. In the end, this inability or unwillingness to organize has hurt the Polish immigrant community. Unlike immigrant groups who are better sociopolitically situated, the needs and interests of Polish immigrants in Chicago are casually recognized, if at all, by policy makers and the larger, immigrant and nonimmigrant communities. Even the Polish American community, which enjoys a degree of socioeconomic security and political recognition, is more interested in increasing the number of educational, business, and government opportunities available to them, than addressing the needs and interests of the Polish immigrant community.

Mexican

Mexican immigrants, like their Indian and Polish counterparts, have organized several types of cultural and national organizations. In Chicago 275 mutualistas (mutual aid organizations) are registered with the Mexican consulate. They are organized into fourteen distinct federations and are represented by CONFE-MEX, a confederation of cultural, mutual aid, hometown, and state organizations. The state federations of Durango, Guanajuato, Guerrero, Jalisco, Michoacan, San Luis Potosi, and Zacatecas are particularly active, organizing beauty pageants, festivals, fundraisers, parades, patriotic celebrations, political events, and soccer tournaments. Although the number of mutual aid organizations registered is impressive, a representative of the Mexican consulate familiar with the organizations admitted that only a few maintain formal contact with the office (usually those that invite representatives of the Mexican government to attend or participate in events), making it difficult to provide an accurate count of Mexican organizations. The official, however, believed that at least 800 mutual aid, home town, and state organizations existed in the Chicago metropolitan area.[11] Aside from these cultural organizations there are 400 different Mexican recreational organizations throughout Chicago, the majority being amateur soccer teams organized by and comprised, almost exclusively, of young immigrant men. Despite the fact they are recreational, as Nicholas De Genova rightfully maintained, "in many ways [they are] analogous to hometown organizations in their capacity to facilitate the exchange of news from the players' communities, locally and abroad" and in their ability to grant friends and family members access to broader, social networks (2005, 256).

Local government officials noted that Mexican immigrants also participated readily in the Chicago Public Schools (CPS) system. One informant described the level of involvement among Mexican immigrant parents in CPS as very high despite the limited English skills of many of them, adding that the high number might have something to do with the relationship between administrators and parents or the translators the district provides to facilitate immigrant involvement. Many attend and participate in school functions (after-school programs, PTA, fundraisers) and help organize local and citywide initiatives.[12] A community organizer agreed with the official's estimation of Mexican immigrants, adding that they play a very important role in organizing themselves and taking an active role in school district governance.[13]

Representatives from larger social service organizations believed that the interests of Mexican immigrants were well represented in the programs, services, and advocacy efforts of social service organizations and city-county government. Many were convinced that representation of the Mexican immigrant community had a lot to do with the ongoing efforts of the Mexican social service community, as well as individual efforts. The director of one community-based organization noted a high level of involvement among immigrants, and women in particular. Although she admitted that most of the immigrant women would not necessarily see themselves as activists or community leaders, they nevertheless played important roles in organizing and publicizing events and community awareness campaigns.[14] Another respondent noted that the number of Mexican immigrants contributing to organizational efforts had increased in the last few years, leading her to believe that immigrant volunteers and participants are a much more recognizable element today than they were a few years ago.

Government officials made similar points with respect to Mexican immigrant involvement, noted that their offices regularly maintained contact and collaborated with many community-based organizations in Little Village (South Lawndale) and Pilsen (Lower West Side), and were working to form relationships with Mexican immigrant communities in other parts of the city. Every city and county official or representative was able to name several prominent Mexican immigrant organizations (at least ten). They were also able to describe in great detail the work of each organization, past and ongoing efforts with the mayor's office and other city departments. For example, the director of Latino Affairs at the city's Commission on Human Relations mentioned that the interests of Mexicans were well represented on city and county boards, committees, and departments, and more so than for Indian and Polish immigrants. The director of a different office at the Commission on Human Relations believed that Mexican immigrants were at a particular advantage compared to other immigrant groups not only because more Latinos occupy public office, but because Latino officials are much more likely to represent and advocate on behalf of Mexican immigrants knowing that the issues affecting immigrants—discrimination, low educational attainment, lack of economic security—also affect the Latino community more generally.

DIFFERENCES IN POLITICAL PRESENCE AND WEIGHT

Members of the Indian immigrant community have struggled to secure resources from prominent community members, who prefer to give to cultural, educational, and national organizations rather than to service organizations. Although the social service community has grown in the last few years and community leaders have gained recognition in the larger service community by working with other organizations and helping organize coalitions, they have yet to gain the same level of recognition from officials in local city and county government or members of the larger, non-Asian community (table 9.2). Service organizations that serve Polish immigrants in Chicago are noticeably absent. This organizational and structural shortcoming has limited the amount of attention social workers and leaders have been able to secure, and made it increasingly difficult to advocate on behalf of the Polish immigrant community. The degree to which this affects the visibility and weight of Polish immigrants, however, is uncertain. Despite having only one social service organization the group appears to enjoy a higher level of visibility than Indian immigrants in various city and county institutions. This political presence and recognition might have more to do with the significant place Polish immigration has occupied in the city's his-

TABLE 9.2   *Summary of Findings on Civic and Political Engagement*

	Indian	Polish	Mexican
Civic participation	high	medium	high
Political participation	low-medium	low	medium-high
Service community	small-medium	small	large
Political presence	medium	low	high
Political weight	low	low	high

Source: Author's compilation.

tory, the large Polish immigrant–American community in Chicago, or the relationships previous immigrants cultivated with political actors than with current immigrant activity. The interests of Mexican immigrants, the largest immigrant group in Chicago, are well represented. Not only is there a large social service network in the Mexican immigrant community and organizations outside of it that support and advance Mexican immigrant initiatives, Mexican interests are also much more likely to be represented by Latino and non-Latino officials than those of Indian or Polish immigrants.

As better-educated predominantly middle and upper middle class English-speaking immigrants, the first Indians to arrive in Chicago had no particular interest in constructing social service organizations or participating in political activity. Many believed their energy and resources were better spent on cultural, educational, professional, and religious associations and initiatives. Community activists have worked hard to convince members of the importance of organizing themselves and participating in the larger, political arena (city-county-state). Although the network of social service organizations in the Indian community is small and struggles to secure funding, organizations and activists in the Indian community are forming partnerships with other immigrants and are beginning to have a recognizable presence on interracial-ethnic coalitions and committees. By participating in increasing numbers in these outlets Indian immigrants are increasing their visibility among the larger, immigrant community and perhaps, more important, among Chicago's policy makers.

Although Polish immigrants are increasingly visible, the absence of organizations that serve the needs and interests of Polish immigrants that could advocate on their behalf in the larger immigrant and nonimmigrant communities has affected their political presence and weight in Chicago considerably. The fact that cultural and fraternal Polish American organizations have yet to incorporate or make Polish immigrant interests a significant part of their missions has made it increasingly difficult for Polish immigrants to capture the attention of local policy makers. It is important to note that even when Polish interests are considered, more often than not they are the interests of Polish Americans, whose interests, as a group than enjoys a certain level of social, political, and economic security, differ significantly from those of Polish immigrants. If Polish immigrants want to become a politically recognized group, an effort needs to be made to convince immigrants that it is increasingly necessary to organize the immigrant community, pressure community leaders (Polish immigrant and Polish American alike) to commit resources and support to social service network, and more aggressively cultivate relationships with the larger community by participating in coalitions, organizational drives, and community awareness campaigns throughout the city.

The fact that Mexican immigration to Chicago exceeds that of Indian and Polish immigrants combined should not be underestimated. Mexican immigrants, unlike their Indian and Polish counterparts, are in a unique position. As the largest immigrant (and ethnic) group in Chicago (estimated at 1.3 million), Mexicans are not only the most visible immigrants, they also have a much larger network of social service organizations (Ready and Brown-Gort 2005). Although the organizations themselves may vary in size, services, and the amount of time and resources they are able to dedicate to serving Mexican immigrant clients, they serve an important role in organizing, representing, and advocating on behalf of the Mexican immigrant community. The fact that the circumstances Mexican immigrants face are also faced by a significant number of Mexican Americans and other Latinos should not be underestimated. Not only does this mean that Mexican immigrants have access to programs and services provided by Mexican American, and to a larger extent Latino organizations, it also means that their interests, at least in theory, are more likely to be represented by prominent members of the larger Latino community. When one takes the number of Mexican American and Latinos with city and county offices into account, it becomes increasingly obvious that Mexican immigrants are the most visible and most represented immigrant group in Chicago. In the end, the dense network of social service and community-based organizations Mexican immigrants have access to; the active role they play, or are believed to play, in organizing and contributing to organizational drives and community awareness campaigns; and the number of people on city and county coalitions not only make Mexican immigrants the most visible immigrant group in Chicago, they also make them the group whose interests are most likely to be recognized and considered by policy makers at the city and county level.

CONCLUSION

The size of the Mexican immigrant community no doubt plays an important role in its ability to bring attention to and advance group interests. However, group size may not be necessary for political influence, as Kristi Andersen explains, for instance, in chapter 3 of this volume, where a small community-based organization in Fort Collins, Colorado, was effective in its efforts to pass an ordinance prohibiting city employees from inquiring about a resident's immigration status. Group size may also not be enough in some cases, as Ramakrishnan and Bloemraad show in chapter 2 of this volume, as Mexican immigrant populations in several California cities who, despite constituting the largest immigrant group, had a disproportionately lower number of organizations and enjoyed considerably less political presence than their Vietnamese, Korean, Armenian, Indian, Chinese, and Filipino counterparts. In light of Andersen and Ramakrishnan's findings, how do we account for the political presence and weight of Mexican immigrants in Chicago?

As part of a larger community that has struggled to gain political recognition since the 1970s, the interests of Mexican immigrants have historically been well represented. Access to a dense network of community-based and social service organizations that have the capacity to organize, represent, or advocate on behalf of (or help bring attention to immigrants so they can advocate on their own behalf) gives Mexican immigrants a distinct advantage and allows them to compensate for some of the factors that may otherwise preclude political activity in the United States, such as limited English-speaking ability, low educational attainment, unfamiliarity with local resources and institutions, and undocumented status. As a group with relatively limited socioeconomic mobility it is very likely that Mexican immigrants view civic and political involvement in local and citywide organizations as a fundamental catalyst to social change. Factors also worth considering include Chicago's immigrant-friendly institutions, interest in facilitating immigrant involvement in local and citywide efforts by providing and promoting events in the immigrant community and providing translators, and the effort of Mexican American activists, leaders, and community-based organizations to gain access to and recognition from city and county government since the late 1970s.

That there are alderman and city-county representatives of Mexican or Latino descent that advocate on behalf of the Mexican immigrant community may also place Mexicans in Chicago in a more favorable position than Andersen and Ramakrishnan describe. In addition, one should not underestimate the fact that long-time mayor Richard M. Daley has formally courted Latino voters and politicians since 1987.[15] Although not one of the primary themes of this chapter, Daley's interaction with Latino voters may help explain the political presence and weight of Mexican immigrants in Chicago, particularly when one recognizes the increasingly important role the Hispanic Democratic Organization has played in upholding the Daley machine.[16]

In the past two decades, the Indian and Polish immigrant communities have both experienced a rise in the number of less-educated immigrants. In the end, the extent to which these groups are able to secure a higher degree of political presence and weight at the local level may depend on following a strategy similar to Mexican immigrants: forming new organizations and increasing participation in organizations that tie the interests of immigrants and native-born ethnics alike, and focusing more attention to the placement of community members in appointed positions. Without such efforts, Indian and Polish immigrants in Chicago risk remaining on the margins of civic and political life in the city.

NOTES

1. For more on the Immigrant Civic Engagement Project (ICEP), see chapter 2, this volume.
2. Government informants included, but were not limited to, representatives of city and county committees and departments and individuals appointed by the mayor.

3. Although religious institutions are important sites of civic, and at times, political activity and organization, their contributions were not taken into account for the purposes of this study, consequently they do not figure prominently in the chapter's findings.

4. Although the incomes of Indian and Polish immigrants correspond particularly well with their educational and occupational characteristics, the case of Mexican immigrants appears to be the exception—especially when one realizes that 24 percent of Mexican households have three or more people contributing to the household's income, compared to less than 15 percent of non-Latino households (Ready and Brown-Gort 2005).

5. The group defended their choice of title by arguing that "since the illegal alien situation in Illinois primarily concerns Mexican nationals . . . [it was quite natural that the] report be restricted to that facet of the problem."

6. Interview, University of Chicago, August 11, 2006.

7. Interview, Advisory Council on Asian Affairs, Commission on Human Relations, December 15, 2005.

8. Interview, Office of Language and Cultural Education, Chicago Public Schools, December 15, 2005.

9. Interview, Polish Museum of America, Polish Roman Catholic Union of America, August 4, 2006.

10. Interview, Polish American Association, October 9, 2006.

11. Interview, Mexican Consulate in Chicago, December 2, 2005.

12. Interview, Local School Council Relations, Chicago Public Schools, December 15, 2005.

13. Interview, Interfaith, March 17, 2006.

14. Interview, Mujeres Latinas en Accion, May 31, 2006.

15. For an example of the types of roles Latinos in Chicago play in Daley's current machine, see Dan Mihalopoulos, "Chicago Rebuilt Machine, U.S. Says," *Chicago Tribune*, May 8, 2006, 1.

16. For more information on Daley's relationship with the Hispanic Democratic Organization, see Dan Mihalopoulos, "Mexico Nabs Fugitive with City Hall Ties," *Chicago Tribune*, September 21, 2007, 1; Dan Mihalopoulos, "Feds Indict Daley Campaign Worker," *Chicago Tribune*, December 2, 2006, 1; Rudolph Bush, "Daley Jobs Chief Guilty," *Chicago Tribune*, July 7, 2006, 1; Dan Mihalopoulos, "Jockeying for Power Amid Scandal," *Chicago Tribune*, March 19, 2006, 2; Oscar Avila, "Symbol of Unity Divides City's Hispanic Politicians," *Chicago Tribune*, January 8, 2006, 1; John Kass, "Memory Malady Always Strikes when Feds Visit," *Chicago Tribune*, October 6, 2004, 2; Oscar Avila, "Political Outsider Now Inside," *Chicago Tribune*, February 27, 2003, 1; "Political Army Wields Clout, Jobs," *Chicago Tribune*, October 31, 2002, 1; "A Message from Latino Voters," *Chicago Tribune*, March 19, 1998, 20; and "Memories Bind Hispanics to Daley," *Chicago Tribune*, December 13, 1988, 1.

REFERENCES

Archdeacon, Thomas. 1989. *Becoming American*. New York: The Free Press.

De Genova, Nicholas. 2005. *Working the Boundaries: Race, Space, and "Illegality" in Mexican Chicago*. Durham, N.C.: Duke University Press.

Erdmans, Mary Patrice. 1998. *Opposite Poles: Immigrants and Ethnics in Polish Chicago, 1976–1990*. University Park, Pa.: Pennsylvania State University Press.

Erie, Steven P. 1988. *Rainbow's End: Irish-Americans and the Dilemmas of Urban Machine Politics, 1840–1985.* Berkeley, Calif.: University of California Press.

Gosnell, Harold F. 1969. *Machine Politics: Chicago Model.* New York: AMS Press.

Kantowicz, Edward R. 1975. *Polish-American Politics in Chicago, 1880–1940.* Chicago, Ill.: University of Chicago Press.

Liu, John. 1992. "The Contours of Asian Professional, Technical, and Kindred Work Immigration, 1965–1988." *Sociological Perspectives* 35(4): 673–704.

Mehta, Chirag, and Nik Theodore. 2002. "Chicago's Undocumented Immigrants: An Analysis of Wages, Working Conditions, and Economic Contributions." Chicago, Ill.: Center for Urban Economic Development, University of Illinois at Chicago.

Ngai, Mae M. 2004. *Impossible Subjects: Illegal Aliens and the Making of Modern America.* Princeton, N.J.: Princeton University Press.

Paral, Rob. 2004. *The Polish Community in Metro Chicago: A Community Profile of Strengths and Needs.* A Census 2000 Report. Chicago, Ill.: The Polish American Association.

Paral, Rob, and Jim Lewis. 2001. "A Profile of Immigrants in the Illinois Workforce." Prepared for the Illinois Immigrant Policy Project, a roundtable discussion. Chicago, Ill.: Roosevelt University, Institute for Metropolitan Affairs. Accessed at http://www.roosevelt.edu/ima/pdfs/immigrant-workforce.pdf.

Paral, Rob, and Michael Norkewicz. 2003. *The Metro Chicago Immigration Fact Book.* Chicago, Ill.: Roosevelt University, Institute for Metropolitan Affairs.

Rangaswamy, Padma. 2000. *Namasté America: Indian Immigrants in an American Metropolis.* University Park, Pa.: Pennsylvania State University Press.

Ready, Timothy, and Allert Brown-Gort. 2005. *The State of Latino Chicago: This Is Home Now.* South Bend, Ind.: Institute for Latino Studies, University of Notre Dame.

Part III

Variations by Organization Type

Janelle Wong, Kathy Rim, and Haven Perez

Chapter 10

Protestant Churches and Conservative Politics: Latinos and Asians in the United States

This chapter is part of a larger project that, focusing on Asian Americans and Latinos, examines the role of growing numbers of evangelical, Pentecostal, and charismatic (EPC) Christian immigrants in American politics and in conservative Christian political movements in particular. The primary question animating the project asks whether growing numbers of evangelical and Pentecostal Asians and Latinos will strengthen or undermine the political influence and policy positions of politically conservative Christians in the United States. We argue that the future role of Asian American and Latino EPC Christians in the political sphere depends in large part on two factors: the degree to which ethnic EPC churches and temples shape the political orientations of and mobilize their members, and the extent to which Asian American and Latino EPC Christians are able to build coalitions with the mainstream conservative Christian movement or other groups.

In the past decade, scholars have begun to focus on the role that civic organizations play in mobilizing contemporary immigrants to participate in the civic sphere. Recent and past literature identifies labor unions, worker centers, ethnic advocacy organizations, hometown associations, and social service organizations as among the most important organizations shaping immigrant civic engagement (Wong 2006a; Fine 2006; Milkman 2006; Levitt 2002). These organizations tend to be visible in debates over immigration policy and in political action aimed at fortifying immigrant rights in the United States. With the critical exception of Catholic churches and associated organizations (Warren 2001), religious organizations have received comparatively less attention in studies of immigrant civic engagement. Research that does investigate the role religious organizations play in immigrant activism tends to concentrate heavily on civic engagement around progressive policies, such as mobilization to liberalize immigrant policies and protect immigrant worker rights (Warren 2001; Wood 2002; Hondagneu-Sotelo 2007). Missing from these accounts is attention to the influence of non-Catholic and nonpolitically progressive religious organizations on the civic engagement of immigrants.

In fact, conservative Protestant churches, particularly those that are evangelical, Pentecostal, or charismatic, are some of the largest ethnic organizations in the nation, with many drawing from 500 to 6,000 worshippers each Sunday, most of whom are first- and second-generation immigrant Asian and Latino. The number of immigrants who attend ethnic EPC churches and temples on any given Sunday vastly exceeds those directly served by any of the lead social service providers or advocacy organizations. Further, there are many more Asian and Latino EPCs in the United States than there are union members. The most comprehensive study of Latino religiosity to date, the Hispanic Churches in American Public Life (HCAPL) survey, estimates that almost one-fourth of all Latinos were Pentecostals or members of other Protestant faiths in 2000 (Espinosa, Elizondo, and Miranda 2003, 15).[1] Many Asian immigrants and their children participate in EPC movements through evangelical churches (Busto 1996; Jeung 2007; Carnes and Yang 2004) and scholars estimate that about 15 to 25 percent of Asian Americans in the United States identified as evangelical Protestants in 2004 (Carnes and Yang 2004).

EPC religious organizations demand attention for other reasons than sheer numbers. First, EPC churches draw people together on a much more regular, consistent basis than other types of civic organizations, such as ethnic advocacy groups. Some EPC adherents in our study attend services or Bible studies four times a week throughout the year. Second, an EPC pastor or religious leader is more than a trusted community member to their church or temple members. EPC leaders are spiritual and religious advisers, and may yield a very different, and perhaps more powerful, influence on political attitudes and behavior than, say, a union local leader or the executive director of an advocacy group. Finally, for many Asian and Latino EPC Christians, conservative interpretations of the Bible, not the liberal progressive political ideology embraced by most other types of immigrant community organization leaders, serve as the basis for political action and beliefs. For these reasons, and because of their importance to future political coalitions with both the larger conservative Christian population and the larger Asian American and Latino advocacy communities, we believe it important to study the role of EPC Asian and Latinos in the civic sphere.

DATA AND METHODS

This project draws on multiple methods, including site visits to EPC places of worship, in-depth interviews with Asian American and Latino EPC Christians, and analysis of survey data. This chapter uses data from a pilot-stage study that included site visits to EPC churches in Los Angeles and Orange counties in California. Members of our multiracial research team visited twenty-one EPC and four Catholic worship sites, twelve predominantly Asian and fourteen predominantly Latino, to collect data.

Site visits provide information on the substantive nature of the relationship between religion and politics for Asian and Latino EPC Christians. How is political participation encouraged, political information shared, and political community created at religious spaces? Site visits took place during worship sessions.

Although most visits were to Sunday services, we also attended weeknight services at some Pentecostal storefront temples. The one-time site visits were designed to give us a sense of the demographic characteristics of members, descriptions of the religious leadership, key themes of the services, rituals or events, explicit and nonexplicit references made to social or politics issues, community-building practices, and community-related announcements, flyers, literature, and visual materials available to church and temple members and visitors. The sites were not systematically selected during this pilot phase of the study. Some were chosen because we were already familiar with a church or temple, some because they were mentioned in media stories, some on the basis of word of mouth from friends and acquaintances, and others more randomly, because we drove past them as part of our everyday routines. At each site, notes and observations were recorded on a standardized intake form that helped us to organize key descriptive information. These visits provided a great deal of useful information, but were limited in important respects. First, they did not allow us to observe changes over time or to compare services within the same site. They only allowed for a snapshot of one activity among many activities that take place throughout the church week and throughout the year. Second, the visits focused primarily on Sunday and other worship services, which are designed in part to draw in new church members. If controversial political issues are discussed overtly at all, the worship service is probably the least likely venue for such discussions given that the leadership would not wish to alienate potential new members. Additional interview data, which we describe shortly, suggests that Asian and Latino EPC Christians discuss politics, but not through sermons. Discussions around social and political issues tend to be reserved for small group discussions or Bible studies and emerge from questions asked by participants in the group studies, rather than direct comments from leaders.

Twenty-three EPC Christians were interviewed in Los Angeles and Orange counties, recruited through snowball sampling techniques that included our social and academic networks and our contacts with religious leaders. For example, Haven Perez, one of the researchers on this project, attended a service at a large Pentecostal church in Wilmington, California. The pastor introduced him to the congregation and encouraged members to take part in the interviews. These semi-structured, open-ended interviews allowed Asian and Latino evangelical and Pentecostal adherents to explain and elaborate on their religious beliefs, religious practices, relationships with religious leaders, racial identities, and to relate the ways in which these and other potential motivations, concerns, and attitudes inform their political thinking and action. Interviews lasted, on average, one hour. Demographic and family background questions, including family religious histories, were asked of all interviewees. A variety of other questions were asked as well: What does being religious mean to you? What does the term *politics* mean to you? Do the members of your church or temple ever talk about community problems (national-local)? How about moral issues? Do you ever talk with people at church or temple about moral values? Do you know how your minister or pastor feels about same-sex marriage or affirmative action? How important are the political views of your minister or pastor to your own political views?

The interviews were not conducted with a random sample of EPC practitioners, and thus the findings based on the interviews cannot be generalized to that wider population. However, a snowball sample has certain benefits beyond convenience. Most important, such a sample may generate higher quality interviews, given that the interviewees were introduced to the project through trusted acquaintances and leaders. Religion and politics are sensitive topics and, without trust between the interviewees and interviewers, conversations about such topics have a tendency to be superficial or even misleading. Second, a snowball sampling technique reveals connections between different people and these linkages are relevant to our understanding of how religious and political communities form. All interviews were recorded and transcribed.

Finally, we incorporate findings from previous survey analysis. The main survey used in these analyses is the 2001 Washington Post/Kaiser Family Foundation/Harvard University survey on race and ethnicity. The survey, conducted by telephone in May 2001, includes 1,575 white, 418 black, 370 Latino, and 254 Asian American respondents. One benefit of the survey for the current study is that it includes questions about beliefs about racial equality and discrimination as well as questions about religious affiliation, attendance at religious services, political orientations, attitudes toward social issues, and political participation. One major limitation of the study is that it does not include questions about immigration status or citizenship status. In addition, the survey was not multilingual: interviews were conducted only in Spanish and English. Nonetheless, it is one of the most recent publicly available surveys that includes large enough numbers of Latinos, Asians, and blacks to allow for cross-racial comparisons and conduct meaningful statistical analysis.

RELIGION AND THE CIVIC SPHERE

Why focus on religious adherents when attempting to explain civic participation among Asian Americans and Latinos? One reason is that researchers consistently find a strong connection between church attendance and involvement in the civic sphere among Americans generally (compare Verba, Schlozman, and Brady 1995; Wald 2003, 36). These studies contend that churches are not only religious spaces, but organizational spaces—housing meetings and encouraging communication, leadership development, and consistent contact between people. In this respect, churches contribute to the accumulation of social capital and can provide the institutional foundations for civic and political action (Putnam 2000). Michael Jones-Correa and David Leal (2001) find that church attendance is important for civic participation, particularly voting, among Latinos because churches provide a space for sharing of political information and recruitment into political networks. According to their research, churches, whether Catholic or Protestant, function as critical civic associations. Consistent with this perspective, Asian Americans also exhibit a strong connection between church attendance and civic involvement. Among this group, attendance at religious services is associated with voting (Lien, Conway, and Wong 2004) and Asian Americans who take part in religious activities or who volunteer for their church are more likely to participate in nonreligious volunteering as well (Ecklund and Park 2005).

WHO ARE LATINO AND ASIAN AMERICAN EPC CHRISTIANS?

Religious categories are dynamic, overlapping, and often contested. Scholarly categories may not mirror categories of religious self-identification among religious adherents. We follow Gaston Espinosa and his colleagues (2003) in distinguishing EPC adherents within the larger Protestant Christian community. Evangelicalism is defined commonly by the following features: an emphasis on sharing one's faith, a reliance on the Bible as the ultimate authority, the importance of Christ's redeeming work through his sacrifice on the cross, and the need to accept Christ to achieve salvation, an act of faith commonly referred to as being born again (Noll 2001, 13; Emerson and Smith 2001, 3; Yang 2004, 208). Evangelicalism can also refer to a religious tradition and style of worship adopted by a range of groups, including African American Baptists, Asian American Baptists, and Pentecostals.

Pentecostalism emphasizes the direct experience of God, the ability of the Holy Spirit to inhabit the body, and gifts of the Holy Spirit (Robbins 2004, 117). Gifts may include speaking in tongues and healing. A distinguishing feature of Pentecostalism is enthusiastic worship and it is not uncommon at services to witness congregants singing, dancing, crying, shouting, and otherwise demonstrating the rapture of being "moved by the spirit."

Pentecostalism is a relatively recent faith, traced in large part to an African American preacher, William Seymour, who began a ministry on Azusa Street in Los Angeles in 1906. Since then, Pentecostalism has spread rapidly throughout the world and is set "to become the predominant global form of Christianity of the 21st century" (Casanova 2001, 435). In Los Angeles, Pentecostalism's birthplace, one can drive along parts of Western Avenue, Olympic Boulevard, La Brea Avenue, and almost any of the major street traffic arteries in the central city and see storefront Pentecostal temples and small and medium-sized churches every few blocks. Major Pentecostal denominations include the Assemblies of God, the Church of God in Christ, and the Foursquare Church (Robbins 2004, 121).

In the 1960s, members of mainline Protestant churches began to experience what they called the gifts of the spirit and adopted some of the beliefs and practices of the Pentecostal movement. Many of these members split off from their mainline churches and established their own brand of charismatic Christianity. Joel Robbins notes that "the term charismatic Christian," which includes charismatic Catholics, "has come to refer to members of non-Pentecostal denominations who believe the gifts of the Spirit are available to contemporary believers" (2004, 121).

It should be clear that the terms *evangelical, Pentecostal,* and *charismatic* are by no means mutually exclusive. Pentecostals are evangelical and charismatic, but not all evangelicals are Pentecostal nor are all evangelicals charismatic. Similarly, not all charismatic worshippers are Pentecostal. Nonetheless, we distinguish those that identify as EPC Protestant Christians from those who identify as mainline Protestants.[2] Some churches within these mainline denominations may be evangelical or charismatic and we include those churches in our definition of EPCs.

Finally, although this chapter is concerned with conservative politics, not all EPC churches (ethnic nor mainstream) are politically conservative. Although those who described themselves as traditional evangelical Christians voted overwhelmingly for Bush in 2004, politically progressive EPC churches do exist. Most have been eager to distance themselves from the media image of evangelical Christianity as synonymous with the political right. For example, the Reverend Gregory A. Boyd, the minister of an evangelical megachurch in Minnesota, has condemned publicly the involvement of evangelical Christian leaders in right wing politics.[3] The *Los Angeles Times* recently profiled Christ Chapel in North Hollywood, California, one of several EPC churches that explicitly welcomes gay and lesbian members and rejects the belief held in many conservative Christian churches that "homosexuality is a sign of man's fallen state."[4]

EPC ASIAN AMERICANS AND LATINOS IN THE UNITED STATES

Because of the fluidity of religious identity, it is difficult to obtain accurate statistics on religious affiliation. In addition, most survey data are only a snapshot of the population, based on distinct samples and different times. Estimates of the EPC population therefore vary from survey to survey. To describe the Asian American and Latino population in the United States, we rely on several sources of data. The data in figure 10.1 are from the Kaiser Survey, which includes a multiracial, nationally representative sample of randomly selected respondents. These data allow us to approximate the relative rates of EPC Christian identity among different racial and ethnic groups. Most survey data do not allow researchers to probe beyond the most general categories of Catholic, Protestant, Jewish, and whether respondents identify as born again.[5] Thus, one rough measure we use is whether one identifies as born again, because the experience is often associated with evangelical and Pentecostal religious identity. Note that compared to their black and white counterparts, Latinos and Asian Americans identify as born again at a lower rate. In fact, more than one out of every four Asian Americans does not affiliate with any religion.

The data in figure 10.1 suggest that compared to the black and white American population, lower rates of EPC affiliation characterize the Latino and Asian American populations. However, what the data fail to show is the tremendous rates of growth among Latino and Asian American EPC Christians. Catholi-

FIGURE 10.1   *Born Again Religious Affiliation in the United States by Major Racial Group*

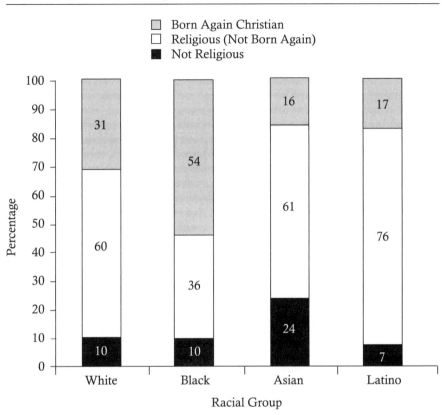

Source: Washington Post, Kaiser Family Foundation, and Harvard University (2001).
Note: N = 1635; data are unweighted; similar results obtained when data are weighted; numbers may not add up to 100 percent due to rounding.

cism remains the dominant religious affiliation of Latinos in the United States, but over 600,000 Latinos convert from Catholicism to evangelical and other faiths annually (Espinosa, Elizondo, and Miranda 2003, 15). According to one estimate by an evangelical polling firm, Asian Americans who identified as born again Christians grew from 5 percent in 1991 to 27 percent in 2000.[6] The tremendous growth of these ethno-racial-religious communities, and their implications for politics in the United States, provides the impetus for this study.

Figure 10.2 shows more detailed figures on religious affiliation among the Latino population from the 2000 HCAPL survey. Although we do not report religious affiliation among specific ethnic groups here, the data underscore the re-

FIGURE 10.2   *Latino Religious Affiliation*

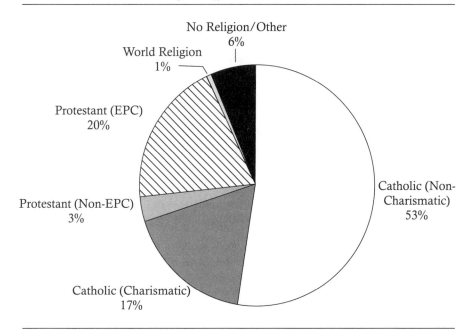

Source: Authors' adaptation of Espinosa, Elizondo, and Miranda (2003).

ligious diversity that characterizes Latinos in the United States today. Field research conducted for this project suggests that Pentecostal identity is prevalent especially among Central American immigrants, but Pentecostal and evangelical places of worship also attract a large number of people of Mexican and Puerto Rican origin. A striking statistic reported by Espinosa and his colleagues is that 25 percent of those who identified as Catholic also reported that they had experienced being born again (Espinosa, Elizondo, and Miranda 2003, 14). Indeed, there is a strong charismatic movement within the Catholic Church.

The 2000 to 2001 Pilot National Asian American Political Study (PNAAPS) represents one of the most comprehensive surveys of Asian Americans' political attitudes and behavior, and also includes questions of their religious affiliation. The PNAAPS includes data on religious affiliation by specific Asian American ethnic group, but the data do not allow researchers to differentiate between Asian American mainline Protestants and those who are EPC Christians. Among the PNAAPS respondents, a little over 25 percent claimed that their religious preference was Christian or Protestant as opposed to Catholic, Buddhist, Islam, Judaism, Other, or None. Because Tony Carnes and Fenggang Yang (2004) suggest that most of these Protestant and Christian identifiers attend an evangelical Christian church, these data give one an idea of the relative rates of

FIGURE 10.3 *Christian and Protestant Identifiers Among Asian American Ethnic Groups*

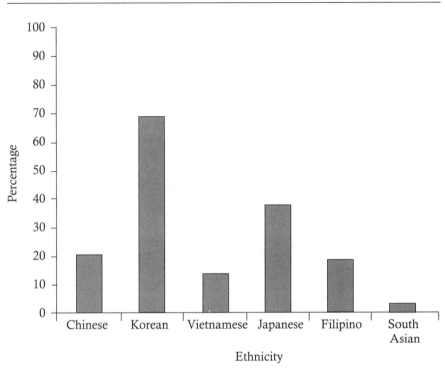

Source: Author's compilation from Lien (2004).

religious identity by Asian American ethnic group. Figure 10.3 shows that Koreans were much more likely to identify as Christian or Protestant than any other group in the survey. In addition, more than one out of every five Chinese and one out of every three Japanese in the survey identified as Protestants or Christians. In contrast, relatively few Vietnamese or South Asians identified as Christians or Protestants.

HISTORIC AND GLOBAL CONTEXT

Tracing the historical roots of Asian American and Latino EPC churches and temples reveals that missionary work was a critical force in the establishment of Protestant Asian and Latino churches and temples in the United States. In the late 1880s, white Christian missionaries established ethnic churches, separate from predominantly white churches, for early waves of Chinese and Japanese immigrant communities in Los Angeles and San Francisco. Some of these became the first Asian American evangelical churches in the United States. Karen Yonemoto (2006) reported that by 1892 there were ten Chinese immigrant Protestant churches in the United States and that twelve Japanese immigrant Protestant churches were founded in California alone by 1919. The first Korean immigrant church was planted in Hawaii when Korean immigrants began to arrive on the island as plantation workers. In the early 1900s, seven Korean immigrant churches were formed on various Hawaiian plantations. During the same period, the Korean Evangelical Society was established in San Francisco. As the number of Asian immigrant churches grew (primarily in the traditional American immigrant gateway cities), immigrant religious leaders and their congregations also began to distance from the assimilationist ideologies held by many of their churches' white missionary founders. They also severed formal administrative ties with their founding denominations. The result is that many contemporary churches are nondenominational (Yang 1998). Further, these churches became sites for maintaining ethnic traditions and a sense of ethnic community. Despite breaking with some critical aspects of the evangelical missionary movement, many of the churches remained theologically conservative.

Gastón Espinosa (1999a) reminded us that Latino Pentecostalism can be traced to a much earlier period in American history as well. Espinosa observed that Mexicans were present at the Azusa Street revival in 1906: "The first supernatural manifestation of the Holy Spirit at the Azuza Street Mission involved a Mexican day worker. The first person allegedly healed at the revival was also a Mexican with clubfoot. Mexicans were the first Roman Catholics to attend the revival and constituted 'many' of the 'hundreds' of Catholics that attended the revival from 1906 to 1909" (1999a, 279). By 1909, Mexican participants in the movement broke with William Seymour and an indigenous Latino Pentecostal movement was born. A critical leader in the Latino Pentecostal movement was Francisco Olazabál, a Mexican immigrant from Sinaloa who studied theology in Mexico and who served as the pastor of a Methodist church in El Paso, Texas, in 1911 (Espinosa 1999b, 600). In 1916, Olazabál left the Methodist Church after experiencing gifts of the Holy Spirit and becoming convinced that such gifts were necessary to Christian life. More than thirty churches across the country—in California, Texas, Arizona, New Mexico, Kansas, Illinois, Michigan, Ohio, and Indiana—were planted as part of the new Pentecostal denomination, the Interdenominational Mexican Council of Christian Churches he founded in 1923 (1999b, 602). Espinosa writes that Olazabál gave sermons to a quarter of a million people over the course of his ministry and, by the time he died in 1937, 150 churches and 50,000 adherents were part of the mainly Latino denomination he led.

The country has witnessed a singularly dramatic growth in Asian American and Latino EPC churches and temples over the last two decades as the population of Asian and Latino immigrants and their children in the United States has swelled. For example, at Young Nak Presbyterian Church, an evangelical ministry on North Broadway Street in Los Angeles, approximately 6,000 Korean

Americans (first and later generations) attend one of six services between 7 a.m. and 2 p.m. on a typical Sunday. An even larger number of Latino worshippers attend Templo Calvario, in Santa Ana. Templo Calvario, also an evangelical ministry, is one of the fastest growing faith-based organizations in the nation. Further, there has been an explosion in the numbers of Asian Americans populating campus ministries. Rebecca Kim observed that campus ministries such as Campus Crusade for Christ and InterVarsity Christian Fellowship that were mainly white in the 1980s are predominantly Asian American today. She wrote that "at one point in the 1990s, Berkeley was said to have had sixty-four separate Asian Christian organizations. . . . In the last 15 years, IVCF's [InterVarsity Christian Fellowship's] 650 chapters at universities across the United States witnessed the number of Asian Americans grow by 267 percent" (2004, 20).

This growth cannot be understood without attention to the globalization of religion more generally (Vasquez and Marquardt 2003; Leonard et al. 2005). EPC religions have grown dramatically in Latin America, Africa, and in parts of Asia (Smilde 1999; Vasquez and Marquardt 2003). Many Asian and Latino immigrants arrive in the United States after being introduced to EPC churches and temples in their countries of origin, and indeed EPC movements are flourishing in both Latin America and Asia.

Paul Freston (2004, 23) observed in 2004 that Protestants accounted for 10 percent of the Latin American population as a whole, and that two-thirds of all Protestants in the region were Pentecostal. This growth of Pentecostalism in Latin America is attributed partially to an enthusiastic missionary movement credited with driving the growth of Pentecostalism worldwide. But the Pentecostal roots established in Latin America can also be traced to the context of civil war and political unrest that came to characterize many Latin American states beginning in the 1960s and lasting, in some cases, into the 1990s.

The late 1960s also marked the introduction of liberation theology, which contends that the gospel requires church followers to actively work to liberate the world's poor and disenfranchised. Many Latin American proponents of liberation theology were murdered for their political and religious views. Traditionalist Catholics were alarmed by the Catholic Church's new role in Latin American politics and many feared government retribution for demonstrating any degree of political involvement. Some of these disillusioned Catholics turned to Pentecostalism, which may have offered a safe haven to practice religion without fear of political prosecution. This is not to suggest that Pentecostal adherents never fought for social justice or that Catholic adherents were always engaged in political activism. Rather, the general theology and doctrine represented by Catholicism and Pentecostalism may help to explain the relative attraction of each for some Latin Americans. Class divisions in Latin American society may also drive religious patterns. Freston noted that "in Latin America, Pentecostalism is associated disproportionately with the poor, less educated and darker skinned, and its entry into formal politics has provided political mobility for some marginalized sectors" (2004, 24).

Asia has also witnessed a wave of EPC growth. South Korea currently houses the largest proportion of Christians in Asia. Protestant Christianity first came to Korea during a period of Japanese rule and the heart of the movement began in what is now North Korea. Refugees from the North helped to fuel its growth in the South. Because a number of resistors to Japanese rule were Christian, Christianity is associated generally with anti-Japanese colonialism (Freston 2004, 27). In the late 1980s, more than one out of every five South Koreans were Christians, mostly Protestant (Min 1992) and the proportion of Christian adherents there has grown. Today, scholars estimate that the Protestant community in South Korea comprises about 20 percent of the population.

In Asia, Christianity has flourished among certain ethnic minority groups. In India, for example, only 3 percent of the population is Christian and two-thirds of that population is Dalit, a group historically discriminated against as untouchables (Freston 2004, 31). Despite the relatively small proportion of Christians across India, it is important to note that the actual number of Christian adherents is quite impressive. Indian Pentecostals alone account for 33 million people (Burgess 2001). Indeed, India has long been considered a critical site associated with the global Pentecostal revival.

In China, Christianity was long resisted because of its association with western imperialism. Today, the Christian population is estimated at 2 to 7 percent of the population (Yang 1998). Yang attributed tremendous growth in the numbers of evangelical Christians in China since the 1980s to the fact that traditional Chinese cultural traditions have been disrupted by rapid urbanization and modernization leaving Chinese open to new religious belief systems. Luke Wesley (2004) suggested that between 30 and 50 million people in China are Pentecostal, and due to the rapid spread of the religion and growth of the population, China may soon house the largest numbers of Pentecostals in the world.

Recent estimates of the spread of Pentecostalism around the globe come from an October 2006 report published by the Pew Forum on Religion and Public Life. According to the report, Pentecostals and charismatics account for 49 percent of all Brazilians, 60 percent of all Guatemalans, and 44 percent of all Filipinos. As the regions sending the largest numbers of immigrants to the United States, it is perhaps no surprise then that the great flows of migration from Asia and Latin America include a fair number of EPC Christians who continue to practice and evangelize in the United States.

Clearly, some Asian Americans and Latinos arrive in the United States as EPC Christians. However, religious conversion in the United States may also be driving the growth of EPC Christianity among Asian American and Latino immigrants and their children (figure 10.4). Espinosa and his colleagues (2003) found clear evidence that Catholicism declined and that Protestantism increased with each Latino immigrant generation. Only 15 percent of first-generation immigrant Latinos identified as Protestant, but 20 percent of second-generation Latinos and 29 percent of third-generation Latinos did so. Among Asian Americans, data from the PNAAPS suggests that Christian or Protestant religious affiliation also increases by immigrant generation in the United States. About 26 percent of first- and second-generation Asian Americans identified as Christians or Protestants, but fully 47 percent of third-generation Asian Americans identi-

FIGURE 10.4   *Protestantism Among Asian Americans and Latinos*

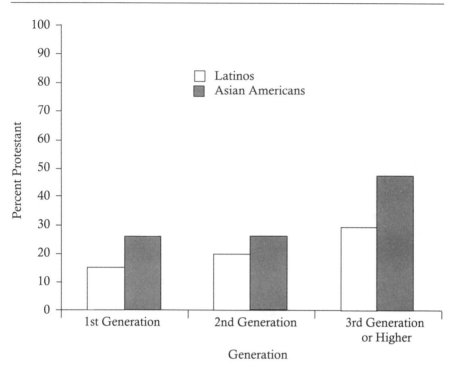

Source: Authors' compilation from Lien (2004); Espinosa, Elizondo, and Miranda (2003).

fied as such. Further, the PNAAPS data show that as length of residence increases, rates of Christian and Protestant identification increase as well. Although these patterns may be partially attributed to differences in EPC affiliation by migration cohort, these and other data (Espinosa, Elizondo, and Miranda 2003; author interview data) suggest that conversion to Christianity and Protestantism is taking place even among the first generation. It seems likely that such conversion is shifting religious orientations within Asian American and Latino communities.

A DIFFERENT MOBILIZATION MODEL? PROSPECTS FOR COALITIONS

Religious organizations have long been viewed as key political mobilizing institutions for minority communities. Historical accounts point to the role of the black church as a critical site for political organizing during the civil rights era and for contemporary black politics (Harris 1994). Traditionally, African American religious leaders such as Martin Luther King, Jr., Jesse Jackson, and Al Sharpton have played a prominent role in politically organizing black communities.

In contrast, the role of religious organizations is largely absent from narratives of political struggle among Latinos and Asian Americans. The dominant view in writing about Latinos' historical struggle in the United States against colonialism and racial oppression is that the Catholic Church failed to offer substantive protection or support for Latinos (Gordon 2001). More recently, though, Timothy Mantovina argued against this perspective, claiming that "Mexican Catholics' heritage and religious traditions provided crucial resources for political and civic activism in the decades following the U.S. takeover of northern Mexico" (2005, 31). For example, he cited explicit references to their Catholic heritage by local Mexican leaders who spoke out against anti-immigrant, and anti-Mexican forces in the 1850s (26–27). His point was that there is a long history of Latino Catholic political resistance in the United States and that the legacy of early religiously based activism was carried on by leaders of the United Farm Workers Union (UFW) and of more recent struggles for human and civil rights among Latinos.

The most prominent Latino civil rights leader in the United States was Cesar Chavez, the founder of the UFW, a major civil rights leader, and a devout Catholic. Recent scholarship contends that Chavez, and by extension the movement he led, was driven by Catholic faith and spirituality (Lloyd-Moffett 2005). Although some Chicano rights activists in the 1960s and 1970s explicitly rejected religion as the basis for protest, images of the Virgen de Guadalupe on UFW strike banners serve to confirm that symbols of Catholic faith played a role in the Chicano movement (Scheper 1999).

Catholic priests were also active in supporting the UFW, though "the institutional Catholic Church did not have a vibrant national ministry to migrant farmworkers" (Espinosa, Elizondo, and Miranda 2005, 8). PADRES (Padres Asociados para Derechos Religiosos, Educativos, y Sociales) was an organization founded by fifty priests in 1969. The organization was dedicated to civil rights and social justice and one its core members, Father Juan Romero, organized support for farm worker strikes and produce boycotts, and, along with other Catholic leaders, participated in civil disobedience on behalf of the workers (Garcia 2005). In part to address gender discrimination within the church and also to fight for Chicano civil rights, Las Hermanas was established in 1971 (Medina 2004). This group of Catholic women, including laywomen and nuns, joined in school walkouts, supported the farm workers, and worked for community change with Alinksy groups such as Communities Organized for Public Service (COPS) and United Neighborhoods Organization (UNO) (Medina 2005). The religious basis for Hermanas was made explicit through the group's melding of religious education and social activism.

Local Catholic leaders in the United States, some mobilized into action by the killing of Oscar Romero, an archbishop in Guatemala killed in 1980 after condemning government and military repression in that country, were also active in the 1980s sanctuary movement. Participants in the movement organized a grassroots effort to protest U.S. policies in Central America and to provide safe haven to refugees from Central America.

Finally, the Catholic Church has been one of the most vocal and visible supporters of contemporary immigrant rights in the United States. Latino clergy have long been strong supporters of immigrant rights, but in the last decade Roman Catholic leaders have been among the most prominent advocates for amnesty and humane immigration policies. Los Angeles Cardinal Roger Mahoney has been an outspoken critic of attempts to cut off access to social service benefits for immigrants in the United States. In 2006, Mahoney vowed to disobey a law passed in the U.S. House of Representatives that would criminalize aid to an undocumented person. At mass marches and rallies for immigrant rights that took place across the nation during the spring of 2006, Catholic clergy were out in force and vocal supporters for immigrant rights in the mass media. In its efforts around worker, civil, and immigrant rights, Catholic Church leaders have not acted independently, but have forged partnerships with other civil rights organizations, worker centers, unions, and ethnic advocacy organizations. In this respect, the Catholic Church has been an important coalition partner with other civic institutions supporting a traditional, politically progressive social justice political agenda.

Perhaps because of the prominent role of Catholic leaders in the historical fight for civil and Chicano rights and in the contemporary immigrant rights movement, the role of Latino Protestants, particularly EPC Christian leaders, organizations, temples, and churches in faith-based activism is less often recognized. Further, in contrast to those Catholics guided by liberation theology, for many EPC Christians, the theological base for their activism is centered on the importance of developing a personal relationship with Jesus and evangelizing. Thus, the language of large-scale, institutionally based change, and social justice may not map onto EPC social action—making it different in character and focus from that of Catholic activists.

Nonetheless, it is unfair to conclude that EPC Christians are so heavenly minded that they fail to engage in activism on earth (Rios 2005, 198). Gastón Espinosa argued that though early Latino Pentecostals "did not consciously create a formal social gospel theology per se, their churches did nonetheless function as religious mutualistas, or mutual aid societies, that attended to the needs of the poor, women, and immigrants (1999a, 285). His historical research showed that during the first half of the twentieth century, Latino Pentecostal leaders, including several important women in the movement, took part in relief work for the poor and started drug rehabilitation programs for prostitutes and other marginalized members of society. For much of their history in the United States, Latino Pentecostals have ministered to the poor and provided social services to those on the margins of American life through individualized outreach. In a study of Latina Pentecostals, Elizabeth Rios contended that "the younger, emerging Latino Pentecostal population believe that just because a better world is expected, they should not accept all injustice with patience while waiting for the Lord's second coming. Rather, their hope is that they can do something about structural evil" (2005, 198; see also Sanchez-Walsh 2003). Latino Pentecostals are at the beginning stages of system-focused social action.

Academic work on Asian American EPCs in the civic sphere is rare, but news reports show that Asian American EPCs have been active in ways that are important to recognize. Some leaders of Asian American EPC churches have been vocal opponents of marriage equality. For example, in 2000, the Reverend Peter Kim gathered the signatures of his parishioners at the Oriental Mission Church in Los Angeles in support of the California Defense of Sexual Responsibility Act of 2000 (CDSRA). Working with the California Christian Coalition, Kim and other Korean American pastors led the effort to get the antigay rights initiative on the November ballot. This was described by one journalist as the "first statewide political campaign by Korean Americans."[7] Don Lattin, a reporter for the *San Francisco Chronicle*, described a protest at San Francisco City Hall following Mayor Gavin Newsom's issuing of marriage licenses to same sex couples in the spring of 2004. According to Lattin, many of the protesters were Asian American Christians. One spokesperson at the protest, the Reverend Thomas Wang, of the Bay Area Chinese Ministerial Prayer Fellowship, proclaimed that radical gay rights activists had hijacked the civil rights movement.[8]

Despite these dramatic examples, the issue of marriage between two people of the same sex has not sparked protest among the whole of Asian American EPC Christians. In particular, young people may deviate from the hard-line antigay views of their parents' generation. Chisun Lee (2000) reports that rather than join highly visible protests against same-sex marriage, young Asian American EPC Christians are more likely to privately oppose homosexuality but remain publicly silent on the issue. Further, some younger Asian American evangelicals have devoted themselves to antipoverty issues, such as obtaining high-quality, affordable housing for low-income racial and ethnic minority groups (Jeung 2007).

To summarize, our research suggests that, historically, Catholic leaders tend to engage in issues that are civil and political in nature, such as farm worker rights, Chicano civil rights, refugee rights, and immigrant rights. These are issues that are not necessarily directly related to religious-spiritual development, rather, they are more traditional social justice issues. For EPC Christians, traditional social justice frameworks are less salient, but EPC Christians do engage in activism perceived as helping people to overcome drug addiction, alcoholism, and other social behaviors considered inconsistent with a healthy spiritual relationship with Jesus or God. For example, Asian American EPCs who organize around the issue of same sex marriage discuss their activism as a response to the (Biblical) Word. Further, in contrast to their Catholic counterparts, Asian American and Latino EPC churches have not joined the traditional civil rights coalition when it comes to taking action in the civic sphere.

Mobilization

It should be noted that EPC ethnic churches and temples may influence their members' political viewpoints, but at the religious sites included in this study, politics was not a large part of their stated mission or an obvious, direct part of any Sunday service or weekday worship service. This may be due to the nature and purpose of such services. Sunday and other worship services are intended to be warm and welcoming to draw people into the organization, and into activities and groups that bring them closer to a relationship with God. Every church aims to grow in numbers, so too much emphasis on politics or controversial political issues might be seen as unwise for the growth of the church. "Seeker sensitive" churches may be especially cognizant of these dynamics and so it is not surprising that they avoid a heavy focus on political debates and issues that may turn new members or visitors off to the organization.

For example, at First Chinese Baptist Church in Chinatown, Los Angeles, a typical service begins with music played by a praise team that includes an electric guitar player, a keyboardist, and a drummer. Three singers at microphones lead the members in upbeat, contemporary Christian hymns. At the back of the church is a sophisticated sound and video system. The lyrics to each song are projected onto a large screen above a stage. A few people sing with their hands raised, eyes closed or focused above. After the hymns and spiritual songs commence, tithes and offerings are made, then the congregation recites the Lord's Prayer. There is a scripture reading, followed by the doxology, and announcements. A guest speaker or missionary might give a short lecture or report. The service ends with the benediction. There is nothing overtly political mentioned by the pastor or the guest speakers.

At one service at First Chinese Baptist Church, the pastor gave a short prayer for peace in the Middle East (this was during the height of the 2006 conflict between Israel and Lebanon). This was also typical. At many services, prayers are lifted up for current issues or crises, but prayers are directed at a very general situation, and do not push worshippers to take sides. Data from our site visits reveal virtually no explicit mention of politics, political issues, or even moral issue topics such as the war in Iraq, abortion, or same-sex marriage.

In the few instances in which the church leadership shared their political viewpoints during a worship service, such statements were brief and easy to miss. At one Sunday service at the Christian Worship Center in Sylmar, a live band played contemporary Christian ballads and eight singers on a stage led the crowd in pop-Christian songs. The crowd was on its feet, singing, clapping, and dancing to the music when Pastor J. R. Gonzalez, wearing jeans, a printed button-down shirt, and his hair slicked back, bounded onto the stage with a shout of greeting. He welcomed visitors and explained that his church was alive. He said he didn't believe in quiet worship time, he believed that God wanted his people to shout and get excited. He ran around the stage and jumped into the aisles, encouraging the crowd to shout their praise. He spoke for about an hour about how the current members of the church represented a new generation—one that was different from its fathers and mothers. The pastor discussed his own background and how his father wanted to do God's work, but couldn't because he drank alcohol and "fooled around with women." Pastor J. R. heard God calling him at age fourteen and said he had faced many challenges—had been the first in his family to graduate from high school, the first to go to college, and at Oral Roberts University. Before a sermon that would focus on developing a personal relationship with Jesus, he said to the congregants, "We know that God created the Heavens and the Earth. There aren't any evolutionists in the house today, are there?!" This was the most overtly political comment heard during the preliminary fieldwork stage of this study.

In a prayer calendar received at Chinese First Baptist Church, two entries included content that might be described as explicitly political. The Thursday, August 24, 2006, entry read: [Pray for] "President Bush and other govt. officials as they lead our nation; America would repent & turn back to God." The Thursday, August 28, entry read: [Pray for] "Prep. of students for new school year (preschool thru grad school); our bros. & sis. who are school teachers/administrators would be strong witnesses of Christ in their classrooms and schools." Yet the norm at all of the churches and temples that my research team visited was for religious leaders to discuss the Bible, a personal relationship with God or Jesus, and to make no mention of any political issue in an obvious manner. This was especially true of small, storefront Pentecostal churches attended by Latino immigrants.

Most examples of civic involvement practiced by many Asian American and Latino EPCs diverge from a more traditional model of social action, which emphasizes collective action directed at systemic change (DeTemple 2005; but see also Rios 2005). Jill DeTemple suggested that EPC churches may be concerned with helping others in need, but in attempting to accomplish that task they may also be "focused less on the overarching strategies that challenge systemic oppression with systematic and organized opposition, and more on tactics designed to address particular experiences of poverty and injustice" (2005, 221). This observation may not be wholly accurate, in that some immigrant EPC leaders may rely on biblical principles to maintain existing policies that serve to systematically marginalize GLBT people. Her claim that EPC leaders and activists tend to focus their altruism on individuals or even groups, and their relationship with Christ or God, rather than on challenging policies that create systematic disadvantages is an important one, however.

This is not to say that politics is absent from Asian American and Latino EPC churches. Although it is not often an explicit focus of most formal services, interview data with Latino and Asian American EPC Christians in Los Angeles and Orange counties suggest that at least among most of the limited sample, worshippers are well aware of the political beliefs of their pastors and fellow congregants. A Mexican American man who had immigrated as a young adult and attended a Pentecostal temple in Wilmington, California, said this about his pastor: "I know that he's a Republican and he likes to vote completely for the party. Sometimes he says, 'Let's vote for this particular issue.' Some people don't like it when he says that, and they're right." A first-generation Korean American woman claimed that her pastor was very political, but was also "really good at being political without completely revealing his own view. Nothing like, 'Oh, I voted for Bush, why don't you all vote for Bush, too.'" Despite the fact that the woman did not have a completely clear idea of the position of her pastor on political issues, she did claim that she knew he did not support same-sex marriage. When asked how she knew this, she said, "Because there was one occasion in a sermon—he was talking about Katrina. . . . He said New Orleans had a lot of gay people. He in a way made it sound like a Sodom and Gomorrah, something bad came about because it was a sin city. And I was like, 'Oh my gosh, I can't believe he's saying that on the pulpit.'" Clearly, political views are sometimes shared by pastors, but congregants are not necessarily adopting such views uncritically. Most congregants made a distinction between the teachings of the pastor and the teachings of the Bible. Pastors are respected, but do not represent the ultimate authority. For example, if the pastor expressed a view that interviewees believed to be inconsistent with the Bible, some interviewees claimed that they would either leave the church or confront the pastor.

Further, political discussion among members does take place, especially in small groups. A second-generation Filipina described her involvement in a church discussion group that meets every week. It was in that small discussion group that she would talk to other members of the church about immigration, poverty, and specific issues affecting the local community, such as homelessness. For example, the group once discussed what their response would be if a gay or lesbian person came to join a church service. "Certain issues like that, I guess morally, we have discussed, typically how would we engage them, how would we serve those kind of—that kind of community. . . . there are issues there we have tried to discuss: What do traditional Christians believe about this, how do Christians react to this? Is that a negative thing, a positive thing?" However discussion about controversial political issues may not always be encouraged. One second-generation Korean American man was asked about whether he ever discussed politics with people at his evangelical and Bible-based church. He responded that he would talk about homosexuality and the war in Iraq, but that such discussion was never seen as the primary focus of the church:

> I mean, for certain issues that come up, like homosexuality. . . . I guess homosexuality is the base issue, not that we focus on that, just because it's a blatant issue that for us we have a clear view on and it seems like it just gets accepted more and more in the secular world, in real life. When I think of any one social issue, that comes to mind. Obviously we would talk about the war, whether we support it or not. But politics doesn't end up being a focal point of our conversation at church, because that pretty much tends to take you away from God and you start to think about just worldly things. In our church, we try not to be worldly, but to focus on God. That would be the primary focus of the church.

Several interviewees also mentioned that their pastor encouraged them to become citizens or vote. It was also not uncommon for interviewees to claim that they voted in the 2004 election because they viewed it as their Christian duty. Others, however, claimed that the church leadership urged them not to get too caught up in worldly matters having to do with politics. Church leaders seem most willing to encourage political involvement when that involvement is seen as linked directly to God's word and commandments. They are less likely to press for involvement for the sake of involvement alone.

Coalition Prospects: Partisanship and Issue Positions

The political role and the coalition prospects of Asian American and Latino EPC Christians will partly be determined by the degree to which they exhibit unique political orientations that may change the agenda of the larger conservative Christian movement. Preliminary evidence suggests that in terms of their theological orientation, these churches and temples align with EPC religious organizations more generally. The politics that flows from their theological commitments is therefore politically conservative when it comes to issues of church-state relations, debates over life issues, including abortion and stem-cell research, and same-sex partnerships. On these issues, Asian American and Latino EPC institutions have formed coalitions with the mainstream conservative Christian movement. But, there may be policy areas in which Asian American and Latino EPC churches force the mainstream conservative Christian movement to modify or expand its political stances. One such policy area may be around racial equality. Congregants interviewed for this project suggested that the leaders of their Asian American and Latino EPC churches and temples vigorously condemned racism and racial hierarchy in their sermons. Although many white EPC church leaders support racial reconciliation, they will have to overcome a history of uneasy race relations and conservative stances toward civil rights legislation if they are to come together with ethnic EPC leaders to advocate for greater racial equality. Another policy area may be immigration. Latino evangelical leaders and worshippers seemed especially dismayed by mainstream EPC leaders' silence on immigration policies, particularly following mass marches calling for liberalizing immigration policy in the spring of 2006. Although we cannot provide a full exploration of the possibilities here, we offer some preliminary background and findings that help to highlight key points of intersection and divergence between Latino and Asian American EPC Christians and the mainstream conservative Christian movement.

One key way in which Asian and Latino EPC Christians coalesce with the larger EPC Christian movement is around support for the Republican Party. According to a report published by the Pew Forum on Religion and Public Life in 2004, a majority of all evangelical Christians identified as Republican, with 56 percent identifying as Republican, 27 percent identifying as Democrat, and the remainder claiming to be Independent. Even more striking, in that year fully 70 percent of traditionalist evangelical Christians identified as Republican (traditionalists are those that hold the most orthodox theological beliefs within their tradition and who also attend church regularly). With nearly 80 percent of white evangelicals supporting George W. Bush in 2004, it comes as no surprise that the Pew Forum on Religion and Public Life concluded that "the 2004 campaign showed once again that White Evangelicals are by far the most important component of the GOP coalition" (2005, 10).

The Pew study found that 37 percent of Latino Protestants (who are mostly EPC Christians) identified as Republican in 2004. This statistic implies that unlike white EPC Christians, the majority of Latino EPC Christians are not Republican. In fact, the Pew study found that 43 percent of Latino Protestants identified as Democrats and 20 percent identified as Independent in 2004.[9] However, it is also true that Latino Protestants were much more likely to be Republican than other Latinos in 2004. For example, only 15 percent of Latino Catholics identified as Republican (61 percent identified as Democrat) in the Pew study. Further, comparisons of exit polls conducted in 2000 and 2004 show that Bush posted some of his biggest gains in support (9 percentage points) between the two election years among Latino Protestants. Based on the National Survey of Religion and Public Life, John Green and his colleagues observed that "Bush's biggest gain came among Latino Protestants," who showed a willingness to move from the Democratic column in 2000 to the Republican column in 2004 (2005, 1). Thus, the evidence suggests that though Latino EPCs appear to be less Republican than their white counterparts, they are also much more Republican than the Latino population generally, and that the GOP has made significant inroads among Latino EPCs over time.

Note also that Green and his colleagues found that in 2004, 56 percent of traditionalist evangelical Protestants (and 42 percent of all evangelical Protestants) claimed that faith was a more important determinant of their presidential vote "compared to other factors." In comparison, 40 percent of Latino Protestants and 19 percent of Latino Catholics made the same claim. These data suggest that religious faith is much more critical to the voting behavior of evangelical Protestants, including Latino Protestants, generally than for any other religious groups (Green et al. 2005, 14).

The Pew studies do not include analyses that allow one to compare the political attitudes of Asian American EPCs to other groups. However, in an analysis of the PNAAPS, Janelle Wong and Jane Iwamura found that Asian Americans who report their religious affiliation as Protestant or Christian tend to identify as Republican much more often than those Asian Americans who claim no religious affiliation (Wong with Iwamura 2006). More striking, though, was that across every religious category, more Asian Americans tended to identify as Democrat than Republican. This is in stark contrast to the general American population. Among Americans generally, Christians (evangelicals, mainline Protestants, and other Christians) are more likely to identify as Republicans than Democrats.

Janelle Wong's more recent study comparing white, black, Asian, and Latino born again Christians confirmed these trends (2006b). Across all groups, those who identify as born again Christian are more likely to identify as Republican than those who do not identify as born again. This suggests a strong association between being born again and Republican identification, regardless of racial background. Although fewer than 10 percent of born again black Americans claim to be Republican, those who are born again are twice as likely to be Republican compared to those who are not born again. Still, among both the not born again Christians and born again Christians, whites are much more likely to be Republican than any other group.

In sum, Latino Protestants, who tend to be EPC Christians, moved steadily toward the GOP camp over the past decade. Asian American churchgoing Christians, who also tend to be EPC in their orientation, are more likely to identify as Republican than other Asian Americans, but still show more favor toward the Democrats overall. These trends suggest that the role of religion in determining political attitudes may vary a great deal across racial groups, but also show that, like their black and white counterparts, Latino and Asian American EPC Christians are more open to Republican appeals than other segments of their racial and ethnic communities.

Where do Latino and Asian American EPC Christians stand in terms of issue positions that might drive their coalition prospects with other groups? Research conducted by Wong (2006b) showed that Asian American and Latino EPCs are staunch backers of the larger conservative Christian movement's position against marriage equality for same-sex couples and abortion. She found a consistent relationship between being a born again Christian and having politically conservative attitudes toward social issues for all racial groups. Similar to blacks and whites, born again Asian Americans and Latinos tend to be much more conservative on social issues such as abortion and same-sex marriage than their not born again counterparts. For example, those Asian Americans and Latinos who identified as born again were much less likely to approve of marriage between two members of the same-sex than those who were not born again. In fact, some born again racial minority group members exhibited higher levels of conservatism than their white born again counterparts. Only 8 percent of born again Asians surveyed approved of same-sex marriage, while 17 percent of born again whites shared the same sentiment. Wong's research suggested that growing numbers of EPC Christians, particularly Asians and Latinos, will bolster support for the hot button social issues that are at the forefront of the conservative Christian agenda.

These findings regarding Latino and Asian American EPC Christians' partisanship and issue position may not be very surprising. Based on the reported results, one might conclude that shared partisanship and positions on social issues would provide a basis for coalition-building between the EPC faithful of different ethnic and racial backgrounds. However, Wong also found that even after taking into account socioeconomic status, age, gender, experience with discrimination, and partisanship, only whites who are born again are more likely to oppose the federal government taking steps to address racial inequality. For blacks, Asian Americans, and Latinos, there was no association between being born again and the role of government in addressing racial inequality. This finding suggests that there may be important divisions between whites and other EPC Christians in terms of support for the government taking an active role in trying to advance racial equality.

As mentioned, a key issue area that may reveal fractures in the traditional EPC coalition is immigration. A survey by the Pew Forum on Religion and Public Life cited in an April issue of *USA Today* found that 64 percent of white evangelical Christians compared to 51 percent of white mainline Protestants agreed that "immigrants today are a burden on our country because they take our jobs, housing and health care."[10] Conservative Christian leaders, including representatives of Focus on the Family and the Family Research Council, have remained largely silent on the issue of immigration. In contrast, Latino evangelical groups and their members have spoken out on the issue, encouraging more liberal immigration policies and the chance for immigrants who enter the country without documents to become citizens at some point. Some, such as the Reverend Sam Rodriguez, president of the National Hispanic Christian Leadership Conference, an organization serving more than 18 million evangelical Latino Christians in the United States, expressed dismay about white evangelical leaders who have advocated for more stringent border-security measures. Following mass protests against such legislation in the spring of 2006, Rodriguez told two *Los Angeles Times* reporters that he had had a hard time convincing white evangelical leaders to support a liberal measures in immigration reform bills last spring: "I had to do a lot of asking: Will Hispanics ever vote for conservative candidates again, or partner with white evangelicals if they were silent while our brothers and sisters and cousins were being sent out of the county [sic] on buses?"[11] In a later interview, Rodriguez claimed that "Hispanics provide key support for such favorite evangelical causes as defending traditional marriage and opposing abortion. Now Hispanics expect reciprocation [on immigration reform]."[12] Although Rodriguez claims that Latino EPCs may be rethinking their support for Republicans, it is not clear that they would abandon the conservative EPC political agenda over immigration issues. In a 2004 interview, he said, "immigration is right up there [as an issue for Latino evangelicals]." But he went on to comment: "However, they're looking at life, they're looking at, you know, the continuity and respect to an institution that has been around since the beginning. You know, if they had to pick one or the other, it's probably going to be life and marriage over immigration. Not that immigration is not important. It's going to be a tough call."[13]

CONCLUSION

Latino and Asian Americans are a growing force in the conservative Christian community. Because the growth in their populations stems largely from post-1965 migration from Asia and Latin America, they are sometimes considered as being new groups in the United States. This review, however, makes two suggestions. First is that their history in the nation predates the current immigration wave. Second is that understanding the potential political influence of Asian American and Latino EPCs requires attention to the extent to which they are able to build coalitions with the mainstream conservative Christian movement or other groups, and to the degree to which their churches and temples shape the political orientations of and mobilize their members.

Regarding the first issue, the preliminary data we highlight here suggests that religious institutions do not make political mobilization a focus of their mission. Nonetheless, members of those institutions do receive information about the political views of their pastors and discuss politics with their fellow members. The interview data collected for this study show that religious adherents are not simply passive recipients of the political information that flows around them. They often view such information with a critical eye.

Political activities and orientations associated with EPC communities often fall outside the progressive framework associated traditionally with minority politics and used at times by the Catholic Church in its stance on civil rights and immigration. Our research so far indicates that Latino and Asian American EPCs will continue to join the Republican Party and support the larger conservative social agenda with regard to abortion and same-sex marriage. As such, we suggest that the political weight of Asian and Latino EPCs in the larger civic sphere may depend in large part on their ability to build coalitions with the mainstream conservative Christian movement, which is itself characterized by ideological and political differences (Noll 2001). These added numbers aside, the potential political weight of Asian American and Latino EPCs may be more clearly revealed in their ability to focus white and black EPC Christians on more progressive immigration reforms and into greater support for systematic policies aimed at reducing racial inequality. Some of the findings in this chapter predict rifts in the coalition if the broader conservative Christian movement does not move in those directions. However, because of their association with progressive positions on abortion and gay, lesbian, bisexual, and transgender (GLBT) rights, is not certain that Asian American and Latino EPC Christians would then join traditional civil rights organizations.

It is interesting that Catholic leaders, who have also been staunch supporters of the pro-life movement and taken a conservative stance on GLBT issues, have joined in coalition with traditional civil rights organizations around the push for liberalizing immigration policies. We speculate that the basis for such coalitions may be attributed in part to historic ties between immigrant communities in the United States and the Catholic Church. For example, Margarita Mooney noted that "the massive immigration of Irish, Polish, and other European Catholics in the nineteenth and twentieth centuries shaped the church in the United States as largely an immigrant church. . . . it means that many of today's members of the Catholic church and its hierarchy are comprised of immigrants and their descendants" (2007, 159). After World War II, the Catholic church actively worked with the federal government to resettle European refugees. Further, one of the legacies of Pope John Paul II was to instill in national and local Catholic leaders a commitment to social justice for immigrants. Mooney observes that Pope John Paul II organized a World Migration Day in each of his last ten years in the Vatican and his speeches encouraged the just treatment of immigrants (2007, 160). Pope Benedict XVI continues the tradition in his papacy. Finally, immigration to the United States from Latin America, the Caribbean, and Asia has been credited with revitalizing the Catholic Church in the United States. Catholic leaders may be responding to the needs and interests of their fastest growing constituencies.[14]

Finally, we argue that one cannot take for granted that religious affiliation always leads to more civic participation, especially among groups that include a large number of immigrants such as Asian Americans and Latinos. Although pastors occasionally encourage their members to become citizens or vote, such encouragement is not a constant theme in EPC churches and may be accompanied by warnings against becoming preoccupied with worldly and political affairs not directly related to biblical imperatives. Those who study religion and civic engagement often fail to emphasize that religion can sometimes discourage political participation. According to Kenneth Wald, "certain types of faith actually depress political involvement" because "some religious traditions regard politics as irrelevant or harmful to their primary task of saving souls. For some faithful, political participation may encourage concentration on 'earthly' concerns at the expense of more pressing needs in the spiritual realm" (2003, 37). The next step in this research is to compare rates of mobilization across white, black, Latino, Asian American, and multiethnic churches. The future relationship between EPC Asian American and Latino Christians and the mainstream conservative Christian political movement is unclear, but provides a critical case for studying the interplay of immigration, race, and religious institutions in the civic sphere.

The authors are indebted to two excellent Ph.D. candidates at the University of Southern California, Sarah Stohlman and Karen Yonemoto, for their research assistance with this project. Both did extensive background research on the topic for which we are very grateful. We would also like to thank Professor Jane Iwamura and the anonymous reviewers for their suggestions. Any errors are our own.

NOTES

1. See also Daniel Wakin, "Ammunition in a Battle for Souls: Evangelical Latinos See Opportunity in Catholic Scandal," *New York Times*, May 22, 2002, A1; Tasha Robertson, "Pentecostalism Luring Away Latino Catholics," *Boston Globe*, April 15, 2005, A1.
2. Mainline Protestant denominations are the traditional Protestant denominations that have been central and mainstream in the United States historically. Characterized by a moderate theology, these include the Methodist Church, Presbyterian Church, Congregationalist Church, Lutheran Church, and Northern Baptist Church.
3. Laurie Goodstein, "Disowning Conservative Politics, Evangelical Pastor Rattles Flock," *New York Times*, July 30, 2006, A1.
4. Larry Stammer, "California: Evangelical Church Welcomes Gays," April 5, 2006, B-22.
5. In terms of questions about religious practices and affiliation, the Kaiser survey asked respondents about the importance of religion in their everyday life and whether they identified as Protestant, Roman Catholic, Jewish, some other religion and no religion. Respondents who initially indicated that they considered themselves some other religion were asked if they considered themselves Christian. All Protestants and Christians were then asked if they considered themselves born again or evangelical Christian. Thus, one limitation of the survey is that respondents

were not asked if they identified as Pentecostal or charismatic. In addition, those who initially identified as Roman Catholic were not asked if they were also evangelical or born again Christians, though some Catholics are evangelical. Although the current study is interested in EPC Christians of all denominations, our analysis focused on those Christians describing themselves as born again or evangelical Christian because they are the most likely to fall into the EPC category.

6. Don Lattin, "The Battle over Same Sex Marriage," *San Francisco Chronicle*, April 15, 2004, B4.
7. Jason Ma, "Straight from the Church: How Korean American Churches in California Rallied Against Gay Rights," *Asian Week*, January 26, 2000, 13.
8. Don Lattin, "The Battle over Same Sex Marriage," *San Francisco Chronicle*, April 15, 2004, B4.
9. The Pew Research Center recently issued a poll analysis suggesting that while white evangelical Christians continue to be the strongest supporters of the GOP, their loyalty to the party is eroding along with the country's general support for Bush and the Republicans (Keeter 2006).
10. Jeffrey MacDonald, "Religious Communities at Odds on Immigration," *USA Today*, April 26, 2006, 9d.
11. Teresa Watababe and Hector Becerra, "500,000 Pack Streets to Protest Immigration Bills," *Los Angeles Times*, March 26, 2006, A1.
12. Jeffrey MacDonald, "Religious Communities at Odds on Immigration," *USAToday*, April 26, 2006, 9d.
13. Sam Rodriguez, "Religion and Ethics NewsWeekly," *PBS* Episode 1006, October 6, 2004, accessed at http://www.pbs.org/wnet/religionandethics/week1006/cover.html.
14. Compare Nichole M. Christian, "Detroit Journal: Mexican Immigrants Lead a Revival," *New York Times*, May 21, 2000, sec. 1, 20.

REFERENCES

Burgess, Stanley. 2001. "Pentecostalism in India: An Overview." *Asia Journal of Pentecostal Studies* 4(1): 85–98.
Busto, Rudy. 1996. "The Gospel According to the Model Minority? Hazarding an Interpretation of Asian American Evangelical College Students." *Amerasia Journal* 22(1): 133–47.
Carnes, Tony, and Fenggang Yang. 2004. "Introduction." In *Asian American Religions*, edited by Tony Carnes and Fenggang Yang. New York: University Press.
Casanova, Jose. 2001. "Religion, the New Millennium, and Globalization." *Sociology of Religion* 62(4): 415–41.
DeTemple, Jill. 2005. "Chains of Liberation: Poverty and Social Action in the Universal Church of the Kingdom of God." In *Latino Religions and Civic Activism in the United States*, edited by Gastón Espinosa, Virgilio Elizondo, and Jesse Miranda. New York: Oxford University Press.
Ecklund, Elaine Howard, and Jerry Z. Park. 2005. "Asian American Community Participation and Religion: Civic 'Model Minorities'?" *Journal of Asian American Studies* 6(1): 1–21.
Emerson, Michael, and Christian Smith. 2001. *Divided by Faith: Evangelical Religion and the Problem of Race in America*. New York: Oxford University Press.
Espinosa, Gastón. 1999a. "Borderland Religion: Los Angeles and the Origins of the

Latino Pentecostal Movement in the U.S., Mexico, and Puerto Rico 1900–1945." Ph.D. dissertation, University of California, Santa Barbara.

———. 1999b. "El Azteca; Francisco Olazabal and Latino Pentecostal Charisma, Power, Faith Healing in the Borderlands." *Journal of the American Academy of Religion* 67(3): 597–616.

Espinosa, Gastón, Virgilio Elizondo, and Jesse Miranda. 2003. *Hispanic Churches in American Public Life: Summary of Findings.* Notre Dame, Ind.: Institute for Latino Studies, University of Notre Dame.

———. 2005. *Latino Religions and Civic Activism in the United States.* New York: University of Oxford Press.

Fine, Janice. 2006. *Worker Centers: Organizing Communities at the Edge of the Dream.* New York: ILR Press and Cornell University Press.

Freston, Paul. 2004. Evangelicals and Politics in Asia, Africa and Latin America. New York: Cambridge University Press.

Garcia, Mario. 2005. "PADRES: Latino Community Priests and Social Action." In *Latino Religions and Civic Activism in the United States*, edited by Gastón Espinosa, Virgilio Elizondo, and Jesse Miranda. New York: Oxford University Press.

Gordon, Linda. 2001. *The Great Arizona Orphan Abduction.* Cambridge, Mass.: Harvard University Press.

Green, John, Corwin E. Smidt, James L. Guth, and Lyman A . Kellsted. 2005. *The American Religious Landscape and the 2004 Presidential Vote: Increased Polarization.* Washington: Pew Forum on Religion and Public Life.

Harris, Frederick. 1994. "Something Within: Religion as a Mobilizer of African American Political Activism." *The Journal of Politics* 56(1): 42–68.

Hondagneu-Sotelo, Pierrette. 2007. *Religion and Social Justice for Immigrants.* New Jersey: Rutgers University Press.

Jeung, Russell. 2007. "Faith-Based, Multiethnic Tenant Organizing: The Oak Park Story." In *Religion and Social Justice for Immigrants*, edited by Pierrette Hondagneu-Sotelo. New Brunswick, N.J.: Rutgers University Press.

Jones-Correa, Michael, and David Leal. 2001. "Political Participation: Does Religion Matter?" *Political Research Quarterly* 54(4): 751–70.

Keeter, Scott. 2006. "Evangelicals and the GOP: An Update Strongly Republican Group Not Immune to Party's Troubles." Washington: Pew Research Center. Accessed at http://pewresearch.org/pubs/78/evangelicals-and-the-gop-an-update.

Kim, Rebecca. 2004. "Second-Generation Korean American Evangelicals: Ethnic, Multiethnic, or White Campus Ministries?" *Sociology of Religion* 65(11): 19–34.

Lee, Chisun. 2000. "Moral Minority." *A Magazine* (April/May): 60–65. Accessed electronically via Proquest database.

Leonard, Karen, Alex Stepick, Manuel Vasquez, and Jennifer Holdaway. 2005. *Immigrant Faiths: Transforming Religious Life in America.* Walnut Creek, Calif.: Altamira Press.

Levitt, Peggy. 2002. "Two Nations under God? Latino Religious Life in the United States." In *Latinos: Remaking America*, edited by Marcelo M. Suarez-Orozco and Mariela M. Paez. Berkeley, Calif.: University of California Press.

Lien, Pei-te. 2004. *Pilot National Asian American Political Survey (PNAAPS), 2000–2001.* ICPSR version. Van Nuys, Calif.: Interviewing Service of America, Inc. (producer), 2001. Ann Arbor, Mich.: Inter-university Consortium for Political and Social Research (distributor), 2004.

Lien, Pei-te, M. Margaret Conway, and Janelle Wong. 2004. *The Politics of Asian Americans: Diversity and Community.* New York: Routledge.

Lloyd-Moffett, Stephen. 2005. "The Mysticism and Social Action of Cesar Chavez." In

Latino Religions and Civic Activism in the United States, edited by Gastón Espinosa, Virgilio Elizondo, and Jesse Miranda. New York: Oxford University Press.

Mantovina, Timothy. 2005. "Conquest, Faith, and Resistance in the Southwest." In *Latino Religions and Civic Activism in the United States*, edited by Gastón Espinosa, Virgilio Elizondo, and Jesse Miranda. New York: Oxford University Press.

Medina, Lara. 2004. *Las Hermanas: Chicana/Latina/Religious/Political Activism in the U. S. Catholic Church*. Philadelphia, Pa.: Temple University Press.

———. 2005. "The Challenges and Consequences of Being Latina, Catholic, and Political." In *Latino Religions and Civic Activism in the United States*, edited by Gastón Espinosa, Virgilio Elizondo, and Jesse Miranda. New York: Oxford University Press.

Milkman, Ruth. 2006. *LA Story: Immigrant Workers and the Future of the U.S. Labor Movement*. New York: Russell Sage Foundation.

Min, Pyong Gap. 1992. "The Structure and Social Functions of Korean Immigrant Churches in the United States." *International Migration Review* 26(4): 1370–94.

Mooney, Margarita. 2007. "The Catholic Church's Institutional Responses to Immigration." In *Religion and Social Justice for Immigrants*, edited by Pierrette Hondagneu-Sotelo. New Brunswick, N.J.: Rutgers University Press.

Noll, Mark A. 2001. *American Evangelical Christianity*. Malden, Mass.: Blackwell Publishing.

Pew Forum on Religion and Public Life. 2005. *A Faith-Based Partisan Divide*. New York: Pew Research Center.

Putnam, Robert. 2000. *Bowling Alone*. New York: Simon & Schuster.

Rios, Elizabeth. 2005. "'The Ladies Are Warriors': Latina Pentecostalism and Faith-Based Activism in New York City." In *Latino Religions and Civic Activism in the United States*, edited by Gastón Espinosa, Virgilio Elizondo, and Jesse Miranda. New York: Oxford University Press.

Robbins, Joel. 2004. "The Globalization of Pentecostal and Charismatic Christianity." *Annual Review of Anthropology* 33(October): 117–43.

Sanchez-Walsh, Arlene. 2003. *Latino Pentecostal Identity: Evangelical Faith, Self and Society*. New York: Columbia University Press.

Scheper, George. 1999. "Guadalupe: Image of Submission or Solidarity?" *Religion and the Arts* 3 (3/4):363.

Smilde, David. 1999. "*El Clamor por Venezuela*: Latin American Evangelicalism as a Collective Action Frame." In *Latin American Religion in Motion*, edited by Christian Smith and Joshua Prokopy. New York: Routledge.

Vasquez, Manuel, and Marie Friedmann Marquardt. 2003. *Globalizing the Sacred: Religion Across the Americas*. New Brunswick, N.J.: Rutgers University Press.

Verba, Sidney, Kay Lehman Schlozman, and Henry E. Brady. 1995. *Voice and Equality: Civic Voluntarism in American Politics*. Boston, Mass.: Harvard University Press.

Wald, Kenneth. 2003. *Religion and Politics in the United States*, 4th ed. Lanham, Md.: Rowan and Littlefield.

Warren, Mark. 2001. *Dry Bones Rattling: Community Building to Revitalize American Democracy*. Princeton, N.J.: Princeton University Press.

Washington Post/Kaiser Family Foundation/Harvard University. 2001. *Race and Ethnicity in 2001: Attitudes, Perceptions, and Experiences*. Accessed March 4, 2008 at http://www.kff.org/kaiserpolls/3143-index.cfm.

Wesley, Luke. 2004. "Is the Chinese Church Predominantly Pentecostal?" *Asian Journal of Pentecostal Studies* 7(1): 225–54.

Wong, Janelle. 2006a. *Democracy's Promise: Immigrants and American Civic Institutions*. Ann Arbor, Mich.: University of Michigan Press.

————. 2006b. "Racial Diversity, Religion and Conservative Politics in America." Paper presented at the American Political Science Association Meeting. Philadelphia, Pa., August 31, 2006.

Wong, Janelle, with Jane Iwamura. 2006. "The Moral Minority: Race, Religion and Conservative Politics among Asian Americans." In *Religion and Social Justice for Immigrants*, edited by Pierrette Hondagneu-Sotel. New Brunswick, N.J.: Rutgers University Press.

Wood, Richard L. 2002. *Faith in Action: Religion, Race, and Democratic Organizing in America*. Chicago, Ill.: University of Chicago Press.

Yang, Fenggang. 1998. "Chinese Conversion to Evangelical Christianity : The Importance of Social and Cultural Contexts." *Sociology of Religion* 59(3): 237–57.

————. 2004. "Gender and Generation in a Chinese Christian Church." In *Asian American Religions*, edited by Tony Carnes and Fenggang Yang. New York: New York University Press.

Yonemoto, Karen. 2006. "Backgrounder on Asian American Evangelicals in the United States." Unpublished paper. University of Southern California.

Rebecca Hamlin

Chapter 11

Immigrants At Work: Labor Unions and Noncitizen Members

Organized labor is an inherently political institution. This is true, not simply in the abstract sense in which worker movements take on political meaning through their very existence, but also in a tangible, day-to-day sense that is intimately connected to their survival. To fulfill their raison d'être—to improve the workplace conditions and socioeconomic status of their members—unions must not only succeed at collective bargaining and contract negotiations, but also sustain victories at an earlier stage, ensuring that policies impacting basic union activities and the lives of working families are shaped in a favorable manner. To that end, American unions must maximize political power at the national, state, and local levels. The success with which unions build relationships with and maintain influence over those in public office has wide-reaching ramifications for the representation of working class interests in the formation of public policy.

For decades, organized labor has been on the defensive in the struggle to maintain political power. Since 1975, union density (the percentage of union members in the workforce) has declined by almost one percentage point every year. In fact, the apex of union density coincided with the formation of the AFL-CIO, when the American Federation of Labor and the Congress of Industrial Organizations merged in 1955. At the time of the merger, 33 percent of the American workforce was unionized. Today, the number hovers around 12 percent (U.S. Census Bureau 2007). This figure is bolstered by high unionization rates among public employees; in the private sector, only 7.4 percent of workers belong to a union; in the agricultural sector, only 3 percent do. Thus the labor movement is faced with the daunting prospect of organizing hundreds of thousands of new members each year to keep pace with the expanding workforce and maintain current density levels. Beyond that, achieving the necessary growth to reverse the trend of decline appears to be impossible.

Organizing noncitizen workers, then, can be a mixed blessing for labor unions. Although increasing membership numbers has clear appeal, unions rely on a combination of political donations and high voter turnout among their members to maintain political power, activities which noncitizens cannot legally do. Moreover, immigrant members may have different political interests than citizens and, if they are undocumented, they may have particular workplace needs about which unions must familiarize themselves. Incorporating immigrants into unions therefore involves a steep learning curve for union staff, without necessarily providing the pay-off that new organizing of citizen members brings.

I argue that mass undocumented immigration over the past twenty years has caused an upheaval at every level of the American labor movement, which, in turn, has affected the ongoing strategies of workplace and political organizing for many unions. First, I chronicle how immigrants have affected change in immigration policy positions in the labor movement via a bottom-up push; then I discuss the emergence of what I call immigrant unions: unions which have large numbers of immigrant members and which give immigrant issues a central place on their political agendas.[1] Finally, I consider the strengths and weaknesses of unions as sites where immigrants can become civically and politically engaged, despite their lack of political power.

In particular, I trace the process leading up to February 16, 2000, when American organized labor underwent a major shift in its official position on undocumented immigrants and their relationship to union power. For this story, I draw on forty-five in-depth interviews with union staff members conducted between 2003 and 2006 about the role of immigrants in the labor movement and the changing position of unions on immigration policy over time. My interviews are predominantly drawn from the San Francisco Bay Area, though a handful of them are with high-ranking labor leaders based in Washington, D.C.

The chapter is focused on California for a number of reasons. First, it is both the most heavily immigrant state and a union stronghold. More than 26 percent of the population of California are foreign-born, compared to about 11 percent nationwide, and compared to the national unionization rate of 12 percent, 15.7 percent of California's workers are union members (U.S. Census Bureau 2007). I also focus on this state because the grassroots mobilization that led to a dramatic shift within the labor movement was initiated there, in part by a loose coalition of concerned labor organizers, immigrant rights advocates and union members, who called themselves the Labor Immigrant Organizing Network (LION).

I focus on the Bay Area's LION, but that choice does not suggest that organizing did not occur in southern California as well. Throughout the period in question, agitation, coordination, and organization began to develop in the Los Angeles area around immigrant issues. Much of it is described in Ruth Milkman's book *L.A. Story: Immigrant Workers and the Future of the U.S. Labor Movement* (2006), and does not require repetition. The story of LION however, is not only an untold story, but an excellent case study of the bottom up change that occurred in the labor movement around the turn of the twenty-first century.

Key insights into the events of 1999 and 2000 came from two interviews in particular: one with Katie Quan, the founder of LION, who gave me access to many LION documents, and one with David Bacon, a photo-journalist who accompanied LION members to the AFL-CIO Convention in 1999, and reported extensively about LION's activities in the left wing media. In addition, I identified ten other key LION members through a snowball sampling method of referrals, and spoke to each one in turn. In later years, I interviewed political directors at immigrant unions in the San Francisco Bay Area, and asked them about the ramifications of the 2000 shift for their ability to represent and organize immigrant workers.

I found that the grassroots pressure leveraged by LION and other labor organizers in California was necessary for changing labor's official position on undocumented immigration policy, and that the shift they fought for enabled immigrant unions to become more explicit about incorporating foreign-born members into their political agenda-setting. However, for many unions that operate in sectors of the workforce with low numbers of immigrants, change at the top did not trickle down. For these nonimmigrant unions, the issue of undocumented immigrant workers remains a low priority, and the 2000 shift is merely symbolic. In other words, the needs of these workers have moved to the forefront of the political agenda for some of the nation's largest unions but not others, resulting in less common ground that can unite working people with differing citizenship status.

IMMIGRATION POLICY AND THE STRUCTURE OF ORGANIZED LABOR

Organized labor is often depicted as an interest group that lobbies government on a variety of policy issues concerning working people (Heinz et al. 1993; Olson 1965). Certainly, projecting a unified front is helpful for maintaining the political clout of labor. However, identifying a common labor interest on some issues is far from clear cut, because the AFL-CIO is an extremely hierarchical, federated organization, made up of millions of constituents who represent a vast range of interests. A labor federation is a group of unions that have banded together to pool resources and maximize political power. It is structured in much the same way as the federal government, with national, state, and county coordination across all sectors of the workforce. Each union belonging to a federation is its own separate entity representing a sector of the workforce, with its own leaders at the international level (representing the United States and Canada), and regional units called locals.

On some policy issues, the general labor position is clear, making choices about how to lobby, who to endorse, and what campaigns to contribute to fairly simple. Other political issues affect different parts of the workforce differently, and affect some regions more than others, creating divisions across internationals in the same federation, and between locals in the same union. Because of labor's large, federal structure, the national leadership of the AFL-CIO is itself occasionally lobbied to take a particular position by a faction within the labor movement with particular interests.

Immigration policy, and in particular, the question of undocumented immigrants, is an issue that has often been divisive within the labor movement. Workers in the United States have frequently viewed immigrants as a threat, despite the fact that new waves of immigrants have traditionally revitalized unions. For example, mass migration to the industrial cities of the East Coast at the turn of the twentieth century brought workers from Eastern and Southern Europe who were largely responsible for founding the American labor movement. Despite immigrant majorities in many locals, however, and perhaps influenced by fears among citizens that immigrants were importing socialism, unions began to take restrictionist stances on immigration policy during the 1910s in anticipation of post–World War I layoffs (Knobel 1996, 256). By 1920, the American Federation of Labor (AFL) officially supported a nationality-based quota system that significantly restricted the number of new immigrant arrivals. When the Conference of Industrial Organizations (CIO) was formed in 1933 during the height of the New Deal, it united low-wage industrial workers from a new wave of immigrant minorities, resulting in a militant class-consciousness that surpassed ethnic divides. The CIO was opposed to the quota system from its founding, but had little leverage because it had far less political power than the more moderate AFL.

After the craft-oriented trades and the industrial arm of labor joined forces in 1955, the newly formed AFL-CIO enjoyed more than a decade of political power and economic prosperity, which gave it the breathing room to approve increased immigration flows. Seeking reforms to the outdated quota system based on national origins, it stated: "The AFL-CIO does not advocate unrestricted immigration. We cannot be indifferent to short-run distress of our people. But we can afford to be much more generous than we are now" (AFL-CIO 1959).

For a number of reasons, labor's support of increased immigration did not last. First, the economic boom of the 1950s gave way to recession by the early 1970s. Second, immigration increased dramatically under the Immigration Act of 1965, which raised the number of annually admitted immigrants and completely revamped the ethnic make-up of new immigrants to the United States for years to come. Mass immigration from Asia, Latin America, and the Caribbean began in unprecedented numbers, creating what has come to be known as the Fourth Wave. During this same period, other forms of migration to the United States increased as well; the flow of refugees from Southeast Asia and illegal immigration from Mexico after the termination of the temporary bracero (guest worker) program in 1964, meant that by 1970 the labor pool of low-wage workers was large enough to cause concern in union circles.

A third reason for displeasure about immigration within the labor movement was that union density levels began to drop in the mid-1970s, as economic pressures led to downsizing, and globalization enabled outsourcing of jobs. Employers stepped up legislative efforts to make union organizing more difficult by limiting union power and by the increased use of union-busting consultants during organizing drives. In short, by the 1970s, union leaders believed that they were under attack from all sides, and began to focus in on the issue of illegal immigration, calling for more enforcement of the southern border to prevent undocumented crossings. As a result, much heated debate within the Democratic Party revolved around the issue of illegal immigration, pitting the AFL-CIO,

Cesar Chavez's United Farm Workers, and the NAACP—which all saw illegal immigrants as an economic threat—against newly formed Latino advocacy groups such as the Mexican American Legal Defense and Education Fund (MALDEF) and the National Council of La Raza, which worked to enforce the rights of undocumented immigrants (Tichenor 2002, 230–32). This controversy marked the beginning of a long-standing divide on the left between organized labor and immigrant rights activists. Despite much congressional debate and several attempts at legislation, these rifts within the Democratic Party coupled with business opposition to stricter enforcement meant that for many years, very little was done legislatively on the question of illegal immigration.

In the early 1980s, the AFL-CIO came out strongly in favor of legislation that would strengthen impediments to illegal immigration. For example, in 1981 the Federation's Executive Council called for a stronger Immigration and Naturalization Service (INS) border patrol and applauded a proposal to introduce sanctions against employers who hire undocumented people, coupled with "a more secure identification mechanism to enable employers to readily determine the legal status of job applicants" that would serve to "discourage continued illegal immigration" (AFL-CIO 1981). At its national convention in 1985, the AFL-CIO claimed that "illegal immigration undercuts job opportunities for unemployed Americans and undermines labor standards for domestic workers." When the legislative process finally gained momentum, the AFL-CIO was intimately involved in the passage of the Immigration Reform and Control Act of 1986 (IRCA), ensuring that employer sanctions were included in the law. The only aspect of IRCA the AFL-CIO opposed was a one-time amnesty for undocumented workers that was included as a compromise with the business community (AFL-CIO 1987).

IRCA turned out to be an incredibly damaging piece of legislation, both to the workplace rights of undocumented immigrants and to unions' ability to organize them. It also did nothing to reduce illegal immigration or illegal employment of immigrants. Employer sanctions were never enforced, but rather were used by employers to bust unions with undocumented members (see Brownell 2005). The union organizers who eventually formed the bottom-up push for immigration reform within the labor movement saw firsthand the impact that nonenforcement of employer sanctions was having on union power, and called for the repeal of the 1986 legislation. Although LION was only a small group of organizers—union staff with no power over policy positions—the network ended up having a profound impact on a notoriously bureaucratic, entrenched institution in a very short amount of time. Armed with firsthand knowledge about the situation on the ground, these organizers were able to temporarily subvert the top-down direction of political weight within the labor movement, and take strategic advantage of concerns within the leadership in order to bring about change. LION responded to the needs of the most powerless people in the labor movement—undocumented union members and potential union members—and made an innovative point to a new cadre of labor leaders: that the flow of undocumented labor into the United States could be more easily unionized than curtailed. How, precisely, LION's strategy was developed and its internal lobbying campaign was waged, is the story I turn to next.

UNDOCUMENTED LABOR: LOBBYING THE AFL-CIO

During the mid-1990s, it became clear to individual union staff working to organize undocumented workers that many employers had found a way around the employer sanctions created by IRCA in 1986, and had introduced a new anti-union tactic—the "no match" letter. Under this strategy, employers used information about which employees did not have legitimate Social Security numbers to frighten workers away from unions. The IRCA provision gave employers access to lists of undocumented workers from the Social Security Administration (SSA), but the INS did not follow up with any enforcement. Instead, employers were allowed to keep the information indefinitely and use it as a convenient union busting tool. Organizers discovered that when they began new organizing drives, many workers (often the leaders of the unionization effort) would be sent a letter from the employer asking for Social Security number verification. If workers could not provide a valid number, they would be fired.

The union staff I interviewed recalled being initially stunned by this new challenge. One said, "we were getting brutalized trying to organize and I knew something was wrong. Employers were using immigration law to thwart organizing, and were exempt." Another organizer explained it this way: "in my new organizing drives, the majority had no papers and employers knew they had no papers. Then they fired them and replaced them with people who had no papers." Employers were able to pursue this approach because enforcement of the sanctions against them was essentially being left to self-regulation. One exception occurred when Service Employees International Union (SEIU) Local 1877, which represents janitors in Oakland, California, and had been an active participant in the nationwide Justice for Janitors organizing campaign, was subjected to a large-scale INS check that resulted in 500 members of the union getting fired on the basis of their immigration status. According to an organizer there, no-match letters "eviscerated the leadership" within the rank and file who had been mobilizing their coworkers for a unionization drive.

Immigration law had not been used to bust unions before the passage of IRCA, and when organizers called around looking for the official AFL-CIO policy for dealing with the issue, they were given no information or guidance. One interviewee recalled telephoning the AFL-CIO national office to speak to the lawyers and being told that they were not familiar with the situation. An organizer said, "I was looking for a strategy around no-match letters, but there was no infrastructure to share strategies." Another recalled, "at that time there was no clear position by the internationals or even the trade locals." Most local unions did not develop any de facto policy in response to no-match letters, they simply refused to deal with the question of undocumented workers. An organizer for such a union said, "unions would say 'we can't do anything.'" Some unions, such as Hotel Employees and Restaurant Employees (HERE) Local 2 in San Francisco, went ahead and fought employers on the Social Security number issue, and managed under a new contract to establish the ability for workers to change Social Security numbers with no questions asked. Through that effort, Local 2 was able to win some workers back their jobs, demonstrating further the extent to which employers had discretion over enforcement (for an interesting account of this process, see Wells 2000).

The official position of the labor movement was becoming more and more disconnected, not only from what was being done in the course of organizing drives, but also from the collective bargaining process. One organizer recalled that, at the time, there was a growing sense among unions with large numbers of undocumented workers that they "wanted to formalize what we were already doing in practice." Another stated that he was tired of dealing with that type of grievance on a one-by-one basis, and wanted to see a broader change. By the summer of 1998, several organizers and activists in the San Francisco Bay area began to discuss the possibility of bringing concerned people together to discuss labor's stance on employer sanctions and strategize around no-match letters.

In August, Katie Quan, director of the John F. Henning Center for International Labor at University of California, Berkeley, convened a meeting. Quan has a background in labor organizing at the International Ladies Garment Workers Union (which later became UNITE), and according to one attendee, she "had clout from UNITE to call leaders to the room. She had relationships with people." A diverse group attended the first meeting, representing many unions, community organizations, cities in the region, and ethnic backgrounds. A few were undocumented immigrants, but most were driven simply by the challenge of doing their jobs effectively and by a sense of injustice. A consensus quickly formed around the belief that AFL-CIO policy was outdated and misguided, and that IRCA had failed to reach the compromise that labor had hoped for when it endorsed the legislation in 1986. Unless that failure was acknowledged, organizers in some sectors and regions were very unlikely to organize any new members at all.

The concept and name of the Labor Immigrant Organizing Network were developed at that first meeting, and it was soon decided that LION would have three committees. One would deal with immediate, on-the-ground crises, helping organizers strategize and mobilize around the employer sanctions issue. This gave LION members who were union organizers a concrete incentive for participation: assistance, advice, and networking around day-to-day immigrant organizing concerns. Several organizers I interviewed referred to LION as a "rapid response network" in the early months because the coalition provided support for local unions in responding to no-match letters and I-9 visa checks. Actions were staged at Bay Area Radisson and Travelodge hotels, where employer tactics had been particularly egregious in using immigration status to fend off unionization.

The second committee was dedicated to education and training. Participants designed workshops for union members to learn about their legal rights. They then traveled around the country giving presentations on the challenges of organizing undocumented workers. LION also provided general resources and capacity-building for local unions interested in addressing the issue of undocumented workers internally, but unsure of how to proceed. Part of the logic behind providing these services, according to interviewees, was to identify potential allies around the country who might be enlisted into the network.

The biggest and most important committee in most LION members' eyes was the policy task force, which ambitiously aimed to both change the official position of the labor movement and lobby for legislative reform. On January 23, 1999, it held a conference titled "Organizing Immigrant Workers—Defending the Right to Organize" in Oakland, attended by more than 300 people, almost all of whom were in favor of change. Attendees drafted a resolution stating that "the ability of workers to organize has been increasingly threatened by current immigration law and its enforcement, which has been used to retaliate against workers who organize and protest against sweatshop conditions" (LION 1999).

The support that arose from the January 1999 conference gave LION members the courage to push their agenda more overtly within labor circles. The attendees decided that the best strategy was for LION to try to get the resolution passed by as many locals as possible in order to build grassroots support. However, the ultimate goal was change at the top. One activist member expressed it this way: "I was looking for a coalition to fight AFL-CIO policy." Another said simply, "we had to go for the head." LION participants went back to their locals to make the case that sanctions were preventing organizing. As one member put it, "each person had the responsibility to move their institution." However, some found more support for the resolution than others. One organizer recalled it this way: "Back then many of our own internationals were not in support of amnesty or repealing employer sanctions. We knew it would be hard but we knew it had to be done through the grassroots." An organizer from United Food and Commercial Workers (UFCW), which provided the strongest resistance to the resolution, made this observation: "If I [hadn't had] some local autonomy and a sympathetic boss, I would have been hung" for bringing the resolution up for debate.

Although there was quite a bit of resistance from union leaders in trying to advocate for the resolution within their locals, LION members came across little opposition from the rank and file, including those who were citizens. Many rank and file members were aware of the large numbers of nonunionized undocumented workers in the Bay Area who were weakening union bargaining power because of the no-match letter campaign and similar tactics to end organizing drives. The resolution, because it focused on protecting the right to organize, offered hope to some union members that these workers could be used to increase union density. LION members worked quickly to pass the resolution within their locals, and then encouraged locals to bring it to their county central labor councils (CLC). CLCs are the local (usually county-level) branches of the AFL-CIO that, in the heyday of organized labor, were responsible for extensive grassroots electoral mobilization and lobbying (Ness and Eimer 2001). This strategy was important because, as one LION member explained, "the grassroots by labor standards are the CLCs. With one institution passing [the resolution], it is not generalized in the labor movement." It was accepted first by the Alameda CLC, then San Francisco, South Bay, and Contra Costa counties followed in early 1999.

The only place in the Bay Area where the resolution was debated and defeated was San Mateo county, due primarily to opposition from the United Food and Commercial Workers, which was very powerful in that area, on the peninsula west of the San Francisco Bay. According to LION members who were UFCW staff, the reasoning behind that union's opposition stemmed from a particularly vicious battle UFCW was waging with the meatpacking industry at processing plants in the American Midwest. Because of the unsavory nature of working on the so-called kill floor, which increases risk of serious injury as well as assembly line speed, meatpacking giants in recent years have resorted to recruiting and shipping workers from Mexico to plants in Nebraska, Iowa, and Colorado to cut costs (Schlosser 2001, 161–65). Incredibly high turnover rates among the immigrant workers and fear of INS detection made organizing these plants virtually impossible. Meager wages made it unworkable for smaller, unionized plants to continue to be competitive. According to one UFCW official, defeats in the meatpacking industry combined with the explosion of the anti-union Wal-Mart chain put the UFCW in a protectionist mindframe in the 1990s. The International UFCW saw employer sanctions law, weak as enforcement was, as the only recourse for addressing the meatpacking plants' union busting strategies.

Despite opposition from the UFCW, during the spring of 1999 sympathetic representatives from the SEIU and HERE Internationals began working closely with LION members to discuss the details of the resolution and put it into the larger context of what one SEIU executive called the ongoing debate within that union that dated back to IRCA 1986. With these behind-the-scenes conversations between LION representatives and some strategic union leadership, LION members began reaching out much more aggressively beyond the local level to get the resolution passed in as many places as possible. Versions of the resolution were passed in Seattle (King County CLC), New York City, and Los Angeles County, building on waves of organizing around immigrant issues that were being undertaken in each of these areas. Eventually, the California State Federation of Labor passed the resolution, and in June of 1999, LION began to discuss the possibility of bringing it to the national AFL-CIO convention in Los Angeles that October.

At that point, the AFL-CIO convention was four months away, but International union leaders were still quite concerned about what a change in the labor position on IRCA should look like, and whether a new amnesty and the repeal of sanctions would truly lead to the unionization of large numbers of immigrant workers and build union power. As one LION member put it, "a northern California strategy is not what moved it [the resolution]. International presidents are elected on a national level and need support from a base. This requires education and training." In the months leading up to the convention, the majority of LION's effort and negotiation centered on Washington, D.C., seeking out allies, creating a labor presence around the issue of undocumented workers, and negotiating with AFL-CIO national leaders about the way in which the resolution would be addressed at the convention. LION members agreed that a vote would only be desirable if passage was sure. Eventually it was decided that the California State Federation of Labor would present the resolution and time would be allotted for floor debate. A vote, however, would be postponed pending public hearings in New York, Chicago, and Los Angeles. A committee would be formed to research the issue further and assess the sentiments expressed at the hearings. Then, the committee would make a report to the AFL-CIO Executive Council at its meeting in New Orleans in February 2000, at which point the council would vote on the resolution. This compromise was especially appealing to supporters of the resolution because the delay was not indefinite—only four months—and would allow time to make the case to key players who were still unsure.[2]

As the October 12 convention date approached, the resolution gained a great deal of support at multiple levels of the AFL-CIO and affiliated Internationals. Still, no one knew exactly how the floor debate would proceed. The floor strategy was to line up a diverse array of speakers in favor of the resolution, representing a range of ethnic backgrounds, union affiliations, and roles. LION also continued its strategy of arranging timely and sympathetic media coverage. In a bold stand against his International, Roger Riviera, LION member and organizer at UFCW 428 in San Jose, chose to be quoted in the *Los Angeles Times* the day of the convention: "The sanctions aren't doing what they were supposed to do. They've become another tool for employers."[3] Observers at the convention claim that UFCW officials were visibly distressed by the article because it singled out the International as the major opponent of a resolution that had increasingly broad support.

During the floor debate of the resolution, the line to speak reached around the hall as person after person demonstrated their support. According to an observer, "the convention was heavily scripted and one of the great things about this issue was it got away from the script. It bubbled up off the floor. There weren't canned responses for it. The movement off of the floor meant that the Executive Council could not bury the issue." Notable proponents were Eliseo Medina, vice president of SEIU, Arturo Rodriguez, president of the United Farm Workers and John Wilhelm, president of HERE. Frank Hurt, president of Bakers, Confectioners, and Tobacco Union—who was the chair of the committee that recommended the AFL-CIO support IRCA in 1986—spoke in favor, saying that employer sanctions "arm employers with additional weapons often wielded with governmental complicity" (cited in Bacon 1999, 33). Finally, Joe Hansen, UFCW's International secretary-treasurer, rose to speak. Reading the writing on the wall, he stated that "current immigration policies just do not work" (cited in Bacon 1999, 34).

LION members who attended the convention believe that it was clear from the floor debate and crowd responses that if a vote on the resolution had been called, it could have passed. However, sticking to the compromise plan, the vote was deferred. Sweeney of AFL-CIO appointed Wilhelm of HERE as chair of the interim committee that would plan the public hearings. This move was viewed as a clear sign of support from Sweeney, because Wilhelm was obviously sympathetic to the resolution. It was also decided that the hearings would actually be postponed until after the February vote to give more time to plan them. This decision all but sealed the victory of the resolution because it changed the practical nature of the hearings from exploratory gauges of union membership opinion to research forums for how to best implement a change in policy.

LION members left the convention with the sense that a reversal of the AFL-CIO position was inevitable. They were proved correct four months later when the executive council unanimously approved the resolution. LION has never officially been mentioned by the AFL-CIO, but, according to one LION member, "as soon as people began to start fighting over who should take credit for the resolution, I knew our job was done." Many Internationals began to weigh in on the particulars of implementation and drafted a statement that was released along with the passage of the resolution on February 16, 2000 (for the full text of the resolution, see the appendix). The statement further detailed the new position and laid out recommendations for changes in American immigration policy.

> We strongly believe that employer sanctions, as a nationwide policy applied to all workplaces, has failed and should be eliminated. It should be replaced with an alternative policy to reduce undocumented immigration and prevent employer abuse. . . . It must allow workers to pursue legal remedies, including supporting a union, regardless of immigration status. . . . The AFL-CIO calls for the enactment of whistleblower protections providing protected immigration status for undocumented workers who report violations of worker protection laws or cooperate with federal agencies during investigations of employment, labor and discrimination violations. (AFL-CIO 2000)

Although it focuses on legal rights for workers and new legislation proposals, the language of the executive council statement also implicitly suggests a commitment to organizing undocumented workers as full-fledged union members. The challenge that this commitment presents to organized labor has proved to be almost as daunting as the commitment to lobby for a policy change in the current political climate.

The AFL-CIO resolution of February 16, 2000, is unique in that it was generated from a loose grassroots coalition. Similar reversals have occurred in recent years in several European countries but, according to a comparative study, "in Spain, Italy and France, changes in labor leader's immigration preferences occurred first among the top leadership at the confederal level, and worked its way down to regional and sectoral unions" (Watts 2002, 154). Although that study was conducted before the AFL-CIO passed its resolution, the epilogue states that the "trickle-up effect" of the movement in the United States "stands in contrast" to the processes observed in Europe. The United States is a much larger and more regionally diverse country than any European nation, with a more fragmented and decentralized labor movement. It is perhaps for this reason that union leaders in the United States had a delayed reaction to the on-the-ground realities occurring in some areas, and relied on local staff to inform them. LION members all emphasized the bottom-up nature of the process. One said, "we weren't completely part of the structure, but close enough to have impact." Another organizer characterized LION's efforts as "the perfect example of the tail wagging the dog." A third interviewee, when asked about the relationship between LION and the labor movement said without hesitation, "we *are* the labor movement."

What would have happened if LION had not been created? In retrospect, it is easy to look at the new faces of labor movement leadership, in particular SEIU's Eliseo Medina and UNITE-HERE's John Wilhelm and assume that change would have come about without a forceful and sustained push from any particular small group. Certainly, their support made the shift possible, but the story of LION makes it clear that the national level leaders were not the driving force behind the change, because they lacked the on-the-ground information about the tactics being used by employers, and their effect on organizing efforts. Thus, the presence of these men at the top of the AFL-CIO was a necessary, but inadequate factor in the 2000 shift. Indeed, it was the combination of LION's lobbying, similar efforts in other parts of the country, and the desperation of these leaders that made them more amenable to an unusual process for policy change. In fact, in confidential interviews, administrators of the AFL-CIO and International unions acknowledge the impact of LION. One SEIU official said that LION "deserves the credit for trying to make the changes" and for pushing the resolution through the "first phase" of the Central Labor Councils. An AFL-CIO official conceded that LION "worked hard to get support for the resolution on the [convention] floor. They did a good job of organizing that." A high-level official from the Teamsters also applauded the work of LION, saying that "they did a lot of lobbying, asking for input from people, asking for support to pass the resolution through different organizations. They were able to bring leadership in and move the resolution to the next level and build momentum."

The work of LION did not just change the position of the labor movement on undocumented immigration, it gave undocumented immigrants a much more favorable view of labor. Because of its close association with community-based organizations and immigrant rights coalitions, LION was able to incorporate the positions of those key stakeholders into the resolution and thus gain the trust and support of the immigrants that made up the base of those organizations. One labor organizer believed that "a social movement institution coming out in support of their issues inspired massive new support for labor in immigrant communities, especially Latino communities because the issue of amnesty resonated sharply." Another observer, assessing the impact of the resolution, suggested that it had "a more unifying effect than a polarizing one. It gave huge credibility to the labor movement in immigrant communities. It positioned us as a vehicle for immigrants to improve their standards of living and become part of the American political system." By incorporating outsider perspectives and opinions, LION directly addressed the problems with stagnation that were preventing immigrant incorporation into the labor movement, and allowed for better relations between labor and community activists on the local level.

STRATEGIES OF IMMIGRANT UNIONS IN THE CURRENT CLIMATE

The impact of LION's work and the AFL-CIO resolution have sparked many changes within the International unions. After the 2000 resolution, many immigrant locals saw a shift in their freedom to pursue pro-immigrant tactics of new organizing and political lobbying without fear of reprisal from their Internationals. UNITE-HERE[4] representatives in particular described a decentralization, by which the International placed more autonomy with the locals to get involved in politics and respond to the local environment, rather than waiting for approval from the International before taking a stand or joining a coalition. This freedom has enabled UNITE-HERE locals to get much more involved in the immigrants' rights question, and subsequently inspire the International to do the same.

In the case of UFCW, once the most bitter opponent of working with and for undocumented workers, the union has gone through a major shift, particularly in terms of how it handles its campaigns in meatpacking plants in the Midwest. Today, the UFCW is working closely with community groups, such as Omaha Together One Community (OTOC) to reach out to immigrant populations in Nebraska and launch a joint effort to unionize meatpacking giants such as Con-Agra (Bacon 2002; Fine 2006). In a striking illustration of the union's about-face, Roger Riviera, the UFCW organizer quoted in the *Los Angeles Times* for his opposition to the International over the resolution, subsequently became the president of his local. Additionally, Joe Hansen, the UFCW secretary-treasurer who spoke up at the convention, is now the International UFCW president.

Teamsters staff still acknowledge that they place much more of a focus on networking between union staff and elected officials than on mobilizing members. However, this union demonstrates the most striking difference in strategies between 2003 and 2006. In 2003, a Bay Area Teamster Business Representative reported that his local was not part of any coalitions with nonlabor groups. In 2006, however, the same regional Teamster organization was able to list several new coalitions with immigrant organizations, advocacy groups and religious institutions. The International Brotherhood of Teamsters also passed its own complementary resolution on the rights of immigrant workers, which endorses the AFL-CIO Executive Council Resolution, but also surpasses it in its commitment to provide resources for services on the local level. Among other things, it pledges to "develop pilot programs that will provide workers with immigration assistance, other legal services, language instruction, job training and outreach programs to immigrant communities, promote a legislative agenda aimed at reforming current immigration laws," and "educate members on this commitment to the rights of immigrant workers" (IBT 2001).

Despite differences in scale and scope, almost all of the interviewees among thirty staff at San Francisco Bay Area unions reported an increase in coalition building and local political activity, especially in the area of political education among members since 2000. Political directors from several unions described a shift away from focusing on collecting campaign contributions and toward grassroots organizing and local level involvement. Union staff described a local level orientation to their political activities, such as working on establishing living wage ordinances. SEIU and UNITE-HERE staff reported having built strong partnerships with a wide range of local organizations, ranging from tenants rights groups to environmental activists and the locally powerful groups East Bay Alliance for a Sustainable Economy (EBASE) and Association of Community Organizations for Reform Now (ACORN). One political director called this type of long-term politically oriented strategizing "smart mobilization," because it is inexpensive and leads to long-lasting, tangible benefits for members.

Another interesting development that affects unions and immigrants on the local level is the rise of immigrant worker centers (for an excellent treatise on worker centers, their history, growth and political potential, see Fine 2006). Despite their missions, membership, and activities varying a great deal, worker centers are characterized by their commitment to advocacy and organizing on behalf of their members, their strong ties to a particular ethnic or racial community and their geographic, rather than work-site focus. Early worker centers were unaffiliated with unions and usually served low-skilled, low-income, nonunionized immigrant workers. Gregory Mantsios explains them this way:

> Worker centers challenge established categories of organization. They are not quite unions although they mobilize workers around employment concerns. They are not quite community organizations, although they are involved in community issues. They are not quite legal or social service agencies although they provide some legal representation as well as training and education. They grew out of the enormous unmet needs of immigrant workers who had no organization or representation as they faced tremendous problems in the workplace. (1998, 134)

Some immigrant advocates within the labor movement chose to establish such facilities outside the traditional union structure in order to address the needs of the undocumented, and the rise of such centers helped LION make its case that immigrant workers had a desire to organize that was not being adequately dealt with by the traditional union approach. Over the past few years, however, some unions have begun to get on the worker center bandwagon. Teamsters Local 890 in Salinas, California, has founded an affiliated immigrant workers center and local 78 in Hayward, California, is in the process of developing one.[5] In 2006, the AFL-CIO announced a new partnership with the National Day Labor Organizing Network, designed to facilitate relationship between unions and worker centers.[6]

As these examples make clear, many locals have embraced the reality that they have become immigrant unions, and have developed innovative strategies to accommodate their noncitizen, often undocumented members. This sets such unions apart from those unaffected by changing workforce demographics. Since 1996, the percentage of foreign-born people in the workforce has grown from 10.8 percent to 15.3 percent, but this shift has been concentrated in just a few sectors. For example, fewer than 1 percent in the education sector are foreign-born, but 23 percent of the service sector are (U.S. Census Bureau 2007). After the 2000 shift, these differences led to diverging priorities between two camps that emerged within the labor movement.

At the end of the summer of 2005, after months of building tensions, seven of America's largest labor unions officially split from the American Federation of Labor–Congress of Industrial Organizations (AFL-CIO) and formed a new federation called Change to Win. The reason for the break, according to news reports at the time, was a disagreement over how to allocate resources.[7] The Change to Win federation claimed that spending money on organizing low-wage workers, rather than giving it to the Democratic Party, was the only way for labor unions to maintain political power and credibility. In an era of globalization, many jobs were being downsized and outsourced, but, argued Change to Win leaders, there were still millions of workers in the agricultural, construction, and services industries whose jobs were tied to American soil and who were in need of the protection that only a union can offer. What went unspoken in the flurry of press conferences and statements released by both sides was that many of these workers are undocumented immigrants.

There is no official data about the foreign-born, let alone the undocumented rates within individual unions, but a quick glance at the unions that chose to break off and form the new federation, outlined in table 11.1, is instructive. When one takes into account the predominant sectors the Change to Win unions must organize, it is no exaggeration to call them heavily immigrant areas of the workforce.

There is evidence that these unions have begun to view political organization in new and different ways. In particular, they seem to be increasingly disinclined to maintain the traditionally unbreakable ties with the Democratic Party. Although the Change to Win unions represent 40 percent (approximately 6 million) of the union members in the United States, they have come to donate to political campaigns at disproportionately low levels. For example, SEIU and the Carpenters, who had consistently been among the top twenty political donors to the Democratic party, dropped off the list in 2006, leaving the Laborers, Teamsters, and UFCW among the top twenty, but at much lower rankings than in previous years. Instead, these unions have shifted their political donations to 527s, which allows them to do political issue advocacy independent from the Democratic Party (Center for Responsive Politics 2007). It remains to be seen what kind of a national political voice the Change to Win federation will develop, and how powerful it will be in bringing about new policies. In theory, this strategy of disengagement could pay off by getting the Democrats to take the Change to Win platform more seriously, but in some senses the labor movement today is eerily reminiscent of the pre-1955 merger, when the CIO, which was heavily immigrant, took a political backseat to the more moderate AFL. If this scenario plays out, the political weight of immigrant unions may be severely diminished in respect to nonimmigrant unions.

When staff members in charge of political mobilization at Bay Area locals in the Change to Win Federation were asked about strategies and approaches to political mobilization, it became clear that changing demographics in the work-

TABLE 11.1   *Sectors Organized by Change to Win Unions*

Change to Win Unions	Sectors
International Brotherhood of Teamsters (IBT)	freight drivers and warehouse workers
Laborers' International Union of North America (LIUNA)	construction, manual labor
Service Employees International Union (SEIU)	healthcare support services, property services
UNITE-HERE	manufacturing, hotel, and restaurant employees
United Brotherhood of Carpenters and Joiners of America (UBC)	carpenters
United Farm Workers (UFW)	agriculture, historically Mexican immigrants
United Food and Commercial Workers (UFCW)	grocery and retail food, meatpacking, and food processing

Source: Author's compilation.

force have forced unions to develop new strategies for building political power. As one organizer in an immigrant union put it, "we have to start thinking outside the box." A few union representatives confidentially reported that when Committee on Political Education (COPE) donations are collected, they often adopt a don't ask, don't tell policy about the members' immigration status. Another organizer made the point that because so many immigrant families are mixed status, it is important not to ignore the influence that noncitizen members can have on family members and friends. "I know that our leaders, even if they're not citizens, they are out there encouraging the citizens to vote, right? And because they can't do it, they feel this obligation to go get five other people." The president of a UNITE-HERE local in southern California stated that she has gotten active participation of undocumented workers precinct walking for pro-labor candidates: "we like to knock on doors because it allows them [the workers] to grow. You know? It challenges them to lose their fear of talking to people, just talking to people about the issues that are important to our union." Another labor leader reported that "we do mobilize huge numbers of folks to a city council meeting if we're having a problem," regardless of citizenship status.

As these examples demonstrate, there are political activities in which noncitizens, and even undocumented workers, can get involved as long as they believe the union has their best interests at heart. Building trust in immigrant communities has been a huge undertaking for immigrant unions. Even immigrants who are citizens may feel alienated from getting involved in politics stemming from experiences with corruption in their home country. Labor leaders reported that many immigrants are suspicious about politics, and that part of the union effort is therefore to acculturate them to have an interest in participating in politics. A study done in 2000 of barriers to new organizing in the United States found that "racial splits between established members and newly organized workers, or between members and leadership, exacerbate tensions" (Fletcher and Hurd 2000, 6). Jose La Luz and Paula Finn (1998) found three mistakes unions make in attempting to unionize immigrants. First was an insensitivity of union organizers to the internal diversity of immigrant communities. Second was overlooking the wealth of experiences and skills among immigrant workers, particularly with regard to union activity in their country of origin. Third was a reluctance to move away from English as the language of meetings and publications, and not hiring bilingual organizers.

Although these problems undoubtedly still exist in many locals across the country, many immigrant unions have begun to counteract historical exclusion by reaching out to immigrant communities in a number of ways. First, they have worked to become more accessible to diverse members by translating all their political documents into other languages, holding workshops on workers' rights in multiple languages, and holding meetings in various locations convenient to a membership that is increasingly dispersed. Other unions reported sending staff to local citizenship day events designed to help people fill out naturalization paperwork, and pass out information about the union's political program. In some cases, unions have hosted citizenship events in their own union hall. Additionally, immigrant union staff reported over and over again the extensive work they have dedicated to building collaborations with immigrant rights and community groups to hold forums on immigrant issues. One Change to Win union organizer said, "our membership is going toward that [being predominantly undocumented], and we have to figure out a way to represent all of our membership."

Another important strategy is for unions to acknowledge that many immigrants have other powerful influences over their political decisions, such as ethnic and religious community leaders, and to build relationships with those people. For example, one UFCW local in a region of the Bay Area with a large Vietnamese community hired a Vietnamese organizer, who has built ties and coordinates Get Out the Vote efforts with that community's Vietnamese organizations, which are extremely politically active. In another interesting example, a Teamster leader described efforts his local is making to coordinate with the local Sikh temple to do Get Out the Vote efforts, based on common interests. As he put it, "their whole idea is similar to labor. They have a community hall. . . . they are very active in politics, and they have a huge voting bloc, because whatever the temple recommends, they're going to follow that. . . . So I think it will pay dividends in building coalitions." But, he added, "it's very, very difficult to break into some of these ethnic groups and build trust. It takes time."

A recent study of immigrant incorporation into unions in Western Europe found that the main issue immigrant unions struggled with was whether the union should "exclusively attend to the common interests of indigenous and immigrant workers, or . . . stand up for the specific interests of their immigrant members?" (Roosblad 2000, 171). Although immigrants make up a substantial percentage of the American workforce, only rarely is a union local's membership predominantly noncitizen, and some locals did report feeling tension as the demographics of the membership changed. Some members have also expressed frustration that dues were being spent on community outreach rather than member representation. In one extreme example, a UNITE-HERE local that was 70 percent immigrant experienced a split in which the members who were citizens (predominantly white, but some native-born Mexican Americans as well) broke away because they had different priorities for resource allocation. For the most part, the staff at immigrant unions seemed unfazed by these types of tensions. They said that educating those members and moving immigrant members up from the rank and file into leadership positions were two strategies they found effective in addressing tensions between citizen and noncitizen members. One SEIU organizer said that the white members have become extremely enthusiastic about supporting immigrants rights and have been very active in lobbying efforts, often pushing for an increasingly progressive agenda on immigration.

In addition to local efforts and collaborations, the Change to Win unions have added immigration to their short list of policy priorities. At the state level, these unions lobby vigorously for bills that would allow undocumented immigrants to get driver's licenses in California. As one organizer put it, "we believe that it's in our membership's interest to support the driver's license bill and then slap the governor around to get him to sign it." Change to Win unions also have begun collaborating with immigrant groups to have an annual immigrants rights lobby day in Sacramento. At the national level, Change to Win unions were among the most staunch opponents to the immigration reform bill passed by the House of Representative (H.R 4437) at the end of 2005. In a March 1, 2006, open letter to the ranking members of the Senate Judiciary Committee, the Change to Win federation rejected employer sanctions and guest worker programs as policies that would "create an underclass of cheap, exploitable labor who will become the indentured servants of the 21st century" (Change to Win 2006). The letter went on to push for amnesty for the nation's 11 million undocumented residents and a system that prioritizes family reunification.

CONCLUSIONS AND SUGGESTIONS FOR FUTURE RESEARCH

As the open letter suggests, the labor movement experienced a dramatic about-face on undocumented immigration between 1996 and 2006. The story is in many ways an ironic one. The (sometimes strategically) poor enforcement of American immigration law regarding undocumented immigration in the aftermath of IRCA 1986 made non-status union members more visible to their unions and taught them that they needed to consider the needs of undocumented workers more generally. This important lesson led to a reversal in the policy position of the extremely entrenched, hierarchical AFL-CIO, which placed great value on traditional political channels of voting, lobbying, and political donation. It has also forced immigrant unions to learn from past experiences of immigrant organizing, to develop new and innovative strategies, and to build coalitions at the local level. These changes are very new, but they promise to be extremely important to the political fortunes of both immigrants and immigrant unions. The impact of this newfound alliance will depend on wide-ranging political and demographic trends, and will necessitate further study.

As the Change to Win Federation continues to develop its agenda, more research is needed as to the differences in political agenda between this new labor federation and the AFL-CIO, and the political weight each federation has within the Democratic Party. Ongoing research could also fruitfully explore the dynamics of this division at the local level. For example, are Change to Win and AFL-CIO locals more likely to collaborate in areas of the country that are heavily immigrant? What about areas that are labor strongholds?

Much of the interesting research on unions working with undocumented workers has focused on California and New York, because these two states, until very recently, have been the locations of the vast majority of immigrant organizing (Delgado 1993; Milkman 2000; Ness 2005). More recent efforts in the Southeast and mountain regions of the United States are going unstudied. This bias in scholarly research results in an overly rosy picture painted by labor scholars of the successes of the labor movement, because the labor regulations in New York and California are worker friendly, especially in comparison to the twenty-two states with restrictive right to work laws. Today, sixteen states, all with strict right to work laws, have density levels below 7 percent (National Right to Work Foundation 2007).

These laws directly affect new immigrant workers, because many right to work states are arising as new immigrant destinations. Fine suggests that since 2000 a new wave of worker centers has begun cropping up in many of these states in lieu of unionization. New research should look more systematically at union efforts in right to work states to see how immigrant workers have shaped on-the-ground strategies, and how antilabor legislation affects the scope of what unions can do for their members (see chapter 4, this volume).

Another interesting finding is the emerging presence of both South and Southeast Asian workers as political participants in immigrant unions. Much of the current research is in the form of case studies that focus on Latinos, who frequently come from nations with powerful labor movements. Future research might examine how Asian workers incorporate into unions differently than other immigrant groups, especially immigrants from Vietnam, Cambodia, or China, who may—on the basis of experiences in their home countries—have negative associations with socialism.

Unions are constrained in what they can do to facilitate immigrant political incorporation by their pressing need for survival—a top-down, often entrenched, and stagnant hierarchical structure—and by the diversity of their members, who require democratic accountability from their union. However, recent events have shown that change is possible within the labor movement, and that many unions are increasingly becoming the sites of immigrant political and civic engagement. Unions are in a unique position to help immigrants get involved in political and civic life because employment is the predominant reason for many to migrate to the United States. Thus unions can speak to immigrants about an issue that is very important to them—their rights at work.

APPENDIX: AFL-CIO RESOLUTION

Defending the Right of Immigrant Workers and the Right to Organize
    (Submitted to the AFL-CIO national convention by the California Labor Federation. Adopted by the AFL-CIO Executive Council on February 16th, 2000)
WHEREAS, our country and its labor movement were built in large part by immigrants that include those Africans who were kidnapped and forced into slavery. Our laws have historically reflected public attitudes about race, with bans and discriminatory limits on legal immigration from Asia, Africa and Latin America, which have only recently been rectified. People have come here seeking economic survival, often driven from their countries of origin by hunger, political repression and the lack of economic opportunity; and
WHEREAS, there are over 100 million people in the world today who have left their countries of origin. Only social and economic justice on a global scale will create a world where immigration is not a means of survival for the world's poor; and
WHEREAS, thousands of immigrants, working both with and without documents, have mounted large and effective campaigns to organize unions in California in the last decade. These efforts have created new unions and strengthened and revived many others, benefiting all labor, immigrants and native-born alike; and
WHEREAS, the ability of workers to organize has been increasingly threatened by current immigration law and its enforcement, which has been used to retaliate against workers who organize and protest against sweatshop conditions; and
WHEREAS, the California Labor Federation resolved in 1994 that employer sanctions should be repealed and we have passed the same resolution in each convention since then. Sanctions cause discrimination against anyone who looks or sounds foreign, because they provide a weapon employers have used repeatedly to fire and threaten immigrant workers who organize unions, and because they make immigrant workers vulnerable and cheapen their labor, violating their rights as workers and human beings; and
WHEREAS, the California Labor Federation stands for the equality of all workers and opposes immigration legislation and its enforcement, which divides workers and undermines their strength. All workers, regardless of immigration status, have the right to form unions, file complaints against illegal and unfair treatment without fear of reprisal, receive unemployment insurance, disability insurance, workers' compensation benefits, and enjoy the same remedies under labor law as all other workers;

THEREFORE, BE IT RESOLVED, that the California Labor Federation supports the calls made by many affiliated unions for the repeal of employer sanctions; and

BE IT FURTHER RESOLVED, that the California Labor Federation opposes all cooperation between the Immigration and Naturalization Services and other government and public institutions in which information provided by immigrants is misused for immigration enforcement purposes. The institutions include but are not limited to SSA, the Department of Labor, unemployment and welfare offices and motor vehicle departments, among others; and

BE IT FURTHER RESOLVED, that the California Labor Federation calls for a new amnesty program, allowing undocumented immigrants to regularize their status, and an inexpensive and expedited citizenship process to allow immigrants to become citizens as quickly as possible; and

BE IT FURTHER RESOLVED, that the California Labor Federation proposes that the budget for immigration enforcement be cut drastically, and the money used instead to increase enforcement of workers' rights and fair labor standards; and

BE IT FINALLY RESOLVED, that the California Labor Federation submits this resolution to the national convention of the AFL-CIO for adoption, and requests the AFL-CIO to forward its position to the national convention for adoption as well.

I thank Margaret Weir, Steven Pitts and Katie Quan at the University of California, Berkeley Institute of Industrial Relations for their advice and support. Thanks also to Bruce Cain at Berkeley's Institute of Governmental Studies for funding an early stage of this research.

NOTES

1. According to my definition, immigrant unions do not necessarily have a majority, or even a plurality, of noncitizen members. They often have many foreign-born members of various immigration statuses—some naturalized, some legal permanent resident, and some undocumented—and they always list immigration concerns as a focus of their political activities.
2. Detailed information about the compromises leading up to the AFL-CIO convention in October 1999 was provided to me by Katie Quan, and confirmed by Eliseo Medina, who is the International executive vice president of SEIU, and was instrumental in selling the LION resolution to leaders of other Internationals.
3. Nancy Cleeland, "Unions Questioning Sanctions Against Employers Over Hiring," *Los Angeles Times*, October 12, 1999.
4. On July 8, 2004, the Union of Needletraders, Industrial and Textile Employees (UNITE), merged with the Hotel Employees and Restaurant Employees union (HERE). UNITE-HERE was a founding member of the Change to Win coalition, and in 2006 had more than 450,000 members.

5. For a detailed description of the Salinas center, see Paul Johnston's (2002) "Organizing Citizenship: Teamsters Local 890's Citizenship Project" at http://www.new citizen.org/paul/publication/organizing_citizenship.doc.
6. Steven Greenhouse, "Labor Federation Forms a Pact With Day Workers," *New York Times*, August 10, 2006.
7. Steven Greenhouse, "Breakaway Unions Start New Federation," *New York Times*, September 28, 2005.

REFERENCES

AFL-CIO. 1959. *The World's Refugees: A Challenge to America*. Publication No. 98. Accessed at http://www.aflcio.org/aboutus/thisistheaflcio/convention/resolutions_ecstatements .cfm.

———. 1981. *Immigration Reform*. Executive Council Action, August 3, 1981, Chicago, Ill. Accessed at http://www.aflcio.org/aboutus/thisistheaflcio/convention/resolu tions_ecstatements.cfm.

———. 1987. *Immigration Policy*. Washington: 17th National Convention, October. Accessed at http://www.aflcio.org/aboutus/thisistheaflcio/convention/resolutions_ ecstatements.cfm.

———. 2000. *Immigration*. Executive Council Action, February 16, 2000, New Orleans, La. Accessed at http://www.aflcio.org/aboutus/thisistheaflcio/convention/resolu tions_ecstatements.cfm.

Bacon, David. 1999. "Labor Grapples with the INS." *The Progressive* 63(12): 33–35.

———. 2002. "Immigrant Meatpackers Join Forces with the Union and the Church." *Labor Notes* 280(July 2002): 1, 10–11.

Brownell, Peter. 2005. "The Declining Enforcement of Employer Sanctions." *Migration Information Source*. September 1, 2005. Accessed at http://www.migrationinforma tion.org/Feature/display.cfm?id=332.

Center for Responsive Politics. 2007. "Top Donors." Accessed at http://www.opense crets.org/.

Change to Win. 2006. March 1, 2006, letter to Arlen Specter and Patrick Leahy. Accessed at http://www.changetowin.org/issues/workers-rights/immigrant-workers-rights.html.

Delgado, Hector. 1993. *New Immigrants, Old Unions*. Philadelphia, Pa.: Temple University Press.

Fine, Janice. 2006. *Worker Centers: Organizing Communities at the Edge of the Dream*. Ithaca, N.Y.: Cornell University Press.

Fletcher, Bill, and Richard W. Hurd. 2000. "Is Organizing Enough? Race, Gender and Union Culture." *New Labor Forum* 6(Spring/Summer): 59–69.

Heinz, John P., Edward O. Laumann, Robert L. Nelson, and Robert H. Salisbury. 1993. *The Hollow Core: Private Interests in National Policy Making*. Cambridge, Mass.: Harvard University Press.

International Brotherhood of Teamsters (IBT). 2001 Resolution on Immigrant Workers, General Executive Board, January 2001.

Johnston, Paul. 2002. "Organizing Citizenship: Teamsters Local 890's Citizenship Project." Accessed at http://www.newcitizen.org/paul/publication/organizing_citizen ship.doc.

Knobel, Dale. 1996. *America for the Americans: The Nativist Movement in the United States*. New York: Simon & Schuster.

La Luz, Jose, and Paula Finn. 1998. "Getting Serious about Inclusion: A Comprehensive

Approach." In *A New Labor Movement for a New Century*, edited by Gregory Mantsios. New York: Monthly Review Press.

Labor Immigrant Organizing Network (LION). 1999. *Program: Conference on Organizing Immigrant Workers*, January 23, 1999. Oakland, Calif.: LION.

Mantsios, Gregory, editor. 1998. *A New Labor Movement for a New Century*. New York: Monthly Review Press.

Milkman, Ruth, editor. 2000. *Organizing Immigrants*. Ithaca, N.Y.: Cornell University Press.

———. 2006. *L.A. Story: Immigrant Workers and the Future of the U.S. Labor Movement*. New York: Russell Sage Foundation.

National Right to Work Foundation. 2007. Web site. Accessed at http://www.nrtw.org/.

Ness, Immanuel. 2005. *Immigrants, Unions, and the New U.S. Labor Market*. Philadelphia, Pa.: Temple University Press.

Ness, Immanuel, and Stuart Eimer. 2001. *Central Labor Councils and the Revival of American Unionism*. Armonk, N.Y.: M. E. Sharpe Publishers.

Olson, Mancur, Jr. 1965. *The Logic of Collective Action*. Cambridge, Mass.: Harvard University Press.

Roosblad, Judith. 2000. "Trade Union Policies Regarding Immigration and Immigrant Workers in the Netherlands (1960–1995)." In *Cultural Diversity in Trade Unions: A Challenge to Class Identity?* edited by Johan Wets. Burlington, Vt.: Ashgate Publishing.

Schlosser, Eric. 2001. *Fast Food Nation: The Dark Side of the All-American Meal*. New York: Houghton Mifflin.

Tichenor, Daniel J. 2002. *Dividing Lines: The Politics of Immigration Control in America*. Princeton, N.J.: Princeton University Press.

U.S. Census Bureau. 2007. Current Population Survey. Washington: Government Printing Office.

Watts, Julie. 2002. *Immigration Policy and the Challenge of Globalization: Unions and Employers in an Unlikely Alliance*. Ithaca, N.Y.: Cornell University Press.

Wells, Miriam. 2000. "Immigration and Unionization in the San Francisco Hotel Industry" in *Organizing Immigrants*, edited by Ruth Milkman. Ithaca, N.Y.: Cornell University Press.

Els de Graauw

Chapter 12

Nonprofit Organizations: Agents of Immigrant Political Incorporation in Urban America

Throughout American history, the religious, charitable, and educational organizations that constitute the category of 501(c)(3) nonprofit organizations have been important providers of services to the poor and other disadvantaged populations in American society. Three developments in the four decades since the Immigration and Nationality Act of 1965 help explain why these organizations have become more prominent as providers of various socioeconomic services to immigrants in particular. First, after the act renewed large-scale immigration to the United States, there was an increased need and demand for newcomer services. With political machines largely vanished, local party organizations not interested in reaching out to the new immigrants en masse, and labor unions divided on the immigration issue, nonprofit organizations catering to newcomers proliferated after 1965 (Berry with Arons 2003; Cordero-Guzmán 2001, 2005; Wong 2006). Second, as part of the Great Society programs of the mid-1960s and the federal government's Community Development Block Grant program enacted in 1974, the federal government contracted with nonprofit organizations to provide services to extinguish poverty and foster community development in poor urban areas where many immigrants resided. Third, the push for privatization of the American welfare state since the late 1970s meant that the government contracted more of its services to nonprofit organizations, which grew more dependent on government grants and contracts (Grønbjerg 1993, 2001; Marwell 2004; Salamon 1999; Smith and Lipsky 1993). Privatization further fueled the growth of the nonprofit sector by making nonprofit organizations the key vehicles for the provision of social services to the poor and other disadvantaged groups, including immigrants (Marwell 2004; Silverman 2005).

Given nonprofits' increased importance as providers of educational, legal, linguistic, health, employment, and other social services to immigrants in recent decades, I ask in this chapter what role 501(c)(3) nonprofit organizations play in structuring the political incorporation of immigrants in contemporary urban America. What role do nonprofit organizations play in mobilizing individual immigrants to civic and political action and what role do they play as political advocates for immigrants' group interests? I rely on an expansive understanding of immigrant political incorporation that includes the mobilization of immigrants' individual participation in electoral and nonelectoral politics as well as group empowerment through the representation of immigrants' collective interests vis-à-vis government institutions and actors (Jones-Correa 2005). On the whole, the current literature on nonprofit organizations has a bleak or negative view of nonprofits' political activism and suggests that nonprofits have a limited presence and little influence in local politics due to their tax-exempt status and government restrictions that limit these organizations' political activities (Berry with Arons 2003; Chaves, Stephens, and Galaskiewicz 2004). However, if yesteryear's ward politics—where effective organization of political power was inextricably linked to the provision of much-needed services to vulnerable populations—are indicative of the political significance of immigrant-serving organizations, then nonprofits may play an increasingly influential role in the local politics of immigrant political incorporation.

I argue that 501(c)(3) nonprofit organizations catering to immigrants— which I refer to as immigrant nonprofit organizations—are important political actors that are heavy lifters of immigrants' incorporation at the local level. Nonprofits not only facilitate the political participation of individual immigrants, as documented in the literatures on social capital and civic engagement, but also function as independent actors in local politics advancing the collective interests of the immigrant community. Immigrant nonprofits develop immigrants' political skills and resources, foster immigrants' political interest, and mobilize immigrants' civic and political participation. As advocates for and representatives of the larger immigrant community, immigrant nonprofits articulate immigrants' needs with government officials, shape the local political agenda with regards to immigrant issues, and engage in advocacy on immigrants' behalf with the local legislative branch as well as the local bureaucracy and the local judiciary. Immigrant nonprofits perform these various political functions within the bounds created by government regulations on tax-exempt entities. They participate in various aspects of local political life often under the guise that they are educating immigrants and local government officials alike. At the same time, government officials frequently invite nonprofits' political activism, and participation in the local political process is also part of many organizations' mission to serve the immigrant population. Although some immigrant nonprofits are active in national and transnational political issues, most of the organizations focus more exclusively on local and state issues. In particular, immigrant nonprofits serve as agents of community empowerment and representation that successfully influence local immigrant integration policies as a result of their knowledge and expertise on the immigrant community and their practical and pragmatic (rather than partisan or contentious) orientation toward the policy-making process.

DATA AND METHODS

I draw on a number of qualitative data sources collected between 2005 and 2007. They include data from semistructured interviews with forty-five nonprofit organizations catering to immigrants in San Francisco and elected officials and other public employees from the consolidated city and county of San Francisco. I interviewed executive directors and other paid staff of the nonprofit organizations. Each interview lasted one and a half hours on average and I conducted more than one interview with some staff members. In these interviews, I inquired after key organizational characteristics such as the nonprofits' service provision activities, composition of the organizations' clientele, various types of advocacy work and other political activities, and collaborations with other community-based organizations. In conversations with members of the San Francisco political establishment, I asked about these officials' interactions with nonprofits and the organizations' role in the local policy-making process around issues directly affecting the city's immigrant population. I complement these interviews with data from newspaper articles from the local mainstream and ethnic press, government reports, and a variety of secondary sources as well as observation of participants in meetings and hearings at San Francisco's city hall.

I focus on urban 501(c)(3) nonprofit organizations catering to immigrants, and those located in San Francisco in particular, for three reasons. First, nonprofits catering to immigrants continue to be located in urban areas even as more immigrants today settle in suburban and rural areas. Second, these organizations are heavily focused on the communities in which they operate and often are involved in the increasingly localized dynamics of immigrant integration. And, finally, San Francisco has a sizable immigrant population, a long history of community involvement in challenging social and political injustices, and a political environment generally hospitable to nonprofit organizations.[1] For these reasons San Francisco makes an opportune site to witness, document, and analyze nonprofits' role in structuring immigrants' political incorporation.

The organizations documented in this chapter do not constitute a random or representative sample of immigrant nonprofits. Instead, they are the most visible in San Francisco's immigrant nonprofit sector, which counts about 300 organizations.[2] I focus on organizations officially incorporated as 501(c)(3) nonprofits due to my interest in how their tax-exempt, not-for-profit status influences the kinds of political behaviors, tactics, and strategies they demonstrate in the local politics of immigrant incorporation. The forty-five organizations consequently are all 501(c)(3) public charities that serve broad public purposes and provide programs to benefit immigrants (see table 12.1). They also all have annual budgets greater than $25,000 and more than 40 percent of their clientele are first-generation immigrants. All but two have multilingual staff and the vast majority have staff and volunteers who are first- or second-generation immigrants. However, as table 12.2 shows, the organizations differ from each other in size of budget and number of paid staff, the range of immigrant nationality groups they cater to, the range and nature of services they offer, the extent to which they

TABLE 12.1   *San Francisco-Based Immigrant Nonprofits Interviewed*

African Immigrant and Refugee Resource Center	Lao Seri Association–Laotian Community Services
Arab Cultural and Community Center	Mission Learning Center
Arriba Juntos	Mujeres Unidas y Activas
Asian Perinatal Advocates	Partnership for Immigrant Leadership and Action
Asian Women's Resource Center	
Asian Women's Shelter	POCOVI
Cameron House	Refugee Transitions
Central American Resource Center	Richmond District Neighborhood Center
Chinatown Beacon Center	
Chinatown Community Children's Center	South of Market Childcare
Chinese for Affirmative Action	Southeast Asian Community Center
Chinese Newcomers Service Center	Upwardly Global
Chinese Progressive Association	Vietnamese Community Center of San Francisco
Curry Senior Center–North of Market Senior Services	
	Vietnamese Youth Development Center
Good Samaritan Family Resource Center	Visitacion Valley Community Center
Homeless Prenatal Program	West Bay Filipino Multi-Service Center
Irish Immigration Pastoral Center	Young Workers United
La Raza Centro Legal	

Source: Author's compilation.
Note: Twelve of the forty-five organizations I interviewed wish to remain anonymous.

combine service provision with advocacy activities, their age, and their sources of income. Although immigrant nonprofits with different organizational characteristics are likely to have variable presence and influence in local politics, I focus here on what unifies 501(c)(3) nonprofits as actors mediating immigrants' political incorporation at the local level.

TYPOLOGIZING IMMIGRANT NONPROFITS AS POLITICAL ACTORS

Although the forty-five immigrant nonprofits I surveyed provide an array of socioeconomic services, it would be a mistake to characterize them solely as service providers. They are increasingly combining service provision with advocacy campaigns and political activism. Some organizations voluntarily choose to enter politics with the realization that service provision and public policy advocacy are two interrelated activities that need to be pursued in unison to fulfill the organizations' mission to serve the needs and interests of the immigrant population. With their service provision activities, nonprofits fight the symptoms of a

TABLE 12.2   *Variety Among San Francisco's Immigrant Nonprofits, 2005*

Period nonprofit founded	Number (N = 45)
1868 to 1899	3
1900 to 1919	2
1920 to 1964	0
1965 to 1974	16
1975 to 1984	10
1985 to 1994	10
1995 to 2004	4
Number of paid staff (less than 20 hours per week)	
1 to 5	9
6 to 10	5
11 to 20	17
21 to 30	6
31 to 40	1
More than 40	7
Percent foreign-born paid staff (less than 20 hours per week)	
0 to 20	7
21 to 40	9
41 to 60	10
61 to 80	6
81 to 100	13
Annual budget	
$25,000 to $100,000	4
$100,001 to $250,000	4
$250,001 to $500,000	7
$500,001 to $1,000,000	13
$1,000,001 to $1,500,000	5
$1,500,001 to $2,000,000	8
Over $2,000,000	4
Government funding as percentage of annual budget	
0	9
1 to 20	1
21 to 40	8
41 to 60	11
61 to 80	8
81 to 100	8
Percent foreign-born clientele	
40 to 60	13
61 to 80	12
81 to 95	10
96 to 100	10

TABLE 12.2   *Continued*

Origins of foreign-born clientele[a]	Number (N = 45)
China and Hong Kong	21
Other Asian Countries	21
Mexico	20
Central and Latin America	18
Africa	6
Former Soviet Union	5
Europe	3
Middle East	2

Source: Author's compilation.
[a] I asked each nonprofit organization to identify up to four countries from which their foreign-born clients came.

limited public service system. With their advocacy activities, they fight the root causes of the injustices immigrants experience in American society. In describing the mission of her nonprofit, which serves Hispanic immigrants in San Francisco's Mission District, the executive director explained, "Our mission is to promote a just and equal society and the way we do that is through the provision of direct legal services and a community empowerment-style of advocacy. And the reason we do it this way is that we recognize that services alone don't challenge the causes of the injustice or inequality; you need advocacy for that as well."[3] Other immigrant nonprofits, however, have entered politics only reluctantly, often out of fear of losing their public funding. As a result of retrenchment of government spending, nonprofits that are dependent on government funding have been forced to advocate for public funding with government officials in efforts to secure the survival of their organizations. As the executive director of an organization catering to Asian immigrants said, "Ideally, we would like to focus more exclusively on service provision to the immigrant community, but with all these funding cuts we need to advocate for government money if we still want to get some."[4] Whatever the impetus behind their greater involvement in local political affairs, immigrant nonprofits are more properly conceptualized as multipurpose hybrid organizations rather than as service providers (Hasenfeld and Gidron 2005; Minkoff 2002). It is because of these organizations' hybridity that they are well situated to affect the civic and political participation of the immigrants they serve and the representation of immigrants' collective concerns with local government officials. It is also because of this hybridity that immigrant nonprofits are able to develop the unique informational resource they leverage with local government officials to have input in the local policy-making process.

As providers of an array of socioeconomic services, these nonprofits meet needs no longer met by shrinking public human and social service programs that face contracting federal and state budgets. Immigrant nonprofits provide services in a culturally and linguistically competent way and offer a nonthreatening environment in which immigrants feel comfortable seeking assistance. Consequently, they have earned immigrants' trust and are able to build support for their organizations and services among the immigrant community they serve. Simultaneously, through service provision and daily interaction with immigrants, immigrant nonprofits collect valuable information about the people they serve, which puts them on the frontline of developing, assessing, and articulating immigrants' needs. As a staff member of a nonprofit serving immigrants in San Francisco's Mission District said, "We know the immigrant community like no one else, and the folks at city hall know it."[5]

Nonprofits' expertise on the immigrant community translates into a source of power vis-à-vis local government officials, who would struggle to learn about the needs and interests of a large portion of the city's residents without these nonprofit allies. As recipients of public monies, immigrant nonprofits naturally enter into communications with various city officials and agencies and they have opportunities to bring the needs and interests of a politically controversial and obscure as well as economically vulnerable population to the attention of top levels of local government. Government-nonprofit contractual relations consequently set in motion a policy feedback loop (Pierson 1993) that provides immigrant nonprofits with opportunities to advocate on immigrants' behalf with the San Francisco Board of Supervisors (the city's legislators), the mayor, city departments, and various other local government agencies. In sum, as hybrid organizations combining service provision with political advocacy, immigrant nonprofits are able to build their political capital from the bottom up as well as from the top down. Due to their position as a bridge between the powerless immigrant community and the powerful members of the San Francisco political establishment, immigrant nonprofits are strategically positioned to have a presence and influence in the local politics of immigrant incorporation.

Immigrant Nonprofits: A Distinct Type of Actor in Urban Politics

The nonprofit and political science literatures pay little attention to immigrant nonprofits as agents structuring immigrants' political incorporation in urban America. The lack of attention can perhaps be explained by the fact that they are still largely conceived of as service providers reluctant to engage in politics because of government regulations limiting tax-exempt entities' political activism. At the same time, the lack of understanding can perhaps be attributed to the fact that they are not easily classified with other collective political actors that partake in local politics and policy making, such as social movement organizations, civic organizations, yesteryear's urban machines, and interest groups. (see table 12.3)

Immigrant nonprofit organizations share with social movements a desire to challenge the American political system and both types of organizations embrace social change. However, most of the organizations I looked at rely more heavily on conventional political tactics and strategies than social movement organizations do, their work is proactive and planned rather than reactive and spontaneous, they work with local government officials rather than around them, and they provide a variety of socioeconomic services in addition to their political activism. At the same time, nonprofits are not like civic organizations either. Civic organizations are mostly member-serving organizations whereas nonprofits are largely client-serving. Both need to maintain good relations with their donors, but the key relationship for nonprofits is not one with their members, but rather one with the larger immigrant community and other disadvantaged city residents. This client or public orientation finds expression in nonprofits' communitarian pursuits and advocacy for policies benefiting public—rather than special or members only—interests. Although nonprofits and yesteryear's urban machines both emphasize a reciprocal relationship with those who receive nonprofit or machine services, partisan ideologies do not color immigrant nonprofits' political work to the same extent as they did for machines. Immigrant nonprofits do not operate on a vote maximization rationale like the urban machines of the past did.

Arguably, immigrant nonprofits most closely resemble interest groups in that both types of organizations—in the language of political theorist Hanna Pitkin (1967)—are motivated to speak for, act for, and look after the interests of their clients or constituents in the political process. Nonprofit organizations, however, are subject to more government restrictions and regulations on their political activities than are interest groups. While the American structure of government actively invites interest groups to participate in the political process, federal law actively discourages 501(c)(3) nonprofits from engaging in overly political activities (Berry with Arons 2003). The financial incentives these organizations enjoy under U.S. tax law—they do not pay income tax on their revenue and donor contributions are tax-deductible—are accompanied by limitations on what these organizations can do in the political realm. Federal tax law bars 501(c)(3) organizations from partisan politics at any level of government (they cannot endorse or directly campaign for a candidate or party, donate money to a candidate or party, or distribute materials aimed at influencing the outcome of an election) and places restrictions on their lobbying activities. Legally, 501(c)(3) nonprofits are allowed to lobby, but the lobbying must be an "insubstantial part" of their overall activities (Lunder 2006).[6] According to Jeffrey Berry and David Arons (2003), these government restrictions—as well as governmental scare tactics warning tax-exempt organizations not to engage in politicking[7]—help explain why many nonprofits are reluctant to engage in public policy advocacy and other overly political activities for fear of losing their tax-exempt status.

Under federal law, lobbying is conceived of narrowly. Only advocacy before

TABLE 12.3   *Immigrant Nonprofits Compared with Other Collective Political Actors*

Social movement organizations	• Similar: challenge the status quo and advocate for social change • Different: immigrant nonprofits rely on more conventional political strategies and tactics of influence; collaboration rather than contention; simultaneously provide services
Civic organizations	• Similar: foster civic engagement; importance of donors • Different: immigrant nonprofits are mostly client-serving (not member-serving) and consequently more publicly spirited
Yesteryear's urban machines	• Similar: reciprocal nature of service delivery • Different: immigrant nonprofits are less partisan; less active in electoral politics
Interest groups	• Similar: speak for, act for, and look after the interests of their clients or constituents in the political process • Different: immigrant nonprofits are subject to more government restrictions and regulations on their political activities; less partisan; more exclusively informational power; more likely to serve the public (rather than special) interest

Source: Author's compilation.

a legislature with the goal of influencing legislation is subject to limitations. Many forms of political activity by nonprofits are not limited under federal law. These unrestricted political activities include advocacy with administrative departments, city commissions and boards, and the judiciary; nonpartisan analysis and research on all sides of a policy or legislative issue; invited public testimony before any government body; and instances when a nonprofit organization engages with stakeholders in discussions of broad social, economic, and political problems (Harmon, Ladd, and Evans 2000; Lunder 2006). With the legal constraints on nonprofits' political activism generally overstated, there are many safe and unrestricted opportunities for immigrant nonprofits to undertake political work at the local level. However, because some nonprofits do not understand the full extent of federal tax law, the psychological barriers to political activism are more genuine. That is why many immigrant nonprofits feel more comfortable directing their advocacy energies at the local bureaucracy and administrative agencies rather than the local legislature. When they do advocate with the local legislature, nonprofit staff make a point of emphasizing that their organization's advocacy does not constitute an instance of politicking or lobbying in the traditional sense of the word, where it refers to the attempt to influence the passage or defeat of legislation. Rather, their advocacy is intended to educate local legislators on all sides of a particular immigrant issue or is in a response to a request from local legislators for that organization's input. The staff member of an organization serving Chinese immigrants in San Francisco's Chinatown, for example, tried to make clear to me that what her organization does is supposedly not political. "We don't really do politics," she said. "Instead we serve immigrants and educate and tell government employees what our immigrants need. Yes, we advocate, but we don't lobby. It's better that way."[8]

Nonprofits also differ from interest groups in that they have a distinct source of power vis-à-vis local government officials. Interest groups are often politicized entities that attempt to influence government officials of a particular partisan persuasion with a combination of votes, campaign contributions, and information. The power of nonprofit organizations in the local political arena derives more exclusively from their informational expertise on immigrants, a population that rational government officials occupied with the maximization of their vote share are more likely to ignore (Aldrich 1993). In communicating with local elected officials, immigrant nonprofits emphasize that city officials need to take into account the needs and interests of the many immigrants who live in San Francisco if the city is to function properly and provide a safe and healthy work and living environment for all city residents. A review of mission statements reveals that many immigrant nonprofits are motivated by social justice and civil rights goals, but they are adept at switching codes and their interactions with government officials tend to be free from such ideological language and emphasize what are practical policies to help the city and immigrant population move forward. In adopting a practical and pragmatic approach to local politics and policy making around immigrant issues, immigrant nonprofits put themselves in a position where they can influence local politics and policies across partisan lines and work with liberal as well as more conservative government officials. Such an approach also pushes the nonprofits to adopt a cooperative rather than a challenging or adversarial stance toward local government officials.

The comparison of immigrant nonprofit organizations with other collective political actors makes clear that immigrant nonprofits form a unique type of urban political actor likely to make a unique contribution to local power dynamics and political outcomes. As 501(c)(3) tax-exempt entities with government restrictions on their political activism, immigrant nonprofits experience pressures to modify which government institutions and actors they target with their advocacy as well as how they frame and package their advocacy claims. They are more likely to direct their advocacy campaigns to the local executive and judiciary, resulting in what might be thought of as delayed or reactive representation for immigrants as these branches are not the policymakers, but rather the implementers and adjudicators of policies passed by the local legislature. At the same time, they are likely to bring a variety of ethnic and cultural diversity issues to the attention of local government officials, but will package these in nonpartisan and practical language while emphasizing the educational and collaborative nature of their intervention in the local policy-making process. This shows that ethnic and cultural diversity issues in urban societies do not necessarily have to translate into contestation and conflictual urban politics, as argued by scholars ranging from Robert Dahl (1961) to Romain Garbaye (2005). Also, as organizations with a unique informational source of power and staff members dedicated to immigrant integration issues, it is difficult for public officials to ignore them; these organizations have an unmistakable voice in the local politics of immigrant integration and are not easily co-opted by other governmental and nongovernmental institutions at the local level. A staff member of an organization serving immigrants and refugees of different nationalities summarized well how government regulations have shaped his organization's advocacy strategy and how his organization is different from other collective political actors at the local level. With an air of humor and resignation, he said, "I don't think we have the same bargaining power that unions and lobby groups do, for example. All we can try to do is killing [government officials] with kindness and information. We take every possible opportunity to tell [government officials] about the people we serve. And we let [government officials] know that we want to work with them so that in partnership we can better serve the immigrants and refugees who come to us for help. What else can we do?"[9]

NONPROFITS AND IMMIGRANTS' CIVIC AND POLITICAL PARTICIPATION

As agents structuring immigrants' political incorporation at the local level, the effects of immigrant nonprofits are two-fold. First, they facilitate access to civic and political participation on the part of individual immigrants. Second, immigrant nonprofits function as independent actors in local politics representing the needs and interests of the immigrant community at large.

The immigrants that the forty-five organizations I interviewed serve tend to have limited English skills and little formal education. Many are not American citizens and some are living in the United States without legal documentation. Most live on poverty wages. These characteristics render immigrants a politically obscure population whose interests often are ignored by mainstream political institutions (Jones-Correa 1998; Ramakrishnan 2005; Wong 2006) and by most studies of political participation and political behavior (Rosenstone and Hansen 1993; Verba, Schlozman, and Brady 1995; Wolfinger and Rosenstone 1980). These characteristics also make immigrants' civic and political participation challenging in the American political system where skills and resources, political interest, and mobilization explain individual-level political participation (Rosenstone and Hansen 1993; Verba, Schlozman, and Brady 1995). Through their service provision and advocacy work, nonprofits help immigrants acquire the language skills and informational resources that facilitate their participation in civic and political life at the local level. They change immigrants' predisposition toward local politics so they become more willing participants in the local policy-making process. They also provide opportunities for immigrants to participate in civic and political life and actively mobilize their participation. In sum, nonprofit organizations lower barriers to immigrants' civic and political participation.

Developing Skills and Resources

Immigrant nonprofits provide a range of socioeconomic services on a day-to-day basis that give immigrants the capacity to participate in local civic and political life. Most organizations, for example, provide English-language instruction and citizenship classes either in-house or in collaboration with other nonprofits at an off-site location. Better command of the English language and a basic understanding of the American governmental process facilitate immigrants' participation in local politics. In interviews, nonprofit staff often mentioned that immigrants' linguistic isolation is the most important impediment to immigrants' socioeconomic and political advancement and makes it difficult for immigrants to communicate with San Francisco city officials even as the city has made great strides in recent years to provide multilingual access to government services. Furthermore, nonprofits are among the first organizations immigrants encounter after their arrival in the United States. As such, they are an important clearinghouse for information on immigrants' access to public services. They educate immigrants about which city officials to contact in response to particular needs or problems and how city agencies work. In this process, immigrants become better equipped to navigate the institutional hurdles of a civically and politically active life.

Fostering Political Interest

Immigrant nonprofits also foster immigrants' interest in local political affairs. The organizations make their clients understand that immigrants—whether American citizens or not—have access to various public services as a matter of right, and that they can and should speak up when the services they receive through nonprofit organizations are threatened with funding cuts. It was not uncommon for me to hear stories about nonprofit staff who emphasized in interactions with their clientele that immigrant participation in San Francisco's allocative process is instrumental in helping to secure continued public funding for the nonprofit service provider. The English as a second language (ESL) instructor of an organization serving elderly Chinese immigrants explained it this way: "During class time we make it clear to our students that their input is crucial for the continued provision of language and citizenship classes, and we invite them to come to city hall with us to let the politicians know just how important these classes are to them. We'll even drive them there; make an excursion out of it."[10] I attended various hearings at San Francisco's city hall where immigrants filled the public stands and provided coached testimony to the Board of Supervisors and other public officials about the importance of a particular nonprofit organization and the services it provides. The nonprofits in effect foster political interest among their immigrant clientele by emphasizing the reciprocal relationship between the organization and its clients and by emphasizing that immigrants' continued enjoyment of nonprofit services in a climate of funding cuts partly depends on their participation in the local allocative process. Although political interest is generated among an organization's immigrant clientele, frequently this is done around a narrow set of issues related to service provision, funding allocation, and organizational survival.

On a more intermittent basis and as organizational resources permit, immigrant nonprofits also try to get immigrants interested in a broader set of political issues. Around election time, for example, nonprofit organizations collaborate with other community-based organizations to organize forums where members of the immigrant community learn about important election issues, candidates running for local and state office, and candidates' positions on issues of specific relevance to the immigrant community. Additionally, a few nonprofit organizations conduct their own research—often on specific issues of importance to the immigrant community, such as language rights, wage disputes involving undocumented immigrants, and consumer fraud involving elderly immigrants—and share their findings with the immigrant community and local government officials. In doing this, nonprofits hope to stimulate a dialogue between immigrants and government officials and activate a policy response to remedy the problem identified as affecting immigrants. Nonprofit organizations thus foster immigrants' interest around a wider set of political issues, but often on the cyclical basis of elections or when issues affecting immigrants have reached crisis proportions and a government response is deemed necessary.

Mobilizing Participation

Nonprofit organizations also function as mobilizing agents that recruit immigrants' participation in local political life. They mobilize immigrants to participate in the election process, but also in the policy-making process and extra-electoral actions such as protests, marches, and demonstrations. These initiatives target naturalized and noncitizen immigrants alike. Nonprofits' efforts to bring immigrants into the political system are important in current times when political parties do not have a strong presence in the mobilization of immigrants more generally and noncitizen immigrants more specifically. Nonprofits become even more important as mobilizing agents in localities where there are even fewer incentives for political parties to reach out to immigrants, such as in California—a state that is not a battleground state—and San Francisco—a city that has neither a clear party structure nor party competition.

With regard to electoral participation, many immigrant nonprofits encourage eligible immigrants to register to vote and turn out on Election Day. They recruit immigrants who cannot vote to volunteer their time for activities such as voter registration drives and precinct walks. In terms of the local policy-making process, nonprofits recruit their immigrant clientele to attend public hearings, provide public testimony, and share with government officials their personal experiences and frustrations of living in the United States as an immigrant. Often immigrants are recruited to participate in the local policy-making process to influence allocation decisions that impact nonprofits as well as policy decisions that affect the larger immigrant community. Finally, nonprofits mobilize immigrants to participate in protests, marches, and demonstrations. In 2006, for example, many nonprofits recruited their immigrant clientele and other immigrants to take to the streets in support of equal rights for immigrants and in opposition to new federal immigration reform proposals.[11] Holding banners and dressed in t-shirts bearing the names of various organizations, nonprofit staff and their immigrant clientele marched through downtown San Francisco and held large rallies at city hall to bring to the public's attention their opposition to proposed immigration reforms.

Evaluating Nonprofit-Induced Civic and Political Participation

The political interest and participation that nonprofits induce, however, tends to be narrowly focused as it largely flows from a nonprofit-client relationship that emphasizes reciprocity or the expectation to give back.[12] As recipients of nonprofit services, immigrants are encouraged to give back to the organization by participation in the political process on behalf of that organization. Immigrants benefit from a variety of socioeconomic services the nonprofit organizations provide. Struggling with funding cuts, nonprofits engage in advocacy at the local level aimed at securing future government funding, continued service provision, and organizational survival. They turn to their clients for support. Immigrants, for example, are recruited to attend activities sponsored by the organizations and testify at public hearings to convey to government officials the important role that nonprofit organizations play in their lives. Immigrants consequently develop an interest in political affairs and are recruited to participate in local civic and political life, but often this happens around a narrow set of organizational issues, resulting in what might be termed organizational incorporation as opposed to a more broadly conceptualized political incorporation. Nonprofits induce immigrants to participate in local politics, but self-interested organizational ends and resource management concerns often form the basis of that participation. It is therefore not certain that there are spillover effects into other aspects of political life and that immigrant nonprofits provide a gateway into participation beyond nonprofit organizational concerns at the local level.

A second important characteristic of the civic and political participation that nonprofit organizations bring about is that it targets not only naturalized citizens, but also noncitizens and undocumented immigrants. Given the inability to vote on the one hand and dubious immigration status on the other, these immigrants find themselves at the margins of the polity and tend to go unnoticed by political parties and elected officials. Because many nonprofits engage in nonelectoral political activities where the inability to vote is inconsequential, noncitizens and undocumented immigrants are also mobilized to participate in local civic and political affairs. Ten of the forty-five organizations stated—in line with postnationalist conceptions of membership—that they also reach out to noncitizens and undocumented immigrants because of their belief that one is entitled to participate in local politics based simply on one's residence in a particular locality. U.S. citizenship and legal documentation, they believe, should not determine one's ability to become politically active in local affairs. This subset of organizations therefore does not inquire after citizenship or documentation status. The executive director of an organization serving Mexican immigrants said, for example, "[immigrants] live here, they work here, they pay taxes here, they have friends here, and they have children that go to school here. I think it is only natural that they can participate in the decisions that affect their community here. I don't think it matters if they're not citizens of this country."[13] Because nonprofits reach out to these immigrants long before political parties take notice of them and because they provide immigrants with their first experience of American government and social institutions, these organizations are likely to be important shapers of immigrants' political interests and participation.

Finally, nonprofit mobilization is often selective and limited (Wong 2006). Nonprofits do not generally have the resources to mobilize a very large number of immigrants. They tend to focus on those immigrants who already have a basic level of skills, resources, and interest that facilitate active political participation. For example, they provide political leadership training to those who already have affinity with the political process and mobilize for public testimony those with the confidence to speak in public and the time to sit through hours of public hearings. Nonprofits, however, were successful in turning out large numbers of immigrants in 2006 to protest federal immigration reform proposals. This effort was possible because nonprofits collaborated with labor unions, religious institutions, and other community-based organizations, and because all these institutions were opposed to the immigration reform proposals for one reason or another. Their consensus was on the harm the proposals would bring to both the immigrant community and the organizations and individuals that help undocumented immigrants. Mobilizing immigrants to political action is more likely when it is a collaborative effort between nonprofits and other community institutions and when it is in response to a broadly shared concern or perceived threat.

NONPROFITS AND THE LOCAL POLITICS OF IMMIGRANT REPRESENTATION

Immigrant nonprofits also interact with a variety of local government officials in four aspects of the policy-making process with the aim of influencing local policy and representing the collective interests of the immigrant community. These stages include articulating needs and setting agendas, seeking access to decision-making arenas, legislative advocacy, and monitoring, shaping, and challenging legislation through administrative and judicial advocacy. I briefly address each of these and discuss San Francisco's Equal Access to Services Ordinance to demonstrate how nonprofits' intervention in the local policy-making process has played out in the case of one policy that directly affects San Francisco's newcomer population.

Needs Articulation and Agenda Setting

Immigrant nonprofits help set agendas by identifying, problematizing, and politicizing key issues that affect the immigrant population. Specific issues that nonprofits in San Francisco have articulated as important to the immigrant community and placed on the political agenda include equal access to government information and services, affordable housing, public transportation, education, neighborhood safety, rights in the workplace, and voting rights for noncitizens.[14] Often in collaboration with other immigrant nonprofits, organizations survey their clientele to assess immigrants' needs, conduct background research for proposed policies, develop pro-immigrant positions, and communicate their research and policy proposals to elected and appointed public officials, local print and broadcast media (especially the ethnic media), and the communities they serve. In doing so, nonprofits function as needs articulators, agenda setters, and public watchdogs in local politics and policy making.

Accessing the System

Immigrant nonprofit organizations also regularly access the San Francisco political apparatus and contact members of the political establishment. Nonprofit staff travel to city hall—acting on an invitation from public officials or of their own volition—to attend legislative and administrative hearings, to testify to provide substantive and technical advice to the Board of Supervisors and city agency heads (such as the mayor's office, the Department of Elections, the Human Services Agency, and the Immigrant Rights Commission), or to participate in task forces and advisory groups (including the Nonprofit Contracting Task Force, the Cultural Competency Task Force, and the Sweatfree Procurement Advisory Group). Likewise, staff members maintain phone, email, and fax contact with elected and appointed officials to express concern about topics such as funding, legislation, and developments in broad policy areas including the lack of affordable housing and increased crime rates in immigrant-dense neighborhoods. Staff members also attempt to stay in touch with officials simply to remain on their radar screen. In addition, immigrant nonprofits host district supervisors, their staff, and department heads at community events (such as important festivities and community organizing events) and nonprofit functions (such as fundraising galas), and often invite public officials to observe specific nonprofit programs and services. My interview data suggest that immigrant nonprofits find it easy to access the San Francisco political system and believe that elected and appointed officials are receptive to their concerns and requests. San Francisco government officials listen to immigrant nonprofits, which—as a result of years of dedicated service to immigrants—have developed an expertise on the immigrant community that government officials willingly use to develop local policies. As one San Francisco legislator put it, "I sometimes don't have enough eyes and ears to learn about the changing needs of the people in my district. Community organizations are indispensable in this regard; they are my eyes and ears on the ground."[15] At the same time, the city's relatively liberal political culture might also explain why city officials are more accepting of input in the policy-making process by nonprofit organizations. "For us nonprofits that want in on local decision making, San Francisco is a Mecca of some sorts," remarked an individual who currently works for a nonprofit organization catering to the Asian Pacific Islander community in San Francisco and who previously worked for a politically active immigrant nonprofit organization in New York City.[16]

Legislative Advocacy

Nonprofit organizations also use legislative advocacy, or lobbying, to influence the local policy-making process. Within the limits set by federal law, nonprofits lobby local government officials to bring about legislative outcomes they favor and resist outcomes they do not favor. Often lobbying activities are an attempt to influence allocation decisions or to secure access to continued city funding for immigrant programs and services. For example, one nonprofit catering to low-income Chinese immigrant families in San Francisco secured a $300,000 grant from the city's Human Services Agency. This grant, however, was not enough for the organization to meet the overwhelming need for its services. The agency's executive director therefore appeared before the Board of Supervisors to advocate for additional funding, brought along clients and staff to provide testimony on behalf of the organization, and succeeded in securing an additional $200,000 from the city's general fund. Immigrant nonprofits also advocate with the Board of Supervisors and the mayor for specific policies with a direct effect on the city's immigrant population (including affordable housing policies, crime prevention policies, the Equal Access to Services Ordinance, job creation programs, and the City of Refuge Ordinance). Immigrant nonprofits engage in a substantial amount of advocacy with the local legislature, but it does not violate federal limits on nonprofits' lobbying. In many cases, local legislators invite immigrant nonprofits to testify before the Board of Supervisors during public hearings and request to be educated on the problems facing the city's immigrant population. Federal law does not limit legislative advocacy by nonprofits that results from invitations by government officials, that is educational, or that provides nonpartisan analysis of a policy issue.

Administrative and Judicial Advocacy

Immigrant nonprofit organizations are even more active in administrative and judicial advocacy aimed at monitoring, shaping, and challenging local policies after their enactment. Specifically, many nonprofits target city departments, city agencies, and the local court system. This type of activity is not limited by law and is distinguishable from legislative advocacy, which is aimed at the city's Board of Supervisors and focuses on issues yet to be codified into local law.

Because many nonprofit organizations contract with city agencies to provide services, they are well situated to evaluate the effectiveness and shortcomings of government programs and policies. As direct service providers firmly rooted in the communities they serve, nonprofits can serve as a barometer of social and economic conditions in the immigrant population and can identify new concerns that should be addressed with updated administrative rules and procedures. Through frequent interactions with city departments and agencies, such as the Human Services Agency, the Metropolitan Transportation Agency, and the Mayor's Office of Community Development, the immigrant nonprofits I surveyed continuously interact with administrative staff to adjust the ways through which policies are implemented. For example, numerous nonprofits engaged in administrative advocacy by challenging the reporting requirements different city departments used to track nonprofits with government contracts. Furthermore, in recent years, nonprofit organizations have monitored the implementation of the city's Equal Access to Services and Minimum Wage Ordinances and coached and pressured city departments and San Francisco employers, respectively, to fully comply with both city laws.

Immigrant nonprofits also use legal action to challenge unfriendly policies and practices at the local level, but this is more likely to happen when the party challenged is not part of San Francisco government. They bring disputes challenging unfair labor practices against immigrants to the small claims court and report violations of the Minimum Wage Ordinance to the city attorney. Additionally, when nonprofits detect a pattern of abuse against immigrants, as has been the case with telecommunications fraud of non–English-speaking Chinese and Hispanic immigrants and violation of tenant rights for elderly immigrants, the organizations have advocated with the district attorney's office and filed class action suits to end the abuse.

Evaluating Nonprofits as Political Actors in Local Politics

Immigrants are likely to hold distinct views on a number of local issues central to their lives but of marginal importance to most Americans. It is therefore important—especially for cities and states with sizable immigrant populations such as San Francisco and California—that immigrants' views on such issues as language rights, housing, policing, English as a second language (ESL) education, and driver's licenses and health care for undocumented immigrants are known to public officials and that their needs are adequately met through government policies. My data on immigrant nonprofits based in San Francisco reveals the important ways in which these nongovernmental institutions make public officials pay attention to the concerns of immigrants and, in doing so, help build a more democratic system of governance that incorporates the interests and needs of immigrants who live in our midst. Immigrant nonprofits are especially notable for their presence and weight in local politics with regard to material issues of importance to the immigrant community—such as language acess, health care, and labor rights. They are also relevant for more symbolic reasons, however. For example, immigrant nonprofits have successfully advocated with local government officials for getting part of San Francisco's Tenderloin neighborhood renamed Little Saigon in 2004 and, in 2005, getting a park in the South of Market district named after Victoria Manalo Draves, to date the only woman of Filipino ancestry to win an Olympic gold medal. Such measures are likely to create a local context where immigrants feel welcomed and appreciated. As is clear from the research demonstrating that immigrants' political incorporation increases in such welcoming contexts (Bloemraad 2003, 2006), immigrant nonprofits are important as organizational vehicles that prod government officials to pass policies of material and symbolic importance that in turn create an environment that invites immigrants' participation in political affairs.

As actors in local politics, immigrant nonprofits engage in activities that give immigrants a voice in the local political process. In many cases, immigrant nonprofit advocacy is elite-led issue advocacy that fits more closely with the republican model of representation—where immigrants are largely spoken for by others—rather than a grassroots empowerment model—where immigrants directly engage with local government officials and speak on their own behalf. A handful of immigrant nonprofits provide political leadership training that helps immigrant recipients of nonprofit services develop the skills and resources to take charge of their political destiny. For the majority of organizations I surveyed, though, nonprofit staff members—who tend to be second-generation immigrants with U.S. college degrees—organize advocacy campaigns from which the larger immigrant community benefits. Although they are important in giving immigrants a voice in local politics, these processes of political representation and group empowerment are not as invigorating as they could be if the immigrants themselves had more agency and played a more prominent role.

San Francisco's Equal Access to Services Ordinance

According to the 2000 census, 46 percent (or 341,079) of San Francisco's residents five years and older speak a language other than English at home. About 13 percent (99,659) have limited English proficiency, meaning that they speak English not well or not at all, and 13 percent of households (43,710) are linguistically isolated and lack proficiency in English. Asian immigrants are by far the most isolated: in 66 percent of all linguistically isolated households (28,840) an Asian Pacific Island language is spoken (see table 12.4). Sustained immigration since 1965 created a linguistic diversity challenge for San Francisco. Given that government business is largely conducted in English, San Francisco's increased linguistic diversity made it challenging for government officials to effectively communicate with city residents. Immigrant nonprofits have long advocated for the need to have government business conducted in languages other than English. In response to these pressures, the San Francisco Board of Supervisors passed the Equal Access to Services Ordinance (EASO) in 2001. This law removes language barriers that limited-English speakers may have in accessing city services. EASO requires city departments to translate their paperwork in non-English languages and hire bilingual staff for public contact positions if enough of those using their

TABLE 12.4   *Language Diversity in San Francisco, 2000*

	Number	Percentage
Population five years and older	745,650	100.00
Language other than English spoken at home	341,079	45.7
Spanish	89,759	12.0
API language	194,584	26.1
Other Indo-European language	49,788	6.7
Other language	6,948	0.9
Speak English not well or not at all	99,659	13.4
Ability to speak English by language spoken at home		
Speak Spanish at home	89,759	100.00
Speak English not well or not at all	23,026	25.7
Speak API language at home	194,584	100.00
Speak English not well or not at all	68,040	35.0
Speak other Indo-European language at home	49,788	100.00
Speak English not well or not at all	7,975	16.0
Speak another foreign language at home	6,948	100.00
Speak English not well or not at all	618	8.9
Linguistically isolated households by language spoken at home[a]		
Total households	329,850	100.00
Linguistically isolated households	43,710	13.3
Total of linguistically isolated households	43,710	100.00
Spanish	7,548	17.3
API language	28,840	66.0
Other foreign language	7,322	16.8

Source: U.S. Census Bureau (2000).
Note: API = Asian Pacific Islander.
[a] A linguistically isolated household is one in which all persons aged fourteen and over speak a language other than English and none speaks English "very well." In other words, all household members aged fourteen and over have at least some difficulty with English.

services do not speak English effectively because it is not their primary language and if they share another primary language. Because of EASO, public information and government services in San Francisco need to be offered in English, Chinese, and Spanish citywide. In certain supervisorial districts with a high concentration of Russian, Filipino, and Vietnamese immigrants, branch offices of city departments are also required to offer city services in Russian, Tagalog, and Vietnamese. A brief overview of the legislative history of this policy demonstrates that immigrant nonprofits dominated the policy-making process from beginning to end. The story of EASO is not intended to create the impression that nonprofits are omnipotent political actors with all types of local policy issues, but it does show the political potential and versatility of nonprofits in the local politics of immigrant representation.

San Francisco's Equal Access to Services Ordinance was several years in the making and finds its origins in an initiative by a statewide coalition of nonprofit organizations to address language rights and access to government services. During the 1990s, many nonprofits received complaints from immigrants that they were not able to access city, county, and state services due to their inability to speak English. Nonprofit organizations consequently ended up doing the translation work that was, according to existing federal and state laws, the responsibility of the government. In theory, Title VI of the 1964 Civil Rights Act and the 1973 Dymally-Alatorre Bilingual Services Act should have been providing access to government services to limited-English speakers, but in reality noncompliance was common and these laws were not enforced. When complaints became widespread and were more systematically recorded in the late 1990s, a number of nonprofit organizations from across the state acted on the collective awareness and organized to ensure proper compliance with existing federal and state laws. This coalition, however, was operating in a political environment characterized by hostility to immigrants and opposition to language rights.[17] It was also not clear that they would succeed if they simply lobbied state officials with data generated by their own organizations. Aware of the constraints under which they were operating, the coalition of nonprofit organizations made the strategic move to successfully ask for a state audit of the Dymally-Alatorre Bilingual Services Act (DABSA) with the help of Senator Martha Escutia (D-Montebello). The 1999 California state auditor's report on DABSA concluded that "state and local governments could do more to address their clients' needs for bilingual services" and gave the nonprofit organizations the objective facts necessary to convince government officials that DABSA lacked enforcement and that there was widespread noncompliance with the law (California State Auditor 1999). The auditor's findings also demonstrated that limited-English speakers did not enjoy access to government information and services on par with those proficient in the English language. After the report was released, various bills were introduced in the California assembly and senate that led to DABSA's being amended in 2002 and 2003 to improve implementation and tighten enforcement mechanisms.

As proposals were circulating at the state level to amend DABSA, policy action in San Francisco created a local law that would ensure equal access to government services for limited-English speakers across a greater number of city departments and on a more consistent basis. Chinese for Affirmative Action (CAA), one of the nonprofits that had been part of the statewide coalition requesting the state audit, took the lead in getting an Equal Access to Services Ordinance passed in San Francisco. CAA is a San Francisco-based 501(c)(3) nonprofit with service and advocacy programs catering to Asian immigrants and Asian Americans. Founded in 1969, CAA has advocated for laws and policies to protect and expand the rights of limited-English speakers for many years. It spearheaded the effort for an equal access law in San Francisco and collaborated throughout the policy-making process with a small number of other city-based 501(c)(3) nonprofits catering to immigrants from different nationality groups. CAA also enjoyed the support of a local labor union with an immigrant membership. Labor unions as well as other types of community institutions, however, remained rather aloof throughout the policy-making process and the enactment of EASO—from setting the agenda to implementing the law—was dominated by nonprofit organizations that had an effective monopoly on policy makers' attention.

The first attempt to get EASO passed in 1999 failed. CAA and collaborating organizations had drafted the language of the bill and found then-supervisor Mabel Teng willing to sponsor the policy. However, the bill never received a hearing with the board and fizzled in the absence of strong leadership from local legislators and the mayor's office. From this early failure, CAA learned that it had assumed more political support than there really was in 1999 and realized that it had to work much harder to get both policy makers and the local community engaged with the issue so the language policy could pass. CAA and its nonprofit allies renewed their efforts to get EASO passed in 2001—after the city switched from at-large to district elections, resulting in an important change to the composition of the Board of Supervisors. This time they were successful. CAA asked then Supervisor Mark Leno to become the lead sponsor of the bill. This was a strategic calculation on the part of CAA. Leno was the chair of the Finance Committee (through which the bill had to travel), he was considered to be a rising star on the Board of Supervisors, he maintained a relatively good relationship with the mayor's office, and he once owned a San Francisco-based sign company that produces multilingual signs. In other words, he would be able to provide strong leadership on the issue and was personally engaged with the policy proposal. As the bill made its way to the full Board of Supervisors, CAA and other immigrant nonprofits frequently met with individual supervisors and the Immigrant Rights Commission to get them engaged with the issue, share the organizations' substantive knowledge on the issue, and answer questions the supervisors and commissioners might have.[18] For example, CAA helped calm concerns that certain supervisors had about the cost of EASO as the policy called for translating a variety of government documents into Chinese and Spanish and hiring bilingual staff who would receive additional pay. CAA also helped Supervisor Leno prepare an adequate response to the criticism from Supervisor Tony Hall, who maintained that the policy amounted to affirmative action for Asians and Latinos who would likely be given preferential treatment for the bilingual public contact positions that EASO called for. The nonprofits recruited their staff and clientele to offer testimony in support of EASO during hearings of the finance committee and the full Board of Supervisors. They also drummed up support by submitting letters to the editor of the *San Francisco Chronicle* defending the policy, accepting interviews from reporters from the local ethnic media, and launching educational campaigns targeted at other community-based organizations in San Francisco. This impressive campaign to engage and educate government officials and the larger public paid off and EASO was approved by all eleven supervisors, with the exception of Tony Hall.

After Mayor Willie Brown signed EASO into law, CAA and other nonprofits did not disappear from the political scene. Rather, they took on the daunting task of getting reluctant city departments to implement EASO and provided technical assistance to help city departments comply with the new law. To these ends, they collaborated with the Immigrants Rights Commission, the government body responsible for monitoring and facilitating compliance with the ordinance and charged with the duty to resolve disputes arising under the ordinance. CAA, other nonprofit staff, and the executive director of the Immigrant Rights Commission met with department heads on various occasions to help them determine which documents needed translation and which positions should be staffed by bilingual personnel. They helped various departments formulate the annual compliance plans they are required to submit to the commission. A few city departments supported the policy and made its implementation a priority, but a larger number were less supportive and argued that they had too few resources and too little time to implement EASO.

Since the enactment of EASO, immigrant nonprofits have continued to hear from immigrants unable to receive city services because of their weak English skills and resulting inability to communicate with public officials. Despite complaints that city departments were not fully implementing EASO, nonprofit organizations only filed two official complaints—one against the Rent Stabilization and Arbitration Board in 2002 and one against the Metropolitan Transportation Agency in 2004—on behalf of immigrants willing to go through the complaint procedure. To date, nonprofits have not taken legal action against the city departments for failure to comply with EASO, even though they might have built a strong case against the city during the years immediately after the law's enactment. Immigrant nonprofits are reluctant to take a more confrontational position with government officials for practical reasons. They do not want to undermine the trust and collaboration they have been able to establish over the years. The nonprofits also receive government funding, which also explains why they prefer to maintain amicable relations with city officials.

When, five years after enactment, the Immigrant Rights Commission and several nonprofits believed that city departments had been given adequate time to fully implement EASO, they collaborated on research and a report. The report, published in February 2006, documented the (partial) noncompliance of various city departments with the ordinance and advised the Board of Supervisors to strengthen the law's enforcement mechanisms and make additional resources available to implement and monitor EASO (San Francisco [California] 2006). The report induced the Board of Supervisors to hold public hearings in May 2006, at which a number of department heads were called on to explain why they had not been able to bring their operations in line with EASO in the preceding five years. The report also got supervisors interested in the possibility of amending EASO and codifying the recommendations that came out of the report. In 2006 and 2007, the Board of Supervisors continued to work with the Immigrant Rights Commission, CAA, and other immigrant nonprofits on proposals to amend EASO.

Nonprofit organizations consequently played a key role in the making of EASO and dominated the policy-making process from beginning to end: CAA and its allies identified the need for EASO, put the policy on the city's legislative agenda, drafted the text of the law, advocated for its passage, monitored the implementation of the ordinance since its enactment in 2001, and negotiated with local government officials in 2006 and 2007 to amend the law. San Francisco government officials are well aware of the critical role the nonprofits played and admit they are not entirely sure what would be the state of equal access to government services in San Francisco today had those organizations not been so dedicated to the issue over the years and had they not expended such efforts on engaging local government officials. As a local legislator working on the amendment in 2006 and 2007 said, "Look at the stacks of files on my desk. I have so many issues I need to attend to and so many things I need to know about. It's hard to prioritize. If it wasn't for CAA and the other community organizations, it might have taken us much longer to legislate language access, I might not have realized the importance of the ordinance, and I might not have been interested in revisiting the issue today."[19]

CONCLUSIONS

Nonprofit organizations, then, are important institutions that structure the political incorporation of immigrants in contemporary urban America. Nonprofits in San Francisco provide numerous socioeconomic services to the city's immigrants, facilitate the political participation of individual immigrants, and engage in legislative, administrative, and judicial advocacy to advance nonprofit organizational interests as well as the collective interests of the immigrant community. One drawback, however, is that they tend to work at the local level, in particular on organizational resource management issues, and might not mediate participation in the larger national polity. A second drawback is that many nonprofits provide elite representation, which continues to sideline many immigrants as public policies that directly affect them are established.

Despite a mixed evaluation, it is clear that these organizations constitute a distinct type of urban political actor. Immigrant nonprofits are most noteworthy for their broad understanding of what constitutes politics and political advocacy. Strategically responding to the federal regulatory environment that restricts their political activities, these organizations have come to see that politics encompasses more than the popular, but narrow, conception of politics as limited to state institutions and legislative and partisan politics. Immigrant nonprofits in San Francisco see politics as including nonlegislative activities on the part of nongovernmental institutions. As a result, these nonprofits engage in administrative and judicial advocacy targeting the city's executive and judicial branches of government. Politics also includes nonpartisan and collaborative politics, where even in a city like San Francisco—which lacks party structure and party competition and where nonprofit organizations perform functions seemingly complementing those of the state—immigrant nonprofits participate in political life at the local level.

San Francisco in many ways provides a unique setting for the study of nonprofit organizations that cater to immigrants. The city has a liberal political culture and is relatively more tolerant of nonprofit political activism around issues affecting controversial populations of immigrants. Its nonprofit sector is mature and entrepreneurial nonprofits have a relatively good understanding of which types of politicking are legal and acceptable and which are not. The city's institutional openness, though, does not make nonprofits' success inevitable or guarantee the passage of immigrant friendly policies. My narrative of the Equal Access to Services Ordinance demonstrates that—despite a hospitable political context—immigrant nonprofits still had to put up a political fight and make strategic calculations and decisions to secure their policy-making success in San Francisco. Having played a critical role in the fight over San Francisco's language policy, these organizations can also be critical in the political fights over immigrant policies in other localities. Indeed, similar developments can be observed in other established American gateway cities. Research by a number of immigration scholars reveals that nonprofit political activism around immigrant issues is taking place in New York, Chicago, and Los Angeles (Cordero-Guzmán 2001; Jones-Correa 1998; Marwell 2004; Wong 2006). San Francisco-based organizations are perhaps the avant-garde of advocacy for immigrants' local integration, but nonprofit political activism on immigrant issues is by no means limited to San Francisco.

NOTES

1. With nearly 800,000 residents, San Francisco is the fourth largest city in California. According to the 2000 U.S. Census, this number includes just over 285,000 foreign-born individuals (37 percent of the population) and about 122,000 noncitizens (16 percent). By way of comparison, only 11 percent of the American population are foreign-born and only 7 percent are noncitizens (U.S. Census Bureau 2000).

2. I base my estimate of 300 immigrant nonprofit organizations in San Francisco on a directory of immigrant nonprofits I put together in the course of my research. My directory brings together information from existing nonprofit databases and referrals from immigrant nonprofits I contacted. Databases and directories I consulted include the San Francisco Community Services Directory (San Francisco Public Library), HelpLink (United Way of the Bay Area), the California Database of the Institute for Nonprofit Organization Management (University of San Francisco), California Charitable Trust, and databases at the National Center for Charitable Statistics (Urban Institute in Washington, D.C.). Included in my directory are immigrant nonprofit organizations that officially incorporated as 501(c)(3) tax-exempt entities and a few organizations that are fiscally sponsored by a 501(c)(3) nonprofit organization (the latter is an indication that they themselves are likely to become an independent 501(c)(3) organization). This directory, like my sample of organizations surveyed for this chapter, is biased towards the more formally organized groups catering to immigrants in San Francisco and is most likely an under-count of the actual number of nonprofit organizations catering to the city's immigrant population.

3. Interview, April 25, 2006.

4. Interview, February 28, 2006.

5. Interview, January 26, 2006.

6. There is a second standard that 501(c)(3) organizations can use to ensure that their lobbying activities are in compliance with federal law. This second standard is known as the "section 501(h) expenditure test" and was added to the Internal Rev-

enue Code in 1976. If 501(c)(3) nonprofit organizations elect for the 501(h) status, they are covered by clearly defined lobbying rules and benefit from more generous limits on lobbying. To date, only a very small percentage (about 2.5 percent) of 501(c)(3) nonprofits nationwide have elected to become 501(h) entities (Berry with Arons 2003). Section 501(h) was enacted to clarify the much-criticized and ambiguous "insubstantial part" test. The 501(h) rule is sometimes referred to as the 20% rule and establishes specific dollar limits that are calculated as a percentage of a nonprofit's total budget. With the 501(h) status, a 501(c)(3) nonprofit can use up to 20 percent of the first $500,000 of its budget for legislative lobbying work. For organizations with larger budgets, these dollar amounts slide upward until they reach a $1 million cap. Cost-free lobbying activities, such as legislative advocacy by volunteers, do not count toward an organization's lobbying limit under the 501(h) expenditure test. However, organizations that exceed their limit will initially receive a steep fine and repeat offenders will lose their 501(c)(3) tax-exempt status (Harmon, Ladd, and Evans 2000; Lunder 2006). Seven of the forty-five San Francisco-based immigrant nonprofits I surveyed told me they have the 501(h) election.

7. For example, over the summer of 2006, the Internal Revenue Service sent letters to 15,000 churches warning them that these tax-exempt organizations' politicking could endanger their tax-exempt status (Stephen Clark, "IRS Warns Churches to Stay Neutral on Politics," *Los Angeles Times*, July 18, 2006, B3).
8. Interview, March 29, 2006.
9. Interview, April 28, 2005.
10. Interview, December 16, 2005.
11. It is interesting to note that H.R. 4437—the Border Protection, Anti-terrorism, and Illegal Immigration Control Act of 2005, the immigration reform proposal sponsored by Congressman James Sensenbrenner—would criminalize support to undocumented immigrants, including information and services immigrant nonprofits provide to undocumented immigrants. Nonprofit staff members who took to the streets in 2006 told me that they were animated to do so because of the harm the reform proposals would bring to both the immigrants they serve and the organizations they work for.
12. Nicole Marwell (2004) similarly speaks of reciprocal relationships between a number of community-based organizations in New York City and their clientele. Marwell, however, does not specifically focus on nonprofit organizations serving immigrants.
13. Interview, May 10, 2005.
14. With regard to these policy domains, immigrant nonprofit organizations have advocated on behalf of such immigrant-friendly local policies and resolutions as the City of Refuge Ordinance (1989), Equal Access to Services Ordinance (2001), INS Raid-Free Zone Resolution (1999), Minimum Compensation Ordinance (2000), and the Sweatfree Contracting Ordinance (2005). Immigrant nonprofits have also advocated for immigrant-friendly city ballot measures (such as Proposition L (2003, passed), setting San Francisco's minimum wage above the federal and California minimum wages, and Proposition F (2004, failed), allowing noncitizens with children in the San Francisco school district to vote in school board elections) and state policies (most noteworthy in recent years is the fight over Gil Cedillo's AB 1463 (2001), AB/SB 60 (2002, 2003), and SB 1160 (2004), allowing undocumented immigrants to obtain California driver's licenses).
15. Interview, December 7, 2006.
16. Interview, February 22, 2006.

17. In 1998, Proposition 227—the English for the Children initiative—passed with 61 percent of the vote. This California initiative virtually ended bilingual education in public schools. Earlier, in 1994, Proposition 187 passed with 59 percent of the vote, denying social services, health care, and public education to undocumented immigrants.

18. The Immigrant Rights Commission was created by the San Francisco Board of Supervisors in 1997 and functions as a consultative body whose primary duty it is to provide advice and make recommendations to the Board of Supervisors and the mayor on issues affecting San Francisco's immigrant population.

19. Interview, December 7, 2006.

REFERENCES

Aldrich, John H. 1993. "Rational Choice and Turnout." *American Journal of Political Science* 37(1): 246–78.

Berry, Jeffrey, with David F. Arons. 2003. *A Voice for Nonprofits*. Washington: Brookings Institution Press.

Bloemraad, Irene. 2003. "Institutions, Ethnic Leaders, and the Political Incorporation of Immigrants: A Comparison of Canada and the United States." In *Host Societies and the Reception of Immigrants*, edited by Jeffrey G. Reitz. La Jolla, Calif.: UCSD, Center for Comparative Immigration Studies.

———. 2006. *Becoming a Citizen: Incorporating Immigrants and Refugees in the United States and Canada*. Berkeley, Calif.: University of California Press.

California State Auditor. 1999. "Dymally-Alatorre Bilingual Services Act: State and Local Governments Could Do More to Address Their Clients' Needs for Bilingual Services." Sacramento, Calif.: Bureau of State Audits.

Chaves, Mark, Laura Stephens, and Joseph Galaskiewicz. 2004. "Does Government Funding Suppress Nonprofits' Political Activity?" *American Sociological Review* 69(April): 292–316.

Cordero-Guzmán, Héctor R. 2001. "Immigrant Aid Societies and Organizations." In *Encyclopedia of American Immigration*, edited by James Ciment. Armonk, N.Y.: Sharpe Reference.

———. 2005. "Community Based Organizations and Migration in New York City." *Journal of Ethnic and Migration Studies* 31(5): 889–909.

Dahl, Robert A. 1961. *Who Governs? Democracy and Power in an American City*. New Haven, Conn.: Yale University Press.

Garbaye, Romain. 2005. *Getting into Local Power: The Politics of Ethnic Minorities in British and French Cities*. Oxford: Blackwell Publishing.

Grønbjerg, Kirsten A. 1993. *Understanding Nonprofit Funding: Managing Revenues in Social Services and Community Development Organizations*. San Francisco, Calif.: Jossey-Bass.

———. 2001. "Markets, Politics, and Charity: Nonprofits in the Political Economy." In *The Nature of the Nonprofit Sector*, edited by J. Steven Ott. Boulder, Colo.: Westview Press.

Harmon, Gail M., Jessica A. Ladd, and Eleanor A. Evans. 2000. *Being a Player: A Guide to the IRS Lobbying Regulations for Advocacy Charities*. Washington: Alliance for Justice.

Hasenfeld, Yeheskel, and Benjamin Gidron. 2005. "Understanding Multi-purpose Hybrid Voluntary Organizations: The Contributions of Theories on Civil Society, Social Movements and Nonprofit Organizations." *Journal on Civil Society* 1(2): 97–112.

Jones-Correa, Michael. 1998. *Between Two Nations: The Political Predicament of Latinos in New York City.* Ithaca, N.Y.: Cornell University Press.

———. 2005. "Bringing Outsiders In: Questions of Immigrant Incorporation." In *The Politics of Democratic Inclusion*, edited by Christina Wolbrecht and Rodney E. Hero. Philadelphia, Pa.: Temple University Press.

Lunder, Erika. 2006. "Tax-Exempt Organizations: Political Activity Restrictions and Disclosure Requirements." CRS Report RL33377. Washington: Library of Congress, Congressional Research Service. Accessed at http://www.ombwatch.org/npadv/PDF/CRSReportonTaxexemptorganizationsRestrictions.pdf.

Marwell, Nicole P. 2004. "Privatizing the Welfare State: Nonprofit Community-Based Organizations as Political Actors." *American Sociological Review* 69(2): 265–91.

Minkoff, Debra. 2002. "The Emergence of Hybrid Organizational Forms: Combining Identity-Based Service Provision and Political Action." *Nonprofit and Voluntary Quarterly* 31(3): 377–401.

Pierson, Paul. 1993. "When Effect Becomes Cause: Policy Feedback and Political Change." *World Politics* 45(4): 595–628.

Pitkin, Hanna F. 1967. *The Concept of Representation.* Berkeley, Calif.: University of California Press.

Ramakrishnan, S. Karthick. 2005. *Democracy in Immigrant America: Changing Demographics and Political Participation.* Palo Alto, Calif.: Stanford University Press.

Rosenstone, Steven J., and John Mark Hansen. 1993. *Mobilization, Participation, and Democracy in America.* New York: Macmillan.

Salamon, Lester M. 1999. *America's Nonprofit Sector: A Primer*, 2nd ed. New York: Foundation Center.

San Francisco (California). 2006. "Report Concerning the Status of San Francisco's Equal Access to Services Ordinance." City and County of San Francisco: Immigrant Rights Commission.

Silverman, Robert Mark. 2005. "Caught in the Middle: Community Development Corporations (CDCs) and the Conflict between Grassroots and Instrumental Forms of Citizen Participation." *Community Development* 36(2): 35–51.

Smith, Steven Rathgeb, and Michael Lipsky. 1993. *Nonprofits for Hire: The Welfare State in the Age of Contracting.* Cambridge, Mass.: Harvard University Press.

U.S. Census Bureau. 2000. Summary File 3 data. Washington: Government Printing Office.

Verba, Sidney, Kay Lehman Schlozman, and Henry E. Brady. 1995. *Voice and Equality: Civic Voluntarism in American Politics.* Cambridge, Mass.: Harvard University Press.

Wolfinger, Raymond, and Steven J. Rosenstone. 1980. *Who Votes?* New Haven, Conn.: Yale University Press.

Wong, Janelle S. 2006. *Democracy's Promise: Immigrants and American Civic Institutions.* Ann Arbor, Mich.: University of Michigan Press.

Chapter 13

Civic Engagement Across Borders: Mexicans in Southern California

"How can we encourage the Latino community to participate in the voting process? Through these hometown associations, you have the potential to inform and educate the community on the value of engaging in the civic process. It is important that immigrants know the impact they can have in the United States."
—Congresswoman Grace Napolitano (D-CA 38), addressing a leader of Jalisco-based Hometown Association at Immigration Hearing University of California, Los Angeles, August 14, 2006[1]

"Before, we would not turn our attention sufficiently towards our communities here in the United States. But the moment we are typecast as criminals, that is the critical point at which we must decide to combat that image and demonstrate that we are contributing members to this society."[2]
—Past president, Federation of Puebla Clubs of Southern California

In the spring of 2006, cities across the United States organized one of the largest public demonstrations in American history to challenge federal immigration legislation proposed by Congressman James Sensenbrenner in December 2005. The content of the Sensenbrenner-King bill, HR 4437, called for—among other things—the criminalization of undocumented immigrants in the United States as well as the individuals and institutions who assist them. This provision was perceived by immigrant rights advocates as outright hostile to immigrant communities across the country. The local level response to this legislation was the mobilization of millions of migrants across various American cities in repudiation of the bill and a call for an economic boycott to call attention to the indispensable role that immigrants play in the local, state, and national economies of the United States. In Los Angeles, this mobilization took place through a coordinated effort that included civic groups, religious organizations, labor unions, immigrant-serving organizations, youth, business, and a wide array of social actors across diverse sectors of the city. Another formidable player in this historic social and civic manifestation was a relatively less well-known and historically invisible segment of the Los Angeles organizational landscape—immigrant hometown associations.

Although not a new phenomenon in Los Angeles, hometown associations are beginning to emerge as visible and important actors in the civic, political, and social discourse around immigration in the United States. For example, the member federations and hometown clubs that form the Consejo de Federaciones Mexicanas en Norte America, or Council of Mexican Federations in North America (COFEM), an umbrella organization that in 2007 united more than ten state federations in Los Angeles, played a critical role in mobilizing immigrants at the base by disseminating information, organizing their constituents, and collaborating in an unprecedented manner in a process of coalition building. In many ways, this represented a milestone in these organizations' efforts to increase their civic presence in the United States. The consejo mobilized its base, which consisted of thousands of members at large, by drawing on a number of innovative grassroots strategies including organizing a rodeo show, concert, and cultural exposition in a local sports arena to galvanize members, and by holding a binational press conference one month later to announce their unequivocal support of the May 1 economic boycott.[3] The General Assembly, composed of the presidents of state federations, communicated not only with U.S.-based Spanish language media, but also with Mexican-based media by telephone, calling for the support of compatriots on both sides of the U.S.-Mexico border.[4] This act served to reaffirm Mexican hometown associations' distinct form of organizing, one that differs markedly from that of established U.S.-based organizations, which cater to immigrants and insist on a binational frame of reference. In the months following the March 25 and May 1, 2006, historic marches, leaders of immigrant hometown associations engaged in a series of public policy dialogues with elected officials both in California and Washington, D.C., to continue raising the profile of their respective organizations and giving voice to the needs of their immigrant constituents.

In essence, the various activities of these hometown groups in southern California are beginning to display what researchers describe as civic binationality—a mode of orientation that captures immigrants' simultaneous engagement with both Mexican and U.S. civil societies (Fox 2005, 11). This binational perspective holds much promise for increasing the level of U.S.-based civic engagement of immigrants since, as others have concluded, Mexican migrants—particularly those engaged in hometown associations—begin their civic participation by engaging in home country activities, and over time, they can potentially translate the skills learned through their homeland-based activities toward their communities in the United States (Fox, Selee, and Bada 2006, 40). This study builds on the recent work on immigrant transnationalism and attendant concepts of civic binationality and simultaneity of immigrant incorporation, to highlight how Mexican immigrant hometown associations represent a viable organizational arena for U.S.-based civic incorporation. These organizations recognize Mexican immigrants' strong desire to contribute to the betterment of their communities of origin even as they seek to integrate into American society. Simultaneity of incorporation and civic binationality, however, can be difficult to measure in quantitative terms. Moreover, as this research suggests, civic engagement can significantly tilt in one direction or the other—toward a Mexico- or U.S.-based agenda at particular social and political moments in the host or home country. Thus, rather than a simultaneous interaction equally weighted between the two societies at once, hometown associations most often display a desire to achieve a stage of civic binationality in which the priorities and activities of their home-land can be successfully interwoven with their growing U.S.-based activities. The simultaneous mode of immigrant incorporation that hometown associa-tions in Los Angeles appear to moving toward reveals that social and political threat—in the form of anti-immigrant legislation, racism, and physical deporta-tion—is not only a factor in how these groups orient their civic activities, but perhaps the very focal point motivating these efforts and influencing the extent to which these groups begin to elevate their civic and political presence in the United States.

THEORETICAL ISSUES: IMMIGRANTS AND SIMULTANEITY OF INCORPORATION

The incorporation of immigrants into their host societies has been the subject of numerous scholarly inquiries across a wide range of disciplines. Most recently, the growing literature on immigrant transnationalism has begun to shed light on the ways in which immigrants engage in modes of organizing that span geo-graphic and political borders. Transnationalism has been defined by some researchers as "the processes by which immigrants forge and sustain multi-stranded social relations that link together their societies of origin and settle-ment" (Basch, Glick Schiller, and Szanton Blanc 1994, 7). As immigrants move back and forth between home and host countries, they produce a transnational social field of deterritorialized nation-states.[5] This paradigm shifts attention away from traditional theories of assimilation that described migrants' identity as shifting to their new host society (Warner and Srole 1946; Gordon 1964). The assumptions undergirding these theories of assimilation rest on a one-to-one cor-respondence between length of residence in the new country and the shedding of cultural, regional, or parochial identities, which occurs as immigrants gradually loosen their ethnic ties and sentimental attachments to their home country. More recently, scholars have endeavored to reactivate the debate around assimilation by arguing for its relevance to contemporary immigrants (Alba and Nee 2003).

From a theoretical perspective, though, transnational theories of migration have offered an important corrective to previously held theories of immigrant adaptation by complicating our understanding of how identities are renegotiated across political and social boundaries. For example, the ethnographic research in this area has presented an invaluable framework and highlighted how ties and ac-tivities are forged across national and political borders (Levitt 2001). Other re-searchers have proposed a distinction between the grassroots, bottom-up model of migrant-led transnationalism that immigrant hometown associations embody, and the state-led transnationalism of federal, state, and local governments that seek to maintain migrants' loyalty through initiatives including matching funds programs and development projects (Goldring 2002).

A related body of literature has explored the increasing role that sending countries have begun to play in promoting and encouraging dual citizenship and the effect of this on prospects for immigrant incorporation into the United States. Traditional views of citizenship, in line with classic assimilation theory, have long held that immigrants must abandon home country attachments and undergo a process of naturalization and allegiance to host society. Recently, some have contended that dual nationality and citizenship seriously undercuts allegiance to the United States and hinders the process of assimilation (Huntington 2004; Renshon 2001). Implicit in this notion is the idea that migrants cannot maintain multiple memberships because doing so would potentially erode the traditional form of citizenship and belonging. Scholars, however, have proposed that dual citizenship may in fact promote incorporation of immigrants into their host society because it may "impart a sense of belonging, reinforcing their attachment to American values" (Schuck 1998, 164). As Irene Bloemraad noted, in some contexts "notions of traditional belonging remain relevant despite globalization" (2004, 420).

Other researchers proposed that Mexican immigrants, particularly those involved in hometown associations, regarded "the recuperation of political rights in the homeland as a first step to gain political rights in the host country" (De la Garza and Hazan 2003, 4). Dual nationality can be positively correlated with higher rates of naturalization, especially among Mexican immigrants in the United States, and particularly given that granting dual nationality for this group has arisen from bottom-up initiatives on the part of immigrants, who represent "a constituency in place ready to take advantage of this policy shift" (Jones-Correa 2001, 1022).

Perhaps most significant for my analysis in this study is Michael Jones-Correa's finding that the dramatic rise of naturalization rates following the anti-immigrant backlash in California and the passage of the Welfare Reform Act by Congress in 2006 suggests that "immigrants are still much more sensitive to changes in policies of receiving countries than to changes in sending country policies" (2001, 1023). In this chapter, I suggest that U.S.-based domestic policy shifts—in tandem with dual citizenship policies—appear to heighten the propensity of Mexican immigrants to thus engage in the civic process, particularly the naturalization process, but also unconventional civic and political activities, including boycotts and protests.

The civic organizations immigrants form can also play a critical role in whether—and to what extent—immigrants begin to simultaneously engage U.S.- and Mexican-based society. Researching findings from the Comparative Immigrant Organization Project undertaken by Alejandro Portes, Cristina Escobar, and Alexandria Radford (2007) revealed that the preponderance of the HTA model among Mexicans is positively correlated with greater Mexican governmental outreach, context of exit and reception from homeland to host country, and length of stay in the United States. Similar findings by other scholars highlight the ways in which the development agenda of Mexican hometown associations is the result of an instituted process that includes home state domestic politics, home state relationship to world system, a transnational civil society of migrants, and context of reception of migrants in United States (Smith 2003, 297; Ayon 2006).

Theoretical differences have emerged within the field of transnationalism, but Portes (2003) concluded that any understanding of the phenomenon must acknowledge its initial grassroots origins, its subsequent macrosocial consequences, and the overwhelming participation of established, first-generation immigrants within them. These theoretical convergences in the literature help lay an important foundation on which to conduct further studies. In his exhaustive study of Puebla migrants in New York, for instance, Robert Smith (2006) found that though first-generation immigrants are indeed the mainstay of Puebla hometown associations, transnationalism cannot be fully understood within this community without reference to the second-generation youth's engagement in transnational activities. Assimilation into New York life and transnational belonging are not incompatible experiences for these youth, argues Smith. Rather, they inform each other and generate complex understandings of immigrant identity and belonging.

Smith's (2006) work is a useful case study illustration of what Levitt and Glick Schiller call simultaneity—a useful model for "thinking of the migrant experience as a kind of gauge, which, while anchored, pivots between new land and transnational incorporation. Median point on gauge is not full incorporation, but rather, simultaneity of incorporation (Levitt and Glick Schiller 2004, 1011). The notion of simultaneity recalls Jonathan Fox's (2005) proposition that immigrants are engaging in new and different modes of integration—what he calls civic binationality, or what Gaspar Rivera-Salgado, Xochitl Bada, and Luis Escala-Rabadán described as the consolidation of a "migrant civil society" between Mexico and the Unites States (2005, 25). The new understandings of immigrant incorporation offered by the concepts of simultaneity and civic binationality, coupled with the emerging body of work on dual citizenship, provide powerful analytical tools with which scholars can now work with.

My research aims to build on these powerful theoretical lenses by proposing that, if, as Peggy Levitt and Nina Glick Schiller explained, the migrant experience is the gauge between here and there, then, more specifically, social and political moments characterized by exclusion and hostility toward the immigrant community in the host country are the pivot shaping a binational civic agenda. The emphasis on specific political and social moments allows us to better understand and assess the degree to which simultaneity represents a transitional moment or a more protracted process of immigrant incorporation. In this regard, hometown associations are an illustrative case study of immigrants' desire to be full participants of both societies and of the manner in which the interplay of immigration, context of reception, and policy shifts in the home and host country with respect to immigrant citizenship and belonging is significantly influencing organizational goals, tactics, and activities across physical and cultural borders.

RESEARCH DESIGN AND METHODS

This chapter explores the manner in which civic binationality has begun to unfold among Mexican immigrant hometown associations by examining the following research questions:

- How do the initial formation of hometown associations and their organizational features influence their degree of civic presence in the host society, as well as their relation to U.S.-based Latino and mainstream organizations?

- What are explanatory factors driving HTAs' attempts toward leveraging their mass membership to engage in U.S.-based issues and concerns that in many ways preceded the mass mobilizations in 2006?

- What role is institutionalization playing in providing Mexican hometown groups a viable channel for translating skills learned through civic voluntarism in their home country activities onto a U.S.-based agenda?

This research draws on in-depth qualitative interviews with hometown association leaders and members across southern California as well as extensive fieldwork conducted from 2005 through 2007, including attending organizational meetings, conferences, and events. Structured interviews were conducted face to face and had an average length of one hour. Organizations were identified through various methods including Internet research and the use of a listing of Mexican hometown federations provided by the Mexican Consulate Office in Los Angeles. Currently, twenty-four state federations are registered with the Mexican Consulate Office in Los Angeles. The consejo currently serves as the umbrella organization for more than ten state federations. The universe of hometown associations that form the backbone of the organization is quite extensive. For example, Nayarit unites thirty-one HTAs, Puebla thirty-nine, Guanajuato eleven, and Yucatan six. Most important, individual HTAs can count up to 300 members within their group. Other large hometown federations in Los Angeles include the Federation of Jalisco Clubs of Southern California, with 128 HTAs, and the Federacion Zacatecana del Sur de California (FZSC), or Federation of Zacatecan Clubs of Southern California, with seventy-five.[6]

Prospective interviewees were contacted by email or phone and organizations were selected through a method of snowball sampling that relied on informant referrals. Organizations from diverse regions in Mexico were targeted for this study, including the recently formed, such as the Federation of Hidalgo Clubs, established in 2004, and the long-standing, such as the FZSC, established more than twenty years earlier. A total of seventeen interviews were conducted with immigrant hometown associations representing the following regions in Mexico: Hidalgo, Jalisco, Nayarit, Puebla, Yucatan, and Zacatecas. The sampling strategy was to conduct interviews with federations, contacted through the website of the Mexican consulate in Los Angeles, followed by interviews with presidents of individual hometown associations. This study consequently does not capture the full range of activities of other state federations and hometown groups that were not reached. Nonetheless, it does cover substantial regional diversity through the state federations. It also relies on reporting in mainstream and ethnic newspapers and participant observation at meetings, festival, and leadership training sessions.

The southern California communities represented in this study include those cities with a long-standing history of immigrant reception as well as new and emerging immigrant receiving localities. Zacatecan migrants, for instance, have a long tradition of migrating to southern California, and several of the hometown associations interviewed for this study, including Club Fraternidad Las Animas, have members living in largely established immigrant communities including East Los Angeles and Norwalk. The same is true of Club San Pedro, with members residing primarily in Whittier and Montebello. This is also the case with hometown groups from Jalisco such as Club San Martin de Bolaños, who, like Zacatecan migrants, have established strong settlement patterns in southern California, particularly in such communities as La Puente, El Monte, and East Los Angeles. Club Cañadas de Obregon, representing long-term immigrant residents from Jalisco, has a membership base primarily in the areas east of Los Angeles, including Pico Rivera and Whittier. In contrast to these organizations, recently formed state federations and hometown associations from Puebla and Yucatan incorporate both newer and more established immigrants. Club Coat, of the Federation of Puebla Clubs, for example, has members residing primarily in south Los Angeles, whereas Yucatecan migrants have developed a strong community base in Inglewood. The areas of eastern Los Angeles—including East Los Angeles, Whittier, Montebello, El Monte, and La Puente—thus represent heavily immigrant-settled communities. The communities in south Los Angeles are in the midst of an influx, primarily immigrants from the state of Puebla and Yucatan. Southeast Los Angeles communities—including Bell, Huntington Park, and Lynwood—include large numbers of immigrants from the state of Colima. Orange County communities—including Santa Ana, Garden Grove, and Anaheim—have also emerged as immigrant destinations in recent decades, with a large number of immigrants from Jalisco, Yucatan, and Nayarit settling in these areas.

HISTORICAL ORIGINS AND LIFE-CYCLE OF MEXICAN HOMETOWN ASSOCIATIONS

Mexican hometown associations in southern California have a long and varied history. A proper understanding of their origins and life cycle entails placing them within a discussion of early twentieth-century U.S.-Mexico history. George Sanchez (1993) provided one of the most definitive accounts of this period by highlighting the central role the Mexican government played in promoting the growth and activities of mutual aid organizations. The Mexican Revolution and the 1911 overthrow of the Porfirio Diaz government propelled the migration of Mexican citizens to the north. In the wake of revolution, the government led by Álvaro Obregón launched a new effort in the 1920s to "shape local institutions and programs and instill patriotism among the Mexicanos de afuera (Mexicans abroad) (1993, 109). This was a major attempt on the part of the Mexican government to reach out to its expatriate community through its consulates. Protecting the rights of Mexicans in the United States figured prominently in the mission statement and duties of the Mexican consulate (as it continues to the present), but, as Sanchez noted, in the postrevolutionary period, another important factor was at play—the promulgation of a national identity to encourage return migration back to Mexico (1993, 113).

Rachel Sherman, in her study of modes of emigrant incorporation by the Mexican state, characterized this period (1917 to 1932) as one of state introversion. "The state was preoccupied with creating modern state institutions and gaining support in the wake of the Revolution: the quest for political legitimacy at home was the primary motivator behind its policies toward emigrants," she noted. "The intense nationalism that dominated public discourse meant that the logical mode of incorporation was introverted" (1999, 859–60). To achieve this objective, the Mexican state, through its consulate offices, bolstered civic and community activities aimed at solidifying the community's Mexican identity. This took the form of sponsoring patriotic festivals and parades organized by committees composed of community and business leaders within the immigrant community. The Comite Mexicano Civico Patriotico, for example, was founded in 1931 by Don Rafael de la Colina, general consul of Mexico in Los Angeles, and prominent businessmen to commemorate Mexican Independence Day through an annual parade in East Los Angeles, the largest Mexican parade in the United States.[7] On September 10, 2006, the comite celebrated its seventy-fifth anniversary by hosting its annual parade, which featured Latino local and state politicians, including Mayor Antonio Villaraigosa, Speaker of the Assembly Fabian Nuñez, and floats led by numerous hometown clubs and federations including Jalisco, Yucatan, Hidalgo, Puebla and Zacatecas. The procession also included prominent radio personalities, Mexican singers, and cultural presentations by hometown clubs.[8]

The enduring legacy of civic groups such as the Comite Mexicano Civico Patriotico in Los Angeles is a reminder of the deep historic roots of Mexican-based civic organizations, but perhaps more important, of the role the Mexican state played in creating some of these community institutions to foster Mexicanismo. In this respect, a form of transnationalism from above as described by Luis Guarnizo and Michael Smith (1998) was already under way in the early twentieth century, namely, the reconfiguration of social space and creation of governmental bodies outside the borders of the Mexican state. Although the aggressive outreach efforts of the Mexican state during the 1920s toward its immigrant compatriots would not resurface again until the late 1980s, the historical record and scholarship on this period of U.S.-Mexico relations reveals the unequivocal desire on the part of Mexico to create a strong institutional apparatus (represented by the consulate) to shape a strong Mexican identity among its expatriate citizenry as well as to defend and protect their rights in an often hostile anti-Mexican social and political environment.[9]

The transnationalism from above—articulated through the consular activities of the 1920s—laid an important foundation for the establishment of Mexican civic institutions whose goal of preserving Mexican culture and identity would continue in the decades to come. However, as Sanchez explained, a convergence of factors, including the Great Depression and the subsequent repatriation of Mexicans, would lead to a decline in the visibility of these institutions (1993).[10]

The Mexican government's interest and intervention in the Mexican-origin community in southern California resurfaced again in the late 1980s and again assumed prominence, particularly in the fifteen or more years beginning in the 1990s. The Mexican government's launching of the Programa para Comunidades Mexicanas en el Exterior (PCME), or Program for Mexican Communities Abroad, housed in the Secretariat of Foreign Relations signaled the first important step toward this new policy, and one that would have a decisive impact on the proliferation of hometown associations and federations in the 1990s and beyond (Leiken 2000). In 2000, a Presidential Office for Mexicans Abroad was created, followed by the Institute of Mexicans Abroad (IME) in 2002. The latter is the successor to the PCME, and is housed in the Secretariat of Foreign Relations.[11]

The formation of larger statewide federations that unite various hometown clubs coincides with this new shift in Mexico's policy toward Mexican immigrants. Yet the birth of the vast majority of hometown associations interviewed for this study predates the Mexican government's policy of *acercamiento*, or increasing closeness and contact with its diaspora. They were established much earlier—in the 1970s and 1980s—but on a grassroots level. These origins would weigh heavily in their life cycle, many of them undergoing periods of inactivity and organizational death, only to resurface again after a few years through the charismatic leadership of new members interested in revitalizing the group.

The origins also attest to the practice of a transnationalism from below that immigrants engage in to negotiate their membership in two nations. As Guarnizo and Smith (1998) pointed out, this transnationalism differs from transnationalism from above through the differences in power, scale, and resources available to transnational actors. Luin Goldring added another analytically useful framework by distinguishing between migrant-led and state-led transnational processes to "draw attention to the distinct role of transmigrant networks and agency in producing and reproducing transnational communities versus federal policies in maintaining transnational social spaces" (2002, 60). She thus provided an explanatory framework for understanding the life cycle of particular organizations. Table 13.1 illustrates this cycle, capturing the initial grassroots orientation of groups, and their increased interaction with state-led transnational activities of the Mexican state. The figure does not capture the life cycle and organizational trajectory of all hometown associations, but rather, the general course of change that some HTAs undergo, as described by the leaders and members interviewed for this study.

TABLE 13.1 *Hometown Associations' Organizational Life Cycle*

	Organizational Development and Resources	Collaborations and Alliances	Civic Presence
Stage 1: "Informal"	Few formal resources.	Groups function in self-contained manner.	Low in host and home country.
	Example: Soccer club is formed by family members and friends from El Rincon, Jalisco, to promote cultural identity and foster unity.		
Stage 2: Club formation	Members expand resources through fundraising dinners.	A few begin to emerge, including local hometown priest and Mexican Consulate Office in host society.	Low in host society; visibility grows in home country.
	Example: A pressing social concern in migrants' community of origin leads to the formation of a club, as is the case of Club Fraternidad Las Animas, Zacatecas, created in response to ecological hazards posed by a water waste treatment plant in Mexico.		
Stage 3: Federation affiliate	Fundraising capacity increases.	Partnerships with local and state representatives in home country are solidified through the three-for-one matching funds program.[a]	High in home country; leadership roles emerge; visibility grows in host society, especially within ethnic community.
	Example: Federation acts as the formal intermediary between individual clubs and Mexican state representatives to carry out social projects. The Federation of Puebla Clubs, for instance, is formed through the encouragement of the Mexican Consulate and eight existing clubs previously operating in an informal manner.		

| Stage 4: Council of federations | Grassroots fundraising continues and is accompanied by technical assistance and leadership seminars. | HTA interaction with home country agencies continues; HTA leaders engage U.S.-based Latino groups. | Institutionalization permits HTAs to attain greater visibility in host society and command attention of elected officials. |

Example: Following the immigrant rights marches in spring 2006, hometown association leaders representing such federations as Nayarit, Puebla, Yucatan, and several others met with members of the Congressional Hispanic Caucus Institute in Washington D.C. to engage in policy discussions around education, immigration, and health and discuss ways to leverage the strengths of immigrant hometown associations.

Source: Author's compilation.
Note: The life cycle of most hometown associations considered in this study is marked by various phases that begin with an informal group of migrants and results into a formal organization over time, a change prompted by social catalysts in the home country, incentives provided by Mexican-led transnational initiatives, and institutional ties with U.S.-based groups.

[a] This is a matching funds program in which every dollar donated by U.S. clubs is matched by local, state, and federal government in Mexico.

Hometown associations are originally established as informal groups of migrants, usually from the same extended family. At this first stage, the groups exist primarily as a social function: to bring migrants together for camaraderie or to maintain cultural and religious traditions. The Club El Rincon, a Jalisco-based association with 350 members at large, for instance, began as a sports club, as the ex-president of the group explained:

> I initially got involved by being president of a sports club. I saw the need for us [immigrants] to keep ourselves busy in a healthy environment. I began to see that the people needed leadership. Sports really helped to unify us. It was in 1982 that we first began to contemplate the idea of creating a more formal club, because I began to see that the people in the sports club would come to me asking for help, like burial services for a family member who had just died. I felt the need to do something. I went to the Mexican consulate to ask how I might go about doing that.[12]

The informal character of these groups in their initial stages is precisely their appeal to new immigrants. Moreover, the entry costs associated with participation are minimal to none. Similar to Club El Rincon, Club Santa Rita, which formed in 2004, began as a group of Jalisco migrants who met regularly in a Garden Grove park to play soccer. The men were later approached by their Mexican hometown's local mayor to form a club to work on social and productive projects to help with the hometown community's economic development.[13] Club San Martin de Bolaños, of the Federation of Jalisco Clubs, began with a group of relatives wanting to help the hometown church by financing annual patriotic fiestas. In 1995, as interest grew in helping the hometown in other ways, the priest of San Martin de Bolaños encouraged the group, which was made up of about five migrants representing families in the United States, to become a more formal club.[14] Initially focused on the hometown church renovation, the group of Jalisco migrants then turned its attention to the needs of the elderly and proposed the construction of a day home, one of the first three for one projects the group has embarked on. Mexico's three for one program is a matching funds scheme by which every dollar donated my migrants is matched by the federal, state, and local governments.

Other hometown associations in the Los Angeles area were related to environmental issues, such as the Club Fraternidad Las Animas of the Federation of Zacatecan Clubs of Southern California (FZCSC) and the Federation of Yucatecan Clubs. As the president of Club Fraternidad Las Animas explained, this HTA was motivated by the hometown church's involvement in exposing the ecological hazards posed by a water waste treatment plant in the community of Las Animas in Zacatecas. The club president alerted friends and neighbors in Los Angeles, which set into motion the creation of a more formal club.[15] The Federation of Yucatecan Clubs had a similar start. Yucatecan migrants in Los Angeles began to work together in response to Hurricane Isidoro, which hit Yucatan in December 2002. The group initially turned to the Mexican consulate for assistance in developing a coordinated response. Because there was no formal group registered, the consulate encouraged them to form an association. The group, initially numbering about fifty, organized festivals (kermés) to raise funds. By October 2003, they incorporated as Club Yucatan de California and later developed a second group, the Club Yucatan de Inglewood. After being invited to participate in the Consejo de Presidentes de Federaciones Mexicanas, an informal group in the Los Angeles area that served as the base for the Consejo de Federaciones, the Yucatecan migrants opted to name their organization Federacion de Clubes Yucatecos.[16]

The organizational features that accompany the initial stages of HTAs' organizational development facilitate the entry of immigrants, particularly those who lack legal status. In fact, as the ex-president of the Federation of Jalisco Clubs of Southern California explained, immigrants are quite aware of the existence of HTAs in southern California even before their migration. Thus, many migrate with the understanding and, to some degree, expectation that there will be a strong network of support once they arrive in the United States: "Jalisco has 124 municipalities. We have 111 clubs. Of these clubs, we have presence in 90 municipalities. In other words, almost all of Jalisco knows about us, and what we are doing. From over there, they are aware that migrants here are realizing projects back home through the three for one program. When these immigrants arrive here, they already know that there is a club here."[17]

The tremendous growth in membership within hometown associations is made possible by the fact that family relatives and friends have established themselves in the United States and can provide a ready source of support and by the transnational ties built through philanthropic projects in Mexico. Moreover, as Levitt (2001) and Jones-Correa (1998) have documented, the growth in communication technology has greatly facilitated the maintenance of social and cultural ties to the homeland. Hometown leaders maintain regular contact with family members in Mexico by telephone, and in some cases by email as well.

CIVIC AND POLITICAL PRESENCE IN THE UNITED STATES AND MEXICO

The initial organic and grassroots mode of immigrant incorporation that characterizes hometown associations is quite effective and successful and requires no interaction with American mainstream organizations or political entities. The safety factor at play here cannot be overstated but translates into invisibility in regard to mainstream and even ethnic civic and political structures in the United States. Figure 13.1 illustrates the major factors contributing to the marked isolation of HTAs.

Not surprisingly, given their initial orientation, the HTAs interviewed in this study enjoy a greater degree of visibility in their communities of origin during the early stages of their formation. Gaining the support of figures such as the local priest, as with Club Las Animas and Club San Martin de Bolaños, has enabled each group to establish credibility. This, in turn, translates into a greater

FIGURE 13.1   *Factors Impinging on Diminished Civic Presence of HTAs*

Resources

Lack of office space; no formal budget; limited financial resources; absence of paid personnel; all-volunteer-based

Characteristic of Members   Organization Mission

First-generation immigrant   Homeland focus
Limited English fluency
Noncitizen population (exception: leaders)
Lack of legal status among some members
  (exception: leaders)
Lack of formal U.S. education

Source: Author's compilation.

degree of civic presence in subsequent stages of the association's life cycle. That the vast majority of organizations are staffed by volunteers, however, has often led to the stagnation of certain groups. This collapse takes place most often at the club stage, when members commit themselves to formalizing their group and engaging in more sustained social projects, which places an inordinate burden on their energy, time, and financial resources. A leader of the Federation of Zacatecan Clubs explained it this way: "The common denominator . . . among the leadership of all the hometown clubs is that the financial costs of running the organization are all shouldered by the president and board members, from gasoline to telephone expenses. Often, clubs will become defunct or inactive for a period of time and eventually resurface again."[18]

Indeed, the lack of resources, limited English of members, and lack of knowledge about the grant-seeking process and nonprofit incorporation have hindered many groups, often leading to their demise or inactivity. The characteristics of the organizations, coupled with the characteristics of members (especially the language barriers) have contributed to their civic stratification. Members of Club Santa Rita and Club San Martin de Bolaños of the Federation of Jalisco Clubs, for example, noted that they would like to be more involved in U.S.-related matters and collaborate with U.S.-based civic groups such as the Rotary and Lions Clubs, but that their lack of bilingual skills, particularly in interactions with the school system, have diminished their participation.[19] Moreover, their organizational mission is significantly at odds with that of the U.S, groups, despite the fact that the leaders of such organizations are often first-generation naturalized citizens and successful small business owners within the immigrant community. Club San Pedro of Zacatecas was formed twenty years ago without a formal leadership structure and monetary resources. It went through a dormant period but was reactivated by a young cohort of migrants with the support of the founders. In its early years, the club was instrumental in helping the hometown rebuild one of its most prominent churches. It recently registered itself as a member of the Federation of Zacatecan Clubs by paying annual dues of $240 to be able to participate in the three for one matching fund grants program.[20] Other federations, including the Federation of Nayarita Clubs, require clubs to pay annual dues of $260.[21]

Hometown associations in the United States have historically operated under the radar and isolated from American civic and political entities. They have been somewhat more successful, however, at capturing the attention of Mexico-based social and political structures. Immigrants' desire to have a greater impact in their communities of origin and leverage even more money toward their social projects in Mexico motivate many clubs to work with Mexican local and state authorities to create a state federation, or affiliate with an existing federation that unites hometown clubs from the same state. In many cases, as with the Federation of Zacatecan Clubs and the Federation of Jalisco Clubs, the ability to participate in the government's three for one program depends on a club's membership in the federation. The formation of many federations including Jalisco, Puebla, and Hidalgo has been spurred on by the Program for Mexican Communities Abroad through the Ministry of Foreign Relations, which coordinates the visits of state governors to hometown clubs in the United States. As Robert Leiken noted, "governors encourage the federation as the most convenient form for dealing with many hometown associations, and in turn, HTAs find that federations help win state funds for their projects" (2000, 17). Since 1991, the PCME has played a prominent role in this process by coordinating visits not only of governors, but municipal presidents as well, working through the consulates. The federations of Jalisco and Nayarit, for example were formed this way (Leiken 2000, 13–14). The past president of the Federation of Puebla clubs described the process by which eight existing hometown clubs that had already undertaken various fundraisers through their own initiative to remodel the hometown church, were encouraged to federate:

> I heard on the radio that they were inviting Poblanos, people from my state, to go to the Mexican consulate and have meetings. I arrived as a volunteer. A committee was formed to organize activities for Cinco de Mayo, our first Poblano event held at the Plazita Olvera. From then on, we formed a committee to get the federation going. We were constituted as a federation in 2004. The governor of Puebla came to officiate us as an organization, as well as the Consul General of Mexico in Los Angeles. We were then invited to become part of the Council of Presidents of Mexican Federations.[22]

The melding of migrant-led transnationalism and state-led transnational activities explain in large part the movement from early stages of informality to subsequent stages of formalization that bring HTAs in close contact with Mexican political officials. Of vital significance too, is the fact that the Council of

Presidents of Mexican Federations, which preceded COFEM, was created through the initiative of individual presidents of existing federations and through the encouragement of the Mexican consulate.[23] The agglomeration of hometown clubs into federations, and subsequently, into a larger umbrella organization is a process neither entirely state-driven nor migrant-led, but rather the merging of state interests and migrant interests. Thus, hometown association leaders' initial grassroots civic engagement in their communities of origin, coupled with the Mexican state's increased desire to reach out to its diaspora in a variety of ways, have played an important role in allowing migrants to gain the attention of political elites and civic actors in Mexico. This, in turn, has increased the level of political engagement Mexican migrants pursue in the formal political arena, with the intention of influencing government policies and practices.

The Transnational Civic Actor: Increased Political Presence and Weight in Mexico

Hometown association leaders of the Federation of Zacatecan Clubs of Southern California represent, in many ways, the rise of the transnational immigrant civic actor. The federation's long-standing history and status as a pioneer in the immigrant hometown association scene in Los Angeles is further exemplified by the civic and political weight the organization has carried, particularly in the symbolic and ideological realm involving Mexican state policy making. The effects of this weight have been far-reaching, not only in the state of Zacatecas, but on a transnational scale as well, in that it has set important precedents for other immigrant-led civic efforts. For example, the creation of the three for one program can be traced to an agreement forged in 1986. The then-governor of Zacatecas, Genaro Borrego, entered into an agreement with migrant leaders of the young federation, and the program was adopted at the national level in Mexico after the strong lobbying efforts of migrants at the Congress of Mexico. A hometown association leader within the federation intimated the ideological underpinning of this political activity: "Through this effort, we empowered Mexican states in a single project by bringing unity, transforming governmental relations, and asking for accountability. We have been able to legislate on different issues. Because, when we come from Mexico, we see what's wrong. People from our town are afraid to speak because they don't believe in the system."[24]

The sense of empowerment felt by Zacatecan immigrants to effect change in their home country from afar led as well to the passage of the Ley Migrante (Migrant Law), which allows immigrants with dual citizenship and their U.S.-born children to participate and run in the election of mayors and representatives from their hometown. Zacatecan migrants and the Frente Civico Zacatecano, a political organization that functions independently of the federation, lobbied and petitioned for the passage of this piece of legislation, which also opened the door for U.S. migrants to be appointed as representatives within the two major political parties in Mexico. This legislative act, approved by the state legislature of Zacatecas, acknowledges the role of migrants as a decision-making population.

The political activities hometown association leaders undertake underscores their recognition that their role in Mexican society goes beyond the economic contributions made through the three for one matching funds program. When queried as to whether they support the proposal to allow Mexicans abroad to vote in the Mexican presidential elections of 2006, all respondents answered emphatically with a yes, adding that it constitutes a right, given the level of commitment to their communities of origin.

Toward Visibility

When queried as to the possible relationships or collaborations with mainstream organizations such as the Rotary, Lions Clubs, or Chambers of Commerce, vast number of HTAs admitted having little to no knowledge of them. The HTAs' organizational distance from these mainstream groups with strong traditions of civic voluntarism and charitable giving translates into significant disadvantage in terms of American civic and political presence. Furthermore, the language barriers and the legal status of members of some hometown associations that contributed to their isolation from mainstream civic groups have also limited their interactions with Latino groups in the United States. As historians have documented, the gulf between immigrants and U.S.-born Latinos has its roots in the specific ideological orientation of the U.S.-based groups. David Gutiérrez (1995), for instance, describes how, from the perspective of established U.S.-based Latino organizations, a focus on homeland issues and concerns has often been seen as incompatible with U.S. incorporation. Rodolfo Acuña (1996) describes how in the southern California social and political sphere, the push for Latino electoral representation has often limited the more direct engagement of Latino elected officials with the immigrant community. Michael Jones-Correa (2005) notes that the limited collaboration between Mexican immigrants and established Latinos has much to do with the types of organizations each has traditionally participated in. Migrants are drawn to transnationally oriented groups, and Latinos to ethnic groups. Moreover, U.S.-based Latino organizations have historically operated within a civil rights framework, as opposed to the human rights framework that guides much transnational migrant activities. One hometown association leader had this to say:

> When you look at the agenda of the Latino Legislative Caucus, the agendas of NALEO [National Association of Latino Elected and Appointed Officials], MALDEF [Mexican American Legal Defense and Educational Fund], and our topics, they are the same. But when you look at our vision of implementing and addressing those issues, it's a bottom-up focus; it's a families-first focus. We've got to focus on families first. We've got to raise their leadership and their ability to help themselves, first, organizationally. These other organizations serve a different role. They provide policy advocacy and are focused on the big picture.[25]

The disconnect is a concern expressed by nearly all hometown association leaders in my study. HTA leaders recognize the civic and political clout that these groups enjoy and the differing vision guiding the work of these groups. A leader of a twenty-year-old Jalisco-based HTA commented on this organizational distance: "We have not really had interaction of any kind. I believe NALEO has a different vision. They are much more in tune with Mexican Americans, not immigrants. But, we have to encourage them to shift their attention toward us, because ultimately, when we improve our organizational capacity, we will serve as an important point of reference, and serve their interests as well."[26]

Immigrant hometown associations in this study and established Latino organizations are evolving in important ways nonetheless, and in so doing are bridging the gap that has historically set them apart. Notably, it is socially and politically contingent factors, including the present context of reception of immigrants, the maturing of the HTA leadership base, shifts in home country policies regarding dual nationality and citizenship, and the coming of age of the second generation, which is facilitating much of these hometown groups' desire to command a strong civic presence in the United States.

EXPLANATORY FACTORS MOTIVATING A BINATIONAL AGENDA

Interviews with HTA leaders suggest that the shift from a singular homeland-focused perspective to a broader one that articulates migrants' relationship to their host society has been largely influenced by the context of reception in the United States. This finding echoes conclusions offered by Alejandro Portes on the extent and form of transnationalism that develops in various immigrant communities. "Transnational activities flourish," he noted, "in highly concentrated communities especially those that have been subjected to a hostile reception by the host society's authorities and citizenry" (2003, 880). Indeed, when queried as to the reasons for the creation of hometown associations, nearly all HTA leaders listed, in addition to economic and social assistance in their hometowns, the need to promote and preserve cultural identity in the United States. Moreover, when queried as to the most pressing issues facing members of their associations, informants overwhelmingly cited such concerns as a path to legalization for immigrants, driver's licenses for unauthorized migrants, and better paying jobs. The turn toward a U.S.-based civic engagement thus appears to be drawing on both a largely reactive stance occasioned by repressive state and governmental policies toward immigrants and a response to the needs and concerns expressed by their members, many of whom lack legal status in the United States. In the case of more recently formed state federations such as Puebla and Hidalgo, legislation such as HR 4437 has played a significant role in prompting the groups to orient their activities and goals to U.S.-based civic incorporation. Rather than remaining passive, these groups have adopted an assertive stance by mobilizing their members to participate in the large immigrant rights marches of early 2006. However, hometown groups had begun to activate their immigrant leaders on several other key immigrant-related concerns. The issue surrounding the potential cancellation of the matricula consular (consular identification card) used for identification purposes by Mexican nationals living abroad, for instance, mobilized many hometown groups in Los Angeles. Members of Club Fraternidad Las Animas testified before the board of supervisors of Los Angeles County on the importance of maintaining this form of identification. Most important, hometown groups received the support of other established civic groups in Los Angeles, including MALDEF and the ACLU.[27] The board of supervisors approved continuation, signaling an important shift in hometown groups' ability to leverage their collective base to advocate on issues affecting their compatriots.

The increased civic presence of hometown associations is thus attributable not only to their reactive stance to immigrant-related policy issues, but also to their dynamic interactions with existing organizations. In 2003, individual presidents of state federations that represented the Council of Presidents of Mexican Federations and the MALDEF engaged in a series of meetings to devise ways to leverage the collective strength of hometown associations by providing leadership training. MALDEF and the federations of Colima, Michoacan, Nayarit, Oaxaca, Jalisco, Yucatan, and Zacatecas, among others, created an advisory group of eleven members, six representing hometown leaders, and five MALDEF members. In the spring of 2005, MALDEF's Immigrant Leadership for Responsible Development and Education program offered its first fifteen-week intensive leadership training session, a significant first step in the subsequent collaborations and alliances that immigrant hometown associations would forge with more prominent U.S.-based Latino groups. The first of these sessions took place on May 18, 2005, and consisted of a citizenship form completion workshop organized collectively by the Council of Presidents of Mexican Federations, MALDEF, NALEO, and the Legal Aid Foundation of Los Angeles. This partnership has continued, as evidenced by the joint American citizenship completion workshop held at the National Council of La Raza's annual convention held in July 2006, co-sponsored by NALEO, National Council of La Raza (NCLR), COFEM, and the Legal Aid Foundation of Los Angeles.[28] A week before NCLR's annual conference, members of the We Are America Coalition, which includes hometown federations in the region, also organized a massive citizenship drive at the Los Angeles Convention Center. Notably, the event was attended by policy makers in Washington, D.C., including Congresswoman Grace Napolitano (D-38).

The joint creation of the MALDEF-LIDER program increased the visibility of hometown groups, especially in relation to established Latino civil rights organizations. The Council of Presidents of Mexican Federations, however, had been operating as an informal group since 2002. At the time, it was beginning to articulate its U.S.-based agenda, which included addressing immigration reform and driver's licenses for undocumented immigrants in California. The latter issue also served to bring hometown association leaders in contact with members of the Latino Legislative Caucus in Sacramento. As the past president of the Federation of Jalisco Clubs of Southern California noted, the efforts to push forward legislation around this issue compelled them to adopt a binational approach: "We did belong to a commission that supported Gil Cedillo with SB60 initially, then SB1160. We have been making noise with regards to this issue and will continue to do it. In fact, we suggested to the state governor of Jalisco that they get involved by visiting the governor, and pleading that together, we do something to advance on this issue."[29]

It is thus important to consider that the participation of hometown associations in the immigrant rights marches of spring 2006 were not the first instance of U.S.-based civic engagement. In 2003, between September 20 and October 4, the Immigrant Workers Freedom Ride took place across the country, galvanizing labor unions, immigrant organizations, religious associations, and other advocacy groups to bring attention to the plight of immigrant workers, the protection of immigrants' workplace rights, and the need to establish a path to citizenship. Five members of the Council of Presidents of Mexican Federations, participated in the cross-country trip caravan.[30] The presence of hometown associations in this historic event laid the foundation for their ensuing collaboration with labor unions such as UNITE-HERE in Los Angeles—which was instrumental in spearheading the Freedom Ride—religious organizations including the Catholic Archdiocese of Los Angeles, and immigrant advocacy groups including the Coalition for Humane Immigrant Rights of Los Angeles and Central American Resource Center. These organizations resurfaced as important social actors in the 2006 immigrant rights marches as well.

These activities helped elevate the civic and political presence of hometown associations. HTA leadership is increasingly gaining the attention of elected officials, who see in the membership of these groups a potentially large base for mobilizing individuals around issues of immigration, health, and education reform. In fact, the California Latino Legislative Caucus had a historic meeting with leaders of hometown associations in August 2005 to discuss how the groups might leverage their collective strength to advance on key legislative issues. Similarly, in January 2006, hometown association leaders convened with Los Angeles Mayor Antonio Villaraigosa, who committed to help them advance in important areas of mutual interest, including educational issues facing Latino youth and the promotion of naturalization workshops within the immigrant community.[31] Such encounters with policy makers and government officials would have been unimaginable a decade ago. This participation in so many U.S.-based issues, the ability to forge alliances and gain visibility and legitimacy are certain precursors to political weight.

Characteristics of Leaders

Jonathan Fox (2005) theorized that the binational agenda that hometown associations begin to pursue depends greatly on the emergence of migrant-led arenas that articulate migrants' desire to remain connected to their homelands even as they become integral members of American society. A significant migrant-led arena, he argued, is represented by "migrants, who as individuals, have gained positions of leaderships within established nonprofit organizations in the United States, including foundations. They are strategically located to make a major contribution to the capacity building of organizations" (2005, 19). The extent to which an immigrant leader is incorporated into American society, by such measures as bilingual abilities and civic skills in navigating the civic and political system, does certainly determine the ability of HTAs to begin to articulate a U.S.-based agenda. In this regard, hometown associations with a long history do not necessarily have a greater advantage over more recently formed associations, especially if the latter are initiated and led by migrant individuals who can do the work of bridge-building because of bilingual skills and U.S.-based schooling. The president of Club Fraternidad Las Animas, a relatively young organization, has, through her unique positioning, been able to bring members of her club in closer contact with other nonprofits in the city. Having migrated to the United States at the age of ten, she enjoys strong credibility within the community because of her bilingual and bicultural abilities, and her positions as a board member for the Legal Aid Foundation of Los Angeles and as chair of the East Los Angeles Advisory Council. These skills have been instrumental in allowing her to create partnerships with the National Association of Latino Elected Officials. Currently, NALEO sponsors four U.S. Citizenship Form completion workshops on a yearly basis at the Federacion Zacatecana.

In addition to the ability to act as cultural and linguistic brokers, immigrant leaders have critical civic skills, gained over many years through their active participation in hometown-based activities. These include running meetings, organizing large-scale events such as the week-long Semana Jalisco that brings Jalisco elected officials to southern California to interact with immigrants, and raising funds through familial networks. In fact, as table 13.2 shows, the vast majority of HTA leaders are male middle class business professionals who have lived in the United States for well over twenty years and whose leadership has matured. Many are also naturalized citizens or permanent legal residents, with no need for apprehension about speaking in public. They are HTA leaders with the time and money to devote to Mexico and U.S.-based activities that they or their membership deem important. The issue of time figured prominently in conversations with hometown association leaders. As to the time spent on HTA-related activities, respondents averaged ten to twenty hours a week—the equivalent of a part-time job, as many noted. As noted, however, leaders' mostly middle class background and self-employed status enables them to devote a substantial amount of time to these efforts.

Dual Citizenship and Promoting U.S.-Based Civic Incorporation

When asked whether they approved of the proposal to give Mexican immigrants the opportunity to vote in the Mexican elections of 2006, all informants emphatically answered yes. They also expressed favorable views of dual nationality and citizenship, not only because such provisions allow them to have a political voice in their home country, but also, and most important, because it opens up the door to U.S.-based civic incorporation. As the president of the Federation of Nayarit Clubs pointed out, "one of our pressing goals within our organization is to encourage our members to become American citizens. Unfortunately, there is

TABLE 13.2   *Profile of Leadership and Membership of Select Immigrant Hometown Associations in Los Angeles*

Hometown Group	Number of Participants	Region in Mexico	Immigrant Generation	Gender
Club El Rincon				
Leadership	8	Jalisco	first	mostly male
Membership	350 to 400		first and second	male and female
Club Cañadas de Obregon				
Leadership	11	Jalisco	first	mostly male
Membership	100's		first and second	male and female
Club Santa Rita				
Leadership	6	Jalisco	first	mostly male
Membership	100		first	male and female
Club San Pedro				
Leadership	12	Zacatecas	first	mostly male
Membership	250 to 400		first	male and female
Club Fraternidad Las Animas				
Leadership	12	Zacatecas	first	male and female
Membership	1,000		first and second	male and female
Club Tuxpan				
Leadership	10	Nayarit	first	mostly male
Membership	150		first	male and female
Club San Martin de Bolaños				
Leadership	5 to 6	Jalisco	first	mostly male
Membership	300		first	male and female

TABLE 13.2   *Continued*

Socio-economic Class	Language Proficiency	Age
middle class business professionals	primarily monolingual	forties to fifties
working class and some middle class business professionals	primarily monolingual first generation; Spanish-English bilingual second generation	teens to sixty-five, 70 percent under thirty
middle class business professionals	primarily monolingual	forty to forty-five
middle class and working class	primarily monolingual; Spanish-English bilingual second generation	teens to fifties
working class	primarily monolingual	forties to fifties
working class	primarily monolingual; Spanish-English bilingual second generation	0 to fifties
working class	primarily monolingual	thirties to forties
working class	primarily monolingual	teens to sixties
middle and working class	primarily monolingual; a few fully bilingual	forty-four to seventy
working class	monolingual first generation; Spanish-English bilingual second generation	teens to eighty
middle and working class	primarily monolingual	thirty to sixty
working class	primarily monolingual	thirty to sixty
middle class business professionals	primarily monolingual	forty to fifty
working class	primarily monolingual first generation; Spanish-English bilingual second generation	forty to fifty; 20 percent under thirty

Source: Author's compilation.

still the notion within our community that if you become an American citizen, you are turning your back on your home country. But this thinking is flawed, and it is one that we must change. Now with the policy of dual nationality, we don't lose our Mexican nationality, and that is a great advantage."[32]

The sentiment captures the belief held by other HTA leaders that, rather than diminishing their interest in U.S.-based incorporation, dual nationality can in fact, facilitate it by removing the cultural stigma associated with abandoning loyalty to the home country. For immigrants involved in hometown associations, the ability to participate effectively in both societies is aided, not hampered, by these policy shifts relating to immigrants' sense of belonging and allegiance.

As Jones-Correa aptly noted, however, it is not only domestic policy shifts such as dual nationality and citizenship provisions in the sending country that can motivate U.S.-based incorporation, but also domestic policy shifts in the receiving country (2001, 1023). Indeed, it may well be that immigrants are responding to these simultaneous shifts, prompting them to devise a "simultaneity of connection" between homeland-issues and concerns and U.S.-based civic activities (Levitt and Glick Schiller 2004, 1011). The case of the Federation of Nayarit Clubs in Los Angeles provides a good example of this. Every August, the federation organizes a Feria Nayarit that includes visits from the state governor of Nayarit and other high-ranking officials to discuss the progress of social development projects in hometown villages and to provide a forum for migrants to air concerns. For the first time, in August of 2006, on the heels of the proposed immigration legislation, HR 4437, and in conjunction with the National Association of Latino Elected Officials, the federation included a citizenship completion workshop among its three day-long activities in Santa Ana, California. Similarly, even as they continued working on development projects in their communities, hometown federations worked through the Consejo de Federaciones to partner with the Coalition for Humane Immigrant Rights of Los Angeles, the Los Angeles County Federation of Labor, and other community-based and civic groups on a national campaign spearheaded by Univision Communications, NALEO, NCLR, and the Service Employees International Union aimed at naturalizing more than 1 million new citizens during 2007.[33] Such coalition building—particularly in the area of naturalization and immigration-reform—is an important indicator of their growing civic and political presence.

The Coming of Age of the Second Generation

Hometown associations are the creation of first-generation Mexican immigrants. Second-generation immigrant involvement is minimal and takes place primarily on the part of young women recruited by their parents and relatives to participate in annual beauty competitions. The winners become, in effect, young cultural ambassadors. They are taken on trips to Mexican hometowns, where they learn about the history and culture of the regions and engage in a kind of U.S.-Mexico cultural exchange meant to promote the second generation's link to their parents' culture, a way of reinforcing cultural ties and steering young women away from what are seen as the negative influences of mainstream U.S.

culture. Similarly, second-generation boys participate actively in sports leagues organized by the first generation as a way to foster cultural pride and provide a healthy outlet for interaction and leisure.

Although many first-generation immigrant leaders once dreamed and hoped for a time that they would be able to return to their homeland after a few years of work, that possibility has become less and less viable. Immigrant hometown association leaders speak in nostalgic terms about this fading hope and with greater urgency and insistence on the need to focus on youth. For this reason, many HTAs have begun to channel their fundraising efforts on providing scholarships to the second generation and finding ways to increase their educational opportunities to attend college and obtain a higher education. The role that the second generation is playing in shaping HTA activities was neatly expressed by the president of the Jalisco-based Club San Martin de Bolaños: "We want to do a study of all the young people in college who need financial assistance, because many of our members are starting to tell us, 'What about the people here?' So, there will be a drastic change in the club. Before, we were devoting our work 100 percent to our hometown. Now we are rethinking this, and considering spending 50 percent on hometown, and 50 percent on communities here."[34]

Although they do not represent the core membership of hometown associations, the second generation is playing a de facto role in encouraging hometown associations to address legislation and policies that directly affect this generation of youth. For instance, the Federation of Zacatecan Clubs of Southern California collected 10,000 signatures in support of AB 540, the DREAM Act, which would make higher education accessible for undocumented youth, and the Federation of Puebla Clubs is embarking on a project to raise money for student scholarships. Several hometown federations took part in the first formal meeting with the mayor of Los Angeles in early 2006 to discuss the role they might play in advancing important agenda issues, including educational reform and civic participation.

THE POTENTIAL AND CHALLENGES OF A BINATIONAL CIVIC AGENDA

Research reveals that long before the proposal of HR 4437 in late 2005, immigrant hometown associations had participated in some form of civic and political activity relating to immigration reform. This activity, however, had been for the most part sporadic and difficult to sustain over time. Carol Zabin and Luis Escala-Rabadán (1998) documented the role of southern California HTAs in mobilizing against Proposition 187 in 1994 by participating in marches. Their primary finding, however, was that this level of engagement was not sustained, particularly after the proposition was ruled unconstitutional. Among the factors that weakened the subsequent participation of HTAs in legislative matters pertaining to immigration and other issues was their "extreme parochialism" and lack of a larger umbrella organization at that time that could unify them in much the same way that Jewish federations in the 1920s and 1930s unified individual hometown groups to build a strong voice of unity (Zabin and Escala-Rabadán 1998, 25). Adding to the limited civic activity of HTAs in the public sphere was the lack of consensus among HTA members regarding the extent to which clubs should focus exclusively on philanthropic issues in the United States and Mexico (Zabin and Escala-Rabadán 1998, 27).

My research with hometown associations reveals that these organizations have historically been insular, a fact that has contributed to their success in attracting new members, particularly those with no legal status. This mode of operation, however, is quickly changing. It appears to be motivated in large part by contextual factors, including the recognition that permanent roots have been established in the United States, the space opened up by the provision of dual citizenship, and—most important—the present context of reception of immigrants in the United States. As David Ayon described it, on the Mexican side, there was "a major step in the redefinition of the terms of Mexican nationality and citizenship, opening up new opportunities for transnational migrant empowerment" (2006, 1). On the U.S. side, the growing recognition on the part of established Latino organizations of the growing social and political clout of immigrants has enabled the construction of an infrastructure that was lacking in 1994. In particular, the Consejo de Federaciones is playing an instrumental role in bringing HTAs in closer contact with U.S.-based elected officials by annually hosting a Binational Conference on Immigrant Affairs. The first of these was held in October 2006, and provided a forum to discuss key issues such as immigration reform, health, and educational access. The event brought together Mexican governors, local mayors, and other influential policy makers from Mexico to meet with U.S.-based elected officials, including the mayor of Los Angeles and representatives of the Congressional Hispanic Caucus Institute and California Latino Legislative Caucus. A panel on the 2006 Mexican presidential elections and migrant vote abroad with representatives of the Mexican Federal Electoral Institute was preceded by a panel discussion with members of the Congressional Hispanic Caucus Institute on the disparities in health access within the Latino community.[35] This binational convention was in many ways a crowning moment in the slow—but seemingly promising—path HTAs in southern California have had to travel to achieve civic and political presence.

Hometown organizations show strong promise in their ability to serve as a link between immigrants' strongly felt desire to participate in their homeland as well as their hope to more fully incorporate into American society. Several key challenges nonetheless loom on the horizon. Most notable is the significant chasm between leadership and members of these organizations. HTA members, particularly the undocumented, are more inclined to participate in large-scale activities, such as marches and protests, that allow them to remain under the radar. It is for the most part the leadership of these groups who participate more directly, for example, in interacting with elected officials. Hometown groups also face the prospects of conflicts relating to the vision of immigrant leadership and organizational models. Integrating more women and members of the second generation into the leadership structures of the organizations presents important challenges as well.

The pivotal role that the current anti-immigrant sentiment has played in prompting hometown groups to turn their attention toward U.S.-based issues is a phenomenon that merits further investigation and longitudinal analysis. If the current impulse toward a binational or simultaneous mode of immigrant incorporation is premised on the negative context of reception immigrant communities face, will the organizational model provided by hometown associations be able to sustain this level of civic engagement across borders, or will it remain contingent on these political and social moments? It remains to be seen whether this flurry of activity will be sustained over time, granting HTAs a civic and political presence that until now has eluded them.

I would like to thank Karthick Ramakrishnan and Irene Bloemraad for encouraging this research on immigrant hometown associations, and for their dedication to this project on immigrant civic engagement. Hector Cordero-Guzmán provided valuable comments on how to conceptualize the life cycle of organizations. I also thank anonymous reviewers, editors, and contributors to this volume for helpful comments on earlier versions of this paper.

NOTES

1. The hearing was sponsored by the We Are America Coalition, a coalition of immigrant rights, community based, advocacy and civic organizations, formed in response to HR 4437 in 2006. The Consejo de Federaciones Mexicanas is a member organization of the coalition's steering committee.
2. Organizational interview, September 15, 2006.
3. Eileen Truax, "Federaciones Se Unen Contra HR 4437" ["Federations Unite Against HR4437"], La Opinion, March 16, 2006, 4B.
4. Gabriel Zaragoza, "Organizaciones en EU Insisten en Realizar el Boicot, Denuncian Acoso" ["Organizations in the U.S. Insist on a Boycott, Denounce Harassment"], La Jornada, April 25, 2006, accessed March 5, 2008 at http://www.jornada.unam.mx/2006/04/25/027n1mig.php.
5. Following the publication of Nations Unbound, researchers proposed more nuanced and detailed analyses of transnationalism and the state. Guarnizo and Smith offered a critical view of deterritorialization, by insisting on the "opportunities and constraints found in particular localities" (1998, 12). Luin Goldring (1998) and Robert Smith (1998) echoed this idea, whereas Luis Guarnizo, Alejandro Portes, and William Haller (2003) stressed the "specific territorial jurisdictions in which transnational actions occur which affect the way immigrants incorporate themselves" (1239).
6. As of this writing, the Federation of Jalisco Clubs and Federation of Zacatecan Clubs of Southern California operate independently, and are not member organizations of the Consejo de Federaciones Mexicanas.
7. See http://www.cmcpla.com. It is important to note that the CMCPLA is governed by a board of directors, many of whom are also hometown association leaders and representatives in Los Angeles.

8. Field notes, September 10, 2006.

9. George Sanchez (1993), Francisco Balderrama and Raymond Rodriguez (1995), and Camille Guérin-Gonzales (1994) all examined the interaction between the Mexican consulate and the local Mexican community in southern California, particularly with regard to labor organizing and politics.

10. It is important to note that the Mexican Consul in Los Angeles during this tumultuous period in American history, Rafael de la Colina, played an instrumental role in coordinating plans with local authorities for sponsoring trains to transport migrants. This activity was consistent with the Mexican government's goal at that time to encourage return migration of its nationals. Abraham Hoffman (1974), Balderrama and Rodriguez (1995), and Camille Guérin-Gonzales (1994) explored this little-known period in U.S.-Mexico history in their respective studies.

11. See http://www.ime.gob.mx. A notable exception to this pattern is the FZSC, which dates to 1972 and is the oldest immigrant-led transnational organization in Los Angeles. Roberto Leiken provides a rich account of this shift in Mexico's increased attention toward its immigrant population, noting that a confluence of factors including the legalization of 2.7 million (mostly) Mexican immigrants through the Immigration Reform and Control Act (1986), a split in the ruling party in Mexico and the transnational political struggle that ensued, as well as the imperatives posed by Mexico's increasing export-economy oriented to the United States, all influenced the Mexican government to take an active role in developing relations with migrant communities in the United States (2000, 9).

12. Organizational interview, August 29, 2006.

13. Organizational interview, April 28, 2005.

14. Organizational interview, April 13, 2005.

15. Organizational interview, April 2, 2005.

16. Organizational interview, April 18, 2005.

17. Organizational interview, April 17, 2005.

18. Organizational interview, April 1, 2005.

19. Organizational interview, April 28, 2005.

20. Organizational interview, April 9, 2005.

21. Organizational interview, June 16, 2005.

22. Organizational interview, August 2, 2005.

23. Organizational interview, April 17, 2005.

24. Organizational interview, April 2, 2005.

25. Organizational interview, August 25, 2006.

26. Organizational interview, August 29, 2006.

27. Organizational interview, April 2, 2005.

28. Rachel Uranga, "Mexican Hometown Groups Wooed—Members Urged to Become U.S. Citizens, vote for Local Politicians," *Los Angeles Daily News*, July 8, 2006, N3, N6.

29. Organizational interview, April 17, 2005.

30. Organizational interview, June 6, 2005.

31. Eileen Truax, "Reunion de Villaraigosa y federaciones mexicanas" ["Meeting Between Villaraigosa and Mexican Federations"], *La Opinión*, January 18, 2006, 3A.

32. Organizational interview, September 24, 2006.

33. The Ya Es Hora Ciudadania! campaign is an interesting model of the interaction of U.S.-based Spanish language media, public and private agencies, established Latino organizations, and emerging immigrant-led organizations. The campaign relies on regular newscasts informing viewers of community-based resources for those seek-

ing naturalization, and provides an important outlet for the dissemination of news regarding the naturalization process. See http://www.yaeshora.info.
34. Organizational interview, April 13, 2005.
35. Field notes, First annual Binational Conference, Los Angeles Convention Center, October 27–28, 2006.

REFERENCES

Acuña, Rodolfo. 1996. *Anything But Mexican: Chicanos in Contemporary Los Angeles.* London: Verso Press.

Alba, Richard, and Victor Nee. 2003. *Remaking the American Mainstream: Assimilation and Contemporary Immigration.* Cambridge, Mass.: Harvard University Press.

Ayon, David. 2006. "The Long Road to the Voto Postal: Mexican Policy and People of Mexican Origin in the United States." Working paper 6. Berkeley, Calif.: Center for Latin American Studies, University of California, Berkeley.

Balderrama, Francisco, and Raymond Rodriguez. 1995. *Decade of Betrayal: Mexican Repatriation in the 1930's.* Albuquerque, N.M.: University of New Mexico Press.

Basch, Linda, Nina Glick Schiller, and Cristina Szanton Blanc. 1994. *Nations Unbound: Transnational Projects, Postcolonial Predicaments, and Deterritorialized Nation-States.* Langhorne, Pa.: Gordon and Breach Publishers.

Bloemraad, Irene. 2004. "Who Claims Dual Citizenship? The Limits of Postnationalism, the Possibilities of Transnationalism, and the Persistence of Traditional Citizenship." *International Migration Review* 38(2): 389–426.

De La Garza, Rodolfo, and Myriam Hazan. 2003. *Looking Backward, Moving Forward: Mexican Organizations in the U.S. as Agents of Incorporation and Dissociation.* Claremont, Calif.: The Tomas Rivera Policy Institute.

Fox, Jonathan. 2005. "Mapping Mexican Migrant Civil Society." Paper presented to Woodrow Wilson International Center for Scholars, Conference on Mexican Migrant Civic and Political Participation. Washington, D.C., November 4–5, 2005. Accessed at http://www.wilsoncenter.org/news/docs/MexicanMigrantCivilSocietyFoxFinal1.pdf.

Fox, Jonathan, Andrew Selee, and Xochitl Bada. 2006. "Conclusions" In *Invisible No More: Mexican Migrant Civic Participation in the United States*, edited by Xochitl Bada, Jonathan Fox, and Andrew Selee. Washington: Woodrow Wilson International Center for Scholars.

Goldring, Luin. 1998. "The Power of Status in Transnational Social Fields." In *Comparative Urban and Community Research Vol. 6: Transnationalism from Below*, edited by Michael P. Smith and Luis Eduardo Guarnizo. New Brunswick, N.J.: Transaction Publishers.

———. 2002. "The Mexican State and Transmigrant Organizations: Negotiating the Boundaries of Membership and Participation in the Mexican Nation." *Latin American Research Review* 37(3): 55–99.

Gordon, Milton. 1964. *Assimilation in American Life: The Role of Race, Religion, and National Origins.* New York: Oxford University Press.

Guarnizo, Luis, and Michael Smith. 1998. "The Locations of Transnationalism." In *Comparative Urban and Community Research Vol. 6: Transnationalism from Below*, edited by Michael P. Smith and Luis Eduardo Guarnizo. New Brunswick, N.J.: Transaction Publishers.

Guarnizo, Luis, Alejandro Portes, and William Haller. 2003. "Assimilation and Transnationalism: Determinants of Transnational Political Action Among Contemporary Migrants." *American Journal of Sociology* 108(6): 1211–48.

Guérin-Gonzales, Camille. 1994. *Mexican Workers and American Dreams: Immigration, Repatriation, and California Farm Labor, 1900–1939.* New Brunswick, N.J.: Rutgers University Press.

Gutiérrez, David. 1995. *Walls and Mirrors: Mexican Americans, Mexican Immigrants, and the Politics of Ethnicity.* Berkeley, Calif.: University of California Press.

Hoffman, Abraham. 1974. *Unwanted Mexican Americans in the Great Depression: Repatriation Pressures, 1929–1939.* Tucson, Ariz.: University of Arizona Press.

Huntington, Samuel. 2004. *Who Are We? The Challenges to America's National Identity.* New York: Simon & Schuster.

Jones-Correa, Michael. 1998. *Between Two Nations: The Political Predicament of Latinos in New York City.* Ithaca, N.Y.: Cornell University Press.

———. 2001. "Under Two Flags: Dual Nationality in Latin America and Its Consequences for Naturalization in the United States." *International Migration Review* 35(4): 997–1029.

———. 2005. "Mexican Migrants and their Relation to U.S. Latino Civil Society." Paper presented to Woodrow Wilson International Center for Scholars at Conference on Mexican Migrant Civic and Political Participation. Washington, D.C., November 4–5, 2005. Accessed at http://www.wilsoncenter.org/news/docs/MJC%20MX%20Migrant%20US%20Civ%20Soc.pdf.

Leiken, Robert. 2000. *The Melting Border: Mexico and Mexican Communities in the United States.* Washington: Center for Equal Opportunity.

Levitt, Peggy. 2001. *The Transnational Villagers.* Berkeley, Calif.: University of California Press.

Levitt, Peggy, and Nina Glick Schiller. 2004. "Conceptualizing Simultaneity: A Transnational Social Field Perspective on Society." *International Migration Review* 38(3): 1002–39.

Portes, Alejandro. 2003. "Conclusion: Theoretical Convergencies and Empirical Evidence in the Study of Immigrant Transnationalism." *International Migration Review* 37(3): 874–92.

Portes, Alejandro, Cristina Escobar and Alexandria Radford. 2007. "Immigrant Transnational Organizations and Development: A Comparative Study." *International Migration Review* 41(1): 242–81.

Renshon, Stanley. 2001. *Dual Citizenship and American National Identity.* Washington: Center for Immigration Studies.

Rivera-Salgado, Gaspar, Xochitl Bada, and Luis Escala-Rabadán. 2005. "Mexican Migrant Civic and Political Participation in the U.S.: The Case of Hometown Associations in Los Angeles and Chicago." Paper presented to Woodrow Wilson International Center for Scholars at Conference on Mexican Migrant Civic and Political Participation in the United States. Washington, D.C., November 4–5, 2005. Accessed at http://www.wilsoncenter.org/news/docs/riverabadaescala1.pdf.

Sanchez, George. 1993. *Becoming Mexican American: Ethnicity, Culture, and Identity in Chicano Los Angeles, 1900–1945.* Oxford: Oxford University Press.

Schuck, Peter. 1998. *Citizens, Strangers, and In-Betweens: Essays on Immigration and Citizenship.* Boulder, Colo.: Westview Press.

Sherman, Rachel. 1999. "From State Introversion to State Extension in Mexico: Modes of Emigrant Incorporation, 1900–1997." *Theory and Society* 28(6): 835–78.

Smith, Robert. 1998. "Transnational Localities: Community, Technology, and the Politics of Membership Within the Context of Mexico-US Integration." In *Comparative Urban and Community Research Vol. 6: Transnationalism from Below,* edited by Michael P. Smith and Luis Eduardo Guarnizo. New Brunswick, N.J.: Transaction Publishers.

————. 2003. "Migrant Membership as an Instituted Process: Transnationalization, the State and the Extra-Territorial Conduct of Mexican Politics." *International Migration Review* 37(2): 297–343.

————. 2006. *Mexican New York: Transnational Lives of New Immigrants.* Berkeley, Calif.: University of California Press.

Warner, William, and Leo Srole. 1946. *The Social Systems of American Ethnic Groups.* New Haven, Conn.: Yale University Press.

Zabin, Carol, and Luis Escala-Rabadán. 1998. "Mexican Hometown Associations and Mexican Immigrant Political Empowerment in Los Angeles." Nonprofit Sector Research Fund working paper. Washington: The Aspen Institute.

Index

Boldface numbers refer to figures and tables.